Thinking Popular Culture

Thinking Popular Culture

JASON HASLAM

Department of English

Dalhousie University

Toronto

Acquisitions Editor: Matthew Christian
Marketing Manager: Lisa Gillis
Program & Project Manager: Madhu Ranadive
Development Editor: Rebecca Ryoji
Production Services: Rashmi Tickyani, Aptara®, Inc.
Permissions Project Manager: Kathryn O'Handley
Text Permissions Research: Varoon Deo-Singh, EPS
Photo Permissions Research: Dimple Bhorwal, Aptara®, Inc.
Cover Designer: Alex Li
Cover Image: Patchanee Samutarlai/Shutterstock

Library and Archives Canada Cataloguing in Publication

Haslam, Jason W. (Jason William), author
Thinking popular culture / Jason Haslam, Department of
English, Dalhousie University.

Includes bibiliographical references and index.
ISBN 978-0-13-270846-3 (pbk.)

1. Popular culture—Philosophy. 2. Culture—Philosophy.
I. Title

CB19.H38 2014   306.01   C2014-905810-1

10 9 8 7 6 5 4 3 2 1 [WC]

ISBN 978-0-13-270846-3

Brief Contents

Contents

Part II Cultural Theories: Beginnings 33

3 Marxism I: Ideology, Hegemony, and Class 34

4 Psychoanalysis I: Freud and Jung 54

5 Linguistics and Semiotics 69

Part III   Cultural Theories: Developments   91

6   Marxism and Psychoanalysis II: Forming Identity   92

7   Disciplining Cultural Studies   111

Part V   Writing About Popular Culture   275

14   Writing About Popular Culture Across the Disciplines   276

15   Opinion, Analysis, Evidence, Theory   283

16   Sample Assignments   291

Preface for Students

The purpose of this book is to introduce you to some of the tools and skills necessary to the critical analysis of popular culture. We focus on what scholars call "cultural theories"— theories that offer different ways of looking at the cultural landscape of our societies. Although popular culture is often considered to be "simply entertainment," the theories you'll learn explain the centrality of popular culture to everyday life, especially but not only in the post-industrial period. They also provide methods of analysis, including the "close reading" of particular popular culture artifacts and moments, wider studies of the socio-economic contexts that inform popular culture and how people interact with it, and ways of discussing how popular culture represents individuals and groups. The book pays attention to the Canadian context as well, through many of its examples and in some of the methodologies and theories examined. In this preface we discuss the basic structure of the text and some of the features that have been included to help you learn about the rich, diverse field of popular culture studies.

STRUCTURE OF THE BOOK

The main text of this book is split into five parts. Part I is a general introduction to the academic study of popular culture, offering students basic definitions of some of the central terms in the field (including *popular* and *culture* themselves, which aren't as simple as one might think!). Part II offers an overview of the foundational studies and theories of culture in general and popular culture specifically. These theories are updated in Part III, which looks to some of the more contemporary methods of studying popular culture (including the creation of the discipline known as cultural studies). Part IV builds on these foundations (and picks up on their discussions of social class) to explore in more detail the representation and construction of certain social or group identities (in particular, gender, sexuality, race, and national and postcolonial identities). Part V applies some of these theories to practice (we'll return to this in a moment).

If you were to sit down and read the book from start to finish, you'd be given a general overview of the field of popular culture studies and its methods. But this book is designed to be used in a classroom setting. Theories and methods are meant to be applied, and a lot of that application will likely happen in class. And so you may even be reading the chapters in a different order than the one presented here. While the book can certainly be read chronologically, and while chapters do refer to each other, each chapter is also self-contained and designed to function in conjunction with the needs of specific courses in order to provide an idea of a particular way of analyzing popular culture. Instructors will likely include certain items of popular culture to analyze with each chapter or set of chapters being read.

LEARNING AIDS

Each chapter includes exercises and other material that will help students think in greater depth about the issues being discussed. These include sections in which the theories are applied to particular forms of popular culture as well as more interactive sections that ask students to apply what they've learned. These aids take the form of keywords, figures, issue boxes and case studies, discussion questions, and further reading. Readers will notice that certain words are placed in bold text throughout: these are considered to be keywords for the discussion at hand, and definitions for them can be found in the glossary at the back. Using the glossary often can help students more quickly integrate these concepts into their own work and knowledge set. The figures or diagrams help explain complicated ideas visually by breaking the theories down into their basic components. The issue boxes (throughout the chapters) and the case studies (at the end of all the chapters, starting with Chapter 3) apply the theories being analyzed to particular popular culture objects (and on occasion offer additional theoretical background). The discussion questions, also at the end of each chapter, can give students a starting point—both in and outside of class—for thinking about how to further explore the issues being discussed. Finally, the further reading lists that follow the questions allow students to explore the issues and ideas at hand in more detail.

Building on these learning tools, Part V provides extended applications of the theoretical material. Specifically, Part V discusses ways of writing about popular culture and how to incorporate theoretical work into that writing. It also offers examples of the types of student work many instructors assign in their courses, as well as samples of student work. These samples aren't provided as "perfect" assignments, but rather as starting points for discussion and other work, or as guidelines that students can use as they learn to analyze popular culture and to incorporate theories into those analyses. Even if an instructor uses different forms of assignments, students can still use the assignments provided here to practise their writing and as practical study aids.

POPULAR THEORY!

As a final note: Students often find the theories discussed in this book to be difficult, and they sometimes think that approaching popular culture in these ways can take the "fun" out of it. But as you go through this book and your course, you'll likely come to a different perspective on these topics: yes, the theories are difficult, but applying their methods to analyze popular culture will take you beyond its surface—and as you learn to engage with it on more levels than you may have previously, these analyses can actually make the experience of popular culture richer and more exciting than before. This book aims to help students approach their cultural surroundings anew, and to challenge commonly held assumptions about our societies and their cultures.

Preface for Instructors

This book aims to offer the instructor of popular culture classes an overview of some of the more foundational and central statements of cultural theory, and to provide students and instructors with examples of the ways in which those theories relate to and can be employed for the study of popular culture. Importantly, *Thinking Popular Culture* draws on many Canadian examples and case studies to explain and employ the theoretical models discussed; some of these theories are also specific to the Canadian context (the textbook does not draw solely on Canadian examples, however, since doing so would, in fact, limit its usefulness for a Canadian classroom).

ORGANIZATION

The organizing principle of the book combines two of the common textbook approaches to the field: chronological-theoretical and thematic. The chronological-theoretical approach focuses on the developments in cultural theory over time by following the development of certain schools or theoretical groups (from the Frankfurt School to the Birmingham School; from structuralist to poststructuralist; from modern to postmodern; and so on), while the thematic organization focuses on concepts surrounding identity (nationalism and postcoloniality, race, feminism, gender, and sexuality). This book joins these two approaches, first discussing the origins and developments of cultural theory and the study of popular culture in the first three parts, and then analyzing theories of identity in the fourth. The chapters often refer to each other in order to allow students to develop a sense of the various relations between the theories and schools, but each chapter also functions as a self-contained narrative on a particular subject, along with relevant case studies showing the potential applications of the theories being discussed. Primarily, the text summarizes and analyzes, in relatively conversational language, what students often find to be dense theoretical texts. As much support as possible—by way of selective quotation and direct application—is provided so that instructors may choose to use the book on its own, or pair it with specific theoretical readings and examples of popular culture, either those mentioned directly here or additional works.

    Thinking Popular Culture thus offers instructors a variety of choices as to how to incorporate the textbook into their classes: the textbook can be read from cover to cover, certainly, but it can also be "broken up," with instructors assigning chapters—or sections of chapters—in any order, as best befits their classes. In general, the textbook is designed to help instructors with the task of introducing difficult theories so that more classroom time can be spent on the discussion and application of those theoretical models. More information on possible classroom uses is provided below.

Pedagogical Features

In addition to the central theoretical discussions, several pedagogical features have been included for use in the classroom, in tutorials, and/or for assignments. Throughout each chapter, instructors and students will find six central learning aids, in addition to the main text:

- Keywords
- Figures
- Issues Boxes
- Case Studies
- Discussion Questions
- Further Reading

Keywords: Each chapter contains several keywords that are placed in bold, which the student can then find in the glossary at the end of the book. These definitions can prove especially useful for the introductory classroom, as students are exposed to an extensive new set of terminology: having the glossary handy can help them learn the usefulness of—and engage with—that terminology quickly and effectively (it can also serve as a useful study tool).

Figures: The figures are primarily designed to help students understand different stages of some of the more complex theories. While not all theories lend themselves to such diagramming, these are included where they have proven especially useful.

Issue Boxes: These boxes appear several times in each chapter; taken as a whole, they fulfill two purposes: they apply individual theories to particular elements of popular culture, and do so at the moment in the text when those theories are being discussed (e.g., an issue box on a "Pregnant Barbie" is provided when discussing heteronormativity and performative theories of gender identity); and they offer some practical background to the theories when necessary (e.g., the brief discussion of the history of Marxism and Communism at the beginning of the section dealing with Marxist theories).

Case Studies: Longer case studies have been included at the end of each of the main chapters, starting at the end of Chapter 3, to demonstrate some of the ways in which the main theories discussed in each chapter can be used to analyze specific examples of popular culture. Unlike the issue boxes, these case studies show how a particular element of popular culture can be analyzed from a variety of theoretical perspectives. The case studies show students that they have choice in how to approach and apply the theories discussed in any given chapter, and also serve as a quick overview of some of the main points of the chapter. Moreover, these are intended to be "open-ended" analyses, to which students and instructors can add with discussion and with further examples brought to class. More information on the examples chosen for the issue boxes and case studies is provided below.

Discussion Questions: Following the case studies, the discussion questions are framed in a number of ways: often they build on the possibility of having either the instructor or students bring in other examples, thus allowing even more direct analysis and application to happen in the classroom. Other questions serve as springboards for a wider exploration of the theories, often by focusing on those areas that experience has shown students to have problems with. Depending on the structure of the class, these questions can be incorporated into the lecture or class discussion or used in break-away tutorials for larger classes. Students can also be asked to prepare formal or informal replies to them, either to bring to class or to post on the course's electronic systems, if any.

Further Reading: This section, finally, is provided for the instructor who may want to assign other texts in related areas as readings, and for students interested in furthering their awareness of the larger field. These examples can be supplemented with an instructor's own list, of course.

On the Use of Examples in the Text and in the Classroom

The text was written with an eye to the interdisciplinary and multi-disciplinary nature of the field, and so examples and objects for analyses in the main text, issue boxes, and case studies are drawn from a variety of materials, including television, film, music, advertisements, political action, common situations, university campuses, and many others. These examples are provided in order to give students some concrete analyses to help them as they read material ahead of class. The examples are also chosen from a range of periods: while many examples are contemporary, more historical ones are chosen when especially appropriate. Likewise, material was chosen with an eye to providing material with which many students will be familiar as well as more specific or "obscure" examples that can expand the range and depth of discussion. To take two film examples, most students will know the international blockbuster *The Matrix* even though it's fifteen years old at the time of this writing. Their knowledge of the film can help start conversation easily. Fewer will know the much more recent Canadian film *Pontypool*, but most will be familiar with the resurgence in the popularity of zombies. Offering an analysis of this film not only allows the injection of a particularly inventive Canadian example of popular culture, but can also allow students to see how somewhat obscure theories can be intimately connected to a particular popular cultural phenomenon.

It is also expected, however, that instructors can and will both build on these examples in lecture and discussion and add to them examples of their own that are especially relevant to particular classes or student and instructor interest—such supplemental work is actually quite important given the rapidly changing nature of the pop culture landscape. No popular culture textbook can stay up to date in its analytical examples. By offering summaries of the theories alongside separate examples throughout, this textbook provides students with the necessary theoretical tools that will allow them to branch out into their own applications, with their instructor's help.

Writing Section

Importantly, the textbook also includes an innovative concluding section that discusses approaches to writing about popular culture. This section is not intended to be a replacement for, nor is it as comprehensive or wide-ranging as, a writing handbook. Instead, it offers students some basic approaches to writing both short and longer assignments about popular culture using the theories discussed in the text. "Combining" theory and critical analysis often proves challenging to students, and so by suggesting a few different approaches, this book aims to give students and instructors useful entry points into that work. As part of this discussion a selection of sample writing assignments is provided, including assignment sheets and model student responses. These assignments were chosen after surveying a variety of popular culture course outlines: common writing assignment types were synthesized into three forms: the theory response, the object analysis, and the research essay. These assignments are described at greater length in the relevant section of the book, but important to note here is that they're described in ways that can easily be incorporated into a number of other specific assignment types (including, but not limited to, writing journals, Wiki-style assignments, presentations and group work, and so on). Using the samples provided here in conjunction with the requirements of a specific course can allow the instructor to incorporate writing and analysis instruction directly into the other material being discussed in class.

Significantly, these sample assignments are intended to be used as interactive tools rather than as static models of the "perfect" assignment. While they should provide strong examples, there are still areas of the application or writing than can be analyzed and critiqued with the students: instructors can identify particular areas of the sample assignments and ask students how they could be improved, or how their structures would need to be modified to meet the needs of the specific course assignments used in their particular course. Getting students to engage actively in such activities could allow for a more engaged relationship with their own writing.

Overall, this book is designed to complement an instructor's own pedagogical choices: a chronological reading of the book would work for many courses, but the various portions can also be arranged onto a course schedule in a variety of ways, with some sections joined together or others lingered over and emphasized, following the needs of the particular course. Likewise, the analytical examples provided in the textbook can be supplemented with ones of the instructors' and students' own choosing.

The textbook is designed to be incorporated into your class rather than the other way around. Teaching the critical analysis of popular culture in conjunction with cultural theory can be a challenge, but it can also be one of the more rewarding classroom experiences one can have, and this book hopes to help instructors and students reach that goal.

SUPPLEMENTS
CourseSmart for Instructors

CourseSmart goes beyond traditional expectations–providing instant, online access to the textbooks and course materials you need at a lower cost for students. And even as students save money, you can save time and hassle with a digital eTextbook that allows you to search for the most relevant content at the very moment you need it. Whether it's evaluating textbooks or creating lecture notes to help students with difficult concepts, CourseSmart can make life a little easier. See how when you visit http://www.coursesmart.com/instructors.

CourseSmart for Students

CourseSmart goes beyond traditional expectations–providing instant, online access to the textbooks and course materials you need at an average savings of 60%. With instant access from any computer and the ability to search your text, you'll find the content you need quickly, no matter where you are. And with online tools like highlighting and note-taking, you can save time and study efficiently. See all the benefits at www.coursesmart.com/students.

Learning Solutions Managers

Pearson's Learning Solutions Managers work with faculty and campus course designers to ensure that Pearson technology products, assessment tools, and online course materials are tailored to meet your specific needs. This highly qualified team is dedicated to helping schools take full advantage of a wide range of educational resources, by assisting in the integration of a variety of instructional materials and media formats. Your local Pearson Education sales representative can provide you with more details on this service program.

Pearson Custom Library

For enrollments of at least 25 students, you can create your own textbook by choosing the chapters that best suit your own course needs. To begin building your custom text, visit www.pearsoncustomlibrary.com. You may also work with a dedicated Pearson Custom editor to create your ideal text—publishing your own original content or mixing and matching Pearson content. Contact your local Pearson Representative to get started.

peerScholar

Firmly grounded in published research, peerScholar is a powerful online pedagogical tool that helps develop students' critical and creative thinking skills through creation, evaluation, and reflection. Working in stages, students begin by submitting written assignments. peerScholar then circulates their work for others to review, a process that can be anonymous or not, depending on instructors' preferences. Students immediately receive peer feedback and evaluations, reinforcing their learning and driving development of higher-order thinking skills. Students can then re-submit revised work, again depending on instructors' preferences.

Contact your Pearson representative to learn more about *peerScholar* and the research behind it.

ACKNOWLEDGMENTS

This book is the result of working with students and colleagues in Cultural Studies, Communication Studies, and English programs at three different universities, and the strengths the book has are the result of their engaging questions and discussions. I would especially like to thank my students at Dalhousie University: over the past decade, their enthusiasm and support both inspired this book and made it possible.

If I were to list everyone I should be thanking, the book would be twice as long, and I worry that I'd inadvertently leave someone out. Suffice to say that many friends, colleagues, and graduate students have always been willing to discuss the range of material covered here, and for that I am eternally grateful. I would be remiss not to single out (so to speak) the teaching teams for my larger pop culture classes—each of you deserves your own page here. I would also like to thank the other members of the steering committee for Dalhousie's interdisciplinary minor in Popular Culture. The team at Pearson has been wonderful to work with: I would like to especially mention Rebecca Ryoji and Karen Alliston for their tremendous work and support, as well as Rashmi Tickyani, the permissions team, and the photo researchers. Of course, I need to thank my family for encouraging all my pop culture consumption. Finally, and especially, Julia M. Wright, for so much, but in this case especially for the hours of lingering over the cultural significance of television shows that no one else remembers.

LIST OF REVIEWERS

Pearson Education Canada, along with Jason Haslam, would like to thank the following reviewers for their feedback and guidance during the development of Thinking Popular Culture, First Edition: Michael E. Sinatra, Université de Montréal; Don Perkins, University of Alberta; Raj Mehta, Camosun College; Daniel Burgoyne, Vancouver Island University; Ruthann Lee, University of British Columbia, Okanagan; John LeBlanc, University of British Columbia, Okanagan; Nick Baxter-Moore, Brock University; William Little, University of Victoria; Christopher Bracken, University of Alberta; and Christopher Lockett, Memorial University of Newfoundland.

ABOUT THE AUTHOR

Jason Haslam is Associate Professor in the English Department at Dalhousie University, where he teaches courses on and researches popular culture and cultural studies, prison studies, as well as science fiction, the gothic, and other popular genres of literature, film, and television. His most recent of several published books on these topics are a collection of essays, *The Public Intellectual and the Culture of Hope* (co-edited with Joel Faflak) and a scholarly edition of Edgar Rice Burroughs' popular novel, *Tarzan of the Apes*. He has served as President of both the Association of Canadian College and University Teachers of English and the Canadian Association for American Studies.

Part I
Reading Popular Culture

Chapter 1
Thinking Popular Culture?

INTRODUCTION

When Justin Bieber was arrested in 2014 for drag racing, driving under the influence, and assault, and Rob Ford, the mayor of Toronto, admitted to smoking crack cocaine the previous year, was there something to learn about race, gender, and social privilege? What do frosh chants on Canadian campuses and the reaction to them tell us about sexism? Speaking of campuses, do the advertisements and website for your university or college tell you something about how the institution wants to be perceived by students? What's shown in these ads? Are actual people presented on the website? Who are they? What are they doing? Do these visions of the campus contradict your actual experience of it? By combining popular culture, politics, identity, personal and group behaviour, and other aspects of social and cultural life, these examples, and the questions that arise from them, show how popular culture can be found at the centre of some of the more pressing questions of our societies.

This textbook aims to help you build the skills necessary to undertake a serious study of popular culture. Its title, *Thinking Popular Culture*, can mean two things. First, it indicates that this textbook will help teach you how to think critically about popular culture and the roles it plays in society. Second, it can be read to mean that popular culture is itself a form of thinking about the world in which we live, that popular culture reflects—and reflects upon—the larger world of which it is a part.

The different chapters of this textbook are intended to introduce you to the academic study of popular culture by exploring the various theories and methodologies critics use to analyze cultural behaviour, cultural products, and cultural sites; each chapter will apply those methods to a variety of Canadian, American, and global examples of popular culture, past and present. Rather than simply explain these theories and methodologies, however, this book aims to actively draw you, as students, into the conversation, and through the examples, case studies, and questions, ask you to continue its discussions both in and outside your classes.

But before we begin our analyses of popular culture, we need to build some common ground—a sense of what our general field of study is and what foundations the following chapters will build on. So Part I will cover some basics: we'll define what the phrase *popular culture* means and what purpose there is in studying it. More specifically, we'll define the three terms of the title, but in reverse order: in this chapter we begin by discussing what constitutes *culture* and how it's different from, but related to, such concepts as society, nation, and art. We'll also look at the exact ways in which we can define the rather nebulous term *popular*, and why we can (and sometimes can't) distinguish "popular" culture from other forms of culture. Next, in Chapter 2, we'll discuss what it means to *think* about popular culture, looking at some of the history of cultural analysis and looking forward to the methodologies and theories of cultural study that the rest of the textbook details.

In short, Chapter 1 defines the subject matter of this book, "popular culture," while Chapter 2 introduces some traditional theories about the relationships between culture and the larger social and material world. Parts II, III, and IV then discuss the specific theories that lie behind and arise from the academic discipline known as cultural studies (which began to be developed in the 1960s), and how they can be used to analyze popular culture.

WHAT IS CULTURE?

In the *Oxford English Dictionary*, the word *culture*, as a noun, has three central definitions, each of which is broken down into more specific usages depending on context. These three central definitions relate to agriculture, religious worship (although this meaning is no longer in general use), and the human intellect and society more generally. It is, of course, the third use of the term that concerns us.

Culture in this sense of the word is tied to the practices of specific groups or societies, such that one regularly hears references to "Canadian culture," to take one example. The ease with which we use such phrases belies the complexities of the word *culture*, however. This is partly due to the complexity of contemporary societies (after all, Canadians are defined as much by their differences from each other as by any shared identity). But even more basically, the word *culture* is itself more contested than a straightforward dictionary definition might suggest. Indeed, the various schools of thought and ideas that this book describes—most of which are engaged in the critical analysis of culture—rarely agree on a specific definition of the term. Cultural critic Terry Eagleton, building on the work of many other cultural critics, makes the case clear: "'Culture' is said to be one of the two or three most complex words in the English language, and the term which is sometimes considered to be its opposite—nature—is commonly awarded the accolade of being the most complex of all" (Eagleton, 2000, p. 1).

As Eagleton goes on to demonstrate, however, we can frame in a general way what the term *culture* represents. He argues that it has evolved from describing the act of cultivating land to a more figurative or abstract sense of cultivating the human mind, both individually and collectively. In this sense, then, *culture* acts metaphorically: if a wild or untamed land can be transformed by human labour into a cultivated farm for the purpose of yielding more and better crops, so too can human activity itself be "cultivated" into something that yields us a social, spiritual, or artistic "crop." If a farmland yields objects that we need to physically survive, the objects of this other kind of "cultivation" give us a more abstract form of sustenance, whether we call it "art," "music," "politics," or "entertainment."

In this sense, then, we can call "culture" those actions or products of human activity that go beyond our basic needs of physical survival and instead add to life elements of pleasure, or thought, or beauty, and so on. One way of understanding the distinction is as follows: although we need food to live, and so food as such may not be considered an element of culture, the practices and beliefs surrounding food—the way we cook it, what spices we add, how we eat it, what rituals we engage in around the act of eating, and even what kinds of digestible things we see as food and what not—may all be considered culture. Likewise, we may need shelter to live, but the specific design of houses or apartments, the material from which we construct them, and the colours we adorn them with may all be considered cultural. Even the act of sex, which may be "hardwired" into our and other animals' genetic codes, could be considered biological rather than cultural, but the specificities of courtship rituals and the proscriptions on where, when, and even how or with whom one should have sex may be considered, in most instances, cultural. We can generally refer to this as the distinction between "nature" and "culture" (see Figure 1.1).

With such a basic definition of *culture*, though, much is left out of the discussion that is necessary for learning how to study culture, and specifically popular culture. For that

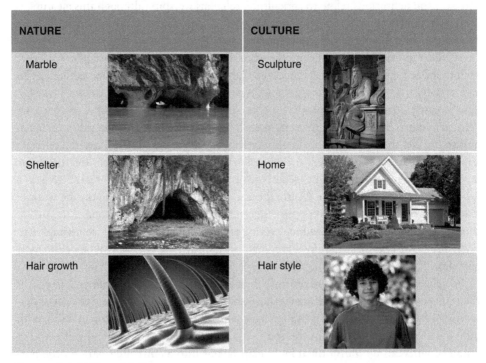

Figure 1.1 Nature/Culture

Source: Serjiob74/Fotolia; Danilo Ascione/Shutterstock; Ljiljana Jankovic/Shutterstock; V. J. Matthew/Shutterstock; Nobeastsofierce/Fotolia; Gareth Boden/Pearson Education Ltd

more focused purpose, it may help to split our definition into three general categories: first, cultural behaviour or traditions—the actions in which people engage that can be considered "cultural"; second, cultural objects or products—the physical creations that humans make and/or use as part of their cultural activities; and third, cultural sites—the places people use, make, and/or transform in order to perform certain actions and/or use certain objects.

Cultural Behaviour, Cultural Traditions

In some academic disciplines, the study of culture focuses primarily on the behaviours engaged in by people who identify as belonging to a larger group. In this sense, "culture" is often equated with large communities—from religious or ethnic groups to regions to nations—such that people can talk about "Roma culture," "Maritime culture," or "Japanese culture." As we'll discuss in later chapters, such distinctions have been drawn to further different political aims, whether these are the liberatory agendas of peoples trying to throw off oppression or assertions that one group has the right to dominate another. For the purpose of defining *culture* in this opening chapter, however, we can set that aside for the moment and say that there are aspects of human behaviour that are cultural in the general terms described above, and that we can study as such.

In anthropology or sociology, for example, students and other scholars examine religious rituals, work habits, leisure activities, sexual and courtship rituals, and so on of various groups of people in order to understand those groups better. The general assumption here is that one can learn more about a society from the ways in which people behave than from asking them to define their own society. In other words, human behaviour can sometimes teach us more about people than even they realize. As Eagleton writes, "If culture means the active tending of natural growth, then it suggests a dialectic between the artificial and the natural, what we do to the world and what the world does to us" (p. 2).

At its heart, then, this form of analysis holds that the cultural activities of a group—those activities that are performed outside of the basic needs of survival—tell us something about how that group is structured, how it perceives the world, and how it differs from or is similar to others in this respect. For example, rituals surrounding puberty vary greatly between different groups: in some cases males and females may be separated for specific activities before or during puberty, while in others such a separation does not take place. In some societies puberty is marked during specific ceremonies, while in other communities it is not. (Such cultural variances aren't always between large social groups—between people from different religious or ethnic backgrounds, for example—since even within an extended family, some members may have a tradition of having "sweet sixteen" parties, while others don't. Cultural analysis does often examine large or "macro" social structures, but it can also focus on behaviour at a smaller scale.)

It's important to note here that the practice of cultural analysis has had its problems. For example, older forms of macro-cultural analysis often focused on cultures that differed from the scholar's own culture, a situation that sometimes led to such scholarship repeating particular biases or assumptions. Scholars from a post-industrial nation who were studying a society based around migratory hunting and gathering activities, for example, might have made the assumption that such a community was "primitive," which could lead the scholars to assume that the community's cultural practices were "simplistic," with the result that they could miss some of the more complex meanings and significance of certain cultural activities. A similar problem could occur even within what seems to be a single culture: an academic from a relatively well-to-do background may make assumptions about a working-class community, for example. Moreover, the group being studied may alter their general behaviour when they know they're being studied: if a professor studying post-adolescent drinking habits was to follow a group of students to a bar, the students may act somewhat differently than they would on their own. Some of the theories we study later in the textbook address these and other problems of cultural analysis.

The study of the **cultural behaviour** of specific groups, however, has at its heart the idea that human beings are constantly shaping the world around them, and are in turn shaped by that world in ways that go beyond our basic physical needs. Or as Eagleton puts it, our behaviour in the world can indicate how we interpret the world around us and in turn how we are constructed by it. Consider religion and politics: cultural practices that, according to some, result from material forces (a society's basic economic needs or structures, for example) but in turn help mould the society around them (the social and cultural lives of people living in a democratic society may be different from a feudal society, for example). We may often distinguish between nature and culture (think of all those debates about whether nature is more important than nurture to an individual's identity), but ultimately, nature and nurture, culture and material life, are constantly reshaping each other. Many of the theories we discuss in this book offer different methods or specific focal points for analyzing this general relationship.

Cultural Objects, Cultural Products

The cultural behaviour of a group can thus teach us important things about how that group perceives the world around it, or about aspects of the society we may otherwise have missed (such as the relative power of different genders in various situations, for example). But cultural behaviour is often associated with certain objects, which themselves often take on a certain societal importance—as objects of veneration, worship, education, aesthetic appreciation, and so on. These objects can include, on the one hand, everything from clothing to tools and to other objects valued for their specific uses, and on the other, those creations we would call art, or literature, or entertainment, which *seem* to fulfill "purely" cultural roles disconnected from day-to-day material life and serving no utilitarian purpose. Somewhere between these two poles lie certain religious objects that may be seen as having a use value but are also seen as often disconnected from the material world, as having a more spiritual nature. Many of the theories we study in this text, especially those most influenced by the Marxist tradition, argue that even such "pure" cultural objects as paintings serve specific roles in relation to material life (for instance, by distracting us from social injustice, or by subtly training us to accept the status quo of society, or by helping us frame revolutionary thoughts).

As with cultural behaviours, however, these objects can be interpreted by a cultural analyst in order to learn something about the people who create, use, or otherwise interact with those objects. Chapter 2 includes an introductory summary of how cultural objects have been traditionally studied, while the rest of the book examines in more detail some of the contemporary forms of cultural analysis. What's important for our purposes now is that critics often differentiate between kinds of cultural objects: obviously there are distinctions between objects that could be called part of **visual culture** (including paintings, for example), **sound culture** (music is the obvious case here), and **print culture** (like literary works). Many distinctions are drawn within these categories, of course, a significant one being between objects that are created by individuals and those that are mass produced, the latter of which can be called **cultural products**. Many of the critics and theorists we will study argue that there is an inherent difference between a unique painting created by an individual and a poster of which millions of copies can be sold. While these distinctions can (and according to some cultural theories, *must*) be made, the fact remains that both sets of objects can be analyzed and studied in order to learn something about the world from which they come. This distinction will be elaborated upon in the chapters that follow.

Cultural Sites

Now that we have a basic understanding of cultural behaviours and objects, there is still one other aspect of culture we can discuss: **cultural sites**, or *where* people engage in their cultural activities and/or interact with cultural objects. Not all spaces can be easily divided into "cultural" and "non-cultural" spaces, of course, and one can make the argument that any space can be a cultural space, since some cultural activities can be performed anywhere a person is, and some cultural objects can be transported or even worn anywhere. While true, there are sites that are specifically intended for certain cultural objects or activities (such as museums or theatres), and those and other sites can also alter how particular objects or actions are perceived. Watching a film in a theatre involves a different set of expectations and effects than watching the same film on a television in your living room or on a computer screen. Likewise, some theorists (such as those we discuss in Chapter 7) would argue that viewing a painting in a museum leads to a very different set of meanings than seeing the same painting projected on a screen in your classroom. Moreover, certain cultural activities, when performed in one place, take on a radically different meaning when performed in another (consider the difference between dancing in a club and standing up suddenly in a classroom and starting to dance). So it's often important to look not just at what people are doing and what they're doing it with, but also where they're doing it. Different sites are often used to distinguish between different kinds of cultural objects or practices, and between different classes or groups of people: when works by the graffiti artist Banksy began appearing in the street they were seen by everyone, but when they became "art" and were sold for high prices they developed a more limited audience. This distinction will be elaborated on later in this chapter when we discuss cultural capital.

Cultural Context

Although we've just discussed cultural activities, cultural objects, and cultural sites separately, it's important to recognize that we often need to analyze these together. In fact, one of the significant changes that the practice and discipline of cultural studies, of which the study of popular culture is one branch, brought to academic scholarship was the very idea that practices, objects, and places all had to be studied in relation to each other.

This critical practice differs radically from other forms of criticism and analysis. A traditional literary scholar may read and interpret a poem all on its own (or at most in the context of other, similar poems, or poems by the same author). A traditional art critic may do the same with a painting, as might a historian of architecture with a building or an anthropologist with religious rituals. A cultural studies critic, however, would say that those poems, paintings, buildings, and rituals need to be analyzed within their larger social context before we can fully appreciate their meanings.

Of course, a *complete* picture of that context is impossible. As the writer Jorge Luis Borges would say, a perfect map of a country would be the exact same size as the landscape it's mapping, and so not be very useful. But all cultural studies scholars, to varying degrees and according to the various methods outlined in this textbook, never look at things in isolation but rather analyze aspects of culture within a larger context.

A general example may help here: different societies and peoples have moulded clay into different shapes throughout much of human history. Some may make pots for carrying corn; others may make vessels for carrying water. Likewise, some may make containers by drying them in the sun while others may use kilns. Some pots may even have evidence of being used only rarely, as if for special occasions, and these might be made slightly differently, or be adorned in specific ways, and so on. Even if we knew nothing else about these groups, the different shapes of these containers, the different ways in which they were made, and even the materials from which they were made may tell us something specific about the ways these societies functioned on a daily, material basis and give us a sense of how they viewed the world. In short, the more we know about the context of the pot's use, the more we know about both the pot and the people.

But if we were to look at one of these containers in a museum, outside the context of its use, we may not interpret correctly how it was used, and our version of what it meant to those people may be wrong. Still, the fact that it's been placed in a museum *may* tell us something about how the culture that built the museum views human history, or what it thinks of other or older cultures, and so on.

In another general example, what if one group makes small people-shaped figures that are always found near burial sites while other groups make small plant-shaped figures that are always found in tilled fields: would these cultural objects—these pieces of art—tell us something about the differences between these groups and their attitudes toward the world? *Perhaps*, but we would likely need much more information, much more *context*, about the material side of these societies (How did they survive and thrive?) and their cultural setting (Were these the only figures they made? Did they make larger numbers of some kinds of figures than others? Did they paint these figures? Did everyone own a set? Were they mass produced in a factory?). Clearly these cultural objects need to be understood as they were used and within the context in which they were used.

A Utah drive-in showing *The Ten Commandments* in 1958.
Source: J. R. Eyerman/Time Life Pictures/Getty Images

The Movie Theatre

Let's think about an object, practice, and site within contemporary culture: the movie theatre. Certainly a traditional film critic could analyze the form of a film, its place in the history of film, and how these help shape the meaning of the film. For example, the specific genre of a film tells us something about its structure and goals: an action-based thriller will affect most audience members differently than would a slower-paced period drama. A critic could analyze a film on its own terms or in a larger film-centred context and offer valuable conclusions about how that particular film is or is not a classic example of the genre, or how it plays with genre expectations, or how it might fail to meet certain judgments of quality relative to other examples of the genre.

A cultural studies critic, however, would argue that the time and place of viewing is just as important: an audience of students watching an action thriller in the classroom may have different expectations of the film than an audience watching it on opening night in the theatre. In other words, the context in which the film is received can be as important as its content in understanding its importance.

Let's consider *The Rocky Horror Picture Show* (1975), which is based on a stage play by Richard O'Brien. Many of you have probably seen or at least heard of this film, given the frequency of its special

A scene from *The Rocky Horror Picture Show* (1975).
Source: Moviestore collection Ltd/Alamy

screenings at Halloween and at LGBTQ Pride events—in fact, *Rocky Horror* holds the record for the longest-running theatrical release, making it in some ways the most popular film of all time!

If traditional film scholars were to analyze *Rocky Horror*, they would likely situate it within the genre history of both film musicals and science fiction and horror films. One of the most popular forms of film in the 1930s into the 1950s, film musicals have become less popular in the decades since then. The science-fiction horror that *Rocky Horror* employs was also very popular in the 1950s, and in somewhat altered form continues to be so. *Rocky Horror* explicitly parodies these films, even as it serves as homage to them. Moreover, its explicitly sexual content points to the often repressed sexual tensions that were at play in those earlier films.

But such an analysis would fall short of explaining why *Rocky Horror* continues to be shown around the world and why it's such an important film. To do that, a critic would have to take a wider, cultural approach, analyzing the role of the cultural site of the theatre as well as the cultural context of sexual liberation movements in the 1970s and later. Such an approach is especially required for this film, given that early in its release certain forms of audience participation, especially at midnight showings, became common and eventually evolved into elaborate forms of audience behaviour that played with the queer sexuality on the screen. As a form of liberation in itself, this audience participation places *Rocky Horror* in a cultural matrix with other cultural acts, such as drag shows.

The audience-participation aspect of *Rocky Horror* makes it an especially rich film for cultural analysis, but it should be stressed that all films can be read this way—all cultural objects are involved in cultural sites with certain cultural behaviours and in larger social and cultural contexts.

This contextualized approach to cultural criticism also has an impact on what kinds of culture are studied. If meaning isn't part of the object or act itself but rather resides in a complex interplay of objects, acts, places, and context, then it doesn't really matter what one studies, since larger cultural meanings can be found anywhere. Of course, some activities may hold more importance than others, but the supposed *quality* of the object or act itself is of less importance than its larger role within the social cultural context: a James Bond movie could be as valuable a source of information for the cultural critic as one of Shakespeare's sonnets. Or, to move away from more "artistic" forms, a cultural studies critic could say that the activities surrounding the preparation and ingestion of food, including what kinds of food are eaten and who prepares it, may tell us more about a group's world view than its philosophical meditations or poetry do. For example, studying the rituals surrounding Canadian Thanksgiving can tell us something about social expectations concerning family structures. In another example, the ways in which a city's restaurant districts are divided, and whether "national" borders are drawn around certain neighbourhoods (such as a Chinatown or Little Italy district), can inform the experience of eating (meaning the context is as important as the cuisine), and could be used to analyze how the notion of "multiculturalism" is deployed (and commodified) in Canadian or other societies.

WHAT IS POPULAR?

The emphasis on context in cultural criticism brings us to the fact that this textbook isn't about culture in general; instead it's about the study of **popular culture**. Like the term *culture* itself, *popular culture* is not as easy to define as it might first seem. The division between which aspects of culture constitute popular culture and which don't can be difficult to make, and is tied up with other kinds of divisions: good vs. bad, or the problem of taste in culture; high culture vs. low culture; everyday culture vs. mass culture; and many others. We'll discuss some of these different divisions and gesture toward why it's important to study popular culture in a serious, careful fashion.

On the one hand, it's quite simple to define what is or isn't popular: something that is enjoyed by a large number of people is, quite clearly, popular. But this basic definition fails us on at least two levels. First, exactly how many people does it take to make something popular? There is no exact line we can draw: we can't say that X number of people enjoy this particular song but it's not popular, whereas X+1 number of people proves that it is popular. Similarly, while there are large categories of culture that are popular (certain styles of music or fashion, for example), not every example of that style is itself popular.

Clearly, then, simple numbers are not adequate for defining popular culture, and yet it's still a category invoked as being meaningful: we tend to know when something is an element of popular culture and when something is not. How is it that we do this? What rubrics or forms of measurement do we rely on, implicitly or explicitly, when we say something is part of popular culture while something else isn't? In what follows we trace out some of the models of judgment commonly used—by both academics and others—to define popular culture.

High Culture/Low Culture

One of the ways people define popular culture is by distinguishing it from other forms of culture, the primary distinction being between high culture and low culture. Generally speaking, **high culture** refers to forms of cultural production or objects that are seen as being unique, well-wrought, and meaningful in themselves, and as helping to distinguish, educate, or enlighten both individuals and the society of which they are a part. Often, this definition of high culture is restricted to specific forms of artistic production. Certain examples of music, painting, literature, or other artistic forms are seen as intrinsically beautiful and uplifting of the spirit and the mind. **Low culture**, on the other hand, is perceived as doing the opposite: it degrades those people who interact with it, and it furthers the larger degradation of society. In Chapter 2 we discuss how traditional forms of the academic study of culture were invested in this distinction and served to perpetuate it.

In our time, especially following what we know as the modernist period (discussed in more detail in Chapter 9), this distinction brings with it certain assumptions: high culture is complex while low culture is simplistic; high culture is intelligent (or best understood by intelligent people) while low culture is not; high culture is original while low culture is derivative; high culture is "refined" while low culture is "primitive" or "base"; high culture can make you a better person while low culture can make you a bad person.

Quite often, popular culture is perceived, with very few exceptions, as falling into the category of low culture. From nineteenth-century pulp crime magazines to comic books and to video games and movies, popular culture is seen as catering to the least informed, basest elements of society. The logic here is simple: in order to appeal to a wide group of people, a cultural object or practice has to appeal to the "lowest common denominator." In effect, then, those who believe this argument would say that the very fact that something is popular makes it likely to be simplistic, unoriginal, and not very complex. Furthermore, if society wants to improve or develop, then the consumption of or interaction with high culture should be encouraged, while popular forms (and the people who like them) should be discouraged.

But contemporary cultural critics question the validity of any division between high and low culture, and in fact the problems with the division are easily made clear. One common method to critique it is to point to works that are considered high culture and yet at the same time are popular: Shakespeare is most commonly invoked here. Seen as the paragon of English literature, his plays are nonetheless popular enough to sell millions of theatre and movie tickets even now. Moreover, his plays often include bawdy or coarse humour in ways not so different from that of an average television sitcom. Finally, while linguistically Shakespeare is undoubtedly original, many of his plots are derivative or are taken directly from other writers.

A poster for Kenneth Branagh's film version of Shakespeare's *Hamlet* (1996).
Source: AF archive/Alamy

Taste and Cultural Capital

Despite the clear problems of adequately distinguishing between high and low (or popular) culture, many people, including academics, still do so. Why? If the division isn't a "natural" or real one, as the Shakespeare example tends to show, then what is to be gained from drawing these divisions? Who benefits from them? There are many answers to these questions, but one of the most important has to do with the ways these cultural divisions relate to divisions in society itself. In other words, cultural taste can relate to the positions of power in society.

This argument has been made most clearly by the French cultural critic Pierre Bourdieu. In his analysis of the concept of **taste**, Bourdieu argues that the seemingly simple act of appreciating culture, such as art or poetry, is anything but straightforward. As discussed earlier, the types of behaviour and judgment we engage in with regard to culture can radically change depending on something as simple as where we are: a tomato soup label in our kitchen will provoke a different reaction from Andy Warhol's exacting reproduction of that label hanging in a museum. We *appreciate* and thus interpret that same image in different ways based on the larger context. Bourdieu would say that, in part, this difference is an effect of our education, and furthermore that different social groups are trained to react differently in relation to culture.

Moreover, some groups (and even objects) are seen as having more value in relation to culture than others. Bourdieu calls this **cultural capital**, with different social groups "maintaining different, and even antagonistic, relations to culture, depending on the conditions in which they acquired their cultural capital and the markets in which they can derive most profit from it" (Bourdieu, 1984, p. 12). Within these relations, certain objects will come to be seen as more culturally worthy, or more significant to society, and so get labelled as high culture. But for Bourdieu, and for many of the writers to be studied in this textbook, there is nothing intrinsic about the object itself that makes it worthier: instead, it is merely its position within the social ladder or hierarchy that makes it so. When people are said to have "good taste," what's really being said is that they have the proper training, and thus cultural access to social power. In this sense, then, the distinction between high and low culture, or between "art" and "popular culture," has nothing to do with the cultural objects and everything to do with maintaining a certain social structure. This relationship between culture and social power lies at the heart of most of the theories discussed in this textbook.

Mass Culture and Everyday Culture

Another term often used interchangeably with popular culture is **mass culture**. The reason they are largely interchangeable is that, from the mid twentieth century forward, most of the objects of popular culture have been both mass produced and designed for mass consumption: film, comic books, popular music, popular fashion, and so on can all be produced on a massive scale and circulated around the world. That doesn't mean that the

Shakespeare, Canada, and Popular Culture: Stratford and *Slings and Arrows*

Shakespeare is certainly an aspect of high culture by any definition, but his plays (and his sonnets) are also extremely popular, and references to them proliferate in popular culture. Did you know that *The Lion King* is a reworking of *Hamlet*, or that there's an episode of *Doctor Who* that features Shakespeare as a character? Tied to these examples are not only all the film adaptations of Shakespeare's plays but also movies like *Shakespeare in Love* and *Anonymous* that, like the *Doctor Who* episode, make Shakespeare himself an object of popular attention.

Shakespeare plays a particular role in Canadian popular culture. The town of Stratford, Ontario, is named after Stratford-upon-Avon in England, Shakespeare's birthplace. Partly because of this, a famous festival—the Stratford Shakespearean Festival of Canada—was launched there in 1953 and continues today. The town's economy largely depends on the tourism generated by the festival. But is this an example of high culture, popular culture, or both? Certainly the name and plays of Shakespeare are central draws, but so too are the many popular Canadian and Hollywood film stars who have performed there. Likewise, the festival now features more contemporary plays as well. One could say, then, that "Shakespeare" serves to lend the festival a certain cultural capital even as it draws some of its popularity from the less "refined" aspects of celebrity culture.

Meanwhile, the Canadian television show *Slings and Arrows* (2003–2006), starring well-known Canadian actor Paul Gross and created by former *Kids in the Hall* star Mark McKinney, fictionalizes the Stratford Festival, calling it the "New Burbage Festival." Focusing on the actors and the production side of the stage performance, the series partakes of traditional television drama and comedy forms even as it tries to challenge certain expectations of mass-marketed American television in its narrative structure.

What to make of *Slings and Arrows*, then? Relying on the association of Shakespeare and Stratford with high culture, the show still participates in popular forms of television entertainment. Does it use Shakespeare just to give itself a gloss of cultural capital? Or is it trying to undermine the class-based assumptions about high art and drama? Or can it be doing both? These are the sorts of questions that can be asked when one focuses on a wider range of cultural objects in academic study and approaches them with the knowledge of the theories discussed in this chapter and the rest of the textbook.

terms *popular culture* and *mass culture* should be seen as exactly equivalent, however. Certainly there were forms of popular culture that existed before the age of mass reproduction. More importantly, though, those critics who prefer to use the term *mass culture* tend to be influenced by what is known as the Frankfurt School of critical theory, which we discuss in Chapter 7. For many of the thinkers from this school of thought, mass culture is empty of the types of depth and complexity of meanings found in earlier forms of original art and high culture. Mass culture serves only to further the goal of maintaining the social status quo because it is necessarily produced by large corporations for the purpose of furthering their own profit, which necessitates the maintenance of current social structures.

Against this idea of popular culture as mass culture, however, runs the idea of popular culture as a form of folk culture, or **everyday culture**, something that arises from the daily lives of the so-called average person or group. Cultural objects such as folk art and folk music, along with more radical practices arising from subcultures or countercultures (groups that follow cultural practices that are not considered "mainstream," which we also discuss in Chapter 7), comprise this notion of everyday or folk culture. Folk cultures are often associated with particular communities, either arising out of a certain region or actually helping to create a self-identified group of people who engage in the same cultural activities (one can think here of certain kinds of hobbyist groups, or folk music or art collectives, and so on). Within these cultural practices, new ideas that challenge the status quo can arise.

Social Media: Mass Culture, Folk Culture, Everyday Culture?

The significance of social media—Facebook, Twitter, Pinterest, Instagram, and so on—in contemporary cultural life in Canada and across the globe can't be overestimated. According to some, Twitter and other social media were instrumental in the democratic movements of the so-called Arab Spring (the series of revolutions and uprisings in the Arab Peninsula and Northern Africa that began in 2010) and helped the activism of the Idle No More movement in Canada. They are also part of everyday life in Canada and around the world.

So how can we categorize these cultural forms according to the rubrics we outlined earlier? Are they cultural sites? Not by any traditional definition, since the "space" of social media exists virtually, but they do form a virtual space as one reads and engages online. Indeed, the space of your engagement in social media can play a role in how you interact with it and gain meaning from it: Are you alone in front of a computer in your dorm room? Are you tweeting in class? If the latter, is it allowed or are you surreptitiously tweeting about the class to your followers? Likewise, the particular device you're using (a computer, a smartphone, a tablet) constitutes a cultural object.

Perhaps more obviously, engagement with social media is a form of cultural behaviour. But what kind of cultural behaviour is it, and does it depend on the form it takes? Facebook, for instance, is heavily "monetized" through advertising, and your status updates and personal information can be mined in order to target particular ads at you. This would seem to be a form of mass culture.

That said, you can form Facebook groups to protest such exploitation in the "real world": various Occupy movements, many of them directed against companies and other capitalist activities, are prevalent on Facebook and other platforms. Moreover, Pinterest and Instagram can link people with similar artistic sensibilities, thus forming particular artistic communities. Even on earlier social media platforms (before the term *social media* was even coined), people would join particular message boards or discussion groups to exchange and comment on each other's writing, for example (one can think here of certain fanfiction communities, or NaNoWriMo, the National Novel Writing Month, which began online in the early 2000s). We could read such behaviour as forming a kind of folk culture, although one not limited to a particular geographical region.

As with most contemporary cultural behaviours, then, our own use of social media is a complex form of cultural engagement that can't be easily pinned down. Still, in analyzing popular cultural behaviour, certain aspects of social media stand out. For example, with every tweet or status update or picture upload, you are defining yourself in terms of your interests (which may or may not be defined in terms of consumerism), your activities, and even your mood.

But are you *choosing* to define yourself in those ways, or are these platforms actually defining you in certain ways beyond your control? Do you find yourself thinking, "This will make a funny status update," or wondering if someone will post pictures of you that you don't want posted? Likewise, we've all read news stories in Canada and elsewhere about social media being used to bully and intimidate people, often in explicitly sexist and sexually violent ways and often in the form of group behaviour. Would such bullying and hatred have occurred without social media? Would it have been as relentless? Would the group dynamic have been the same?

In these ways, the cultural behaviours associated with social media are actually shaping, or at least helping to shape, identity—of both individuals and groups—rather than allowing people to express some inner truth about themselves. In Parts II, III, and IV we'll discuss theories relating to the ways in which popular culture shapes identity.

No matter which particular definition of popular culture we follow, it's clear that popular culture plays a central role in society and in relation to social structures as such, and so is an important area for study and research. If we are to understand our societies and ourselves, the significance of the study of popular culture should not be underestimated. But what does it mean to study popular culture, or to study culture more generally? How does one do so? In Chapter 2 we trace a general history of the study of culture, and use that to lead into the rest of the textbook, where we focus on current methodologies used to analyze popular culture.

Discussion Questions

1. Can you think of cultural objects or acts that mean one thing in a particular space and something else in another? Can you think of situations where the meaning wouldn't change with context? Does that meaning sometimes change depending on the audience or on its gender, racial, or sexual identity?

2. Look at the photograph of the 1950s drive-in theatre earlier in this chapter. What cultural objects, behaviours, sites, or contexts can you identify here? Does the photograph comment on them? What does it tell you about this society or culture?

3. Can you name an example of high culture that's also popular, besides Shakespeare? What about the other way around—are there examples of popular culture that are or have become high culture?

4. When you hear someone described as having "good taste" or "bad taste," what exactly do you picture in your mind? List some items or behaviours a person might exhibit that are in "good taste" or in "bad taste." Do they signify anything else (for example, economic position, education, or background)?

5. Can you think of a *current* example of popular culture that is *not* also an example of mass culture?

6. Look through this book's table of contents. What aspects or particular examples of popular culture seem to be missing? What might that gap tell you about the expectations of the book or its assumptions about readership? Textbooks don't usually ask you to think about what they don't cover: Why might this one draw attention to it?

Further Reading

See end of Chapter 2.

Chapter 2
The Study of Culture

INTRODUCTION

Now that we have briefly defined both the sweeping notion of culture and the more specific subset of popular culture, we turn to the third word in the book's title, and discuss what it means to *think* about culture in general and popular culture in particular.

To make an overly broad generalization, as long as humans have created cultural objects or participated in cultural rituals or performances, it's safe to say that they have also discussed their culture. More to the point, various societies around the world have developed, throughout history, methods of analyzing their own and others' cultures. Whether it's practised informally as a general discussion or more formally as contemporary professional criticism (such as that of book or film critics, or academic scholarship), cultural analysis forms part of any given society's cultural practice. Some would argue that criticism can function to help change cultures, while others would say that such criticism is itself, like the objects or practices it studies, merely a reflection of its surrounding social milieu.

Of interest to us, of course, are the particular forms of cultural analysis that have attempted to formalize both their own methodologies and specific definitions of what counts as "culture." While it would be impossible to discuss all the significant forms of cultural study that have been developed over the millennia, this chapter will provide a brief overview of a selection of traditional methods for the study of culture, focusing on those that have been especially influential in the Western traditions of cultural analysis. While it is necessarily incomplete (the subjects of this chapter could be the basis of entire books), this overview will give us a foundation on which to build an understanding of the newer methodologies of contemporary cultural studies, especially as they relate to popular culture, and how they offer a different understanding of the role of culture in contemporary life.

THE ESSENCE OF CULTURE

In general terms, all forms of cultural analysis frame culture as having a deeper significance than its simple appearance would denote. Thus, a painting is more than just pigments placed on a surface. The specific organization of those pigments (whether they're splattered randomly or shaped like sunflowers, for example) can create different meanings, just as the context of the painting's creation or its viewing, as we learned in Chapter 1, can change that meaning or create new meanings altogether. The study of culture is the attempt to understand those various meanings.

In order to analyze culture, though, the cultural critic must first have an idea of how to define culture and an understanding of how it creates meaning. As we've already learned, one's definition of culture (for example, whether one divides it into high and low, or whether one is talking about a cultural practice, object, or site) can alter one's analysis of culture. This fact implies that at least part of the meaning of any given cultural object or moment—and maybe all of that meaning—is the product of the different relationships that this object or moment has to its surroundings.

This form of cultural analysis, which views meaning as being the result of a dynamic interplay of a cultural object and its various contexts, isn't the only one, however. Several theories instead posit a more **essentialist** notion of meaning, in which culture is defined by an absolute essence, a meaning that ultimately cannot be altered. In such theories, culture either contains or reflects some inherent truth about the world. Opposed to such an approach, contemporary cultural theories tend to be **anti-essentialist** in that they see the meanings of culture as more dynamic and alterable—as being constantly constructed and reconstructed in social settings. As we will learn, this applies to such social identities as gender, race, and sexuality because they are part of our cultural and social practices rather than standing separate from them as pre-existing, essentialist, biological truths.

Put more succinctly, while theories more traditional to European and North American cultural study (such as those explored in this chapter) would hold that great ideas, or the recognition of absolute Truth, shape the world, later theories (such as many of those studied in the rest of this book) hold that the world shapes ideas, and so there is no such thing as an absolute Truth but rather a series of contingent and contextual truths that are always in flux.

In what follows, we trace a brief history of some of the more influential essentialist theories so that we can recognize the foundation on which (and assumptions against which) later thinkers build their own analyses of culture. It should be recognized, though, that this history necessarily leaves out the finer detail you would be given in a philosophy or history of criticism class or textbook. Additionally, the narrative offered here is decidedly European and decidedly male in focus. This is owing to the fact that the forms of philosophy and cultural analysis in North American and other Western universities have traditionally been Eurocentric and patriarchal (among other systemic forms of bias). Understanding these theories can, however, help one to understand later developments in cultural theory and the study of popular culture, in part because one aspect of later cultural theory is precisely to decentre such biased structures of authority such that they no longer serve as the sole models for cultural analysis.

Plato's Cave

One of the clearest philosophical expressions of the argument for the existence of an inherent and absolute Truth lying behind the world, and one that would be seen as an influence on much of Western philosophy for millennia to come, was written by the

Greek philosopher Plato (c. 424 BCE–c. 338 BCE). Plato is one of the most famous philosophers of classical Greece, surpassed only, perhaps, by his teacher Socrates (c. 469 BCE–399 BCE), whom we know of mostly through Plato's writings. Plato's thought is known primarily through his written works, which take the form of dialogues between Socrates and his students. This form is the basis for what is now known as the "Socratic method" of teaching, whereby a teacher educates students by asking them questions and helping to guide their answers. Plato's subjects range from creation myths to political theory, to mathematics and beyond. One of the most enduring of his works, *The Republic*, sketches out a model for society based on what Plato saw as the solid foundations of his philosophy.

Plato's Allegory of the Cave

In *The Republic*, Plato writes that Socrates tells the Allegory of the Cave to Plato's brother, Glaucon, in order to explain the difference between the enlightened and unenlightened mind. Socrates asks Glaucon to imagine a cave in which several prisoners are chained such that they can't escape; their heads are chained so that they're always looking at the cave wall in front of them, and they've been in this position all their lives. Behind the prisoners is a fire that lights up the cave, and between the fire and the prisoners are people walking, holding objects. Because of how they're chained, the prisoners can only ever see the shadows of these objects, not the objects themselves or the fire. Socrates conjectures that these people, having been chained in this way their whole life, would see the shadows in front of them as real objects, as the only reality they can know, and that they would devise names and theories about the various shadows they see.

But at some point one prisoner escapes, and he turns around. At first the brightness of the fire blinds him, but eventually he starts to see the people and the objects and realizes that it was they that caused the shadows. This realization makes these people more substantial, more real than the shadows, and so the prisoner now thinks he's discovered the final truth of reality.

But then, Socrates says, perhaps the prisoner manages to escape the cave, and he sees the sun! Now the prisoner realizes that the fire is only a smaller version of the sun, and that the sun is the true cause of light and beauty.

For Socrates (and Plato), this story serves as an allegory for philosophical enlightenment. In our daily lives, we are like the prisoners. The things we see in front of us and picture as "reality"—our desks, our houses, our culture more generally—are just shadows, or reflections, of a larger reality. How do we know this? Socrates would say that we can all recognize a desk, no matter what shape it is—our desk at home and our desk at school may be different in colour, size, and even shape, but we still know that they're both desks. This is because, Socrates would say, we have an inkling of an Ideal Form of the desk in our minds, of which these actual desks are just a reflection, like the shadows on the wall.

But the notion of the Ideal desk is really just a way to understand the Ideal Forms of concepts like goodness, beauty, and truth. We recognize something as beautiful or true because it reflects a larger, universal, or absolute Good. Like the prisoner who escapes from the cave, the philosopher's job is to try to find Absolute Good and explain it to other people. (Unfortunately, though, such a philosopher, like the escaped prisoner who returns to the cave, may be initially considered insane by the other prisoners, who have only ever lived in the life of shadows.)

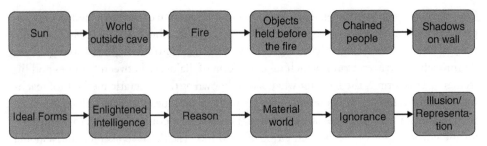

Figure 2.1 Plato's Allegory of the Cave (Simplified)

Significant for our purposes is the so-called Allegory of the Cave that Plato offers in *The Republic*. This allegory maps out a vision of how meaning is both created and understood in the world. The story follows a basic narrative, as traced in the "Plato's Allegory" box and in Figure 2.1.

This allegory asserts that our understanding of the world is shaped by absolute, unchanging Ideals, such as those of Truth or Beauty, and that we must try to discover those absolutes if we are to live a fully meaningful life.

What does this have to do with culture? Well, in this view, only those activities that further our appreciation of those Ideals are seen as useful or good activities to engage in. For Plato, many cultural activities—like painting, for example—fail to live up to these ideals: since an actual tree is merely a shadow of some absolute concept of the perfect Tree, which is itself a reflection of the Ideal of the Good in the world, then a painting of that tree doesn't help get us closer to understanding Truth, because it becomes a mere copy or shadow of the actual tree that is itself a mere shadow of Truth. The same holds for poetry and plays: these artistic, cultural activities serve merely to place us further into the cave and away from true Beauty or Truth. For Plato, the best activity—the only "good" activity—to participate in is philosophy itself. Better yet if it's his kind of philosophy! Other forms of culture—whether they are high or low—only make us further deluded. As we will see, this negative view of culture, especially as it applied to popular culture, pops up again and again throughout the history of Western cultural analysis.

The Enlightenment

Leaping ahead two thousand years to the eighteenth and nineteenth centuries (the beginning of the period this book is interested in), we can find arguments that, while distinct in their approach, agree with Plato's basic assertion: that there is an essential Truth and Beauty to the world, and that we must understand this Truth if we are to better ourselves and our societies.

The German philosopher Immanuel Kant (1724–1804) is one such thinker. Kant is most often identified as one of the pre-eminent philosophers of the Enlightenment, and is seen as offering the primary philosophical foundation for empiricism as a mode of understanding the universe around us. Attempting to define the processes of human thought and its relationship to the world, Kant discusses human observation and thinking. Like Plato, Kant divided the world into objects we can experience with our senses (objects we can see, touch, taste, and so on) and a more ethereal realm of the abstract concepts of those things. He refers to an object in the sensible realm as a **phenomenon** and to the abstract concept as a **noumenon**, which we can roughly correlate with the shadows on the wall of Plato's cave and the Ideal Forms, respectively.

But there is a significant difference between Kant's view, written during the period generally known as the **Enlightenment**, and that of Plato. Whereas Plato argued that, when properly philosophically trained, a human could directly experience the concepts of the Ideal Forms, Kant argues, in his *Critique of Pure Reason*, that humans are bound by their senses and thus can experience only the phenomenal realm. This position doesn't mean that Kant didn't believe in such universal ideas, however. He argued that, through the use of reason, people can work to understand the relations between the objects they experience through their senses. In other words, while we can never move completely beyond our senses into a purely abstract realm of Ideal thought, human rationality can nonetheless piece together the phenomena around us and develop a rational understanding of how the world works, and so approach the Ideal structure of the noumenal realm. Our ability to observe the world and use our reason can allow us to conjecture about the overall structure of the world and the universal laws that tie it together. In other words, for Kant, as for Plato, the world follows a certain set of rational, perfect structures; but for Kant, we can't appreciate these structures directly, but only learn to understand them through a rational explanation of our direct observations.

Kant thus defends human reason and empirical, scientific study as a way of understanding the world, even as he assumes that a logical structure lies behind it that we can never fully grasp (since the limitations of human existence make such omniscient knowledge impossible). This kind of thinking is the foundation of modern scientific thought and the scientific method.

Importantly, though, Kant focuses on the individual's senses and ability to reason based on observations. This places the human individual at the centre of Kant's philosophy. Whereas the Ideal Forms in Plato's work are what give the world meaning, Kant says that we can derive that meaning only through our own mental work. This is a subtle shift of thought but one with profound effects, as it puts the individual at the centre of a rational universe. It is one's power of reason that allows one to see and create meaning in this world. As we'll see in later chapters, this notion of the individual is something that more recent thinkers have begun to move away from, while others note that Kant restricted his belief in reason to certain kinds of people (notably, to European men such as himself).

What about culture in Kant's world view, then? If for Plato culture was merely a reflection of Truth or Beauty and served to further our distance from those ideals, how does Kant see it? For Kant, as for Plato, we do have a conception of the Beautiful, but we can understand it only through objects that are presented to our senses. In other words, while there is a universal concept of Beauty, we can learn to appreciate it only through objects in this world rather than, as Plato would have it, meditating on the concept directly.

And since for Kant the act of aesthetic judgment is best done objectively, it also means that the realm of aesthetics or beauty is likewise an objective category: beauty is not in the eye of the beholder but is instead an autonomous realm, beyond the influence of society or history, and can be appreciated only through an analysis done by an objective viewer of a particular object.

But this dependency on the individual's senses may cause a problem for Kant's belief in a universal Beauty: What happens when two people disagree about what is beautiful? Wouldn't that disagreement mean, following Kant's argument, that there is no such thing as a universal Beauty, and by extension, Truth? Kant would say no, and instead argue that one of those people is simply wrong or mistaken in his interpretation. For Kant, the appreciation of culture, like the practice of science, must be done in an objective, rational manner, and if we approach culture with such objectivity then we can agree on a certain "common sense" as to what is beautiful and what is ugly, and so on.

Romanticism

Kant's rationalist vision of the world, like that of other Enlightenment thinkers, places an objective rationality at the centre of human life. Anything that moves us away from objectivity and reason—such as passionate feelings of anger or love, or subjective beliefs not backed up by observation—is thus pushed to the side of what it means to be human, and is even seen, in some cases, as having a negative effect on our lives. But, clearly, people are not always (or ever) *purely* rational creatures. Is this always a bad thing?

In the decades following Kant's work, a new system of thought emerged, which was later termed **Romanticism**. Like the Enlightenment thinkers before them, Romantic philosophers, poets, and other artists saw the individual as the centre of the philosophical and natural universe. Unlike Enlightenment philosophers, however, the Romanticists emphasized the necessity (and universality) of feeling over that of reason, arguing that emotions—such as love, and more generally sentiment expressed toward other human beings—actually defined who we were as people. Many Romantics emphasized spirit over rationality, and, contrary to Kant's transcendent rational life, claimed that through a return to nature humans could experience a transcendent spiritual enlightenment.

The Romantics took the individualism of the Enlightenment in a different direction in another way. They believed in a universal notion of sentiment or emotion—that all people, if they are properly attuned to themselves and their surroundings (especially their natural surroundings), will feel the same sympathies and emotions under similar circumstances. And some Romantics took their individualism further than this. If humanity is, at its best, in tune with its natural surroundings, then different natural surroundings will lead to different character traits. Thus, modern theories and politics of nationalism begin to develop in the Romantic period of the eighteenth and nineteenth centuries. In Chapter 13 we discuss Johann Herder, who helped develop this Romantic nationalism. Likewise, Romantic scientists like J. S. Blumenbach drew distinctions between races of humans based on Romantic notions of the natural world and beauty. If for Kant (in theory, if not in practice, as we'll see in Chapter 12 on race) objective rationality was a universal trait that finds its expression in a common sense that everyone can share, for the Romantics, universal sentiment or feeling led to a division in how people experience the world. Many of the foundational theories we look at in Part II arise from or respond to the idealism and individualism of the Romantics.

To ask our central question again: How do these theories relate to culture? Building on their belief in the need for the individual to connect to the land, the Romantics—including such English poets and philosophers as William Wordsworth (1770–1850) and Samuel Taylor Coleridge (1772–1834), and, in North America, Ralph Waldo Emerson (1803–1882) and Margaret Fuller (1810–1850), as well as such visual artists as German painter Caspar David Friedrich (1774–1840) and English painter and printmaker J. M. W. Turner (1775–1851), among many others—placed a high value on natural beauty. In particular moments, the natural world could allow you to experience the **sublime**, or a moment of transcendence wrought by the ineffable beauty and terror of the natural world: a lightning bolt striking in a field, or a massive waterfall, or even a simple leaf could open up the wonders of the universe to your senses. Whereas for Kant this moment would gain meaning only if approached through reason, for the Romantics it would be a singular moment that could lift your *spirit*.

Der Wanderer über dem Nebelmeer (*The Wanderer Above the Sea of Fog,* 1818) by Caspar David Friedrich (1774–1840) is an often cited Romantic painting that tries to capture the sublime.

Source: INTERFOTO/Fine Arts/Alamy

Art and cultural objects, especially those that tried to echo natural beauty, could also lift you up in this way. Conversely, cultural objects that emphasized artificially imposed structures, like particular poetic metres or rhyme schemes, removed us from that sublime experience. Many Romantic thinkers thus emphasized the need for individuals to develop their own approach to poetry, art, and life itself. Far from the universally objective rationality of Kant, we are led now to an individualistic approach to life that would nonetheless allow one to experience the universal nature of the sublime.

In this way, then, the Romantics are far removed from Plato. Where he saw the individual expressions of culture as merely chaotic shadows or reflections of the Truth of the Ideal Forms, the Romantics saw in an individual's purposefully unique actions or creations a way of capturing the universal nature of beauty. Beauty and Truth were one and the same for the Romantics: as poet John Keats wrote in "Ode on a Grecian Urn," "Beauty is truth, truth beauty." Like Plato, the Romantics valued the quest for such universals, and believed that people could actually experience them, but unlike Plato they saw the individual's capturing of that truth in art as a means of helping others see their own path to transcendence.

CULTURAL CRITICISM I: THE ESSENCE OF HIGH CULTURE

This brief history has been necessary to lead us to modern forms of cultural criticism. In the remainder of this chapter we'll discuss some of the more traditional definitions of culture and its roles in society as they were practised in the later nineteenth century and early part of the twentieth century, and against which modern forms of cultural studies react.

Specifically, some late nineteenth- and early twentieth-century critics built on Kant's idea that the aesthetic sphere must be judged objectively, separate from worldly concerns, and on the Romantic vision of the ways certain forms of art can lift us up, making us appreciate beauty and truth in their truest forms. Combining these approaches, such critics argued that while culture and art can lift us up and make us better people, cultural criticism must focus on the work of art as an object separate from the world, or outside of its contexts. The first approach is epitomized by the nineteenth-century thinker Matthew Arnold, while the second is encapsulated best by the Leavis school of cultural criticism and by formalist literary critics.

Matthew Arnold: Culture and Civilization

The British author and critic Matthew Arnold (1822–1888) is often held up as a defender of the role of high culture (and its criticism) in the development and maintenance of a functional society. His defence of literary culture and its role in society has had longstanding effects in the West, particularly in the university teaching of literature and in the general view of high culture. Arnold wrote at a time when the British Empire was at its height, but also at a time when control of the functions of government and the state was being opened up through the enfranchisement of the working classes and early women's rights campaigns. Hand in hand with these changes came the Industrial Revolution and transformations in the population wrought by immigration and emigration throughout the Empire. These radical transformations also brought about cultural shifts, such that some, like Arnold, saw traditional forms of high culture as losing their central role in the development and education of the English people, much to the detriment, he argued, of civilization itself. Against this view, Arnold set out to defend high culture and the study thereof.

In the preface to his best known work, *Culture and Anarchy* (Arnold, 1869), he lays out what he sees as the attacks being made against culture by its political critics. Quoting a political speech by someone arguing for a more progressive and open politics, Arnold summarizes the general critique of the academic study of culture:

> "People who talk about what they call culture!"; said he contemptuously; "by which they mean a smattering of the two dead languages of Greek and Latin." And he went on to remark, in a strain with which modern speakers and writers have made us very familiar, how poor a thing this culture is, how little good it can do to the world, and how absurd it is for its possessors to set much store by it. (p. 39)

Against this position, Arnold defends not only the traditional study of the "high culture" classics of Greek and Latin, but also the isolation of that culture from the quotidian concerns of politics and material life in general:

> For as there is a curiosity about intellectual matters which is futile, and merely a disease, so there is certainly a curiosity,—a desire after the things of the mind simply for their own sakes and for the pleasure of seeing them as they are,—which is, in an intelligent being, natural and laudable. Nay, and the very desire to see things as they are implies a balance and regulation of mind. (p. 44)

Following both a Kantian and Platonic vision, Arnold argues that by focusing on traditional high culture we can experience a freer play of the imagination, learn to "perfect" ourselves by achieving this harmonious "balance and regulation," and thereby improve not only ourselves as individuals, but society at large. He continues:

> There is a view in which all the love of our neighbour, the impulses towards action, help, and beneficence, the desire for stopping human error, clearing human confusion, and diminishing the sum of human misery, the noble aspiration to leave the world better and happier than we found it,—motives eminently such as are called social,—come in as part of the grounds of culture, and the main and pre-eminent part. Culture is then properly described not as having its origin in curiosity, but as having its origin in the love of perfection; it is a *study of perfection*. (pp. 44–45)

For Arnold, then, the study of culture can lead people to a more perfect realization of their potential (both individually and in terms of their "civilization"), but only if that culture is of a particular kind (a "high" culture that focuses on or helps to further particular moral traits), and only if the study is a "pure" study, isolated from the petty concerns of daily life. As such, proper culture, for Arnold, is pitted against the industrial or "mechanical" focus of his society. "Proper" or high culture and the "proper" study thereof are thus situated against the industrial society and the mass culture it creates. This is why many people see Arnold as defending a very particular form of "ivory tower" academic research of a very limited canon of works. In this way, a properly cultivated culture protects society from the anarchy of the masses, and trains people into becoming good citizens.

The Leavises and the New Critics: Canons of Culture

Arnold lays the groundwork for a cultural criticism that focuses on a privileged set of high culture materials (often literary) that are seen to both embody and encourage the development of a higher quality of life and civilization. In this approach, we can say that Arnold returns to our opening definition of culture, from Terry Eagleton, wherein culture helps to *cultivate* a better crop of human thought and life. On this foundation were built several twentieth-century academic schools of thought, including, notably, the literary critical approaches of F. R. Leavis (1895–1978) and Q. D. Leavis (1906–1981) as well as the group of American literary analysts known as the New Critics.

The Leavises' overall critical approach to culture is summarized at the beginning of F. R. Leavis and Denys Thompson's *Culture and Environment*. Writing that "many teachers of English" are "interested in the possibilities of training taste," they argue that such teachers may be "troubled by accompanying doubts. What effect can such training have against the multitudinous counter-influences—films, newspapers, advertising, indeed, the whole world outside the classroom?" (Leavis & Thompson, 1948, p. 1). However, they continue,

> the very conditions that make literary education look so desperate are those that make it more important than ever before; for in a world of this kind—and a world that changes so rapidly—it is on literary tradition that the office of maintaining continuity must rest. (p. 1)

This brief statement of purpose makes several claims, both implicit and explicit: first, that there is a clear distinction between forms of popular culture and of high culture (specifically literature); second, that the very prevalence of those popular forms makes them somehow dangerous to the minds of students and others; third, that a proper "training" of students' taste can possibly help stem the negative effects of popular culture; and finally, albeit more implicitly, that high culture "maintain[s]" the "continuity" of culture—that is, that certain kinds of literature can help to solidify and conserve certain kinds of social and cultural values that would otherwise be lost. As we discussed in Chapter 1 when defining taste and popular culture, this approach can clearly be read as a form of elitist championing of a particular kind of social and cultural norm, a norm that Leavis and Thompson (not to mention Arnold, decades earlier) did not want to see change.

However, while F. R. Leavis in his other works does go on to champion a specific canon of "high literature" that can serve to maintain a sense of cultural tradition (and superiority for certain groups), *Culture and Environment* does something different: it offers a critical analysis of popular culture itself, specifically in the form of advertisements, the culture of mass production, the forms of leisure activities in which people engage, and other popular cultural activities. Leavis and Thompson analyze these activities in order to show how, in their opinion, popular culture was destroying civilization as such. Like Arnold, they see "machinery" and the technologization of modern life as a negative influence, one that separates a society from its traditions, and its citizens from the ability to lead a fulfilled, meaningful life.

Like Leavis, the writers of the American critical school known as the **New Critics** championed the notion that a particular canon of literary works needed to be recognized, and that this canon can help, as in Arnold's project, further the culture and civilization of the United States and the West more generally. Rather than focus on the value of tradition and education, however, these critics sought to separate the work of literature from the corrupting surroundings of modern culture. Thus, such New Critics as Cleanth Brooks and I. A. Richards argued that literary works, and especially poetry, needed to be examined as complete wholes, where each poem contained a unified meaning that the critic could discover only through careful, objective close analysis of the structure of the poem itself.

Combined, then, these two approaches bring us back to Plato, Kant, and the Romantics, as well as to our definitions of culture and the popular. High culture, in these arguments, can lift up human spirit and intellect so that we can fully appreciate the true Ideals of Truth and Beauty; high culture is thus separated from popular culture, which can only drag people down to the mundane and the everyday. In order to function properly, then, this high culture must be seen as a distinct aesthetic realm, the meaning of which is fully self-contained within the cultural work itself. Popular culture, meanwhile, is always looking outward, to the degraded world of technology and mass production, and cannot inculcate the inward reflection necessary for true self-knowledge.

CULTURAL CRITICISM II: THE REVENGE OF POPULAR CULTURE

Clearly, this approach to popular culture has not remained standard in academic or other circles. In fact, many modern forms of the study of popular culture explicitly react against this view, placing popular culture in a central role in artistic, social, political, and other debates. While the somewhat negative view of popular culture remains in some critical schools—even among those not directly influenced by, and some opposed to, Arnoldian or Leavisite arguments (one can look here to pronouncements made by some Frankfurt School thinkers, as discussed in Chapter 7)—still others see in popular culture, and in people's reactions to it, a space for invention, resistance, and complex political and artistic thought. Specifically, as we'll see in Chapter 7, a group of British scholars from the 1950s forward formed what is now often referred to as British Cultural Studies, or the Birmingham School, which analyzed the ways in which popular culture helped to shape, and in turn was shaped by, contemporary politics, social formations, class structures, and so on. Meanwhile, in the 1960s and especially from the 1980s forward, North American scholars began to turn to the ways popular culture informed our understandings of social identity—including class, but also gender, race, sexuality, and other categories. It should be noted that there is a lot of movement between these two traditions, and while any summary is overly general, we can say that Canadian cultural studies often blends these two approaches. Canadian courses in popular culture therefore take place in a number of disciplines: from departments of English, French, and other national language and culture programs to music, sociology, and anthropology, and to dedicated cultural studies programs. This book analyzes all of these traditions in a way that will be useful across these programs, with sections focused on the origins of cultural studies as a discipline as well as on issues of identity.

If Leavis saw in popular culture the antithesis of civilized, or *cultured*, thought, then these later critical schools take their cue more from Algernon, a character in Oscar Wilde's 1895 play *The Importance of Being Earnest*, who exclaims, "Oh! it is absurd to have a hard and fast rule about what one should read and what one shouldn't. More than half of modern culture depends on what one shouldn't read" (Wilde, 1999, p. 360).

In Parts II, III, and IV of this book we'll learn about the methods that have been developed to think about popular culture, first by exploring the foundations of such study in the theories of Marxism, psychoanalysis, and structural linguistics and anthropology, and then by examining contemporary theories, specifically in relation to social and cultural identity. In this process we'll likely come to appreciate Algernon's sentiment, seeing the importance of the popular culture that these earlier thinkers would dismiss.

Discussion Questions

1. Plato's Allegory of the Cave is often cited in artistic works, both popular and otherwise. Does the film *The Matrix* (1999) retell the Allegory of the Cave? Why or why not?

2. Arnold and Leavis separately argued that popular culture is dangerous. Can you find similar discussions now? What kinds of popular culture are seen as dangerous, and why?

Further Reading (Part I)

Collini, Stefan. *Matthew Arnold: A Critical Portrait*. Oxford: Oxford UP, 1994.

Gans, Herbert J. *Popular Culture and High Culture: An Analysis and Evaluation of Taste*. Rev. and updated edition. New York: Basic, 1999.

Gilmore, Richard A. *Doing Philosophy at the Movies*. Albany, NY: SUNY, 2005.

Jancovich, Mark. *The Cultural Politics of New Criticism*. Cambridge: Cambridge UP, 1993.

Kraut, Richard. "Plato." *Stanford Encyclopedia of Philosophy*. Ed. Edward N. Zalta. Web. Summer 2012.

Levine, Lawrence W. *Highbrow/Lowbrow: The Emergence of Cultural Hierarchy in America*. Cambridge, MA: Harvard UP, 1988.

Meisel, Perry. *The Myth of Pop Culture from Dante to Dylan*. Oxford: Blackwell, 2010.

Mukerji, Chandra, and Michael Shudson, eds. *Rethinking Popular Culture: Contemporary Perspectives in Cultural Studies*. Berkeley: U of California P, 1991.

Nicks, Joan, and Jeannette Sloniowski, eds. *Slippery Pastimes: Reading the Popular in Canadian Culture*. Waterloo: Wilfrid Laurier P, 2002.

Rohlf, Michael. "Immanuel Kant." *Stanford Encyclopedia of Philosophy*. Ed. Edward N. Zalta. Web. Summer 2012.

Storer, Richard. *F. R. Leavis*. New York: Routledge, 2009.

Part II
Cultural Theories: Beginnings

Chapter 3

Marxism I: Ideology, Hegemony, and Class

INTRODUCTION

As we learned in Part I, one of the foundational principles of the study of popular culture is the idea that its products—films, novels, television, music, sporting events, visual art, and so on—have connections to the social, political, and personal aspects of our lives, sometimes in direct ways, but often in more indirect ways. In other words, the objects of popular culture are not just the imaginative creation of an artist, nor are they simply "entertainment," but instead they are directly connected to their surrounding contexts.

The theoretical works we'll be examining in the remainder of the book elaborate on the reasons why we can draw those connections and give us the critical language through which to describe and analyze the roles and meanings of popular culture in the larger world. Now, you may well be thinking, "Of course popular culture relates to the real world; why wouldn't it?" But we need to understand *why* we can say that. Let's take the films *Star Wars* (1977) and *Avatar* (2009): their stories have no direct connection to our world (after all, they're set on different planets), and yet many people have said that *Star Wars* is a commentary on the Vietnam War and that *Avatar* discusses the importance of environmentalism (even as others decry it for employing an implicitly racist narrative). We need to explain to ourselves why we can make the leap from a "galaxy far, far away" to a discussion of things happening in our societies. Why and how can an imaginative idea with no obvious connections to our world still tell us something about our surroundings or ourselves? The theories we examine in the rest of the book help to answer such questions.

In Part II we discuss some of the foundational figures and works on which the later theories are based: Marxism, psychoanalysis, and linguistics and semiotics. Arising at the end of the nineteenth and early twentieth centuries, these schools of thought provide some of the basic conceptual frameworks and tools that contemporary cultural theory and the study of popular culture use to this day. This is not to say that every cultural analysis in the wide field of cultural studies is either Marxist, psychoanalytic, or linguistic in its approach: in fact, while many cultural theorists trace their influences back to one or more of these schools, many others also take issue with these approaches, selecting parts of them, altering others, and rejecting some of the original tenets of these theories altogether. As we saw in Chapter 1, the study of popular culture is a wide and diverse field.

But there is no denying the influence of these three fields, and the economic theories of Karl Marx and Friedrich Engels have been among the most—and perhaps *the* most—influential of them all. In what follows, we discuss some of Marx and Engels's central ideas and their impact on the practice of cultural analysis, and then move on to one of their more important intellectual descendants, Antonio Gramsci. First, though, we'll discuss three of the central terms in the study of popular culture.

CULTURE AND THE PERSON: INDIVIDUALS, SUBJECTS, AGENTS

One of the things that Marxism, psychoanalysis, and linguistics and semiotics tell us is that culture and specific artistic works are not the product of a single, creative person's own mind; that is, they are not necessarily the artist's or producer's own conscious creation. Instead, popular cultural products are, in important ways, more directly the creation of the world around us. How? For these theorists, just as none of us is self-contained, neither is any creative work: "no man is an island" (to quote John Donne, writing in 1624).

Why do they argue this? These thinkers wrote at the end of the nineteenth and into the early twentieth century—the beginning of the modern industrial and technological world, a time when a number of scientists, philosophers, political theorists, and others were putting forth similar ideas and a lot of old beliefs were falling away. For example, at the end of the nineteenth century, German philosopher Friedrich Nietzsche proclaimed that God is dead and that notions of right and wrong are not absolutes. In the early twentieth century, new schools of human science called psychoanalysis and psychiatry began to be developed; along with the new field of sociology, these disciplines assert, in part, that we are not fully in control of our actions or lives, that we are governed to a degree by our unconscious or by large social forces, neither of which can we fully control. Then there is Marx, who, along with his colleague and collaborator Engels, argued that we're not, individually, in control of our lives, that the economics of our societies control us. In other words, Marx and Engels argued that all of us, and therefore all our cultural creations, are the product of our surroundings: our economic and other surroundings shape who we are and how we think and act. Freud argued that our psyche is shaped both by an unconscious we can never fully understand and by the relationships we form when we are infants; in either case, our thoughts and actions are influenced by something beyond our control. Because of the development and influence of these arguments, previously dominant understandings of the world—primarily religious in basis, including the ideas that we were created with a moral sense of absolute right and absolute wrong, and that we have absolute free will that allows us to consciously act on this sense—were undermined.

At their core, then, these influential theories reposition the relation between individual human beings, their actions, and the surrounding society of which they are a part. Analyses of society and culture that arise from these foundational thinkers therefore always involve discussions of human identity, which is why Part IV focuses explicitly on theories of identity. So before going any further, we'll define the three basic terms—*individual*, *subject*, and *agent*—to use when discussing human beings, terms that will immediately tell us what "flavour" of theory we're using.

One of the clearest definitions of these terms comes from Paul Smith's *Discerning the Subject*. According to Smith, the term **individual** describes the person as "undivided and whole," as the "source . . . of conscious action." The **subject**, meanwhile, "is not self-contained" and is always in "conflict with forces that dominate it in some way or another" (Smith, 1988, pp. xxxiii–xxxiv). For our purposes, *identity* is the general term used to discuss what it means to be human. In other words, talking about the human identity as the "individual" is a way of describing each of us as being fully in control of our thoughts and actions, as "self-contained"; using the term *subject* means that we're following the theory that identity is controlled or determined to some degree by various outside forces—and that these forces can be social, psychological, biological, or what have you. Basically, a "subject" is someone who is *subjected* to these various forces.

The agent, finally, falls somewhere between the other two categories. If we discuss human beings as **agents**, we mean that although they are subjected by forces beyond their control, and are placed in what some theorists call **subject positions** (the "places" in society we identify ourselves with: student, teacher, son, daughter, worker, and so on), they can creatively use those positions to create a semblance of control over their lives. The agent isn't fully in control, as the individual is, but is not fully determined, as the subject is (see Figure 3.1). For agential theories, social forces are generative, not simply oppressive, in their relation to human identity; it may seem paradoxical, but for agential theorists, social forces, insofar as they determine our identities, necessarily also give us the tools and frameworks through which to act creatively within the world.

Someone who thinks we are completely controlled by the biological structures of our bodies (including our brain) sees us as subjects, as does someone who sees us as completely

The Individual	The Subject	The Agent
• Self-controlled (personal will controls actions)	• Subjected (determined and controlled) by forces outside of your control (economic, psychological, biological, etc)	• Social role(s) determined by multiple forces, but can creatively act within/between those roles
• Self-determined (outside forces do not affect you in any way)	• Not fully self-aware (may act for reasons beyond your knowledge)	
• Self-aware (fully conscious of why you act the way you do)		

Figure 3.1 Individual, Subject, Agent

shaped by our surroundings. Someone who thinks we can completely overcome our biology or our circumstances if we just put the effort in would see us as individuals. Finally, someone who thinks our biology shapes us to a degree, and/or that our surroundings shape us to a degree, but that we can use the different skills and tools we develop over time to change some aspects of our being, would see us as agents. What's important to remember here is that these are all general theories of how human identity works, and that the terms (*individual*, *subject*, and *agent*) are just shorthand for those theories. In this chapter we'll discuss human identity mostly as the subject; in the theories discussed in later chapters the agent takes on more importance.

MARXISM

Marxism, Communism, and History

Few of the theorists to be studied in this book have had as profound an impact on the world as Karl Marx (1818–1883). Marx was born and educated in Germany, where he was influenced by the philosophy of G. W. F. Hegel (1770–1831). Marx then moved around Europe, spending a significant period of time in England, where he began to develop his theory of **historical materialism**. During this time, he often co-wrote with his friend and collaborator, Friedrich Engels (1820–1895).

Marx is best remembered today for his theories of economics and politics. These theories focus on the corruption of **capitalism** and what he saw as the inevitability of a **communist** revolution. This process is most clearly articulated in the political text *The Communist Manifesto* (1848), co-written by Marx and Engels. Marx believed that the history of the world has been characterized by **class** struggle, a struggle that would end following the formation of first socialist and then communist societies. Marx's theories would go on to form the political inspiration for revolutions in many countries, most notably in Russia (which subsequently became the USSR), China, and Cuba, the latter two of which still describe themselves as communist states. These revolutions, following the arguments of Marx and others, placed most or all industries and property under public, or government, control; the government would then (as

the argument goes) run them for the public good, as opposed to how they were run by private owners, who were interested only in profit.

For many decades, and arguably up until even today, it was difficult to discuss Marx and **Marxism** objectively—or at all—in parts of the West. Indeed, during the Cold War between the USSR and the United States (and the Soviet bloc and the Western capitalist democracies in general), discussion of Marxist works and ideas could be read as a form of treachery. The deep political and ideological divide between communist and capitalist states made even academic interest in the other system seem suspect.

Following the collapse of the USSR at the end of the 1980s and early 1990s, many people claimed a victory for capitalism over communism and even **socialism**. Others have pointed out, however, that the USSR was never a "communist" state as Marx described it (with the complete abolition of private property and a public governance); it could also be said that the major Western countries were not, by the end of the twentieth century, purely "capitalist" states, either (Canada, for example, has several publicly owned corporations and programs—financed by a graduated taxation system—such as the post office and health care, which in a purely capitalist system would be under private control).

Nevertheless, Marx and some of his contemporaries have profoundly shaped not just those nations that refer to themselves as communist or socialist, but also those that see themselves as primarily capitalist. Most recently, the issues Marx discussed came to the fore of public debate during the Occupy demonstrations around the world, many of which were pointing to the very issues Marx was analyzing a hundred years earlier.

Of course, this isn't a textbook about economic or political theory, but just as they have in politics and economics, Marx's theories have had a profound effect on the study of culture, especially over the past fifty years. And just as Marx's writings, and responses to them, continue to shape debates about the role and level of government involvement in daily life, from unemployment insurance to health care and to military service, so too do they lie at the heart of cultural studies debates about whether the meanings of popular culture are completely determined by market forces or have a more self-contained, aesthetic value.

Division of Labour

Marx moves away from conceptualizing people as "individuals," as cohesive units of conscious action, and toward seeing them as "subjects," as people who are defined or limited by forces they can't fully control. He focuses on how the movement of what he calls the "material conditions of . . . life" (Marx, 1976, p. 31) affects the construction of human subjectivity. At its most basic, this "material life" can be defined as a person's economic situation. Although for Marx the definition of *economics* is much more complex than just how much money one has, in general Marxist theory holds that we are determined by the economic forces around us.

In *The German Ideology* (written in 1845–46), Marx offers a history of the development of civilization. According to this text, earlier historians always started with the idea that different periods of human history were characterized by different ideas and philosophies. These earlier historians used these philosophies to characterize particular societies and to explain why they were structured in the way they were. Such a historian might say that a feudal society was ruled by a king because people at the time believed that the universe was ordered in a rigid hierarchy or ladder, starting with God, then the king as God's representative, and all the way down to the peasant. As ideas about how the universe was formed began to change, so too did the social structure to reflect those changing ideas.

Marx holds that this type of history is exactly backward: "In direct contrast to German philosophy which descends from heaven to earth," he writes, his approach "is a matter of ascending from earth to heaven. That is to say, not of setting out from what men say, imagine, conceive, nor from men as narrated, thought of, imagined, conceived, in order to arrive at men in the flesh; but setting out from real, active men, and on the basis of their real life-process demonstrating the development of the ideological reflexes" (p. 36).[†]

In other words, what people *think* their social world is like and what it's *actually* like can be very different. In his late 1850s work *A Contribution to the Critique of Political Economy*, Marx writes, "The mode of production of material life conditions the general process of social, political

---

[†]Source: "Collected works of Marx and Engels volume 5" by Karl Marx. Published by Lawrence & Wishart (1976). Reprinted by permission.

and intellectual life. It is not the consciousness of men that determines their existence, but their social existence that determines their consciousness" (Marx, 1987, p. 263). Similarly, in *The German Ideology*, Marx and Engels argue that "It is not consciousness that determines life, but life that determines consciousness" (p. 37). The key word in both of these quotations is *determines*. Marx sees people as subjects, as being determined by their surroundings. A society functions, says Marx, first to produce the means of its own survival; then it must continually reproduce those means of production in order to maintain social stability. In this way, people are determined by the material means they have to produce their means for survival, which in turn are determined by the real-world conditions dictating that production.

So, in an agricultural society, people's actions—and therefore, for Marx, people's sense of self—are determined by the fact that they have to spend most of their day in the field, and more time still working on their home and their tools, and so forth. Their cultural habits—their art, politics, religion, and so on—are determined by the amount of time they can spend on them, by the types of needs and materials they have, and ultimately by the way their daily lives have conditioned them to think. In turn, the type of work they do is determined by the material realities around them—including things like the weather and soil, but also the amount of exchange with others, the conditions of their farms, and the ways in which the labour on those farms is structured.

At the personal level, people's subjectivities, their identities, are determined to a large degree by their surroundings—both physical and economic. But this approach doesn't mean that everyone in society is the same, because every kind of economic system creates a division in society between the people who control the means of production and the people who do not.

In *The German Ideology*, Marx offers a potted history of the development of civilization, which he argues is actually a history of the development of the division of labour and of different definitions of property. His history moves from the "tribal" stage, with communal property, to feudal states, to the formation of cities, and forward. The important part of this history is that Marx sees a historical progress of the division of labour: "The division of labour inside a nation leads at first to the separation of industrial and commercial from agricultural labour, and hence to the separation of *town* and *country* and to the conflict of their interests. Its further development leads to the separation of commercial from industrial labour. At the same time through the division of labour inside these various branches there develop various divisions among the individuals co-operating in definite kinds of labour" (p. 32). As the needs of society change, leading to different forms of labour being needed, people get broken up into different groups, each responsible for a different kind of labour. Because of this, people's identities are determined in different ways in a society whose division of labour has stratified them into different groups with different needs.

Political and class struggle therefore become part of life—the division of labour leads to the division of thoughts, of needs, and of ideas, the latter of which Marx calls **ideology**. Ideologies can be generally defined as the dominant ideas of a given society and time, ideas that both arise from and help to shape the economic world. More specifically, an ideology is a particular set of ideas (and codes of behaviour) regarding a particular aspect of life, and so we can talk about gender ideologies and political ideologies, or ideologies regarding race.

Taken together, these ideologies offer particular world views that serve to keep society structured in particular ways. The way in which the society is structured leads to certain groups being in power, and those groups then control the dominant beliefs of that society.

But Marx warns that ideology and the division of labour shouldn't be seen as passive social forces, given that people's identities are determined by their world views, and that these world views are controlled by the structures of society. When different groups then express different ideas arising from their relationship to that social structure (according to the division of labour), they fight with other groups—both physically and in terms of ideas—for control. This struggle leads to divisions in both cultural and economic power in the society: a hierarchy, or social ladder, is formed. As a result of these divisions, the working classes become alienated from their own work and lives: they perform jobs that are deemed unfulfilling and create products that they themselves can't access. This division of labour exists across the spectrum of society. Marx uses the example of a particular relation of labour to explain this last point: "The gradually accumulated small capital of individual craftsmen and their stable numbers, as against the growing population, evolved the relation of journeyman and apprentice, which brought into being in the towns a hierarchy similar to that in the country" (p. 34).

We can map this vision of the social world as follows:

First, people produce the means of their subsistence (e.g., craftsmen create the tools needed for farming).

Second, the necessities of production combined with social realities lead to a division of labour (e.g., a large society with a small number of craftsmen leads to those craftsmen having power).

Third, the division of labour in modern society leads to differing and opposing groups of subjects, who are then divided into a valued social hierarchy, leading to the alienation of the working class.

Taken together, these factors mean that the economic life of society determines people's social (and therefore personal) identities. Marx sums up this process:

The fact is, therefore, that definite individuals who are productively active in a definite way enter into these definite social and political relations. Empirical observation must in each separate instance bring out empirically, and without any mystification and speculation, the connection of the social and political structure with production. The social structure and the State are continually evolving out of the life-process of definite individuals, however, of these individuals, not as they may appear in their own or other people's imagination, but as they *actually* are, i.e., as they act, produce materially, and hence as they work under definite material limits, presuppositions and conditions independent of their will. (pp. 35–36)

Notice how this passage is framed scientifically: rather than assuming that society works in a particular way because of what people in that society say or write about themselves, Marx aims to demonstrate his theories of society through direct observation of people living their actual lives. Why would he want to do this? Because those writings and other ideas about society, he would say, are the products of ideology rather than unbiased observations. Marx argues that people act under certain conditions—physical and ideological—that limit their choices in life. In other words, the structure of society as a whole determines who people are, not the other way around: people, for Marx, are *subjects* of their surroundings, not individuals in control of themselves.

Base, Superstructure, and Ideology

In Marxist theory, certain groups dominate over others, and so societies get formed into hierarchies. Marx sees this process as a matter of class structure: the ruling class are those who govern the means of production, and can therefore control the lives of the people who need those means. So, to again use an overly simplified example, in a society that functions solely on farming for its subsistence, the people who own the land ultimately control the means of production, and can therefore dictate the way in which the society works. To understand this, we need to understand what is known as Marx's **base–superstructure model** of society, as shown in Figure 3.2.

For Marx, all modern societies are composed of two basic elements: 1) the *base*, and 2) the *superstructure*. The base, or foundation, of a society is the space of its economic forces. The base is composed of both the material from which people create their subsistence and the labour necessary for that subsistence. It includes the basic (*base* refers to "basic") economic relations between groups, the division of labour necessary for society to function. The superstructure is made up of things like art, literature, and philosophy, and certain social institutions like politics, law, family, religion, and so on. These should sound familiar to you from Part I: they are all elements of culture as we have been defining it. (Students who are new to Marx often assume that the base is the working class and

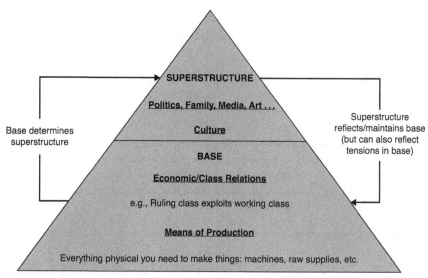

Figure 3.2 Base–Superstructure Model of Society

the superstructure the upper class: that is not what Marx intends at all.) One way to look at this model, then, is to say that the base of society includes all the things we need and all the actions we perform in order to survive. The superstructure is composed of all the other, more socially complex things we do after our basic survival is assured.

This model may make the superstructure seem disconnected from the real world, but this isn't the case: for Marx, the base determines the superstructure. In other words, for Marx, our culture is determined, or created, by the economic base of the society. Why does Marx believe the base determines the superstructure? He writes,

> The ideas of the ruling class are in every epoch the ruling ideas: i.e., the class which is the ruling *material* force of society is at the same time its ruling *intellectual* force. The class which has the means of material production at its disposal, consequently also controls the means of mental production, so that the ideas of those who lack the means of mental production are on the whole subject to it. The ruling ideas are nothing more than the ideal expression of the dominant material relations, the dominant material relations grasped as ideas; hence of the relations which make the one class the ruling one, therefore, the ideas of its dominance. (p. 59)

To phrase this more simply: the ruling class controls the ways in which the society pictures itself, or its ideas. These ideas tend to support the status quo, keeping the ruling class in power. In a society where, for example, the ruling class needs a large number of manual labourers, such work might be associated with a spiritually or physically valued connection to the land; or in a society where highly skilled workers are necessary to maintain the social structure, education may be seen as a way of truly "improving oneself." Both of these ideas are, in Marx's eyes, completely unrelated to what these jobs are, and are tied instead to the maintenance of the existing social structure. And both ideas can exist side by side, as they do in contemporary Canadian culture, because both forms of labour might be necessary.

The important point, for Marx, is that the idea that society has of itself—its culture—does not exist outside of its relation to the economic forces of a society. The passage above continues:

> The individuals composing the ruling class possess among other things consciousness, and therefore think. Insofar, therefore, as they rule as a class and determine the extent and compass of an historical epoch, it is self-evident that they do this in its whole range, hence among other things rule also as thinkers, as producers of ideas, and regulate the production and distribution of the ideas of their age: thus their ideas are the ruling ideas of the epoch. For instance, in an age and in a country where royal power, aristocracy and bourgeoisie are contending for domination and where, therefore, domination is shared, the doctrine of the separation of powers proves to be the dominant idea and is expressed as an "eternal law." (p. 59)

In other words, for Marx, things we take to be universal truths, or common sense ("eternal law"), are in fact simply ideas that are needed to keep the status quo of class relations functioning. So, for example, in a generally capitalist society like Canada's, ideas about "paying your own way" or the possibility of becoming a "self-made person" are seen as positive, honourable things, and are tied to the idea of the necessity and honour of hard work and sacrifice. Now, many manual labourers may work at very demanding jobs for fifty years and never achieve much beyond a living wage (if that), whereas the child of a banker may never work and still be rich, but we still see "hard work" as a valuable thing in and of itself. The proverb "Early to bed and early to rise makes a man healthy, wealthy and wise" by Benjamin Franklin (one of the great proponents of the "work ethic") is another example of this mentality. Following Marx, we can trace the reasons behind the prevalence of this "eternal law" as in fact being the social necessity of having a manual-labour class that's willing to work inexpensively (and to pay things like rent, service charges, and so on) in order to support the dominant banking class. So that little rhyme tells us that hard work is a good thing, and holds out the carrot of possible wealth, even though most people won't achieve such wealth through work alone. To pick up on one of the phrases used in the Occupy movement, 99 percent of the populace won't ever be rich—and yet we still often hear the truism that work can lead to other, more spiritual gains, like health (tell that to a coal miner) or, most intangibly, wisdom. Another example of this is the oft-repeated sentiment "Well, so-and-so might be rich, but he's not as happy as we are." The commonly held belief that "money can't buy happiness" is one that helps maintain the status quo of class division.

People's identities are constructed by the material relations of society, Marx argues, such that those at the top of the social hierarchy want to maintain the existing relations of production. It's important to remember that this isn't necessarily an evil conspiracy: the ruling class too is determined by that economic base—according to Marx, everyone is. One of the central ways in which this subjection takes place is through the representation of existing social structures as "natural" and "universal." We can see a version of this theory when Marx writes that "each new class which puts itself in the place of one ruling . . . is compelled, merely in order to carry through its aim, to present its interest as the common interest of all the members of society, that is . . . it has to give its ideas the form of universality, and present them as the only rational, universally valid ones" (p. 60). Note that Marx isn't saying that the ruling groups (or the people trying to become those ruling groups) are relying on "actual" universal truths; anything that calls itself a "universal truth" is instead a mask for a ruling class's ideas. This is ideology: anything that "sells itself" as a "universal truth" is likely a mask for an idea that supports the interests of a particular group.

The Universal Will Be Televised

By its very nature, the dominant ideologies of a given time and place are largely invisible to most of the inhabitants of that time and place, for the simple reason that it's difficult to point out the ways in which something that appears to be *common* sense can work to the benefit of only *particular* groups. That said, because modern societies are divided (in their division of labour and their resultant class divisions, as well as their divisions of gender, race, and so on), it is possible for some of the dividing lines of that society to be made apparent on occasion—when one group realizes that it's being exploited, for example. Likewise, knowing that declarations of universal

truth can often cover over ideological formations, we can look for those moments in any
given example of popular culture and examine
them closely for ideological assumptions (this
doesn't mean we're *always* capable of doing so:
cultural critics are subjected by ideology just like
everyone else!).

But we can do so sometimes. For example,
let's think about the classic television show *Leave
It to Beaver*, produced in the 1950s and 60s. In
this show, Dad works, the two sons go to school,
and Mom stays home all day. The show often
presents moral lessons when the youngest boy,
Beaver, does something wrong and has to be
corrected by his parents and/or teachers. In this
way the show expresses as a universal truth the
idea that children need to respect and obey
authority figures, and that if they do so, they will
lead better lives. But when you consider that in the
United States during that time there were marches
in the streets over civil rights, the racial segregation

of school boards had only recently been declared
unconstitutional, and there were any number of
other countercultural challenges to authority, the
message that young boys should always obey
authority figures takes on a more ideological tone,
suggesting that those in authority (who at the time
were mostly white, and mostly male) are always
right. Thus, the show tacitly supports the status
quo, and reproduces it ideologically.

Or think about a feudal monarchy, where the
monarch and his immediate subordinates control
a vast amount of land worked by unpaid serf
labour—in such a society, the idea that "everyone has a place, and people should know their
place" might be seen as a universal. The 1975
movie *Monty Python and the Holy Grail* includes
a scene in which a peasant yells at the king,
"Help, help, I'm being repressed!" This scene is
funny precisely because the peasant figure is
stepping outside of the ideologies of the feudal
monarchy the movie is parodying.

Commodity Fetishism

Clearly Marx created a sweeping theory of the development of modern economies, but he
was most interested in the specifics of capitalism in the late nineteenth century. Marx saw
capitalism as an inherently flawed and unjust system, one that would eventually be overthrown through revolution, in large part because of the competing class interests that
capitalism both engenders and relies upon.

One of the particular aspects of modern capitalism that Marx was interested in was
the role played by commodities, those items that we purchase and retain ownership of,
from decorations to clothing to cars. Basically, Marx argues that a commodity is a product, made by human hands, that gains a certain value through its social relationships.
This argument is markedly different from the more traditional economics of the eighteenth and nineteenth centuries that Marx critiques. In those theories, objects contain
an intrinsic value, or at least have a relationship to some other object that has
an intrinsic value. The most common basis of this argument was gold: gold has long
been held to have intrinsic value, so much so that for many generations (starting
around the time Marx was writing) national and international trade was based on what
was known as the "gold standard," a standard, fixed price for gold around which the
value of all other commodities was based. Today, however, the gold standard is no

longer used, replaced by a more open system of financial markets. This makes the contemporary market economy much more complex in some ways than the one Marx was responding to, but to this day many people argue that gold has an intrinsic value; indeed, during times of financial crisis, people often turn to gold as a supposedly safe investment. In his work *Capital* (first published in 1867), Marx describes the belief in intrinsic value this way: "Whence arose the illusions of the monetary system? To it gold and silver, when serving as money, did not represent a social relation between producers, but were natural objects with strange social properties" (Marx, 1996, p. 93). In traditional understandings of value, this value might have social uses, but it is a property of the commodity itself.

But for Marx, this value is not intrinsic: the value of a commodity comes into being only in a social moment. Objects do not have value until they enter into a relationship of exchange. Value is therefore dependent on the social relations of our world. Furthermore, this value is not, for Marx and Engels, a function of how useful something is, nor of how much work went into making it; instead, objects that are produced by people gain value only in relation to other exchanges:

> Since the producers do not come into social contact with each other until they exchange their products, the specific social character of each producer's labour does not show itself except in the act of exchange. In other words, the labour of the individual asserts itself as a part of the labour of society, only by means of the relations which the act of exchange establishes directly between the products, and indirectly, through them, between the producers. . . . It is only by being exchanged that the products of labour acquire, as values, one uniform social status, distinct from their varied forms of existence as objects of utility. (pp. 83–84)

If the value of an object isn't connected either to the object itself or to the labour put into it, then it is only a product of the social relations surrounding it. Whereas the average non-economist may understand something of "supply and demand" and the ways that relationship generates something's price, Marx places importance not on the individual object or how much work it takes to create but rather on the entire system of exchanges that makes up the marketplace.

Marx addresses this disconnect between the object itself and its value as a commodity:

> Could commodities themselves speak, they would say: Our use value may be a thing that interests men. It is no part of us as objects. What, however, does belong to us as objects, is our value. Our natural intercourse as commodities proves it. In the eyes of each other we are nothing but exchange values. Now listen how those commodities speak through the mouth of the economist.
>
> "Value"—(i.e., exchange value) "is a property of things, riches"—(i.e., use value) "of man. Value, in this sense, necessarily implies exchanges, riches do not."
>
> "Riches" (use value) "are the attribute of men, value is the attribute of commodities. A man or a community is rich, a pearl or a diamond is valuable . . ." A pearl or a diamond is valuable as a pearl or a diamond.

So far no chemist has ever discovered exchange value either in a pearl or a diamond. (pp. 93–94)

We might think of something as valuable in itself, as part of its inherent nature, but Marx says that that isn't what determines its value, or its cost; value is determined solely by its place in this whole system of exchange.

This conclusion also has implications in terms of the "value" of people. If the value of an object is tied only to the value of other objects in a system of exchange, then how much people work to create it is meaningless in terms of how much they should be paid for that labour. Instead, it is the various social relationships that determine the value of the labour, and, in turn, the amount of social capital or prestige or power that is associated with particular labour.

As the example in the "Food and Social Value" box should make clear, the purely social aspect of value is why Marx refers to commodities as a "fetish": arising from an understanding of certain religious practices, a fetish is an object endowed with spiritual power, and which therefore exceeds its actual "objectness." A carving of a human-like figure could just be a doll, but if it is said to have magical powers, it is no longer a doll even though it retains the exact same shape. Likewise, a commodity may seem to have a certain value (or "power"), but that value is completely disconnected from the object as such, and from the labour that was used to create it.

Food and Social Value

In order to grasp Marx's idea of exchange value and its relationship to culture, let's think about the act of food preparation: a cook in a fast-food restaurant can work twelve hours a day in a rush trying to get food on the tables for customers, expending the same amount of effort and providing the same service as a chef who prepares food in a five-star restaurant. What's the difference? Well, for one thing the food itself in the second situation is more expensive. But why? In some cases because it's a rare food, like white truffles. But why is rarity seen as something good? We may come back to the supply and demand argument here (which ultimately situates value as a function of exchange rather than a characteristic of the object), or to the idea that truffles inherently taste better than French fries, but Marx would say that the high cost results from the fact that, in the exchange system, truffles are more socially valued. Lots of things in this world are rare yet not valued; lots of things taste good but are inexpensive.

By way of illustration, when my father was in grade school in Atlantic Canada in the 1940s, his family didn't have a lot of money, so the only thing he could take for lunch was . . . lobster. Lobster was considered a "poor" food then: he used to tell me that he would trade his lobster on home-made brown bread for bologna sandwiches on store-bought white bread. This story points to the ways in which different values can accrue to the exact same object, based solely on its social exchange. As Marx writes in *Capital*, "The existence of the things *qua* commodities, and the value relation between the products of labour which stamps them as commodities, have absolutely no connection with their physical properties and with the material relations arising therefrom" (p. 83).

HEGEMONY AND CLASS CONSCIOUSNESS

Hegemony

How do Marxists account for the persistence of the idea that value is "natural" and "universal"? Why don't people just rebel against it? Why don't we question and rebel against the fact that, say, bankers make more money than teachers? Obviously, sometimes people do rebel, and Marx's goal was to call for a communist revolution, but such events are clearly rare occurrences that often require a massive economic or social upheaval to take place. What is it, though, that makes the status quo so tempting, even when it seems unfair?

Ideology is one answer to this question, and several later Marxists develop that theory in different ways (we'll see one particularly important redefinition of ideology in Chapter 6). One of the more influential developments of the concept of ideology, known as **hegemony**—sometimes referred to more specifically as *cultural hegemony*—comes from Italian Marxist Antonio Gramsci (1891–1937), in a series of pieces he wrote both shortly before and while imprisoned. After rising in the Socialist Party, Gramsci and others formed the Italian Communist Party, and he became a leading voice against the rise of the fascist government of Benito Mussolini. He was arrested by the fascist regime, and sentenced to a prison term of twenty years. During this time he wrote philosophical, historical, and political tracts in a set of notebooks that had to be smuggled out of the prison. Not published for decades, these works, collectively known as *The Prison Notebooks*, are now seen as one of the major contributions to Marxist political thought.

In part because of the situation in which he composed his thoughts, some of Gramsci's ideas can be difficult to pin down or define exactly, and this is nowhere truer than in his use of the term *hegemony*, which is never defined precisely. That said, it is clear that Gramsci uses *hegemony* to describe an ideological framework through which society functions, and that helps to maintain the status quo in which particular groups exercise control over others. Hegemony operates through culture: the ideas of the dominant class are constantly reflected in culture, which in turn renders them into "common sense," such that people end up agreeing that the status quo is the proper and only way for society to be organized.

This definition clearly echoes the way in which we've been discussing ideology, and like ideology, hegemony is intrinsically tied to notions of the dominating and determining forces of the dominant society. If we can talk about different ideological forms in society (for instance, those of gender, or class, or race), then hegemony is the overall matrix that allows all of them to culminate in the specific forms of dominance visible in society as a whole, on the cultural (superstructural) and material (base) levels. Raymond Williams, a Marxist cultural theorist, articulates the relationship between hegemony and ideology in this way: "hegemony supposes the existence of something which is truly total, which is not merely secondary or superstructural, like the weak sense of ideology, but which . . . saturates the society to such an extent, and which, as Gramsci put it, even constitutes the substance and limit of common sense for most people under its sway" (Williams, 1980, p. 37). Hegemony thus goes beyond simple uses of the term *ideology*, which often refers to a specific set of conscious ideas that a society has about itself and that simply reflect the social structure.

Hegemony is a more overarching phenomenon that contains those ideologies, frames the very way in which we look at the world, and reinforces existing social structures. It helps to maintain the structures of dominance of particular groups over other groups. In *Marxism and Literature*, Williams writes that whereas ideology can be read as the set of "ruling ideas" used to control the subordinate classes, hegemony, while it "resembles these definitions" of ideology, goes beyond the conscious, "formal" ideas of a society (Williams, 1977, p. 109) to incorporate every process of being and existence, both conscious and unconscious. In this sense, then, hegemony, operating through the tools of culture, reinforces a world view that is very difficult to critique: "Hegemony is then not only the articulate upper level of 'ideology,' nor are its forms of control only those ordinarily seen as 'manipulation' or 'indoctrination'"; instead, the term describes "a whole body of practices and expectations, over the whole of living" (p. 110). Hegemony, moreover, is not just a function of particular forms of community (cities, towns, nations) but can function internationally as well, reinforcing a global vision of the relations between countries, continents, and peoples.

Canadian Multiculturalism and Hegemony

In many ways, Canada's official policy of multiculturalism would seem to work directly against the formation of a truly hegemonic order in this country, one that would suppress the rights of one or more groups for the benefit of a particular ruling class. After all, in its description of the policy, the federal government says, "Multiculturalism ensures that all citizens can keep their identities, can take pride in their ancestry and have a sense of belonging. Acceptance gives Canadians a feeling of security and self-confidence, making them more open to, and accepting of, diverse cultures" ("Canadian Multiculturalism: An Inclusive Citizenship"; see Further Reading). As described, this policy would seem to give power to specific groups under categories of identity (e.g., national origin, religious beliefs, race, sexuality), many of which are protected under our Bill of Rights. Isn't this the exact opposite of hegemony? Doesn't multiculturalism work to ensure that no one group holds all the power?

In theory, yes, but some critics argue that in practice this policy does anything but. Instead of giving power and voice to groups who would otherwise be marginalized, "official" multiculturalism allows the ruling class (who are still, by and large, white, generally well-to-do men) to claim a form of multicultural openness while still oppressing other groups. In Chapter 13 we discuss one such example: in its use of First Nations cultural forms, the opening ceremonies of the 2010 Vancouver Olympic Games conveyed an image of a Canada that was accepting of First Nations as a sovereign people, even as many Indigenous peoples live in extreme poverty. In this way, multicultural policy could be said to provide a "cover" for the functional hegemony of white Canada.

Another way of reading Canadian multiculturalism as a hegemonic force has been proposed by Himani Bannerji in her book *The Dark Side of the Nation: Essays on Multiculturalism, Nationalism and Gender*. She writes that "the proclamation of multiculturalism could be seen as a diffusing or a muting device for francophone national aspirations, as much as a way of coping with the non-European immigrants' arrival. It also sidelined the claims of Canada's aboriginal population, which had displayed a propensity toward armed struggles for land claims, as exemplified by the American Indian Movement (AIM). The reduction of these groups' demands into cultural demands was obviously helpful to the nationhood of Canada with its hegemonic anglo-Canadian national culture" (Bannerji, 2000, p. 9). Like Marx, in other words, Bannerji doesn't start with the ideas expressed in the multicultural policy, but instead places Canadian multicultural policy in its material context in order to understand its actual effects. She demonstrates how, instead of supporting all cultural groups, the policy served the goals of a federalist English Canada against a separatist Quebec nationalism, and likewise served the interests of a predominantly white, Euro-Canadian population against non-white and First Nations populations. In other words, the ideas of multiculturalism are one thing, but in effect, Bannerji argues, the policy plays an ideological and hegemonic role by justifying acts that serve anti-multiculturalist ends.

For Gramsci, the first step in critiquing hegemonic cultural norms is to recognize them as such, to be able to see them not as "universal" truths but as historically contingent ideas that work to support the interests of particular groups of people. Gramsci writes that the "basic innovation introduced by Marx into the science of politics and of history . . . is the demonstration that 'human nature,' fixed and immutable, does not exist and that therefore, the concrete content . . . of political science must be conceived as a historically developing organism" (Gramsci, 1996, p. 150). Likewise, one cannot speak of the singular "character" of a people or a nation: for Gramsci, to talk of *the* Canadian identity would be impossible unless one was uncritically speaking from the realm of hegemony: "As long as society is divided into groups," he writes, "one cannot talk of the 'spirit' [of that society] without necessarily concluding that one is dealing with the 'spirit' of a particular group" (p. 188). Cultural hegemony thus serves to universalize particular interests, and the job of the critic is to point to the fallacies of this equation, and to the contradictions inherent in any society. Such critical work can thus point to the ways in which universalizing assertions actually benefit one group at the expense of the other. This insight is one that lies at the heart of contemporary cultural studies.

Class Consciousness and Identity

The flip side of the ideological coin, however, is the creation of a class identity and the related concept of class consciousness, most famously analyzed by Georg Lukács (1885–1971), a Hungarian communist best known for his literary criticism and Marxist philosophy.

The belief that the current system is "natural" or "universal" forms what is referred to as **false consciousness**: the ruling class, for example, believe that they understand the world and how it functions, and that they do so objectively. Marx would argue, however, that they have only been conditioned by their place in the social world to believe these ideologies to be true—hence they have a false consciousness, because what they believe to be true and natural is only an ideological effect of the material relations in their society. The working class is also subject to such false consciousness, but because they are formed as a group only in relation to those who rule over them, they necessarily recognize the division of labour on which society is based. This recognition, Lukács argues, can form the basis of a true consciousness of the social world, which, given the right conditions, can lead to revolution.

Important to note here, though, is that Marx would not say that people can somehow just "wake up" and realize their positions in society: they are still determined by their economic and ideological surroundings. However, the division of labour that forms these surroundings determines the proletariat or working class in such a way that the possibility is available for a recognition of their condition, and possible actions against it.

The concept of **class consciousness** shouldn't be confused with class identity: **class identity**, from a Marxist perspective, is a set of ideological beliefs and acts that one associates with one's own class. When we use terms like *blue collar*, *white trash*, and *middle-class values*, we're not only identifying people based on their economic position in society but invoking a set of shared beliefs, attitudes, behaviours, and so on—i.e., a shared culture, as the use of *values* in the last example indicates. Class identity can help lead to class consciousness in the working class insofar as it provides an identity around which workers can unite, but it can also serve to maintain the status quo: the term *white trash*, for example, clearly serves to reinforce the hierarchical valuing of the division of labour, with a certain class of workers being associated with "trash." Even as the term can be used in other ways, and perhaps reappropriated to help raise class consciousness, still the negative associations remain.

CASE STUDIES: MARXISM AND POPULAR CULTURE

What does this discussion of Marxism have to do with popular culture? If we return to the beginning of the chapter, we'll recall that Marx's theory can allow us to explain how popular culture, which seems to be simple entertainment, can tell us something about society. When we place popular texts in their specific historical contexts, we can understand more fully the political and class divisions of the time (see Figure 3.3).

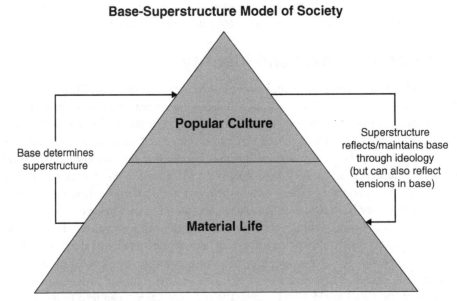

Figure 3.3 Marxism and Popular Culture

This analysis can take many forms: many Marxist studies of popular culture focus not on the content of a given object but on how it's used by people, or how it's marketed to them, who funds it, and, importantly, how it's produced. This is because, as we learned above, the "ideas" about a given object, or those presented by it, are less meaningful for Marx than the actual lived experience or use of an object. In what follows, we offer the first of our case studies in which the theories we've discussed are applied to specific examples of popular culture. These should be read alongside the more specific examples for particular theories above.

This is not to say that all Marxist analysis ignores the content of popular culture: obviously, in the video games example, their war-game content is significant to their ideological function. A Marxist content analysis might examine a given item of popular culture (be it narrative, visual, audio, or so on) for some of its assumptions in order to expose moments of ideological work being done, or it can study the content for its contradictions, analyzing how it reflects different power struggles of its time, as discussed in our second case study on *Trailer Park Boys*.

Military Video Games

A Marxist analysis of a particular video game wouldn't necessarily examine its game play or narrative (if any), and may not even ask the players what they thought of the game, but may instead look to who was funding the research and development of the product, in combination with who the product was marketed to and how it relates to other, similar products. While numerous video games involve war scenarios, if we were to look only at the games themselves, or talk to the people playing them (many of whom would see them as "entertainment"), we might be tempted to say that they engage only in fantasy violence and don't encourage actual warfare. After all, not all the children or adults playing these games go to or start wars. However, if we consider the fact that some military recruitment centres have used these games to attract new recruits, and that the U.S. Army has released a free online game called "America's Army" complete with graphic novel tie-ins and stories of actual soldiers, we begin to see a more direct relationship between military video games and the recruitment of soldiers; or, more generally, we can situate these games within a larger ideology of militarism, an ideology that may be necessary for a nation with a volunteer armed forces to maintain, a nation that uses its military force as a direct means of maintaining its hegemonic position in world politics. Such a material analysis would thus point to the ideological structure of these games as they function in contemporary society.

An ad for "America's Army 3."

Source: Moviestore collection Ltd/Alamy

Ideology and *Trailer Park Boys*

The Canadian television show *Trailer Park Boys* satirizes, to the extreme, a particular vision of economically poor, regionalized Maritimers. The laughter the show invites can be read in a few different ways, but they boil down to laughing "with" and laughing "at" the show's central characters. Filmed as a documentary, the form of the show thus either reinforces the "realism" of its portrayal of trailer park residents in the Maritimes or serves as a "mockumentary" to make fun of those stereotypes. As John McCullough has argued, this dual interpretation also mimics the role of Canadian cinema in the increasingly Americanized global entertainment industry. In order to sell Canadian films to the larger market, filmmakers have to create movies that either appear not to be Canadian (and often films and TV shows shot in Canada are supposed to take place in the U.S.) or purvey a particular set of stereotypes of Canadian identity (think Bob and Doug McKenzie). In this way, *Trailer Park Boys* could be said to play into American globalization, providing a poor, regionalized "other" to laugh at. But, as McCullough also argues, the plots of the series highlight how these othered figures are constantly pulling one over on the authorities around them, thematizing "what it means for Canadians to 'get away with something' in the context of being an underdog in global capital" (McCullough, 2009, p. 167). When we laugh with Ricky, Julian, and Bubbles as they try to smuggle weed in a toy train, we're laughing at a potentially subversive humour that points out how Canadians (and the poor and regionalized "other" in general) can work from the margins of global capital to undermine its power. In other words, the show is a contradictory piece that can be read as both playing into American cultural hegemony and as subverting that hegemony—and given the show's local production and resounding success, it does in fact effect that subversion.

The three central actors (in character) from *Trailer Park Boys*.

Source: EXImages/Alamy

As the video games and *Trailer Park Boys* examples show us, Marx allows us a model to follow whereby we can see how culture (the superstructure) reflects social forces (the base). Of course, this isn't necessarily simple; modern society is never divided into just two classes, and so culture can reflect not just the ruling ideas but the debates between these different forces.

Discussion Questions

1. Can you think of popular representations of "Canadian identity" that may actually serve an ideological purpose (i.e., that support the specific interests of one or more dominant groups)?

2. More specifically, do you agree that the official policy of multiculturalism in Canada serves hegemonic ends, supporting the interests of a ruling class? Can you think of other examples to make this point, or to argue against it? Think about forming a classroom debate on the topic.

3. What item of popular culture do you view as "simple entertainment" with no larger meaning? Looking at it after reading this chapter, can you see any ideological function that this work might have?

4. In 2011, *The Muppets* film was the subject of a political discussion because some commentators thought that making the villain into an oil company executive amounted to engaging in class warfare and pushing an environmentalist ideology. Do you agree? Why or why not?

Further Reading

Bennett, Tony, Colin Mercer, and Janet Wollacott, eds. *Popular Culture and Social Relations*. Open UP, 1986.

"Canadian Multiculturalism: An Inclusive Citizenship." Citizenship and Immigration Canada. www.cic.gc.ca.

Carrington, Ben, and Ian McDonald, eds. *Marxism, Cultural Studies and Sport*. New York: Routledge, 2009.

Nelson, Cary, and Lawrence Grossberg, eds. *Marxism and Interpretation of Culture*. Urbana: U of Illinois P, 1988.

Williams, Raymond. "Base and Superstructure in Marxist Cultural Theory." *New Left Review* 82 (1973): 3–16.

Chapter 4
Psychoanalysis I: Freud and Jung

INTRODUCTION

While Marx and Engels were transforming the study and practice of economics and politics, a similar revolution in thought was taking place in relation to the human mind itself. Although the study of human motivation, reasoning, and behaviour has existed for millennia, in the nineteenth century a particular scientific analysis of human beings began to form, focusing on what has come to be known as human psychology: the basic structures and functions of the human mind, and how they manifest in individual thought and behaviour. These are the same topics covered by philosophy and religion, but modern psychology places them in an explicitly scientific framework, where the human mind becomes the *object* of study and not just the subject performing the study. In this chapter we begin by briefly discussing the history of this field; we'll then discuss the origins of modern psychology, focusing especially on the founder of modern psychological thought, Sigmund Freud, along with Freud's contemporary and sometime collaborator, Carl Jung.

Before we dive into these theories, though, a quick word about the use of psychology in cultural studies and some of the ways it differs from the practices of psychology as such. The first, most significant difference between psychology as a discipline and the role of psychology in cultural studies has to do with subject matter, obviously. Psychology—and its related field, psychiatry—are medical, scientific disciplines that are primarily aimed at analyzing *people*, whereas cultural studies and related disciplines analyze *cultural objects and practices*. While both are a form of analysis of human activity, it would of course be problematic—not to mention unethical and potentially dangerous—to equate the two. As cultural studies scholars, we are not trained to psychoanalyze or medically diagnose human beings.

Also important, however, is the form of psychological discourse used by these different fields. To put it bluntly, you will find few psychology or psychiatry programs that still teach Freud or Jung, or at least that teach them outside of a "history of psychology" course. The field has, naturally, developed and moved on from these foundational figures. Even later psychologists, whom we discuss in Chapter 6 (notably Jacques Lacan), while influential, are not perceived as "up to date." After all, with some exceptions, all medical practices have changed dramatically since the end of the nineteenth century and the beginning of the twentieth. The development and sophistication of psychopharmacology, for instance, or the use of computer-imaging equipment to map the cognitive processes of the brain, would have been unimaginable in Freud's time. In this way, then, although Freud is still seen as a foundational figure (even *the* foundational figure) of their field, many practising psychologists and psychiatrists rarely employ strict Freudian practices. This is not to say that there aren't still some practising psychotherapists who follow Freudian models and techniques, but that these have been substantially changed and added to over the past century.

Why, then, do cultural theory texts, such as this one, and practising cultural critics still return, again and again, to Freud and related figures? If the discipline Freud helped found has moved on from and even discredited some of his theories, why do we still see them as important? The answer here is a complex one, but it can be boiled down to two points. First is the significant fact that Freudian thought—like Marxist thought before it—changed the world and the way many people think about it. To put it simply, people continually employ Freudian ideas to make sense of their world, whether consciously or unconsciously. Read that last sentence again: Do you understand roughly what is meant by people "unconsciously" acting on a certain world view? Do you have a general awareness of what "unconscious" actions are? If so, this is because you've been raised, to one degree or another, in a Freudian world. While it didn't originate with Freud, his development of a theory of the mind that includes a vast area of unconscious desires and motivations has changed the way we think of ourselves. Therefore, we can surmise that it has also affected the way cultural products have been created. As the well-known philosopher and critic Jacques Derrida put it, one cannot underestimate how much of a modern critic's view of culture has been impacted by Freud; as he writes, speaking of his own critical work, "psychoanalytic theory itself is . . . a collection of texts belonging to my history and my culture," and as such one can't "abstract" one's critical practice from that specific context (Derrida, 1974, p. 160).

Second, and even more importantly, psychoanalysis (which is what Freud called his science) is a field that is explicitly focused on critically interpreting even the smallest detail of a piece of discourse, usually the words of a patient but also stories, myths, dreams, paintings, and so on. Beyond its impact on the field of psychology, psychoanalysis has significantly affected the practices of cultural interpretation. As *textual* and *critical* practices, then, Freudian psychology and its offshoots are still very relevant.

A BRIEF HISTORY OF PSYCHOLOGY

As it is with any discipline, it's difficult to pin down psychology's exact "origin." It's even more difficult in psychology's case because the questions it asks and its object of study—the human mind and behaviour—are central to other disciplines (notably philosophy), to other sciences, and to such cultural fields as art, literature, and religion. Humans are often engaged in the study of what it means to be human, and some of the questions psychology tries to answer are precisely the questions asked by these other disciplines and institutions: Why do we act the way we do? What is the goal of our lives? What is the relationship between the self and other people? What makes us human?

Because of these similarities, many textbooks and other studies of the history of psychology (including some of those in the Further Reading section at the end of this chapter) trace its origins back to the ancient world, in classical Greece, Mesopotamia, Egypt, and elsewhere. It would be outside the scope of this chapter to trace these possible starting places, but it is commonly held that the modern origins of the field, especially as it was later shaped by Freud into the practice of psychoanalysis, begin in the nineteenth century. Canadian literary critic and theorist Joel Faflak discusses the ways in which Freud's vision of psychoanalysis has its origins in the Romantic-period poetry of such writers as William Wordsworth and Samuel Taylor Coleridge. Indeed, it was Coleridge who, as Faflak writes, "coined the term 'psycho-analytical' in a September 1805 notebook entry" (Faflak, 2008, p. 7). As Faflak notes, the Romantic period was characterized by a reaction against the earlier Enlightenment period's definition of the human as a necessarily rational animal, so well summarized in René Descartes's famous aphorism "cogito ergo sum" ("I think, therefore I am"). For the Romantic writers, such a reduction of human experience to pure rationality ignored the more emotive elements of our lives; the rational "light" of the Enlightenment likewise ignored the more irrational aspects of human life, including the spiritual as well as the lustful or violent, to mention only a few examples.

Mesmerism, Hypnotism, and the Unconscious

One of the early Romantic visionaries in what would become the field of psychology was Franz Anton Mesmer (1734–1815); he invented the practice of "mesmerism," which has come down to us as hypnosis. Mesmer, a German medical doctor, based his practice on his theory of "animal magnetism." According to Mesmer, people are physically affected by other living beings in much the same way as magnets react to each other and to metal. Therefore, physicians could cure a number of illnesses by developing and using their own animal magnetism to affect the flow of these forces in their patients. Mesmer thought his ability to control people's actions while they were "mesmerized" had to do with an actual physical connection between every object in the physical world (more like "The Force" and the "midi-chlorians" in the *Star Wars* movies than, say, gravity). Mesmerism became largely a parlour trick in the nineteenth century. And yet it was a significant part of popular culture—and remains so, in some ways, when you consider the hypnotism shows that still tour Canadian university campuses.

Still, mesmerism did help later psychoanalysts understand that lurking beneath our rational minds are motivations, desires, and thoughts of which we are somehow unaware in our daily lives. Freud, in fact, used hypnosis early in his career as a psychoanalytic tool, but "abandoned" its use because he was "[a]nxious about scientific legitimacy" (Faflak, 2008, p. 52). And yet the notion of the unconscious would go on to be central to Freudian psychoanalysis. While his theories about the physical nature of the human body proved false, Mesmer's technique remained influential in the developing understanding of the unconscious and how it functions.

Coming out of a cultural milieu that asked these questions, many nineteenth-century thinkers started to develop theories about the less rational aspects of our nature, and did so using basic methods of early scientific inquiry. One of the concepts developed in this period (though it, too, finds much older, even ancient, sources) is the notion of the **unconscious**. The unconscious came to be seen as a part of the human mind that contained thoughts and desires of which the individual was unaware but that could still have an effect on behaviour. This reservoir of instinct and desire, Freud argues, is the driving force of our lives, providing us with the motivation to do things. But because it lurks below the threshold of conscious thought, we can never actually understand it. We can only witness echoes and shadows of our unconscious indirectly, through dreams, for example, or through analyzing our behaviour and actions, especially those for which our motivations may at first be completely unclear.

FREUD I: THE PSYCHE AND DEVELOPMENT

As we discussed in Chapter 3, Marx and Engels's theories could lead us to see popular culture as something that doesn't question the status quo of society but rather helps to justify it. Indeed, popular culture, like religion, is often associated with that famous phrase from the *Communist Manifesto*, "the opiate of the masses." In such a reading, popular culture reflects the dominant vision of society, the vision that protects and maintains those in power.

A standard objection to this view of culture is that people are thoughtful, that their surroundings don't determine their thoughts in such a crude fashion. How can popular culture affect us so strongly? Does it really shape our basic view of how the world works? Marx might say yes, and Freud would agree. For both Marx and Freud we are not really "individuals," people in control of our own lives, but rather subjects in that we are *subjected* to forces beyond our control. For Marx, we are subjected by the economic relations of society; for Freud, we are subjected by the very structure of the human psyche. To understand this, we'll first examine Freud's analysis of our internal, mental functions and the ways in which they relate to cultural norms of behaviour. We'll then examine the Freudian understanding of culture's impact on people's vision of themselves, and what this means to the study of popular culture.

The Psyche: Id, Ego, Ideal Ego

Freud saw the human mind as being irrevocably shaped by the relationships we form as children, even as infants. His essay "On Narcissism: An Introduction" lays out his basic model of the human psyche. In the third section of that essay, he deals with the transformation of the infant into a child and then an adult. Freud writes, "Observation of normal adults shows that their former megalomania has been damped down and that the psychical characteristics from which we inferred their infantile narcissism have been effaced" (Freud, 1953–1974, vol. 14, p. 93). Let's unpack the background of this sentence, which invokes several of Freud's theories of childhood. The main point here is that Freud thinks infants don't see beyond their own needs—that is, their own selves—at all. Their bodily and emotional needs take up their entire world. Freud is not arguing that infants are selfish in the adult sense of that word, where selfish adults *ignore* the needs of others over and above their own needs. Instead, he's saying that an infant's world is centred completely on itself. Other human beings don't exist for the child as subjects: the child doesn't see other people as people, but only sees and understands itself as such. Freud refers to this as "infantile narcissism," where narcissism is a complete focus on the self and an inability to recognize the needs of others.

That's the background for the quotation above, but Freud argues that this infantile narcissism disappears in adulthood (or in what Freud calls "normal" adulthood). He asks the question, "What has become of their ego-libido?" (p. 93). We'll turn to definitions of Freudian terms below, but at this point this question can be rephrased more simply: Freud is basically asking, "What has become of the desire for the self?"—the desire that fuelled the infant's narcissism. For Freud, such a basic drive and the energies that fuel it can't just disappear; they have to be redirected. So, given that babies see only themselves as people, love only themselves and themselves alone, and that "normal" adults recognize the needs of others and don't focus solely on themselves, where, Freud asks, has the narcissistic desire of the child gone? Where has all the love gone?

Freud answers this question, writing that the "ideal ego is now the target of the self-love which was enjoyed in childhood by the actual ego" (p. 94). This is where we need to turn to terminology. Freud's vision of the human mind is composed of several inter-related structures that, once we understand their interactions, can be used to explain all human behaviour. Taken together, these structures compose what Freud called the *psyche*, his general term for the entirety of our individual psychological makeup. In Freud's conception, the individual's psyche is made up of two basic components, the id and the ego. Basically, the **id** is composed of our instinctual drives, our basic biological needs to eat, have sex, evacuate our waste, and so on. Freud calls the sexual drive the **libido**. These instinctual drives are part of our unconscious; we are not directly aware of their functioning, since we can only access the unconscious through indirect means. The **ego**, conversely, is the part of our mind that contains our sense of self and reacts consciously to things around us. Now, in society, we cannot act on our libidinal, instinctual urges whenever the desire takes us, and this is where the **ideal ego** comes in. If we are to have self-respect, what Freud refers to in the essay as "the self-respect of the ego" (p. 93), then we need to repress, or deny, our instincts until the proper, socially acceptable moments.

Culture and the Psyche

But how do we know what a proper moment is and isn't? This is where cultural norms, social expectations, and our sense of our surroundings and other people come into play. Infants don't have this sense because they're in the stage of primary narcissism. But how do adults function in this way? We don't walk around too often consciously thinking to ourselves, "Hmm, it wouldn't be acceptable for me to spit on the classroom's floor, so I'll have to wait until later," or anything like that. For Freud, the repression of our instincts, the knowledge of social norms, is a basic function of our minds, and this is what he calls the function of the ideal ego:

> As always where the libido is concerned, man has here again shown himself incapable of giving up a satisfaction he had once enjoyed. He is not willing to forgo the narcissistic perfection of his childhood; and when, as he grows up, he is disturbed by the admonitions of others and by the awakening of his own critical judgement, so that he can no longer retain that perfection, he seeks to recover it in the new form of an ego ideal. What he projects before him as his ideal is the substitute for the lost narcissism of his childhood in which he was his own ideal. (p. 94)

To put it more simply, within each of us there is a picture of an ideal self against which we measure our actual sense of self based on our feelings, our behaviour, and so on. This ideal self is intrinsically connected to cultural norms.

This doesn't mean that we are aware of this ideal, and set up a picture of our ideal selves that we constantly go home and compare ourselves to. It's a more unconscious structure than that; in fact, Freud compared the human psyche to an iceberg: the vast majority of it is hidden, or unconscious, with only a small portion of it—aspects of our ego and a sliver of our ideal ego—being part of our conscious awareness. So, we unconsciously internalize cultural expectations. We don't have merely an intellectual recognition that we shouldn't behave in certain ways in certain situations; instead, those cultural norms become part of our sense of ourselves. Most people *know* they shouldn't behave in the same ways in a classroom as they do when in a bar with friends, but that doesn't mean they have to make a conscious decision every time they walk into a classroom—it's a largely unconscious act. Freud would argue that this change in behaviour is based on our unconscious desire to live up to an ideal we've formed over the years based on lessons and conditioning from our parents and the larger society. Figure 4.1 provides definitions for, and maps out the relationships between, the id, ego, and ideal ego.

We constantly try to live up to our ideal ego by obeying what we call our conscience, which acts as a policeman, unconsciously forcing us, or trying to force us, to behave as our culture—and therefore our ideal ego—dictates. However, the simple fact that you have such an ideal doesn't necessarily mean you'll do anything about it: as Freud describes, "A man who has exchanged his narcissism for homage to a high ego ideal has not necessarily on that account succeeded in sublimating his libidinal instincts" (p. 94). **Sublimation** and **repression** are the tools we use to live up to our unconscious ideal vision of ourselves. To sublimate means that you take your desire to fulfill your instinctual urges and put it onto a more socially acceptable activity or object. So, instead of people acting on their instinct to have sex whenever the mood strikes them, that desire is sublimated into the desire to get good grades, or to succeed in business, and so on. The ideal ego, our internalization of

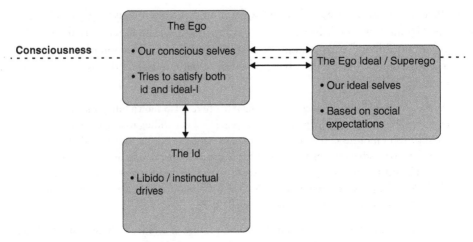

Figure 4.1 Id, Ego, and Ideal Ego

cultural norms, tells us what kinds of activities are acceptable in whatever context we're in. Repression, conversely, happens when your conscious mind suppresses the libidinal urges, refusing to give them any outlet at all. In later works, Freud would use the more commonly known term **superego** to define a mechanism that combines the ideal ego and the conscience.

If you have an ideal ego saying one thing and you behave in the exact opposite manner, you become, in Freud's eyes, neurotic. This can be a problem of either too strong (or weak) an ideal ego or too strong an instinctual drive, or a combination thereof. If you think that to be a good student you need to study twenty-three hours a

The Psyche as Car

Following Freud's description of the relationship between the ego and the id as being like that between a rider and his horse, many people have used the metaphor of a car or carriage to describe Freud's vision of the psyche. That is, for Freud, our id is the engine of our car: it's what powers us to move forward and it's always on, making the car constantly move. While some would say that the ego is the driver of the car, it would be more accurate to say that the ego *thinks* it's the driver: we think of ourselves as being in control of our actions, as guiding ourselves toward certain goals, but for Freud that's not really the case. The conscious self, the ego, is more of a backseat driver, constantly yelling at the id, trying to tell it where to go. Sometimes the ego manages to grab the wheel and direct the car, and sometimes it doesn't. The ideal ego, meanwhile, is like the GPS or map in our car: it provides the route for our id to follow in order to get us where we want to go. Sublimation and repression, meanwhile, are like the steering wheel and the brake: sublimation allows us to steer our id toward a positive goal while the brake allows us, seemingly, to stop the id's movement. But given that the engine is always on, if we repress too much our brakes will wear out and the id's desires will take over.

Freud, Body Image, and Popular Culture

What does Freud's account of the structure of the psyche have to do with popular culture? Analyzing both the ways people act (in relation to media consumption, for example) and how they're represented in particular cultural texts can tell us what norms and expectations are at play, which in turn allows us to form hypotheses about the structure of their society and about the specific texts involved. For instance, consider some of the texts surrounding body image in our culture, such as those in the photograph: How might they affect the internal norms that people try to live up to? Advertisements, television, movies, and other cultural objects tend to emphasize thinness in girls and buffness in boys, and we can see how these images can lead to unrealistic expectations that can play into eating disorders, steroid use, and so on. So, if we were to analyze an ad for a gym, we could discuss how certain ideal body types and behaviours are portrayed, or how undesirable bodies are portrayed, and see how that figures into the way we read and understand the text in the everyday world.

An image typical of fitness advertising.
Source: White Room/Shutterstock

day, which of course you can't possibly live up to, then you're potentially just as neurotic, in Freud's eyes, as those who know they should study but can't stop washing their hands or checking to see if the door is locked.

We have to remember, though, that psychoanalytic criticism might not be as easy as the body-image example in the box makes it seem, because for Freud the ways in which these cultural norms function to create our ideal ego is unconscious: we internalize them. And this is where understanding sublimation can help our interpretations. When we sublimate we replace one thing with another, one object of desire for another. Sublimation, therefore, functions very much as metaphor does, where one word or image serves in place of another. So, if we look at the use of metaphor in some cultural texts, we might be able to see how those texts point to a larger, culturally accepted sublimation of certain (sexual) desires. We shouldn't think that sublimation *is* metaphor, but that if there is a cultural pattern of metaphors that relate to social norms, then they could be pointing to a common form of sublimation.

To take a slightly facetious example, look how many chocolate ads incorporate sexual imagery. We could read this pattern of images, following Freud's view, as setting up a cultural norm in which we sublimate our sexual desires into a desire for chocolate, or indeed any other product, making possession of that product part of our ideal ego. As Freud argues, what prompted the subject to form an ego ideal, on whose behalf his conscience acts as watchman, arose from the critical influence of his parents . . . to whom were added, as time went on, those who trained and taught him and the innumerable and indefinable host of all the other people in his environment—his fellow-men—and public opinion. (p. 96)

If we analyze cultural objects in order to help us to understand "public opinion," we can also start to see how those texts make us want to act in certain ways. Or, in an analysis of a narrative such as a novel or a traditional Hollywood film, we can analyze the portrayal of a character's actions within the particular cultural context being offered, or look at how a text portrays a given social setting, to determine whether there are certain social ideals that a character has or hasn't internalized and thus see how this affects our understanding of the overall text.

Of course, as with all theories, we can analyze texts, social situations, events, objects, and so on to see how they support, critique, or undercut the premises made by the theories. A word of warning, though—try not to psychoanalyze characters in literature, film, or television as if they were real people, but instead look to see how these fictional constructs support or elaborate on certain psychoanalytic models. Likewise, don't treat the author, photographer, or advertiser as someone who is completely in control of all the cultural and psychological dynamics at play in a particular society. After all, culture creators, like the rest of us, are subject to unconscious or cultural forces of which we may not be aware.

FREUD II: CULTURE AND THE UNCANNY

Although Freud's work is primarily aimed at developing and practising the science of psychoanalysis, it became central to later developments in cultural analysis as well. The groundwork for this relationship was laid by Freud himself. In several of his works, he uses literary and other cultural objects as both inspiration and source material for his conclusions. From his analysis of Leonardo da Vinci's paintings and writings to his studies of Shakespeare, Goethe, and Dostoevsky, Freud was continually interested in his cultural surroundings. Nowhere is this more evident than in his highly influential essay, "The Uncanny." While "On Narcissism" gave us a general understanding of Freud's model of the human psyche, "The Uncanny" offers an analysis of a specific psychological state and the ways in which cultural objects can affect us. "The Uncanny" is not, therefore, applicable to all texts or to all situations, but it can provide us with a model for how Freudian analysis can work.

Freud begins the essay by saying that he wants to try to define and understand the mechanisms behind the certain feeling of the uncanny. By the **uncanny** he means a particular kind of fear: not terror or the immediate fear for one's life, and not fear of a particular outcome (as when you're afraid of a test because you didn't study), but rather a sense of intense creepiness. In order to understand the feeling, Freud turns to the dictionary (a useful thing to do in your own essays when defining your central terms!). In

German (the language Freud was writing in, of course), the word for "uncanny" is *unheimlich*, which translates as "unhomelike" but carries with it associations of the unfamiliar, the strange, the hidden, the scary. But in reading the dictionary, Freud discovers something interesting. Under the definition for *heimlich* (homelike, familiar), he finds that, in certain circumstances, *heimlich* and *unheimlich*—homelike and unhomelike, familiar and unfamiliar—can mean the exact same thing: "'unheimlich,'" Freud writes, "is in some way or other a sub-species of 'heimlich'" (vol. 17, p. 226). What does this strange paradox, where *homelike* and *unhomelike* both mean "scary," mean? Well, for Freud, it characterizes that creepy sensation of the uncanny. Something is uncanny not just when it's scary, but when it's both scary and familiar at the same time. (The uncanny is what one feels at night when a jacket hung over a door, or a simple lamp in the bedroom, looks like a person: one knows rationally that it's not, that it's just something familiar, but how many of us turn on the light to check anyway?)

The Double and the Uncanny

Freud himself examines popular culture—in his case, fairy tales and literature—for the way in which certain stories can evoke feelings of the uncanny. One of the significant literary tropes he discusses is the figure of the double. In many horror or gothic stories and films, there is a figure that turns out to be the "double," or, in German, the *doppelgänger*, of one of the characters. For example, in Robert Louis Stevenson's popular nineteenth-century gothic novel *The Strange Case of Dr. Jekyll and Mr. Hyde*, Dr. Jekyll, through a misguided scientific experiment, unleashes his *doppelgänger*, Mr. Hyde, who inhabits Jekyll's body and commits all sorts of nefarious crimes. And in Oscar Wilde's *The Picture of Dorian Gray*, the title character has his portrait painted, which then functions as his double, taking on all the physical effects of Dorian's sinning such that Dorian continues to look young and beautiful while the portrait becomes hideous. In both of these popular works—which have gone on to inspire other novels, films, cartoons, and musicals—the double serves to unleash something that the main character would rather have hidden, and in the process renders strange, or *unheimlich*, the person's own familiar, or *heimlich*, self.

But for Freud, something else is going on here. Recall that in his theory we all have generally the same psychical structures: we all have an id, which provides the driving energy of our being, and an ego, or a conscious vision of ourselves, which is "watched over" by our conscience and ideal ego. In this sense, then, the double in gothic and horror texts echoes the functioning of our psyches: characters watch their doubles behaving badly just as our consciences "watch" over our id's desires. And often, as is the case in *Dr. Jekyll and Mr. Hyde*, the double is acting almost as pure id, fulfilling what were previously "hidden"—*Hyde* being an obvious pun on *hide*—or repressed or sublimated desires. The doctor—the proper, successful person—is, like everyone, repressing and sublimating these desires, and the double that acts on them is the repressed id returning to the surface. This is why the uncanny is both "strange" and "familiar" at the same time: our libidinal desires are part of us, and so are familiar to us, but since we moved beyond the stage of infantile narcissism they have become "strange"—that is, most people will no longer act without sublimating or repressing those desires according to social norms.

As our discussion of the double demonstrates, Freudian cultural criticism is a means of exposing the dynamics of the human psyche through a careful examination of cultural texts and audience reaction to them. Other Freudian-inflected readings take different directions, depending on which aspect of Freud's theories they use. But they all share the idea that people act on unconscious motivations that they either rationalize or repress but that nonetheless come to the surface and can be analyzed. In psychoanalysis itself, this can mean closely studying what a person says or how that person behaves, and seeing whether there are certain words or actions that keep being repeated; such repetition can be read as a symptom of an unconscious desire or trauma. The so-called "Freudian slip," where a person means to say one word but continually replaces it with another, is an example of such a "return of the repressed," another famous phrase of Freud's (vol. 14, p. 154), just as the figure of the double could be. Likewise, readings of cultural material can look for what is "hidden" in plain sight. Freudian and other psychoanalytic analyses are thus often "symptomatic" readings that look for the repetition of particular objects, images, and so on in order to develop a larger explanation of the role or meaning of that text. Every action and utterance has, for Freud, a larger meaning: if that meaning is unclear, it's only because we don't understand the larger unconscious forces at play.

JUNG: THE COLLECTIVE UNCONSCIOUS AND CULTURE

While Freud is certainly the best known and most influential figure in the development of modern psychology and psychoanalysis, he was not alone. His daughter, Anna Freud, as well as Melanie Klein and many others both before and after Freud, also significantly influenced the field and, importantly for our purposes, its role in the study of culture. In Chapter 6 we discuss some of the later figures and their developments of Freudian theory, but for the remainder of this chapter, we turn to a psychologist whose work was integral to the development of the field and still resonates with cultural study: Freud's one-time friend and colleague, Carl Jung.

Twenty years Freud's junior, Jung was very much influenced by Freud's theory of the psyche, and the two agreed in many ways on its structure. Both saw people as being largely driven by their unconscious desires and motivations, and so both decentred the notion of individual free will from the definition of what it means to be human. Jung's theories moved away from Freud's over time, however, and Jung went on to develop what has since come to be known as analytical psychology.

Both viewed the unconscious as a realm of the psyche that could only be accessed indirectly, though analysis of a person's behaviour, creations, and so on. But whereas Freud was interested in discovering through psychoanalysis the individual's hidden or repressed trauma (trauma that usually occurs in childhood), Jungian psychology focuses on the conflicts in a person's life and psyche in the present. As Beatrice M. Hinkle wrote in an early introduction to Jung's *Psychology of the Unconscious*, Jung "places the cause" of a person's pathologies "*in the present moment,*" and sees the desire to trace them back to a past trauma as the person's attempt "to withdraw himself as much as possible from the present important moment" (Jung, 1947, pp. xxxiv–xxxv). Jung expands this difference, developing Freud's notion of the libido (for Freud largely a sexualized energy) into an even wider energy for development and growth, and, importantly, for the development of the self through uniting conscious and unconscious desires. For Freud, then, the unconscious is a chaotic place, full of desires we can't let out, unchanged, into conscious life. Jung, conversely, saw in the unconscious a place from which human culture itself springs. As he writes, "In Freud's view . . . the unconscious contains only those parts of the personality which . . . have been suppressed only through the process of education," whereas Jung sees the unconscious as an active force that "is ceaselessly engaged in grouping and regrouping its contents." These contents include not just repressed desires but also "subliminal sense-perceptions" (i.e., things we see, smell, touch, etc. without consciously realizing it) and other things that have "*not yet* reached the threshold of consciousness" (Jung, 1971, pp. 70–71). For Jung, then, the relationship between the conscious and unconscious mind is much more mobile and interpenetrating than in Freud's model, and, ultimately, more positive. For example, for Jung, dreams are one method whereby "unconscious reactions or spontaneous impulses," rather than trauma, are brought to conscious awareness (Jung, 1968, p. 56).

The Collective Unconscious

In addition to what Jung calls our personal unconscious—the reservoir of our personal experiences that Freud describes—we all, Jung says, have a **collective unconscious**. This is perhaps Jung's best known concept. It doesn't mean that people are somehow psychically connected to each other, but rather that, because the structure of the psyche is the same in all humans, our unconscious desires, fears, and motivations often make themselves known in similar ways. These similarities, often expressed in images and pictures, are what Jung called **archetypes**. If, for Freud, gothic literature can make us feel the uncanny only because it echoes a function of our psyche, for Jung the literature, religions, folklores, and cultures of the world develop directly from our unconscious minds. Looking forward to Claude Lévi-Strauss (see Chapter 5), Jung argued that myths from different cultures around the world have similarities because they are expressions of the archetypes that exist in our collective unconscious. It's not that specific images (birds or spiders, for example) exist in our heads from the moment we are born and mean the exact same things to all of us. Instead, the common image of spiders or other creatures in folklore, if described similarly, could be read as a particular manifestation of a deeper, unconscious archetypal feeling we all share. In *Man and His Symbols*, Jung writes,

> Just as the biologist needs the science of comparative anatomy . . . the psychologist cannot do without a "comparative anatomy of the psyche." In practice, to put it differently, the psychologist must not only have a sufficient experience of dreams and other products of unconscious activity, but also of mythology in its widest sense. Without

this equipment, nobody can spot the important analogies: it is not possible, for instance, to see the analogy between a case of compulsion neurosis and that of a classical demonic possession without a working knowledge of both. (p. 57)

As for Freud, the unconscious for Jung is not directly analyzable because it never makes it to the conscious mind unchanged. Mythologies and common dream motifs and images are merely the "symptom" of a larger archetype. But we can begin to understand those archetypes, and so, for Jung, understand "human nature" as such, through the analyses of these common images and narratives.

So, for Jung, the unconscious is a source not just of individuals' neuroses but of the spiritual and creative life of the species. Many cultural critics would go on to develop Jung's theories, especially through such fields as comparative mythology, which seeks to understand "human nature" by analyzing the supposed archetypes that many different religions and mythologies have in common. Jung's theories remain influential, and traces of them can especially be seen in later structuralist schools of thought, which are discussed in Chapter 5.

Case Study

The Sopranos

Like much of mainstream film and television, *The Sopranos* series (1999–2007) draws explicitly on Freudian and, to a lesser extent, Jungian psychoanalysis. Such reliance on Freudian theory is often seen as outdated by practising psychologists and psychiatrists. That said, *The Sopranos* proves an interesting case study for the application of psychoanalytic readings to popular culture precisely because it enacts just such a reading. In other words, *The Sopranos* itself analyzes popular culture from a psychoanalytic perspective, dramatizing that method's benefits and failings alike.

The Sopranos follows the exploits of small-time organized crime figure Tony Soprano, his immediately family, and the larger "crime family" of which he is a part. In the opening of the series, Tony has a panic attack and seeks out psychiatric help to deal with it. Over the course of the show's six seasons, Tony leaves and restarts psychotherapy several times. In the process of his therapy he comes to recognize that his mother had a profoundly negative influence on his life, and that his

father's violence shaped who he was. In this way the show relies both on Freud's emphasis on childhood development and on Jung's notion of the archetype (since nurturing or unnurturing mother and father figures both fill that role). In other words, Tony's violence and his inability to connect with people are tied to the ideal ego that was shaped by his parents.

But if that was all the show did, it would be less interesting. Instead, the series highlights a division between the ideals framed by his parents and his violent surroundings, and those framed by popular culture itself. On the one hand, Tony's generation of mobsters all identify themselves through popular renditions of the mafia: certain characters are always quoting from or rewatching the famous *Godfather* series of films, for instance. On the other hand, Tony and his family are clearly shaped by certain dominant expectations of upper-middle-class life: Tony and his family echo, in many ways, the presentation of the stereotypical American television family, such as that on

Leave It to Beaver (discussed in Chapter 3), and Tony is always trying to capture the "American dream" of prosperity and happiness (buying a beachfront house and a bigger boat, sending his children to college, even investing in a race horse, and so on). But his "ideal," traditional family life is brought about through drug dealing, violence, murder, prostitution, and other criminal and anti-social behaviour. And it is this paradox that brings about Tony's panic attacks.

What is the show trying to do, then, in using a psychoanalytic framework to present these competing ideals? One could argue that it's offering a psychoanalytic critique of American popular culture: by presenting as ideals both family life and violence, American popular culture demonstrates a split ideal ego just as Tony's life does. By showing the characters themselves interacting with popular culture (gangster movies, television commercials, music, and so on), the show argues that the "ideal ego," or collective identity of the United States (or Canada or elsewhere), is shaped equally by violence, capitalist desire, and unrealistic notions of "ideal happiness" and "perfect families."

In some ways, then, *The Sopranos* argues that we need to step away from the television if we are to "cure" ourselves of panic. For example, an episode that deals explicitly with how American popular culture presents Italians and Italian Americans as criminals (something *The Sopranos* itself was criticized for) explores precisely the complexity of the way popular culture can shape people's world views, and how that is problematic.

The final episode of the series brings this home: in its closing scene in a restaurant, largely presented from Tony's perspective, we see another "ideal" family moment in which Tony and his son remark on the need to "remember the good times" they've had, just as they're having this very moment. Then suddenly the screen goes blank and silent, and stays that way for several seconds before the credits roll. Some have interpreted the ending as Tony's death while others see it as being more ambiguous, but what the final scene does is refuse to give the viewer any logical closure, frustrating the identification between the viewer and the characters, particularly Tony, on screen: Is Tony punished for his crimes? Is he murdered in a random act? Is the show simply indicating that there is no narrative closure? We don't know. The series refuses to give us a moral judgment, leaving it in our hands. *The Sopranos* uses psychoanalytic theories of identification in order to complicate the way in which we allow popular culture to tell us (consciously or otherwise) what is ideal and what is not. The fact that the episode is titled "Made in America" highlights this critique of American popular culture and people's relation to it.

When we return to later versions of psychoanalysis and Marxism in Chapter 6, we'll revisit the ideal ego and television criminals, this time through the character Dexter.

A stylized rendering of *The Sopranos* cast.
Source: AF archive/Alamy

Discussion Questions

1. The photograph in the "Freud, Body Image, and Popular Culture" box comprises two body-image photos of the kind that may reflect and help to form a "public opinion"

about body type. In so doing, according to Freud, they affect the formation of our ego ideal. What other such "public opinions" can you find reflected or shaped in advertisements?

2. Jung argues that some structures of the human psyche are universal, and therefore that certain archetypal desires, fears, and so on appear across cultures and can be represented in similar ways. Can you think of such archetypes? How are they expressed? Do you think Jung is correct?

3. Do you think popular film and television present problematic ideals that we try to consciously or unconsciously live up to? Can you find examples to discuss in class?

Further Reading

Robinson, Daniel N. *An Intellectual History of Psychology*. 3rd ed. Madison: U of Wisconsin P, 1995.

Shamdasani, Sonu, and Michael Münchow, eds. *Speculations After Freud: Psychoanalysis, Philosophy, and Culture*. London: Routledge, 1994.

Shiraev, Eric. *A History of Psychology: A Global Perspective*. London: Sage, 2011.

Thwaites, Tony. *Reading Freud: Psychoanalysis as Cultural Theory*. London: Sage, 2007.

Chapter 5
Linguistics and Semiotics

INTRODUCTION

While popular culture can affect (and effect) the relationship between people and their surroundings (as we saw in Chapters 3 and 4), this chapter concentrates on something perhaps even more foundational to our lives and popular culture in general: How is it that language, symbols, and the other basic structures of culture actually make meaning?

There are many answers to this question, depending on what field one is studying: cognitive psychiatrists' and neuroscientists' answers will differ from those of anthropologists or archaeologists, for instance. In this chapter we'll first discuss theories of the structure of language, and then the ways in which the structures of popular culture help to make meaning. In other words, we're not as interested in the *content* of language and culture as in their *forms*, because the manner in which something is put together is often as important as what it says. Linguistics and, later, semiotics became primary methodologies for understanding those structures, not just in verbal language itself but in other meaning systems in culture (such as visual systems, "body language," and so on). These theories developed into a larger school of thought in the study of culture that has come to be known as structuralism: as we'll see, this school sees culture as being structured much like language itself, where particular objects or actions gain meaning only in their larger context. This chapter therefore will take us into some specific, detailed theories about the structure of language and give us some vocabulary and techniques for talking about the multiple layers of meaning that particular instances of popular culture, when placed in context, can generate.

A BRIEF HISTORY OF THE STUDY OF LANGUAGE

Language may seem to be a simple term to define. But the word *language*, like most words, can mean many different things (this multiplicity of meaning is something we'll be returning to in this chapter). For example, when people speak about "language" they often mean a particular "natural language"—that is, a language that has developed over time among a large group of people in a specific region of the world. These include such language groups as Arabic, English, French, Farsi, German, Hindu, and so on. Such languages often have both oral and written components, and they change over time. Tracing the development of modern languages allows researchers to analyze and discover the relationships among, for example, the Germanic languages and the Latin languages. Other linguists study so-called "dead languages," those that are no longer spoken by people as part of daily life and so are no longer changing or developing. Still others try to trace the origin of human language as such, often seeing this development as a significant step in the process of human evolution.

But people also use the term *language* to describe, for example, computer languages, which set the rules for processing the information and commands that make a computer function in particular ways. So-called "constructed" or "artificial" languages are also created consciously by people, either as an experiment or as a means of developing a new community. One prime example of such languages is Esperanto, which was developed in the nineteenth century in an attempt to create a universal language for all people on the planet. Another significant example developed directly out of popular culture: Klingon, a language based on a few words and phrases uttered by the Klingon characters from the *Star Trek* television and film franchise.

All of these forms of language follow specific rules of syntax, grammar, and so on, and function to allow communication between people. But how does language transfer that meaning from one person to another? One way to answer that question is to examine the structure of languages as such, and this branch of linguistics is called **semiotics**: the study of the basic building blocks of language per se. Instead of analyzing the different structures of natural languages and how they relate to each other, the semiotician studies the structures of what makes something a language, the building blocks that create all language (including verbal or written languages, body languages, and so on). We'll first discuss the theories of the founder of semiotics, Ferdinand de Saussure, and then turn to how those theories were put to use by people who study popular and everyday culture. Finally, we'll turn to a thinker, Mikhail Bakhtin, who proposed a way of understanding why languages change and what that means for the study of popular culture.

WHAT'S YOUR SIGN? SAUSSURE AND SEMIOTICS

One of the most famous linguists of the twentieth century, Ferdinand de Saussure (1857–1913), is best known for a book he didn't write. Saussure's *Course in General Linguistics* was composed by his students based largely on their notes of lectures he gave between 1906 and 1911. While he'd said he was working on a book based on the theories of language he described in those lectures, he died before he completed it, and until recently it seemed he didn't even leave any notes behind (in 1996, a draft manuscript was discovered in his family home and has since been translated and published as *Writings in General Linguistics*). Knowing that their professor's ideas were significant and could have a profound impact on the study of language, some of his students painstakingly recomposed his lectures into *Course on General Linguistics*, which went on to become one of the most influential academic works of the past century.

Saussure's major innovation was to place language at the centre of human life. Before Saussure, as he describes, most linguists were interested in either tracing the historical developments of language or comparing the grammars of different languages in order to describe different "families" of languages, the way biologists describe different categories of living creatures. For these earlier linguists, language was simply a tool used to describe the world and, more importantly, a simple fact of nature: people use language to describe the world that exists around them, and those descriptions are themselves natural and trustworthy. Words mean what they mean, and the process was seen as perfectly natural.

Saussure, conversely, said that proper linguistic study should aim to understand precisely those larger structures of language as such. And, just as importantly, he moved away from seeing language as a "natural" set of representations of reality, and instead saw it as a set of social conventions. Language, for Saussure, doesn't naturally describe an outside world in a direct and linear way; instead, humans living in society have a set of linguistic conventions, which we (more or less) agree on, to describe that world.

The difference here might seem subtle, but it profoundly alters the role and place of language in human life. Instead of language being a transparent tool for describing in clear ways a reality that exists around us, language instead shapes the very way we see that reality. Ultimately, for Saussure, what this means is that the words we use to describe things are completely arbitrary: *blue* means a particular colour only because we happen to agree that it does. It is simply social convention that gives words meaning.

A particular myth may help us understand this. In some versions of the Abrahamic religious story of the Garden of Eden, we are told that God brings all the animals on earth to Adam, "and whatsoever Adam called every living creature, that was the name thereof" (Genesis 2:19). Generally, this biblical passage is read to indicate that the words Adam gives to the animals, and the nature of the animals, are one and the same: each word perfectly describes those animals. For Saussure, however, such a direct link between words and the objects they describe simply doesn't exist: the word *pig*, for example, describes a particular four-footed animal only because we agree that it does, not because the word has any **essential** connection to that animal.

As Saussure's translator, Roy Harris, writes, what Saussure was arguing amounted to a Copernican revolution in linguistics (Saussure, 1986, p. ix). Before Copernicus, people thought the sun revolved around the Earth; he proposed that the Earth revolved around the sun. Likewise, before Saussure, people thought language revolved around reality, but he proposed that our understanding of "reality" was always mediated by language: language, in a way, comes first, and we can grasp "reality" only through language. As Saussure says, we should not "assume . . . that ideas already exist independently of words" or that "the link between a name and a thing is . . . unproblematic" (pp. 65–66). Instead, he says, all our concepts of the world depend on our use of language, and the words in that language have no natural connection to the objects they describe. This conclusion would go on to influence and shape not only linguistics but also anthropology, psychology, and cultural studies for the next century, leading to what has been termed the **linguistic turn** in social and cultural study.

Signs, Signifiers, and Signifieds

Because language is, for Saussure, the most important aspect of human life, it becomes very important to understand precisely how it works. Therefore, it is necessary to study not just the superficial aspects of a given natural language but to understand the very structures that lie behind all languages, that make up language itself. And, for Saussure, these structures aren't the same as grammar, words, and letters. Instead, he breaks up language into the symbols we use and the concepts we're trying to explain. Every time we use a word, a gesture, and an image to express a *meaning*, we are using a symbol to express a concept; Saussure is interested in breaking down this process to its most basic parts.

The most common translations in English of the terms Saussure used to describe these parts of language are *sign*, *signified*, and *signifier*. The **signifier** is the symbol we use when we want to transmit meaning to another person: for our purposes we can think of this as a word, or what Saussure calls the "sound pattern" (p. 67). The **signified** is the concept that that word points to. Taken together, the signifier and signified (the word and the concept) create what Saussure calls the **sign**: the basic unit of meaning in language. (See Figure 5.1.)

To help explain this abstract idea, let's consider a common example: the sign CAT. (To distinguish the sign from the signifier, the SIGN is capitalized and the signifier is lowercase.) When you see the word, or signifier, *cat*, you get an image in your head of a particular kind of animal. That image, or concept, is the signified. Taken together, the

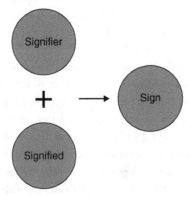

Figure 5.1 Sign, Signifier, and Signified

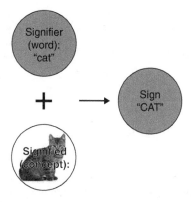

Figure 5.2 The Sign CAT

Source: Jagodka/Shutterstock

signifier and the signified form the sign CAT. In other words, every time we use the signifier *cat* we rely on our listener or reader to know the sign CAT. Figure 5.2 should clarify this.

So, for Saussure, this basic unit of language, the "linguistic sign," is "a two-sided psychological entity"; the "two elements are intimately linked and each triggers the other" (p. 66). If you see a cat, you think the word *cat*, and if you hear or read or sign the word *cat* you'll picture the animal because the word and the concept are fundamentally linked in the sign CAT.

Text and Context

The Many Meanings of *Cat*

The definition of the sign CAT in Figure 5.2 might seem pretty straightforward, but if we push this structure a little further, we'll see that the relationship of signs and meaning is much more complex. After all, if one person says "cat" to another, that second person might picture a tabby, a Siamese cat, a Sphynx cat (the hairless ones), or even a mountain lion or tiger. How do we ensure that the person we're talking to knows which one we mean? Or are there situations where it wouldn't matter?

Saussure argues that signs take on meaning only in context. In the context of one conversation (say, two children discussing their pets), *cat* may refer to a general image of a domestic house pet. In another (people talking about endangered animals), *cat* might mean any number of larger predators. In yet another (in a David Bowie song, or in a movie that's set in the 1950s), *cat* might refer to a person. Meanwhile, on a construction site, *Cat* might refer to a particular manufacturer of heavy equipment. Fishers might use the word to describe a particular kind of fish. In other words, a cat who works construction might sit in a Cat truck, eat a cat sandwich for lunch, and think about giving money to a charity to help protect cat habitats, all while a cat purrs nearby, waiting for leftovers!

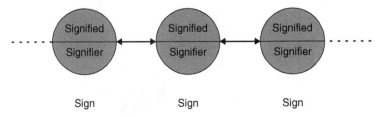

Figure 5.3 The Relations of Signs

Source: to come

As should be clear from our cat example, any individual word can have multiple meanings, which for Saussure proves that signifiers do not have a natural and direct link to their signifieds. This brings us to the role of *context*. Remember that, for Saussure, "reality" is something that is always mediated by language. In any given situation we are constantly "reading" the signs around us. If we walk into a room that has a set of tiered seats pointing down to a stage featuring such items as a chalkboard or a console for using computer displays, we interpret those signifiers to mean that we're in a classroom. How do we do that? Saussure would say that we share a language, that we are part of a "language community" (p. 226) that agrees on what those signifiers mean. But some of those signifiers combined with others would mean something quite different: a set of tiered seats all pointing to a stage where someone is singing or putting on a play could combine to tell us we're in a theatre.

In other words, we are constantly reading the signs around us in relation to other signs in order to generate meaning. In this way we read signs to understand the "real world" context of our lives. Figure 5.3 shows how Saussure diagrams this process.

Each sign gains meaning only in relation to other signs. Words don't have fixed and stable meanings and don't relate directly to the concepts they signify, but instead become meaningful only in relation to other words. You can think of a dictionary here: if words had direct links to their concepts, then a dictionary would be impossible—if you opened up the dictionary to the word *cat*, a cat would have to leap out at you. Instead, when you look up *cat* the dictionary points you to other words that you can also look up; this referentiality continues endlessly. In short, language is a complex structure that references only itself.

Semiotics and Popular Culture: Clothing

What does this discussion of semiotics and language mean for the cultural critic? Why is Saussure's theory of semiotics so important to many theories of popular culture? Although we've been discussing Saussure's theories in relation to verbal languages, they actually apply to all other semiotic (that is, "sign-based") systems. Advertisements, different genres of music, even clothing rely on certain types of signs, and so can be considered semiotic systems in themselves.

Think about how often people are identified as being part of a particular community or subculture based on their clothing, and how people within and outside the community interpret that clothing differently. As signifiers, items of clothing can mean very different things to different people because the contexts are different. Thus, a woman wearing a formal skirt suit or a man wearing a business suit at work will indicate "professionalism," while either wearing the same at the beach might signify "overly formal"; if these two people switched outfits, it may indicate a new set of gender codes or identities (although in some situations, and with some suits, perhaps not).

As Wendy Leeds-Hurwitz writes, "Clothing was one of the first cultural products studied by semiotics," in part because of its "simultaneous demonstration of individuality and of group membership" (Leeds-Hurwitz, 1993, pp. 108, 113). She discusses an example, cited by Rick Horowitz, of someone "pairing bright yellow socks with a proper business suit." On their own the yellow socks could simply be a matter of personal taste, but the combination with the suit, especially when worn at a workplace, could indicate that the person "knows what is expected" of a professional but still wants to be seen as an individual rather than just another suit. Meanwhile, the fact that the socks are relatively "minor" can show that the person "not only knows the rules but also . . . just how far they can be bent" (p. 113).

In other words, "We use clothing as a vehicle to convey identity" (p. 113). Taken more generally, this example demonstrates that certain signifiers and "texts" will have multiple meanings, and so multiple interpretations of any cultural object are therefore possible. The cultural critic, acting as a semiotician, must learn how to read the relationships between these different signs in order to analyze any given text or cultural moment. The case study at the end of this chapter provides such a reading.

LIVING MYTH: STRUCTURALISM AND CULTURE

Saussure's analysis of language and other semiotic systems places such systems at the foundation of our knowledge of the world itself. Popular culture, because it's mediated by language and can form semiotic systems of its own, can thus be described in terms of signifiers and signifieds. Two of the central critics to expand Saussure's model into cultural analysis are Claude Lévi-Strauss and Roland Barthes, the former an anthropologist, the latter a literary and cultural critic. Together, they are seen as founding figures in the interdisciplinary school that is known as **structuralism** and that arises out of Saussure's theories of the structure of language. If, as Saussure argued, our knowledge of the world is inescapably mediated by language, then it follows that our cultural representations and engagements with that world are also structured as language. Lévi-Strauss and Barthes take this basic assumption and develop complex theories about the structures of culture and societies themselves.

Lévi-Strauss: Myth, Meaning, and Structural Anthropology

While Saussure's discussion of semiotics was largely limited to language, scholars and practitioners from other disciplines recognized that his vision had many ramifications for their fields. One of the foremost among these was anthropologist Claude Lévi-Strauss

(1908–2009). Just as Saussure said there were basic structures to language that could be applied to all natural languages, so too did Lévi-Strauss think there were basic structures to human society that one could see operating in any society. Lévi-Strauss did not want to start with any assumptions as to what those basic structures were, insisting that they could be discovered only through careful and detailed empirical observation.

As Saussure did with linguistics, Lévi-Strauss was attempting to correct what he saw as fatal flaws in anthropological methodologies. He begins his early work, *Structural Anthropology*, by describing two different methods of anthropology that came before him: one based on sociology, the other on history. The former focuses on particular societies' practices and stated beliefs regarding the functions of different societal aspects (that is, what specific, necessary role particular objects or customs perform to keep that society working); the latter examines and compares the development of different societies in order to understand how their cultures have evolved. In other words, earlier anthropologists either focused on the functioning of a particular group and tried to describe that group in detail, or examined how certain cultural practices evolve from "primitive" to more "advanced" cultures.

Lévi-Strauss moves beyond both of these practices, arguing that the specific functions of a given society could be related to larger universal structures of human society and that the differences between so-called "primitive" and "civilized" social functions are superficial ones that cover up an underlying, more basic similarity. The obvious hierarchy of earlier anthropology, which positioned so-called "First World" societies—the ones the anthropologists came from—as being better than "Third World" societies, is radically undermined by Lévi-Strauss's assertion that all societies function according to the same basic structures and principles.

Building not only on Saussure but also on structuralist psychology, Lévi-Strauss argues that anthropology needs to study the "unconscious foundations" of the "expressions of social life" (Lévi-Strauss, 1963, p. 18). He takes as his foundation the idea that language is one of the basic components of any culture, and that, like language, many other cultural practices occur largely at the level of the unconscious and take the form of a system of symbolic representations. Culture is a semiotic system for Lévi-Strauss, and should therefore be studied using the tools that Saussure and other structural linguistic theorists provide. Using the work of linguist N. S. Troubetzkoy, Lévi-Strauss summarizes what he sees as the "four basic operations" of structural linguistics that should be equally important to anthropology:

> First, structural linguistics shifts from the study of *conscious* linguistic phenomena to study their *unconscious* infrastructure; second, it does not treat *terms* as independent entities, taking instead as its basis of analysis the *relations* between terms; third, it introduces the concept of *system* . . . ; finally, structural linguistics aims at discovering *general laws*. . . . (p. 33)

Lévi-Strauss then works to apply these principles to the study of societies. Thus, rather than base an analysis of a social group on what they consciously think of their society, he is more interested in the processes of the society that function below the level of conscious thought (he uses his own Western society for examples of certain customs, such as "table manners, social etiquette, fashions of dress, and many of our moral, political, and religious attitudes" that people engage in without consciously knowing anything about "their real origin and function" [pp. 18–19]). "We act and think according to habit," he writes (p. 19), and it is these unconscious habits that often give insight into the functioning of a society.

In other words, we can't just examine a society by looking at different aspects of how it functions on a material, physical level, because each aspect of a society is part of a larger symbolic whole. In a society that relies primarily on fishing for its subsistence, for example, a fishing net may have obvious material uses to keep that society functioning. But it will likely also have larger symbolic value: a family may be interpreted as being "like a net" that holds different members together. Likewise, in a society that functions on a knowledge economy, a book or a computer will have obvious practical uses, but each may also have larger symbolic functions. Such symbolic functions can be understood only through a larger structural analysis of that culture. For Lévi-Strauss, however, these symbolic structures come down to certain basic and universal structures of the human mind, such as the need to cope with or understand death.

Equally important for our purposes, though, is the emphasis Lévi-Strauss places on the non-material aspects of society. Speaking of the "different types of orders" in a society, Lévi-Strauss points out that the social models he discusses "are 'lived-in' orders: they correspond to mechanisms which can be studied from the outside as a part of objective reality" (p. 312): in other words, they are composed of material objects or activities that can be physically observed. But structural anthropology, he argues (and by extension cultural studies), cannot be complete "without acknowledging the fact that social groups" also look to "the 'supernatural'" or "'thought-of' orders": these thought-of orders could include "myth and religion" on the one hand and "political ideology" on the other (pp. 312–13).

Lévi-Strauss's structural analysis of myth is one of his more influential contributions to cultural studies. He saw that earlier studies of mythology wavered between two camps. On the one hand, there were those who argued that mythology is a way for a given society to "express . . . fundamental feelings common to the whole of mankind, such as love, hate, or revenge" or "to provide some kind of explanations for phenomena which they cannot otherwise understand—astronomical, meteorological, and the like" (p. 207). "On the other hand," Lévi-Strauss writes, there were those who argued that mythology simply "reflects the social structure and the social relations" of a given society: "If a given mythology confers prominence on a certain figure, let us say an evil grandmother, it will be claimed that in such a society grandmothers are actually evil" or that they "provide an outlet for repressed feelings" against the power that a grandmother holds in that society, for example (pp. 207–08). Both explanations have problems: the first doesn't explain why particular societies develop such unique and "elaborate" mythologies, or why in any given mythological story, events seem so arbitrary, with "no logic, no continuity"; the second doesn't explain why there is an "astounding similarity between myths collected in widely different regions" (p. 208).

Lévi-Strauss claims that Saussure's semiotic theory solves this problem. Just as the meaning of individual signs in a given language is arbitrary and makes sense only when seen as part of the larger structure of language, so too does each mythological story seem arbitrary until it's studied in relation to the larger structure of the mythology as a whole and in comparison with other mythologies that share certain elements. Likewise, just as Saussure breaks language down into its basic structures, with no attention to the actual content of language or the meaning of words, so too does Lévi-Strauss break down mythology into its constituent parts, paying little attention to the specifics of individual stories. Instead, he wants to find out what those stories share—the basic elements, or "mythemes," that appear across a number of individual stories. This method, he writes, "not only has the advantage of bringing some kind of order to what was previously chaos; it also enables us to perceive some basic logical processes which are at the root of mythical thought" (p. 224). In other words, myth doesn't simply offer an explanation of the world, nor is it simply a reaction to the society from which it comes. Instead, myth offers a set of logical, if symbolic, methods through which people can interpret their world and their lives.

Trickster Semiotics

One example Lévi-Strauss uses is the trickster figure found in the mythologies of the various First Nations in the Americas. Across the mythologies of many disparate nations, the coyote and raven often trick humans and other animals into doing things against their own self-interest. For Lévi-Strauss, these figures don't simply display such universal emotions as love or hate (the trickster is too contradictory for that: sometimes being kind, other times cruel, often with no explanation for either), nor do they simply reflect sociological or psychological specifics of the societies that tell the stories (the figures appear in too many Indigenous peoples' myths, and their societies are too different from each other to account for it). Instead, Lévi-Strauss argues, they represent a basic, underlying structure of how the human mind functions to understand its world.

What precisely is that function, according to Lévi-Strauss? Looking to the myths, he notes that the trickster figure is always a mediator: both carrion animals, the raven and coyote exist between animals of prey and herbivores, exhibiting features of both. These oppositions are mirrored in the more universal human oppositions between agriculture on the one hand and hunting and war on the other, which in turn mirror the opposition between life and death, a basic structure of human existence. The trickster stories, presenting figures who mediate these oppositions, thus offer the societies that tell them a way of understanding and dealing with the basic opposition between life and death. Lévi-Strauss goes on to show how a similar dynamic works in other stories, including European folktales like Cinderella and religious tales of messiahs: "Not only can we account for the ambiguous character of the trickster, but we can also understand another property of mythical figures the world over, namely, that the same god is endowed with contradictory attributes— for instance, he may be *good* and *bad* at the same time" (p. 227). All of these myths, Lévi-Strauss says, pivot on a figure who mediates between two oppositional terms, because the attempt to remedy basic oppositions is one of the foundational structures of human thought. And since this structure is so foundational, there is no real distinction in purpose, Lévi-Strauss says, between "primitive" mythology and "advanced" contemporary science: they are simply looking at different aspects of the world, while the quality of thought put into both is the same.

It is possible to critique Lévi-Strauss's analysis: the universalizing tendency of his structuralism, while it does place different cultures and peoples on an equal footing in ways that can challenge racist or nationalist assumptions, can be seen to ignore specifics of history and place in ways that can deny the identity of a given culture. Consider the novels of Thomas King, which employ Indigenous North American mythology, realism, fantasy, and contemporary settings as a means to play with these differences. In *Green Grass, Running Water* (1993), King pits Indigenous peoples' creation myths against Judeo-Christian creation myths—literally! Canonical European and North American literary and religious works are rewritten such that the supposed Eurocentric aims of those narratives are undermined: Moby Dick, for example, becomes a black female whale attempting to escape the original novel's fixation on whiteness. Likewise setting the oral trickster Coyote against Judeo-Christian myths, the novel demonstrates in a comical way how storytelling and narrative help shape people, and how they are invested in specific social power dynamics in ways that could work against the "universal" notions of "human nature" that Lévi-Strauss argues for.

Barthes: Denotation, Connotation and Mythology

The connection between the anthropological study of various cultures' mythologies and the analysis of the contemporary world is taken a step further by Roland Barthes (1915–1980). Again building on Saussure's discussion of signs, in his book *Mythologies* (Barthes, 1957) he attempts, like Lévi-Strauss, to discover the underlying structures of meaning in mythologies, but in his case he looks to another set of myths: those represented in dominant Western popular culture. Just as Lévi-Strauss does with myths and folktales, Barthes analyzes a number of events and objects: each chapter focuses on one item or a set of items—including wrestling matches, the representation of Romans in contemporary cinema, the portrayal of food items ("Wine and Milk," "Steak and Chips"), "Ornamental Cookery," and Albert Einstein's brain—all of which can be said to be part of popular culture. Barthes contends that each of these seemingly mundane objects can be interpreted as having a larger social and cultural significance. He uses Saussure's theory of the sign to develop these interpretations, but takes the earlier theorist's arguments a step further, arguing that larger meanings adhere to these everyday objects because of their connections to what he calls particular cultural myths.

Before examining these myths, it's important to understand how Barthes uses Saussure's theory. The central distinction is that while Saussure focuses on the form of language, avoiding content, Barthes is interested in the actual meanings of words and images. And yet, as a structuralist, he holds that the content of language, like its form, is still part of an overall structural whole.

In *Elements of Semiology* (Barthes, 1964), he argues that there are two primary layers of meaning in a language: denotative and connotative. The **denotative** is the basic, superficial, literal meaning (or signified) of a word, phrase, or other signifier. Look again at how Figures 5.1 and 5.2 illustrate Saussure's model of the sign. This model is what Barthes would call the denotative level. The signifier, the word *cat*, points to the signified, the concept of a furry feline. This is the literal meaning of the word.

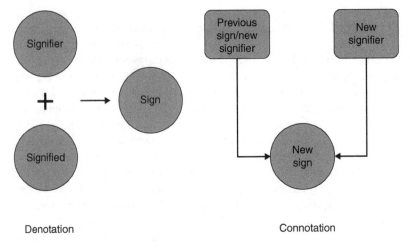

Denotation

Connotation

Figure 5.4 Denotation and Connotation

The **connotative** refers to a second order of meaning. At the connotative level, the whole sign (the signifier and signified together) can become a new signifier for a larger meaning. Figure 5.4 illustrates the denotative and connotative levels of meaning.

A phrase or word or image can have both a literal, denotative meaning, and a larger, connotative meaning.

Denotation vs. Connotation: Protest vs. Riot

To help explain the difference between denotation and connotation, let's turn to the situation that occurred in June 2010 during the G20 summit in Toronto (the G20 is the group of twenty finance ministers and central bank governors from most of the world's largest economies). As often happens at this event, there were demonstrations in the streets that ranged from peaceful marches to the violent smashing of windows. The people in the streets were described by the media in several ways: as "demonstrators," "protesters," "rioters," and "anarchists." On the literal, denotative level, these words were often used to describe the same people. But on the figurative, connotative level, they have different symbolic meanings: *demonstrators* implies a more neutral or even positive image than does *rioters*. The first implies people with a specific objective who are assembling peacefully to get their message across, while the second implies violent and chaotic groups who have no real political objective in mind. Both may be true of specific people in that situation, but if a media outlet emphasized one over the other, it was implying something specific about the events. Similarly, one person might say "I watched the protests on the news last night" while another person might say "I watched the riots on the news last night." At the denotative level, the signs PROTEST and RIOT mean the same thing: the two people would both be indicating that they watched the events at the G20 on the news. But at the connotative level, something else happens. Here we can see that what had previously been signs, "PROTEST" and "RIOT," become signifiers in another chain of meaning. Figure 5.5 illustrates this connotative level.

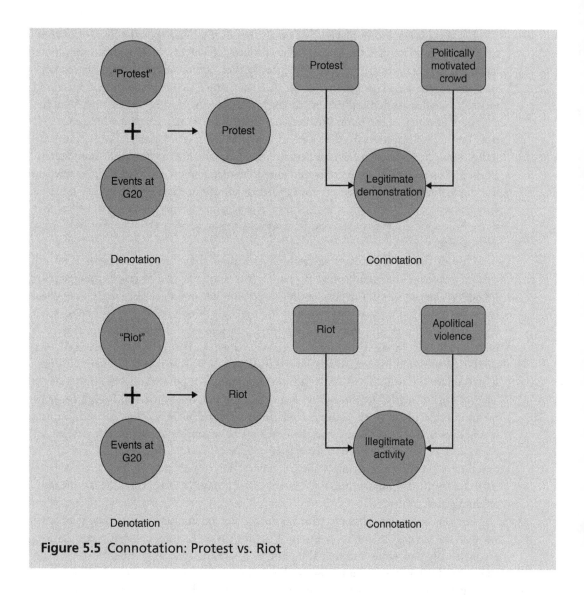

Figure 5.5 Connotation: Protest vs. Riot

It's easy to get lost in the chains and diagrams of signs. The simplest way to understand the difference between denotative and connotative is that the former is the literal meaning and the latter is the larger or symbolic meaning. Barthes explains the difference well in his essay "The Rhetoric of the Image," in which he discusses photographs. Photographs always seem denotative: they are, after all, a direct representation of an actual object at a given moment in time. They seem "true to life," and so have a distinctly literal feel. But Barthes and others argue that every image can be symbolic, or have larger connotative meanings, based on how the photograph is composed: how it's focused, angled, filtered, and so on.

But there is yet another layer of meaning that Barthes discusses: the level of mythology. Where denotation is the literal, direct meaning of a given object and connotation is its larger, conceptual significance, myth, for Barthes, is a common, socially shared connotation that is based on cultural codes and that generally reinforces dominant world views. When discussing Barthes's "mythology," then, we need to keep it distinct from the common meanings of the term. We often use the word *myth* to mean something that isn't true. But mythologies—as in "Greek mythology," or the mythologies of North American Indigenous peoples (which Lévi-Strauss discusses), or Christian mythology—are also religions, and as such they are patterns of belief that shape how a group of people view the world. Barthes's use of the term is closer to this definition, though he's not using it in a religious sense. He is, though, using the term *mythology* to mean a shared set of beliefs that shape how a society views itself and its world. In this way, *myth* is similar to the Marxist term *ideology*.

One of the more interesting examples of myth that Barthes discusses is an art exhibit entitled "The Family of Man," which was composed of a series of arranged photographs. One set of photographs shows three families: one African, in Bechuanaland (now Botswana); one European, in Italy; and one East Asian, in Japan. On a denotative level, these pictures are, individually, representations of different families. But each photograph is composed in roughly the same way, with the families arranged in a similar pattern and in similar relation to the camera. Taken together, then, and presented under the title "The Family of Man" in museums around the globe, they express a larger liberal "myth." Combined with sets of photographs of births and death ceremonies and of people at work—always from different parts of the world—the exhibit as a whole says that all people are the same: we all have families, we all work, we are all born, and we all die. It's a narrative that goes hand in hand with the idea that any differences between us are simply superficial and don't really matter. This myth we can call the myth of humanism. For Barthes, such myths are expressed as natural, unchangeable truths.

But this also means that myths are non-specific and unquestionable. The myth that we're all the same is difficult to question: What if we want to point out that particular jobs are physically dangerous and that the person performing such a job might not get paid adequately? What if we want to discuss the exploitation of much of Africa by Europeans? Or that famines and conflict in different parts of the world are caused by actions of one particular group against another? The "Family of Man" myth doesn't give us an entry point to discuss those specific, material problems. The myth that those differences are merely superficial allows us to ignore the inequities caused by specific political and economic policies, and so allows those policies to continue unchecked. In the case study at the end of this chapter we'll look at how one particular photographic image engages a specific myth of "Canadianness."

The distinction between "connotation" and "myth" is sometimes difficult to make, but generally speaking, "myths" are connotations that are shared by a large group of people (a majority of citizens in a nation, for example) and generally serve to uphold the status quo. "Myth," Barthes writes, "is depoliticized speech" (Barthes, 1972, p. 143). For Barthes, myth takes the specificity of political situations and "makes them innocent, it gives them a natural and eternal justification, it gives them a clarity which is not that of an explanation but that of a statement of fact" (p. 143).

LIVING LANGUAGE: BAKHTIN

Semiotics, and structuralism more generally, had a profound impact on a wide range of disciplines, as we have seen. From literary study and philosophy through to anthropology and even social geography, it's impossible to overestimate the importance of structuralist thought. Some later critics and thinkers, however, point to problems with the structuralist conception of culture. As the example from Lévi-Strauss's analysis of myth may make most clear, structuralism as a whole is a somewhat universalizing theory. It also tends to be rigid in its mode of analysis, even as some of the specific readings it offers are truly innovative and insightful. In Chapter 9 we'll examine some of the specific critiques of structuralism that came in the 1960s and later from what is often called the "poststructuralist" philosophies of Jacques Derrida and others.

But even in the immediate decades following Saussure there were others who were taking a quite different, if equally innovative, approach to language and culture, including Mikhail Bakhtin (1895–1975). A Russian literary critic and linguist, Bakhtin wrote primarily in the 1930s and 40s, developing ideas he'd worked on in the 1920s after the Russian Revolution of 1917. When his first book, about Russian novelist Fyodor Dostoevsky, was published in 1929 during the rule of Joseph Stalin, Bakhtin was exiled to Kazakhstan. It was there that he wrote some of his more famous essays, which began to gain widespread recognition in the West only in the 1980s.

Bakhtin's central argument also concerns the nature of language. Like the structuralists, he argued that any signifier, or "utterance," is always engaged in a variety of discussions with other such utterances. Saussure saw this structure as primarily a formal relation between units of language. Bakhtin, conversely, saw this context as immediately and always social in origin. In other words, starting with the idea of social context, Bakhtin created a framework for understanding how certain cultural forms, especially the novel (at the time considered part of "popular culture"), create meaning. In the process of creating this theory, though, Bakhtin also created a theory of how language functions to allow us to communicate ideas—and how the context in which something is said can also create meanings that can have very little to do with what we intend to communicate. Whereas a common complaint against structuralism is precisely its rigidity and universalizing tendencies—tendencies that some argue make it difficult for a structuralist to account for change or transformation in language and culture—Bakhtin's linguistic theories take transformation as their basis.

One of the more influential theories of criticism and literature to come out of this period has come to be known as Russian Formalism. As their name suggests, formalists, somewhat like Saussure, were interested in form. That is, they focused their analysis on the structure of a literary work (one of the most influential formalist studies is Vladimir Prop's study of folktales, which Lévi-Strauss discusses). The formalists wanted to transform the study of literature into a linguistic science. They wanted objective categories by which to analyze and judge a literary work, and by extension any form of art. Opposed to the conclusions of the formalists as well as of Saussure and Lévi-Strauss, Bakhtin's theory is, as he writes in his essay "Discourse in the Novel," an attempt to "overcome the divorce between an abstract 'formal' approach and an equally abstract 'ideological' approach" to "the study of verbal art" (Bakhtin, 1981, p. 259). Formalists tend to focus only on the form of a work or of language (the relationship of signs, the structure of myth) while "content people" focus on the content (what the work is "about").

Bakhtin argues that both types of readings—those that focus only on form and those that focus only on content—are too abstract: they make the mistake of looking at the text or language as an isolated, self-contained entity. "Form and content in discourse are one," he writes, "once we understand that verbal discourse is a social phenomenon—social throughout its entire range and in each and every of its factors, from the sound image to the furthest reaches of abstract meaning" (p. 259). Moving away from Saussure, then, Bakhtin analyzes language not simply as an abstract structure but as a lived experience (the term **discourse** has since come to be associated with the social side of language). Every statement, every utterance—whether it's a novel, a billboard, or a textbook—is always engaged in a social moment. He goes on to argue that every text, every word, is always and forever in contact with other texts and words.

Basically, then, Bakhtin is arguing against critics who, in his eyes, see language as a "unitary" structure: "Philosophy of language, linguistics and stylistics . . . have all postulated a simple and unmediated relation of speaker to his unitary and singular 'own' language, and have postulated as well a simple realization of this language in the **monologic** utterance of the individual" (p. 269). In other words, earlier linguistics posited a unitary system of language that everyone speaking that language shared, in which each sign means one thing; when people speak, their intended meaning is clear no matter the context in which they are speaking. This is what Bakhtin means by a "monologic" language: a language that is always the same. In a monologic system, "everything has a meaning relating to the seamless whole, a meaning one could discover if one only had the code" (Morson & Emerson, 1990, p. 28). A monologic theory of language says that language is essentially ordered, that there is a unified and understandable structure to how language works.

Bakhtin argues that if language has a unified order, then anyone using language creatively (in a poem, in a newspaper, etc.) is part of that order—so critics, if they have a solid understanding of the structure of language, can almost scientifically decipher any use of language and discover the meaning of any particular text. This is how Bakhtin sees the formalists—and, to a degree, how they saw themselves: as critics who could devise a near scientific approach to language and to literature in order to interpret texts "correctly." It's also a good way to characterize some structuralists, including Lévi-Strauss.

This critique of the formalists echoes Saussure's own critique of those who think signs are not arbitrary. But unlike Saussure, Bakhtin isn't necessarily interested in discussing "universal" structures that lie behind all languages. He's more interested in discussing how language is used in daily life. Bakhtin adds social context to Saussure's notion of the arbitrariness of signs. Bakhtin doesn't see the monologic theory of language as simply wrong, but instead incorporates it into a larger theory. He argues that there are forces that attempt to maintain a unity to language and forces that pull that unity apart. "Unitary language," he writes, "constitutes the theoretical expression of the historical processes of linguistic unification and centralization, an expression of the centripetal forces of language" (p. 270). But against these centripetal forces in language are also what he calls the "centrifugal forces" that pull language apart: "At any given moment of its evolution, language is stratified not only into linguistic dialects in the strict sense of the word . . . , but also . . . into languages that are socio-ideological: languages of social groups, 'professional' and 'generic' languages, languages of generations and so forth" (pp. 271–72). Any given natural language or professional discourse (like the language of cultural studies, say, or physics) is never static, but is constantly changing, and, more importantly, it never comprises only one set of practices. Someone's great-grandparents may speak the same language as their grandchild (English or French, for example), but the slang, syntax, and even definitions of certain words can be radically different. Likewise, someone who works as a lawyer will use an entirely different set of words on a daily basis than someone who works as a psychologist, and words they share—guilt, for example—could mean radically different things.

Bakhtin refers to this multiplicity of meanings as **heteroglossia**, meaning that any given language always contains "multiple voices" or "multiple tongues." Heteroglossia means that language is precisely not unitary but instead more chaotic—that there is no understandable, unitary structure behind language or, therefore, criticism. Unlike Saussure, then, Bakhtin is interested in understanding how the content of language and its form constantly interact, and he says they do so always within a social context. Bakhtin sees the literary form of the novel as the proof of heteroglossia, because novels use all different forms of a language: a science fiction novel can use the language of physics, and put it right next to a traditional romantic use of language, and then go on to discuss things in terms of political science.

Bakhtin's notion of heteroglossia basically means that language is a chaotic system, that it is inherently multiple and split up. In a heteroglossic theory of language, as opposed to a monologic one, there is no ultimate, final, unified structure of language that we can pin down in a grammar textbook or dictionary. Instead, language is alive, it moves, meanings and structures shift and alter. And, for Bakhtin, this "centrifugal force" is a property of every word and every utterance. As discussed above, we might be tempted to think that when someone says "cat," the word *cat* refers to one idea, one form. But for Bakhtin, every time I say "cat" that word is tied up with everything that has ever been referred to as a "cat." He writes:

> But no living word relates to its object in a *singular* way: between the word and its
> object, between the word and the speaking subject, there exists an elastic environment
> of other, alien words about the same object, the same theme, and this is an environment

that it is often difficult to penetrate. It is precisely in the process of living interaction with this specific environment that the word may be individualized and given stylistic shape. (p. 276)

Basically, Bakhtin is saying that we don't live in isolation and are constantly interacting with other people. It's the same for language—a word doesn't exist in a vacuum, and so it doesn't have a complete and stable meaning that, once defined, remains unaltered forever. He argues that when we interpret a piece of language, we need to take context into account—and this is significant for the study of popular culture. In order to understand a word, or a text, we need to see what lies around it, what affects it and touches it, historically, politically, linguistically, and so on. And there is no way we can exhaust or use up these readings, because there are always new contexts—we can offer only one or a few facets of a text. See the discussion of the film *Pontypool* for an example of how a work can sustain several interpretations.

Pontypool (2009)

The Canadian film *Pontypool*, based on Tony Burgess's 1995 novel *Pontypool Changes Everything*, functions in large part as an allegory of the problems with language and the difficulty of clear communication and understanding—and does so in terms that directly echo both Saussure's and Bakhtin's theories.

The film takes place in Pontypool, Ontario, and is set almost completely within a small local radio station. The station has a morning show hosted by Grant Mazzy, a disgraced American radio host. It's mostly a phone-in show, and as the morning wears on, the new host gets to learn about the small-town concerns of his new listeners.

Then the station starts to receive calls about, and eventually reports from, a riot taking place outside the office of Dr. Mendez; it quickly becomes clear that certain of the town's citizens are becoming violent and killing people. They are, in fact, acting like the typical zombies of popular culture: losing the ability to speak, they become seemingly mindless and shambling, and gain a taste for human flesh.

Part of the renewed popularity of the zombie in both literature and film (following the 2004 release of *Shaun of the Dead* and the success of the graphic novel and then television show *The Walking Dead*), *Pontypool* relies on the oft-used plot of a zombie virus that runs unchecked among the human population.

But what *Pontypool* does differently is make the virus part of language, and specifically part of the English language. People get stuck on certain words and, unable to find the correct word in a sentence they're trying to form, they repeat an incorrect one until it's all they can say. They turn into violent zombies, drawn to wherever they hear someone speaking. Near the end of the film, the radio host realizes that he can inoculate people by changing the meaning of words: when a woman gets stuck on the word "kill" he repeats "kill is kiss!" until she changes the meaning of the word "kill" to mean "kiss."

In short, the film plays with the semiotic nature of words: people suffer from the zombie virus when the signifier (the word) becomes disconnected from any signified (its proper meaning), at which point they can no longer function in the world. But because language *is* semiotic, meaning there is no *natural* or *essential* connection between words, Mazzy can stop the virus by forcing certain signifieds onto other signifiers.

Put another way, the heteroglossic nature of language here threatens to explode language completely, until every individual speaks only one word that is meaningless to everyone else. But by engaging in a dialogic process, Mazzy is able to find common ground, where language can change but people can still communicate.

The film uses this linguistic approach in part to discuss Canada's cultural and linguistic politics. While talking to BBC news (an icon of the imperial domination of both England and English), Mazzy is repeatedly asked about tensions between French and English Canada. Dr. Mendez, meanwhile, is represented as an immigrant to Canada, and speaks Armenian to protect himself from the virus. Depending on how one reads the film, then, it could be suggesting that English is "under attack," especially in Canada, that the imperial power it represents is fading (thus connecting the film to others that use a zombie virus to comment on globalization and immigration, such as the film version of *World War Z*); or it could be suggesting that English appropriates other languages (as in heteroglossia) and so doesn't have as strong an identity as others; or, conversely, that contemporary English Canada is too restrictive, trying to police its borders in a monologic way. Watch the film yourself, and see which of these contradictory positions you think it supports: Is it an anti-immigrant, reactionary narrative, or is it trying to suggest a need for English Canada to be more linguistically and culturally open than it currently is?

But Bakhtin argues that both centripetal and centrifugal, monologic and heteroglossic, forces are always at play in language: "Every utterance participates in the 'unitary language' (in its centripetal forces and tendencies) and at the same time partakes of social and historical heteroglossia (the centrifugal, stratifying forces)" (p. 272). How, then, are these forces mediated? How does language end up working on a daily basis? For this, we need to turn to another term, *dialogism*, or the dialogic nature of language. Heteroglossia by itself sounds all well and good, especially at a time when pluralism and openness are important and necessary issues in the academy as they are elsewhere in society. But while Bakhtin sees heteroglossia as generally better and more positive than monologism—one is alive and growing while the other stagnates thought—he doesn't make it, on its own, an ultimately good thing: "stratification and heteroglossia widen and deepen as long as language is alive and developing" (p. 272). Taken to an extreme, heteroglossia is like the mythological Tower of Babel: society becomes so stratified, so split up, that people can't bridge the gap and aren't able to communicate.

But this is where **dialogism** comes in. Think about the word: it comes from *dialogue*, the process of more than one voice talking, communicating. So we have *monologue/monologism*, meaning one perspective talking to itself, and *dialogue/dialogism*, meaning many perspectives talking with each other. Dialogism is the theory of how a heteroglot or multiple-voiced system can function. Heteroglossia by itself would be chaotic, and would mean that we couldn't understand anything, so there needs to be a balance of centripetal and centrifugal forces. We can map Bakhtin's theory out, as seen in Figure 5.6.

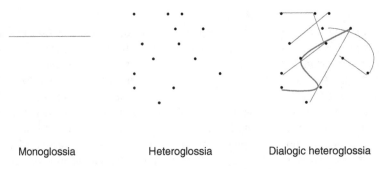

Monoglossia   Heteroglossia   Dialogic heteroglossia

Figure 5.6 Monoglossia, Heteroglossia, and Dialogic Heteroglossia

The first image, the line, represents the idea that language is monologic: everything gets mushed together. At its extreme you have a singular, completely understandable language, but also only one correct world view and one correct interpretation of texts. Language becomes one voice, a *monologue*. The theoretical danger of this vision is that it relates to and threatens to become a totalitarian enforcement of "proper" points of view. The theoretical benefits of this vision of language are that everyone can understand everyone else and all people can make themselves understandable.

The second image, the multiple, disconnected points, represents the theory that language is always a heteroglossia: language is multiple and constantly dividing into different stratifications. At its extreme, this theory would posit that language would eventually blow apart—there would be infinite dialects, discourses, and languages, meaning there would also be infinite world views and infinite interpretation of texts. The theoretical danger of this view of language is that the world would descend into chaos: no one would understand anyone. Conversely, the theoretical benefits of a heteroglossic language would be that no one is silenced; no point of view is denied on the basis of its variance from the dominant point of view.

The third image represents what Bakhtin actually thinks language is: a dialogic heteroglossia. Language is constantly dividing, but the dialogic forces draw connections between those heteroglot discourses, meaning they can communicate with, affect, and impact each other without reducing everything to one discourse. Different parts of language "talk" to each other, as in a dialogue. So, for example, the first time you hear the word *semiotics* you might not know what it means, but after your professor explains it, using examples you can follow, you understand its meaning. You start off with a heteroglossia, but through the dialogic forces of explanation, you come to make it part of your own language.

So, Bakhtin writes, "The authentic environment of an utterance, the environment in which it lives and takes shape, is dialogized heteroglossia, anonymous and social as language, but simultaneously concrete, filled with specific content and accented as an individual utterance" (p. 272). In other words, languages and social groups are individualized and stratified, but they can still communicate with each other.

How can Bakhtin's theories help you interpret cultural texts and objects? By learning to recognize the stratifications of discourse, you can see how different discourses (whether specific ones like legal discourses or more general ones like discourses of class or power differentials in society) can work together to create meaning in a given cultural text, or how they can contradict the stated aim of a work. Likewise, combining this with Barthes's and Lévi-Strauss's theories of myth, you can see how cultural material combines certain discourses to try to get its audience to respond in particular ways.

The Mountie

Let's analyze the photograph here using some of the tools we've developed in this chapter. We can begin with Barthes's distinction between denotative and connotative. At the literal, denotative level, the image is of a mounted police officer and his horse overlooking a valley next to a mountain. But as Barthes discusses in "The Rhetoric of the Image," the composition of the photograph also has meaning. Notice that the Mountie is positioned so that he's higher than most of his surroundings, and so is looking down over the valley and can see a wide range of the landscape: such a composition often implies that the subject of the photograph has power (much as an adult looking down on a child or a guard positioned in a tower has power). It's a particular kind of photographic code that many of us learn to understand. Also, notice that the Mountie is looking not at the camera, but off into the distance. This implies that the Mountie isn't concerned that his photo is being taken, that he's watching for other things. He's focused not on himself but on his investigation of his surroundings. Therefore, this isn't likely to be a personal photograph of this individual but rather a representative photograph of what Mounties do. Finally, notice that the Mountie is in the wilderness, alone. He seems not to need anyone else around him in order to do his job. Thus, the photograph could be said to connote that Mounties are powerful figures who are always in

Mountie mythology.
Source: Underwood & Underwood/Corbis

control, and always watching or investigating: that they're always, in fact, ready to "stand on guard for thee."

Mounties have also become a common symbol for Canada itself: images of them have appeared on our currency; they're often present at major national events (such as the Olympics in Vancouver); people from around the world recognize the uniform as a Canadian icon. Given these connotations, we can say that the Mountie is part of a larger myth, in either Barthes's or Lévi-Strauss's sense, of what it means to be Canadian, and that this picture participates in and helps to construct that mythology. The Mountie, standing in for

Canada, is steadfast, self-reliant, and represents "order." Likewise, the landscape—a pristine wilderness with no apparent pollution or large cities—presents Canada as a rural, unspoiled country; it is "pure." In this way the photo conveys not only specific connotations about the RCMP but also a larger myth of Canada and "Canadianness." It's a particularly male image, too, implying that this norm of Canadian order is one centred on masculine power.

We could use Bakhtin's theories to analyze the photograph and come to similar conclusions. We could point out that while the picture presents a monologic image of Canada (there's no urban space, or crowds, for example), it's still dialogically combining discourses of justice, the environment, and gender to present a very static image of the nation. The lack of movement even implies that "Canadian identity" is an unchanging, monologic entity.

This picture thus participates in the myth of Canada as a pure, unadulterated wilderness, implicitly reassuring us that pollution isn't something we have to worry about—and that even if it was, our government and its male officials are always on the lookout for evil-doers.

Discussion Questions

1. Fashion often has connotative qualities: high school "cliques" are frequently represented as being identified with particular clothing choices. Can you analyze the connotations of your own clothing?

2. The massively popular film *Avatar* employed several different discourses, with military and environmental discourses being particularly opposed to each other. Why would it do this? Is there a larger myth being engaged there? Or is it an example of a dialogic heteroglossia?

3. Think about a novel or story you've recently read or a TV show or film you've watched: Can you identify different discourses used in it? Did it use terms from particular disciplines, such as psychology or environmentalism?

4. Look at your university website: What larger myths does it participate in?

Further Reading

Francis, Daniel. "The Mild West: The Myth of the RCMP." *National Dreams: Myth, Memory, and Canadian History*. Vancouver: Arsenal Pulp Press, 1997.

Green, Eric. *Planet of the Apes as American Myth: Race and Popular Culture*. Middletown, CT: Wesleyan UP, 1998.

Jakobson, Roman, and Morris Halle. *Fundamentals of Language*. 2nd ed. Berlin: Mouton de Gruyter, 2002.

Metz, Christian. *Film Language: A Semiotics of Cinema*. Trans. Michael Taylor. Chicago: U of Chicago P, 1974.

Part III
Cultural Theories: Developments

Chapter 6

Marxism and Psychoanalysis II: Forming Identity

INTRODUCTION

In Part II we analyzed the origins of cultural theory and the study of popular culture by turning to some of the foundational theorists of the late nineteenth century and early twentieth. Now, in Part III, we turn to the contemporary developments of cultural theory, and specifically to the formation of cultural studies as a discipline, with the study of popular culture as one of the most significant elements of that discipline.

Many of these more recent theories combine some of the foundational works we've already discussed: this type of combination is something you may well do in your own analyses as you become more expert in using such theories. In this chapter we examine some influential twentieth-century developments in psychoanalytic and Marxist theories. In particular, we'll discuss Jacques Lacan's use of Ferdinand de Saussure's structuralism to reinterpret Freudian models of the psyche, and then move on to discuss Louis Althusser's combination of psychoanalysis and Marxism. Both of these theorists were instrumental in developing a concept of human identity in relation to its cultural context. In turn, their works influenced theories that came later.

LACAN

French psychoanalyst Jacques Lacan (1901–1981) is the most important psychoanalyst for many cultural critics; his work has influenced a wide number of other theorists, from linguists to an entire generation of feminist psychoanalytic critics (who critique or otherwise analyze Lacan's emphasis on masculinity and the Father figure). In many ways, Lacan follows Freud's model of the psyche, discussed in Chapter 4. Indeed, Lacan's psychoanalytic theories often comprise his rereadings and new interpretations of Freud's foundational texts. For instance, one of Lacan's most often cited works, his theory of what he calls the "mirror stage" of human development, is a reworking of Freud's Oedipal theory and the development of the ideal ego.

Lacan's importance to cultural studies also lies in his emphasis on language, and particularly the way he imports Saussure's semiotics (see Chapter 5) into psychoanalysis. It would be fair to say that for Lacan there is nothing outside of language, because the moment the infant becomes a self-aware being and begins to recognize that it's part of a larger human world is the moment that it enters language.

The Mirror Stage

In Chapter 4 we discussed Freud's theory of "infantile narcissism": during infancy, Freud says, the child acts as if it is the entire world; it doesn't recognize other people as such, but sees others only in relation to its own instinctual needs. But as the child grows up, this narcissistic impulse is refocused onto an ego ideal, or an ideal sense of self: a picture of who we want to be is formed by cultural expectations and norms. Our conscious self (what Freud calls our **ego**) then has to mediate between the desires of the id and the demands of the ideal ego.

Lacan's essay, "The Mirror Stage as Formative of the *I* Function as Revealed in Psychoanalytic Experience," is about that moment when the child recognizes itself as (and therefore becomes) part of the surrounding social world. Lacan calls this moment of transition the **mirror stage**. As with Freud, it is important to recognize that the science of psychology has moved away from these older ideas and now understands the human psyche in different ways. Scientifically, there are parts of Lacan's essay that seem very dated, even to non-scientists (for example, he discusses locusts and the gonads of pigeons in order to medically "prove" that the mirror stage exists in us). Yet these older theories can still be relevant in a discussion of culture, and are in fact necessary for understanding later cultural theories.

Lacan's emphasis on a person's relation to a larger framework (one that can include pigeons, perhaps) is related to his overall project in that he takes an anti-humanist stance. In other words, Lacan's theory of the psyche is one that denies the central importance of the **individual**, as we defined that term earlier, and instead sees each person as a **subject**, part of a larger system of forces—forces that, to varying degrees, shape and determine our sense of self. From a humanist standpoint, the individual is the centre of the world and the centre of meaning—of comprehension and conscious action. The underlying theory of humanism is René Descartes's famous philosophical statement, "cogito ergo sum" ("I think, therefore I am"). In other words, humanists argue that each of us exists as our own centre: we are self-contained and cohesive units.

If we think back to Freud and Marx, though, we can see a beginning of a collapse in a humanist world view. For Freud, remember, our ego (our self, we might say) is constantly under fire from our id, which wants us to act on libidinal, instinctual drives. Our ego represses these desires through the functioning of the ideal ego, which is formed through our relation to society: our families, city elders, etc. When we move into Marxism (and Althusser's rereading of Marx in this chapter), we will see a similar function being filled by **ideology** and certain social institutions. Freud's theories, when reread closely as Lacan does, are all about the disempowering of the ego, of the conscious self, in the face of forces acting upon it. But Freud's conception of the ego risks seeming to describe a familiar humanist centre to our being—a structure that acts consciously, of which we are aware, and in which we recognize what we think of as our "self."

Lacan views this as a central mistake in much of psychoanalysis, and so he goes back to Freud's original texts in order to further demonstrate what he sees as the radical decentring of notions of the individual. Basically, Lacan details the moment at which the child becomes a subject; that is, the moment when the infant develops a subjectivity. This is why, in the title of the essay, the "I" is referred to as a "function": the sense of being an undivided, whole and conscious self is merely an effect of our actual subjectivity, of being subjected to forces around us.

Lacan makes his opposition to the notion of the "individual" explicit: "The conception of the mirror stage" "[sheds light] on the *I* function in the experience psychoanalysis provides us of it. It should be noted that this experience sets us at odds with any philosophy directly stemming from the *cogito*" (Lacan, 2006, p. 75). Here, Lacan is saying that the actual process of the formation of the "I," the creation of a sense of "identity" in people, works directly against the notion of the Cartesian "cogito," what we're referring to as the individual. So the question is, *How* does he see the process of the creation of identity and subjectivity work? Lacan uses the story of what he calls the mirror stage of childhood development to answer this question.

The mirror stage is Lacan's term for the moment when a young child first *recognizes* itself in a mirror:

> This event can take place . . . from the age of six months on; its repetition has often given me pause to reflect upon the striking spectacle of a nursling in front of a mirror who has not yet mastered walking, or even standing, but who—though held tightly by some prop, human or artificial . . .—overcomes, in a flutter of jubilant activity, the constraints of his prop in order to adopt a slightly leaning-forward position and take in an instantaneous view of the image in order to fix it in his mind. (pp. 75–76)

Lacan goes on to interpret this moment in terms of the creation of subjectivity. He says that we must "understand the mirror stage . . . *as an identification*, in the full sense analysis gives to the term: namely, the transformation that takes place in the subject when he assumes an image. . . . This form would, moreover, have to be called the 'ideal-I'" (p. 76). The **ideal-I** is another way of translating Freud's "ideal ego." The reflection in the mirror functions as an early form of this ideal that the subject will try to "live up to" for the rest of her life, which will help her repress any anti-social, unconscious desires.

But if this ideal-I is the same as Freud's ideal ego, then don't we seem to have a problem? We discussed in Chapter 4 that the ideal ego is formed socially, that it is created through the subject's relationship to authority figures and others in general: family, church, government, media, and so on. But this ideal-I in Lacan is situated in terms of a physical reflection of the child's body. How are the two the same?

Lacan answers this question early in the essay: he says that the term is proper because the image the child sees in the mirror "will also be the root-stock of secondary identifications. . . . But the important point is that this form situates the agency known as the ego, prior to its social determination, in a fictional direction that will forever remain irreducible for any single individual" (p. 76). Since Lacan sees this moment as occurring before the child has full motor control, we could say that the child is constantly at war with its own body. The reflection, because it's frozen in time, appears not to have this problem, and so the reflection becomes an ideal image of the self as fully controlled, as "self-contained" and individual.

Significantly, Lacan says, this idea of self-containment and self-control is a fiction, and so the child can begin the process of comparing itself to other idealized images, to other fictions separate from itself. Lacan argues that this is the basic process involved in "secondary identifications"—that is, identifications with parents, siblings, authority figures, and so on. So, what Lacan is describing in the "mirror stage" is the beginnings of the process of the formation of Freud's "ideal-ego."

The Split Subject

For Lacan, the process by which we gain a sense that we are complete, self-contained individuals is precisely a process that denies the very existence of such an ideal because it is always a fiction. The notion of true individuality is, Lacan says, a myth. Our first "identification" of ourselves takes place in a "fictional direction." We must look outward to gain a sense of inwardness and completeness. This is the eternal paradox of humanity for Lacan: the moment when the child sees itself in the mirror in this way "symbolizes the I's mental permanence, at the same time as it prefigures its alienating destination" (p. 76). That is, the mirror stage gives us an internal, ideal sense of our individuality at the very same time as it's directed outward, either to our reflection or to our recognition of the other subjects around us.

This happens because, for Lacan, we can recognize ourselves only in comparison to something exterior—whether it's a fiction of completeness in our reflection or the fiction of authority and completeness in our parents or society. What this means, centrally, is that we are always alienated from ourselves; each of us is a **split subject**. We can never really be self-contained, because we need something outside of ourselves to define that self against.

Let's switch gears here to make this clearer. Lacan relied heavily on the semiotic theories of Saussure, which we discussed in Chapter 5. As we learned there, for Saussure each word in a language gains meaning only in relation to the other words in a language. At the risk of oversimplifying the argument in that chapter, the word *cat* on its own would be meaningless without the word *dog*. That might seem simple, but it involves one radical move that a lot of people still react against. Before Saussure, people saw words as gaining meaning in relation to the object they referred to. So *cat* has meaning because it points to an actual animal. That is, the signifier, the word, has meaning because it relates directly to the signified—the object. For Saussure, however, the signifier is detached from the signified—the object isn't what gives the word meaning. The word gains meaning only in relation to other words, other signifiers.

Lacan picks up on this, and says that any given person has a *sense* of being an individual not because she has a core—an actual cohesive self, or **essence**—that exists within her and her alone. Instead, building on Saussure, Lacan says we have a sense of individuality only in relation to other people. We are ultimately subjects, not individuals, because our sense of self is constantly in a dynamic play—consciously and unconsciously—with others. And since everyone's psyche functions like this, there is no real, irreducible "human nature": we are always involved in a fictional and dynamic play with everyone around us.

But that unessential, "fictional" aspect of identity doesn't make it seem any less real to us. Remember, this is Lacan's central paradox of identity: we *do* feel like individuals, but only because we are engaged in a matrix of relationships with others. The mirror stage, he says, is the "moment that decisively tips the whole of human knowledge into being mediated by the other's desire" (p. 79). Our sense of self is constituted by our relation to others insofar as we see ourselves in the "desires" that those others feel toward us.

But we do still act and think as individuals. Lacan refers to this feeling as the "*function of misrecognition* that characterizes the ego" (p. 80). We "misrecognize" the image in the mirror as an actual idealized self, and this allows us to become properly constituted subjects, solely because it is a fiction that directs us into a social framework. In this way, then, for Lacan our psyches and our unconscious selves function very much as a language, as we understand it through Saussure.

Lacan and Popular Culture: *Dexter*

Lacan's mirror stage has significant implications for cultural studies. Expanding Freud's notion that our unconscious is shaped by others, including "public opinion," Lacan argues that our very notion of self is constituted by those others. In a profound way, then, for Lacan our internal sense of who we are is fully composed of our unconscious identification with what is around us— which includes the images of popular culture. As we'll see in the case study at the end of the chapter, this theory has profound implications for the role of such aspects of popular culture as advertisements, which can help shape our sense of self in relation to certain commodities.

We can also see how some popular culture explicitly and implicitly echoes or analyzes such theories. A case in point is the television show *Dexter* (2006–2013), based on the popular novel *Darkly Dreaming Dexter* (2004) by Jeff Lindsay. The series follows a serial killer, Dexter Morgan,

who was raised by an adoptive police detective father after Dexter as a young child watched his mother murdered. Dexter's father trained him to take out his murderous urges only on violent criminals who had escaped the criminal justice system (although this "code" transforms over time).

Like many post-Freudian representations of serial killers—especially those after Alfred Hitchcock's *Psycho* (1960)—*Dexter* offers a relatively simplistic vision of childhood trauma and its later sociopathic manifestation: Dexter is represented as having no emotional connection to other human beings as such; he has learned to only mimic human emotional response. However, the show goes beyond this narrative by representing images of Dexter's dead father as his "dark traveller," a presence that haunts him during his daily life, reminding him that he's supposed to follow a certain code. By presenting a character with such clear psychological problems, the show can explore how parental figures and others help to form a child's ideal-I, and how that then helps to shape a person's inner self. In this case, Dexter is presented as a split subject, divided between his ideal "dark traveller" and his murderous instincts. While such a representation is sensationalist, it can help explain how, for Lacan, we all look outward to such a fictional representation of our ideal selves, and how that ideal is constructed by those around us.

One could also note how Dexter's "cover" life—in which he holds down a job, tries to have a family, and generally goes through the "regular" problems of an "everyman"—represents the social vision of an ideal self, one that functions in an ideological way to present a "perfect" middle-class existence as the "norm" against which everything else falls short and is

"abnormal." Dexter is always comparing himself with others to make sure he's acting "properly," thus consciously mimicking the unconscious process Lacan says we all go through—like Dexter, we have no "inner core," but only one that gains meaning in comparison with all those around us (though most people do so unconsciously, unlike Dexter).

As the series progresses, however, Dexter begins to experience feelings for others (such as in the episode where he protects his stepdaughter and her friend from another abusive stepfather), and so the show reproduces those ideals of self-sacrifice and protection associated with parenting and proper socialization. In other words, the show also serves as part of the symbolic matrix of gender and social identity, providing a model of its own for our "proper" behaviour.

The Real, the Imaginary, and the Symbolic

This semiotic psychology has another important implication for the study of popular culture. You'll recall that, for Saussure, the signifier (or word) never refers to the actual object it signifies, but gains meaning only in relation to other words. If the same holds true for the human psyche, then what does that mean about our relations to each other—and to ourselves? Lacan says that we have to divide up our experience of the world into three categories, or orders. The first order is what he calls the **Real**. If our mature sense of self exists only in the referential way he describes, in relation to others, then when we think of ourselves we cannot see the Real self but only the false images, as in the mirror. The Real self is that self before the mirror stage, when everything was united and there was no "split" in the subject: "the real is absolutely without fissure," Lacan said in a seminar (Lacan, 1954–1955, p. 97). After that split, after we enter into language and the social world, we can never fully access the Real again.

Instead we live at the level of the image, of what we think of ourselves—and this, for Lacan, is very much like what the baby sees in the mirror: we have only this fictional image of ourselves and our behaviour to work with. Lacan calls this the level of the **Imaginary**. For Lacan, borrowing from Saussure, this is the realm of images, or the signified: the Imaginary is the world we live in, where we gain a sense of self in relation to the other selves we meet. We "imagine" that we have a coherent self that relates to other coherent selves in a meaningful way, as if our identities all related unproblematically to a clearly signified essence. However, just as Saussure's signified and signifiers are only arbitrarily related, so too is our conscious sense of self only an empty reflection. To quote poet T. S. Eliot, the Imaginary is the world where you "prepare a face to meet the faces that you meet" ("The Love Song of J. Alfred Prufrock").

But, as we discussed in Chapter 5, such writers as Saussure, Claude Lévi-Strauss, and others still believed that, despite the inability to access the signified, or the Real, we could make sense of the world because language and culture have an overarching structure that, for lack of a better word, "contains" all of those self-referencing signifiers. Lévi-Strauss examined the structure of mythologies, for example. Lacan calls this overarching structure the **Symbolic Order**: "the imaginary economy has meaning . . . only in so far as it is transcribed into the symbolic order" (p. 255). For Lacan, the Imaginary is made possible by this Symbolic Order, which is the system of free-floating signifiers, all gaining meaning through their differences from each other. After the mirror stage, he says, the role of the symbolic is filled for the child by the Father figure (feminist psychoanalysts and cultural critics would critique Lacan, as they would Freud, for this patriarchal vision). The Father lays down the rules of the house, and the child's Imaginary relations exist only within that larger structure of the rule. Later, this role takes the form of larger social authorities and institutions, which still follow this basic structure. For Lacan, the Symbolic structures our Imaginary (or everyday) lives, which we live without direct connection to the Real.

This model is significant for much later cultural theory. In Chapter 9 we'll see how later thinkers try to do away with the Law of the Father and instead focus on the freedom (or terror) of a world with a lack of order, where we still can't access the Real. Many of these later cultural critics place popular culture as often repeating the demands of the Symbolic Order, even as it repeats the emptiness of the Imaginary. As Marx would say, popular culture reflects back to us the rules of the status quo. We now turn to Louis Althusser, who combines psychoanalytic, structuralist, and Marxist theories in order to explain how society maintains the status quo; culture takes on a very important role in his theory.

ALTHUSSER

Stepping aside from psychoanalysis briefly, we can recall that Marx sees culture as reflecting and maintaining the economic status quo of society. In other words, culture serves to support the current social organization, thus helping the ruling class maintain its position at the top of society. But how does that work? Marx has his own answers for that, but psychoanalysis can also respond. Freud says that public opinion, or culture, shapes our sense of who we are. Likewise, Lacan's "Symbolic Order" relates at least in part to the structure of cultural norms. It's fair, then, to say that popular culture can help to form our perceptions of the world, help to shape our sense of what is right or wrong, what is proper or not, and so on.

We see a development of this idea in Marxist theorist Antonio Gramsci's notion of hegemony and its relation to ideology (see Chapter 3). This is part of Gramsci's larger discussions of how the ruling class maintains order in society. In general, he draws a distinction between a populace's or a person's "spontaneous" consent and "enforced" consent to the domination of the ruling class. This consent, he says, is necessary to the maintenance of the ruling hegemony, or the smooth operation of dominant forms of social relationships, and so on. This point comes out of Marx's assertion that the ideological functions of society serve to universalize the particular social organization that needs to be maintained for the ruling class to maintain its dominance.

The French political theorist and philosopher Louis Althusser (1918–1990) takes these conclusions from psychoanalysis and Marxism and combines them in an attempt to describe the processes through which such universalization is achieved. Moreover, he analyzes how this universalization impacts, and is enacted by, concrete, existing people like you and me.

State Apparatuses

Following Marx, Althusser sees society as being stratified into a hierarchy of competing classes. Also like Marx, he's interested in understanding how the ruling class in society maintains its power. Specifically, Althusser investigates the methods used by the ruling class to maintain control. In his essay "Ideology and Ideological State Apparatuses" (Althusser, 1971), he discusses the institutions that are entrusted with actually exercising and enacting that control. Althusser splits up these apparatuses into two groups (see Figure 6.1): the **Repressive State Apparatus** (or RSA) and the **Ideological State Apparatuses** (or ISAs).

These two types of institutions or organizations function very differently. Althusser first defines how he's using the term "State apparatus," and then defines the specifics of RSAs and ISAs:

> What are the ideological State apparatuses (ISAs)?
>
> They must not be confused with the (repressive) State apparatus. Remember that in Marxist theory, the State apparatus (SA) contains: the Government, the Administration, the Army, the Police, the Courts, the Prisons, etc., which constitute what I shall in future call the Repressive State Apparatus. Repressive suggests that the State Apparatus in question "functions by violence"—at least ultimately (since repression, e.g. administrative repression, may take non-physical forms).

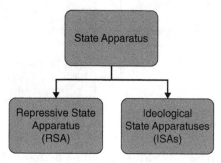

Figure 6.1 Althusser's Model of State Apparatuses

I shall call Ideological State Apparatuses a certain number of . . . distinct and specialized institutions . . . :

- the religious ISA (the system of the different Churches),
- the educational ISA (the system of the different public and private 'Schools'),
- the family ISA,
- the legal ISA,
- the political ISA (the political system, including the different Parties),
- the trade-union ISA
- the communications ISA (press, radio and television, etc.),
- the cultural ISA (Literature, the Arts, sports, etc.). (pp. 136–37)[†]

Both ISAs and the RSA serve to maintain the social status quo. The main distinction between them is that the latter maintain control through direct physical force while the former function through ideas: the dominant group can force you to follow them (as in a police or fascist state), or they can convince you that they're doing what's right for you so that you'll want them to stay in power (see Figure 6.2).

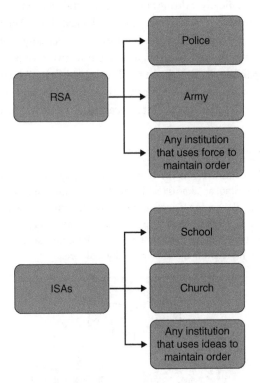

Figure 6.2 RSA and ISAs

[†]Source: Althusser, Louis. Lenin and Philosophy and Other Essays. Trans. Ben Brewster. London: New Left Books, 1971. Reprinted by permission of Verso Books.

Althusser maintains that the RSA and ISAs are distinct in this way, but he does note that the division between institutions that use violent repression as a tool and those that use ideology is not clear-cut: all state institutions use some combination of ideology and violence, he writes, but the difference is that the institutions that are part of the RSA (the army, police, etc.) "function massively and predominantly *by repression* . . . while functioning secondarily by ideology," while the reverse balance is true of ISAs, which "function secondarily by repression. . . . Thus Schools and Churches use suitable methods of punishment, expulsion, selection, etc." if people stray too far from acceptable standards of behaviour (p. 138).

Althusser focuses on the ISAs: these are the general, more common, and more socially and culturally extensive forms of state coercion, whereas the RSA—the violent and superficial exercise of state power—is limited because it's difficult to use constantly. Think about it this way: if the government had to send a group of soldiers to your door every year to collect taxes, it would probably end up spending more money and resources than it would if you yourself "freely chose" to pay your taxes because it's "obviously" in your own and everyone's interest. If you're convinced that taxation (within a democracy) is generally a necessary thing, then the state can spend less money and energy collecting those taxes. For Althusser, it is the Ideological State Apparatuses that make you think this way. In short, the use of ISAs helps negate the need for the use of the RSA.

Ideology and Institutions

Althusser was thus interested in the mechanisms through which the ISAs can make us think and act in certain ways without resorting to force. Specifically, he was interested in how these institutions make us feel as if we're choosing to maintain a system of our own free will, even if that system is unfairly skewed against us.

Let's focus on the reasons for, or the end result of, the functions of ISAs. Althusser's essay shows that the people at the top of the social ladder are there because they control the means of production—we discussed this with Marx. So, if a society is focused on farming, the people who control the land could end up on top of the social-economic hierarchy, and thus control how social relations get structured. In order to maintain their power, this class of people needs to reproduce continually the same means of production: after all, if people could suddenly farm without using the land belonging to the upper class, the upper class could no longer maintain their power.

But, for Althusser, people at the top aren't ultimately interested in the modes of production or the means of production—they're interested in maintaining their place in society. They're focused, then, on maintaining and reproducing the **relations of production**. Figure 6.3 illustrates the basic process of this reproduction, as Althusser describes it.

First, in the centre, we have the economic forces of society, the base that Marx discusses. From this arise the relations of production, or the economic relations between

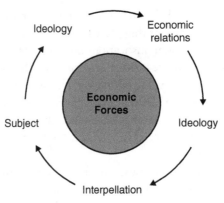

Figure 6.3 Interpellation

groups in society. If the dominant class can maintain the basic structures of these relations they can continue to reproduce these relations, and so maintain their power even if the means of production, or the basic economic forces, change. This is where the ISAs enter into the game. The dominant class must make the hierarchy of society seem natural—something that Gramsci (on whom Althusser relies) says about hegemony. Althusser, however, discusses exactly how he sees this being done. If the RSAs keep people in their place through threat of violence, the ISAs keep people in their place by making that place seem natural and inevitable. Moving clockwise down Figure 6.3, we can see that ISAs maintain the structure of society through ideology. And Althusser doesn't just make this a general theoretical point—instead he concretizes his notion of the existence of ISAs with the examples listed above.

We need to recall here what we mean by *ideology*. We may often talk about ideology in terms of politics—so-and-so has a particular ideology, we'll say—but for us the term is more significant. Ideology, the way Althusser uses it, means a particular world view, and for Althusser, as a Marxist, that world view is shaped by our class position in society. But there are other forms of ideology besides class, including gender ideologies, national ideologies, and so on. Althusser gives a specific if complex definition of how all of these things work: "Ideology represents the imaginary relationship of individuals to their real conditions of existence" (p. 153). In other words, our ideology, our world view, is the vision we have that explains our place in the world to us.

So, let's imagine a situation. We have a world composed of only two people, a boss and a worker; we'll call them Ebenezer Scrooge and Bob Cratchit, respectively. Scrooge is rich and never comes into work; Bob Cratchit is poor, gets up at four a.m. every day to go to work, and stops working only at midnight. Now, there is no reason why Bob shouldn't be boss: he's just as smart as Scrooge, knows just as much about the world, and (since there are only two of them) there's no physical reason keeping him in his place.

If he wasn't ideologically convinced that this job was somehow good for him, he would quit. But Bob honestly believes that "early to bed and early to rise makes a man healthy, wealthy, and wise": this is the dominant ideology. In his world view, his relation to the world is one in which he needs to work in order to be fulfilled on every level, even though, in actuality, it's not. So, instead of quitting his job or rebelling against Scrooge, he goes in even earlier to work and works even harder. The reality of Bob Cratchit's situation is that his position in this job is never going to make him healthy or wealthy or wise, but he has an imaginary vision of his relationship to his work that keeps him going back every day. Scrooge, meanwhile, propagates this ideology because it keeps him in his position of power.

Sometimes ideology can function very specifically, too. You're likely in university because you believe that education will make your life better: you could be working in a factory job with a good union and making money, but instead you're in class learning about ideology. Why? Because in a certain view of the world, education will improve you, even if it doesn't actually change your position in life. Many of us believe that education is a universal good, even if the university and the education system in general also function to maintain the social structure (see "The School as ISA" box).

The School as ISA

The primary example of an ISA that Althusser sees in contemporary Western society is the school. Althusser lists his definitions of the purpose of ISAs, their relationships to each other and to the dominant hegemony, and then the reasons why the school is the dominant ISA. He sees the school as the most important of a group of ISAs, and uses an interesting musical metaphor to describe this group: for Althusser, the ISAs function as a concert "dominated by a single score, [and] occasionally disturbed by contradictions" (p. 146). This "single score" we can relate to Gramsci's notion of hegemony, the term he uses to describe the operation at all levels of society of the dominant class's world view. So, the various ISAs all circle around the same large theme—that of ideologically dominating the populace to maintain the hegemony of the ruling class. But different ISAs achieve this through different means, just as different instruments use different sounds to play the same musical score.

But, says Althusser, the music of ideology is a silent one. As we learned when discussing Marx and Gramsci, the various aspects of the dominant ideology pass themselves off as universals, as common sense, and so most of us, most of the time, fail to see that we're being acted on in an ideological fashion. And the school, Althusser says, is the most silent of all. We've all learned to value education: most people see grade school and high school, at least, as necessary tools without which we would be unable to function as fully "productive" members of society and citizens. And, increasingly, an undergraduate degree is coming to hold that same value.

According to Althusser, the school can function as the dominant ISA because we're all in it for a significant portion of our formative periods; we begin to learn some of what the dominant society wants of us, and we take it as more or less true. So we learn, for example, to function within a nine-to-five day, and how to obey and trust figures whose authority comes from a rigorously structured hierarchy in which knowledge and experience are figured as the reason for that authority. Also, we learn certain skills, says Althusser, that are figured as necessary for our existence as socially responsible adults: language skills, mathematics, certain of the so-called "hard-sciences," and so on. Whereas in previous decades many people were taught in high school how to type or repair car engines, now many learn computing and electronics skills. People also used to see proper handwriting as necessary for a productive life, but as digital communication technologies have replaced pen and ink, so-called proper handwriting is no longer valued as highly, and a number of schools are eliminating the teaching of cursive handwriting altogether.

Also significant is what is considered in many school districts to be electives, in other words non-essentials: art, music, even some languages. In some cases the use of the school as an ISA is more explicit, teaching civics classes on the "proper" functioning of our government, for example; some people have even pushed for "manners" or "behaviour" classes. A Marxist would also say that we need to look at the money the provincial and federal governments put into research grants at the post-secondary level: technology and applied sciences get the most money, while arts often gets the least. So, if you want to make a good living and be respected in the world, you go into applied sciences or business, which has the most connection to the business community, which in turn has a clear and concrete connection to the ruling class—which may then support and finance the elections of the politicians who determine education funding. There are some generalizations here, of course, but the basic model indicates some of the ways the school functions as an ISA.

Of course, according to Althusser, the arts in school also function to maintain the dominant ideology—think about what literary works you were expected to read in high school, and some of the ways they were taught. Common examples include Shakespeare (*Romeo and Juliet*—perhaps to teach the tragic consequences of relationships that aren't permitted?); *Lord of the Flies* (which teaches that children need adults, and that rules keep you alive); *Inherit the Wind* (about the so-called "Scopes Monkey Trial" concerning the teaching of evolution, which basically reinforces the importance of science education, and education more generally). And to call these *ideologies* is not to say that they're "bad" or "good," "wrong" or "right"; it's simply a way to describe how they function.

We could offer many more examples pointing to the ideological functions of the school, but suffice it to say that its position in society gives it the power to "shape and train young minds," and that people generally see this as a good thing—which tells you how powerful a tool it can be. And even if parents don't want their children taught in the public school system, these children are usually home-schooled—meaning that even if people question a particular institution, they don't question the need for formal education, and indeed often follow a curriculum very similar to that of the formal school.

The school is thus in the central position from which to turn certain notions into common sense—by training us to think in certain ways.

Photo 6.1 Children in class (c. 1910). How does the classroom pictured here lend itself to being an example of an ISA?

Source: Thislife pictures/Alamy

This is how Althusser combines Marx and Freud in ways that connect to Lacan: ideology is that which justifies and maintains class structures, and it does so by making us internalize this structure as an ideal. Further, that ideal is a fiction, just like Lacan's infant's view of itself in the mirror. Ideology for Althusser, like our sense of self for Lacan, is an imaginary figure that structures our vision of the world.

Interpellation

Althusser describes what he sees as the precise mechanisms through which an ISA directly affects each of us as social beings, and in doing so further refines his theory of ideology and its relationship to psychology. He writes that, first, "there is no practice except by and in an ideology," and second, that "there is no ideology except by the subject and for subjects" (p. 159). Althusser says here that ideology exists only through us, through our engagement with each other. But, for Althusser, it's not just a matter of us acting out or acting against the dictates of a dominant ideology. Instead, we can act as social beings only within the realm of ideology, and as such, we exist only as social beings because of ideology. This is due to what Althusser calls **interpellation** (see Figure 6.3). For Althusser, ideology is like the air we breathe: we don't exist without it, and we can't exist outside of it. We both enact ideology and are enacted by it: "the category of the subject is constitutive of all ideology, but at the same time and immediately I add that *the category of the subject is only constitutive of all ideology insofar as all ideology has the function (which defines it) of 'constituting' concrete individuals as subjects*" (p. 160; emphasis in original). Althusser is here using *subject* in the way we have defined it. He means the social subject, the person who, in whatever way, is *subjected* to the forces of society. His argument is that ideology is a tautology—something that is self-evidently true—in which we as social beings are created by the ideological forces surrounding us and in turn help to create them.

But Althusser takes this argument to another level. He makes the distinction between the "individual" and the "subject" with much the same definitions as we've been using. But he almost immediately complicates this distinction by writing that "you and I are *always already* subjects" (p. 161; emphasis in original). Being "always already" a subject means that there was never a time when we weren't subjected by ideology, and that there will never be a time when we aren't subjects. There is no "individual" free of society or ideology. The ideological nature of society is always forcing us to recognize ourselves and others only within the ideology itself.

Althusser refers to this as *interpellation*. We are interpellated—meaning we are recognized, named, subjected—constantly and consistently by our names, our position in the classroom, in the workforce, in our families, and so on; we are always positioned and subjected to ideological structures (say if you're a youngest child or an only child, etc.). For Althusser, even before a person is born, that person's identity—the person's being—is subject to certain family structures and cultural expectations:

> That an individual is always-already a subject, even before he is born, is . . . the plain reality. . . . Freud shows that individuals are always "abstract" with respect to the subjects they always-already are, simply by noting the ideological ritual that surrounds the expectation of a "birth," that "happy event." Everyone knows how much and in what way an unborn child is expected. . . . Before its birth, the child is therefore always-already a subject, appointed as a subject in and by the specific familial ideological configuration in which it is "expected" once it has been conceived. I hardly need add that this familial ideological configuration is, in its uniqueness, highly structured, and that it is in this . . . structure that the former subject to-be will have to "find" "its" place, i.e. "become" the sexual subject (boy or girl) which it already is in advance. (pp. 164–65)

In other words, there is no time when we are free of ideology. Another, more specific example would be people who paint a nursery for an unborn child pink or blue depending on what sex they're told the child is going to be, thus already transforming the child into a gendered and sexed subject before it is even born. Building on Freud, who says that "public opinion" shapes our ego-ideal, and on Lacan, who recognizes that the "individual" is always a fiction, Althusser sees us as gaining a sense of self only within a larger social matrix that is out of our control.

This might seem negative and inescapable—but being always already a subject is not the same as having your thoughts and actions completely predetermined and controlled by one ruling ideology. In his essay, Althusser does hint that there are ways to resist the *dominant* ideology—that contradictions and discords can be introduced within the system that allow subjects to resist the dominant social order as agents if not individuals. He writes,

> [T]he Ideological State Apparatuses may be not only the *stake*, but also the *site* of class struggle, and often of bitter forms of class struggle. The class (or class alliance) in power cannot lay down the law in the ISAs as easily as it can in the (repressive) State apparatus, not only because the former ruling classes are able to retain strong positions there for a long time, but also because the resistance of the exploited classes is able to find means and occasions to express itself there, either by the utilization of their contradictions, or by conquering combat positions in them in struggle. (p. 140)

In other words, no society is simple; there will always be different groups and people fighting for power—and those discords can get represented and reproduced in popular culture.

IDENTITY, IDEOLOGY, AND POPULAR CULTURE

How do Lacan's and Althusser's theories of subjectivity relate to analyses of popular culture? Well, one can, for example, analyze texts to look for "hidden" power relations. One could look in, say, newspapers or ads for the uses of euphemism, or inclusive and exclusive pronouns, and so on, as Marxist cultural analyst Norman Fairclough does. Fairclough goes into tremendous detail about how one can analyze texts to look for "hidden" power relations, which is another way of saying looking for traces of ideological structures that pass themselves off as common sense or universals or otherwise make themselves invisible as ideology. He explores the creation of the "contradictions" and "resistances" Althusser mentions, and discusses how we might all be subjected in various ways. Still, we can be creative in our existence as subjects in order to effect change in the world— what we've been defining as **agency**. This is where the fact that we're the vehicles and not just the products of ideology comes into play. Fairclough uses an ambiguity in the meaning of the word *subject* to explain this: "In one sense of *subject*, one is referring to someone who is under the jurisdiction of a political authority, and hence passive and shaped: but the *subject* of a sentence, for instance, is usually the active one, the 'doer'" (Fairclough, 1989, p. 39). Different forms of language, discourse, and culture, as well as the different identities we are interpellated as (student, child, parent, worker, boss, etc.), "are a resource for subjects," Fairclough writes, and "the activity of combining them in ways that meet the ever-changing demands and contradictions of real social situations is a creative one" (p. 39).

Likewise, we can use the tools cultural theory gives us to explore the ideological dynamics of particular aspects of popular culture. We can never stand outside our culture and analyze it objectively, these theorists would say, but our various positions and skills in this world can still allow us to creatively analyze certain effects and aspects of that culture.

For example, whenever you see something about human relationships being assumed as natural, Althusser would say that that's where ideology is functioning. Similarly, Fairclough notes that whenever cultural texts and objects draw on what we can call cultural "conventions," these texts and objects thereby "embody ideological assumptions which come to be taken as mere 'common sense'" (p. 77). Roland Barthes's analysis of "mythology," discussed in Chapter 5, is another example of this type of analysis.

Case Study

Molson/Canadian?

Althusser's combination of psychoanalysis and Marxism, especially when read through Lacan's anti-essentialist vision of the psyche, offers a profoundly useful way to analyze the ideological functions of popular culture. In some ways, this vision informs many of the different theories and applications we'll see in the rest of this textbook, especially when we turn to discussions of identity in Part IV.

Here we examine two advertising campaigns that construct a notion of national identity and can be used to tease out the relationships between nationalist and consumerist ideological apparatuses and identities.

For two decades, since 1994, Molson's beer advertising has pivoted around an "I am Canadian" campaign, with print, radio, television, internet, and other campaigns focused on the relationship between Molson products and a Canadian identity. In 2000 Molson released a popular "Joe Canada Rant," in which a young man stands on a stage and, with increasing confidence, lists a series of actions, verbal tics, words, and products that make him "Canadian." Framed against stereotypes often associated with American opinions of Canada and Canadians, this commercial portrays a reactionary but supposedly universal Canadianness, one that asserts itself against a seemingly hegemonic American identity.

However, as Althusser teaches us, whenever something is presented as a universal or an "ideal"

identity, we should look for the functions of ideology that support a particular ruling class. This commercial delimits Canadian identity: "Joe Canada" is white, male, and young, and the activities he describes are commonly associated with a middle-class suburban or semi-rural life. Left out, implicitly, are poor Canadians, Canadians of colour, recent immigrants, and regional identities (which led to such radio spoofs as "I am an Albertan"). White, middle-class, male Canadians are thus ideologically represented as the "norm" or "universal."

A more recent take on the "I am Canadian" theme tries to avoid these problems, but engages in similar ideological constructions. These ads, known as "The Canadians," feature young men and women of different nations and races, seemingly in their home countries, discussing with each other wild evenings or funny occurrences instigated by a person who isn't present in the commercial. In these conversations, that person is always a little "crazy," but "funny" or "wicked," and everyone "love[s]" or "cheer[s] for" the person. These conversations all end with the revelation that the mystery person is "Canadian," a fact that's met with incredulity. The commercial then cuts to the tagline "So, what happens when Canadians get together?," followed by raucous party scenes.

Rather than defining "ourselves," Canadians are here defined by "others," but in a universal way: Canadians are all funny, they're all carefree, implicitly they all drink, and they're all able to have fun.

But non-Canadians are also defined here: they're not as much these things as Canadians are! So, "when Canadians get together" (implicitly in Canada), life must be better than in those other countries without Canadians.

In both ad campaigns, then, Canadians are represented as something of a paradox: they don't like to brag about their nationality, but do at heart think it's better than others; they're cosmopolitans who are at home and welcomed everywhere and by everybody, but whose own home is better. A national pride that denies itself—an arrogance, even, that refuses to see itself as such—comes out here. Canadianness is an ideal because it only hesitantly admits to being ideal (unlike, one supposes, the stereotype of the "ugly American"). A non-American but equally nationalist and chauvinist vision appears here.

This second campaign, though, adds an international dimension to such nationalism. Canadians are universally welcomed everywhere, the ads imply; they're never seen as cultural or military imperialists or as otherwise unwelcome guests, and they're always helping the local people. How? Through consumerism itself, by buying drinks and partying. This could be read as supporting an economically imperialist ideology that rivals that of the world's superpowers: Canadians should feel at home everywhere, can buy things everywhere, and thus feel the right to be anywhere.

The purpose of these commercials is, of course, to sell bottles and cans of Molson Canadian. By participating in the consumer culture the commercial is selling, we can feel like the "ideal Canadian." Thus, rather than find an inborn or essential Canadianness, it has to be marketed to us as a fictional ideal that we then internalize.

Photo 6.2 Molson Canadian, Molson Canadiana?
Source: Christopher Drost/ZUMA Press/Newscom

For another discussion of these advertisements, and links to the commercials themselves, see Susan Krashinsky, "I Am Canadian, and So Are They: Molson's New Nationalist Pitch" (*The Globe and Mail,* 6 February 2013, www.theglobeandmail.com).

Discussion Questions

1. Keeping in mind the final paragraph concerning ideological analysis as well as the case study, look back at the picture of the Mountie at the end of Chapter 5. What "conventions" is that picture drawing on, and what "ideological" work is it doing?

2. What ideal characteristics does the Mountie photograph present regarding Canada, or masculinity? Could these serve to reinforce psychological expectations of behaviour, as Lacan discusses?

3. In our discussion of ideology, we learned that ideologies are often represented as "common sense" or as "unquestionable": Did you question whether or not university was something you should do? Did you explore other options? What do your answers tell you about the place of education in society, or your relation to it?

4. Look for an ad on campus for a product commonly associated with university life: What assumptions does the ad make about university? Do these assumptions call into question your answers to the preceding question about the role of education? What subject position do these ads place students in, or what ideal-I do they try to construct? Why?

5. Look at the photograph of the schoolchildren in the "School as ISA" box: How is this picture different from or similar to your own experience of grade school? Can you extrapolate from that to larger ideological differences between the time and/or location of that school and your own?

Further Reading

Althusser, Louis. "Freud and Lacan." *Lenin and Philosophy and Other Essays.* Trans. Ben Brewster. London: New Left Books, 1971. 177–202.

Mitchell, Juliet, and Jacqueline Rose, eds. *Feminine Sexuality: Jacques Lacan and the École Freudienne.* Trans. Jacqueline Rose. New York: Norton, 1982.

Roudinesco, Élisabeth. *Jacques Lacan & Co.: A History of Psychoanalysis in France, 1925–1985.* Trans. Jeffrey Mehlman. Chicago: U of Chicago P, 1990.

Valente, Joe. "Lacan's Marxism, Marxism's Lacan (from Žižek to Althusser)." *Cambridge Companion to Lacan.* Ed. Jean-Michel Rabaté. Cambridge: Cambridge UP, 2003. 153–72.

Žižek, Slavoj. *Looking Awry: An Introduction to Jacques Lacan Through Popular Culture.* Cambridge, MA: MIT Press, 1991.

Chapter 7
Disciplining Cultural Studies

INTRODUCTION

As we noted in Chapter 1, the 1960s saw the formation of an academic discipline known as cultural studies, of which the study of popular culture was a major component. In this chapter we'll discuss the formation of two of the major schools of what came to be known as cultural studies. We'll investigate the ways they use the earlier theories we've discussed, how they transform those theories, and the precise ways in which cultural studies came to view popular culture. Named after the locations in which they began, these two schools of thought are known as the Frankfurt School and the Birmingham School. While these schools are often seen as the primary origins of popular culture studies, we would be remiss not to turn to another massively significant figure in the field, Canadian media theorist Marshall McLuhan, whose work on the forms of media has similarly influenced much current study; this chapter therefore uses McLuhan, in part, as a bridge between the two other theoretical camps. In subsequent chapters, we will see how these early disciplinary methods have, in turn, changed from the later twentieth century through to today.

THE FRANKFURT SCHOOL

In some ways, the theorists of the **Frankfurt School** should be included in Chapter 6. Like Louis Althusser, the thinkers associated with this group grew out of a primarily Marxist background, but attempted to rearticulate Marxist conclusions and methodologies in light of new discoveries in psychoanalysis, philosophy, social science, and so on. Unlike Althusser, however, the members of the Frankfurt School were much more interested in the critical analysis of mass culture, which ties them more clearly to the academic, disciplinary study of culture.

The term *Frankfurt School* refers primarily to a group of scholars who worked at the Institute for Social Research in Frankfurt am Main, Germany, founded in 1923. Primarily associated with some of its earliest members, including Max Horkheimer, Theodor W. Adorno, and Walter Benjamin, the Institute moved to New York's Columbia University in 1935 owing to the rise of Nazism in Germany. The Institute, now back in Germany, is still running today.

While later members of the Institute—even those who moved away to a greater or lesser degree from its founding Marxist principles (including such famous theorists as Jürgen Habermas)—are occasionally referred to as belonging to the Frankfurt School, the term generally serves now to identify that group of theorists from its opening decades, most of whom understood popular and mass culture from a Marxist perspective. They saw popular culture as a means of creating the consent of the populace to social structures, even when those structures are not in an individual's or group's own interest. The critical practice they developed is often referred to by the (somewhat too general) term **critical theory**.

Popular Culture as Culture Industry: Adorno and Horkheimer

Perhaps the best known of the members of the Frankfurt School—and the two whose arguments are most often used to represent it—are Theodor Adorno (1903–1969) and Max Horkheimer (1895–1973). Their study, *Dialectic of Enlightenment*, along with Adorno's separate essays, analyzed what they called the **culture industry**. This analysis still frames much of the work being done today in popular culture studies. Starting from a Marxist perspective, they point out that popular culture in the twentieth century is mass produced by an entertainment industry. So, unlike the high artistic productions of the individual genius, mass culture is much more subject to the ideological structures of production and class relations. In other words, the objects of mass culture must fit within the larger **hegemonic** structure of society, and serve a larger social purpose in maintaining that society. Whereas for Marx religion was the "opiate of the masses," for Adorno and Horkheimer that role was taken over by television.

In both his larger body of work and in his collaboration with Horkheimer, Adorno continually lamented the decreasing freedom that aesthetics, or the beautiful in art, had from the marketplace. The Romantic poets and artists of the eighteenth and nineteenth centuries, and many of their descendants in the centuries thereafter, saw art as a means of going beyond the concerns of the daily world and finding transcendent truths (much as Plato saw as possible through philosophy). As John Keats wrote in his poem "Ode on a Grecian Urn," "Beauty is truth, truth beauty," meaning that art can offer people a truth not sullied by the material world. Works of genius were also seen as necessarily unique and unreproducible.

But Adorno, looking at his cultural surroundings in industrial Germany (and at the rise of Hitler and fascism in that country), saw a world where aesthetic beauty and truth were no longer possible. One of Adorno's more famous statements was his proclamation that "To write poetry after Auschwitz is barbaric" (Adorno, 1983, p. 34). This often-repeated line can mean, on the one hand, that beauty is impossible in a world that has experienced the evils of the Holocaust. On the other hand, Adorno frames this memorable statement within his larger critique of mass culture. He saw the entirety of modern popular culture as barbarous, and as helping to create social climates in which terrors like fascist Germany could arise. Beyond those extremes, however, he also saw popular culture as simply flattening the social and cultural spheres, stripping the world of the possibility for larger truths like the ones Keats found in poetry. "Traditional culture," Adorno writes, "has become worthless today . . ., its heritage . . . expendable to the highest degree, superfluous, trash. And the hucksters of mass culture can point to it with a grin, for they treat it as such" (p. 34). Mass culture strips everything to the lowest common denominator, making all culture homogeneous and supportive of the status quo rather than unique and possibly challenging.

The Culture Industry   To clarify their vision of popular culture, Adorno and Horkheimer coined the term *culture industry*. In his essay "Culture Industry Reconsidered," Adorno later wrote,

> The term culture industry was perhaps used for the first time in the book *Dialectic of Enlightenment*. . . . In our drafts we spoke of "mass culture." We replaced that expression with "culture industry" in order to exclude from the outset the interpretation agreeable to its advocates: that it is a matter of something like a culture that arises spontaneously from the masses themselves, the contemporary form of popular art. From the latter the culture industry must be distinguished in the extreme. The culture industry fuses the old and familiar into a new quality. In all its branches, products which are tailored for consumption by masses, and which to a great extent determine the nature of that consumption, are manufactured more or less according to plan. (Adorno, 2001, p. 98)

The culture industry's creations originate with a few large corporations and capitalist interests; their products are uniform and serve primarily to turn their audiences into a uniform mass of consumers. The primary goal of the culture industry is thus not to educate or entertain but rather to make money—and it must continually reproduce itself, in a homogeneous form, in order to do so. "Culture now impresses the same stamp on everything," Adorno and Horkheimer write, such that "Films, radio and magazines make up a system which is uniform as a whole and in every part. Even the aesthetic activities of political opposites are one in their enthusiastic obedience to the rhythm of the iron system" (Adorno & Horkheimer, 1994, p. 120).

Even beyond this claim, they argue that the culture industry serves only to reduce thought altogether, to turn culture into an endless creation of an unthinking mass population bent only on buying more products: "The culture industry turns into public relations, the manufacturing of 'goodwill' per se, without regard for particular firms or saleable objects. Brought to bear is a general uncritical consensus, advertisements produced for the world, so that each product of the culture industry becomes its own advertisement" (Adorno, 2001, p. 100). The true function of mass culture is to flatten all meanings and to create the consent of the populace. In the process, it makes all cultural and material objects the equivalent of each other: films are no different from paintings are no different from comic books are no different from sinks or toilets. Everything must become a consumer object—including the consumers themselves.

This flattening of culture also results in popular culture's repetition of certain "conformist" messages. These messages may have existed in earlier forms of popular culture, Adorno and Horkheimer argue, but they become even starker and more simplistic in the products of the culture industry, which are only ever imitations of each other: "In the culture industry this imitation finally becomes absolute. Having ceased to be anything but style, it reveals the latter's secret: obedience to the social hierarchy" (Adorno & Horkheimer, 1994, p. 131). While older forms of popular culture may have been equally conservative in their messages, Adorno and Horkheimer argue, still those earlier forms presented the possibility of a resistance to those norms. In the modern culture industry, there is no debate. Adorno goes on to argue that this message is repeated so often that even those conservative values are emptied of meaning: they are no longer values that should be followed; they are instead presented as necessary controls, without which the world would fall into chaos, as if "people would really follow their instinctual urges and conscious insights unless continuously reassured from outside that they must not do so" (Adorno, 2001, p. 164).

Adorno uses an example from the popular television of his day to prove the importance of the hidden, conservative messages of popular culture:

> [T]he heroine of an extremely light comedy of pranks is a young schoolteacher who is not only underpaid but is incessantly fined by the caricature of a pompous and authoritarian school principal. Thus, she has no money for her meals and is actually starving. The supposedly funny situations consist mostly of her trying to hustle a meal from various acquaintances, but regularly without success. . . . The script does not try to "sell" any idea. The "hidden meaning" emerges simply by the way the story looks at human beings. . . . In terms of a set pattern of identification, the script implies: "If you are as humorous, good-natured, quick-witted, and charming as she is, do not worry about being paid a starvation wage. You can cope with your frustration in a humorous way; and your superior wit and cleverness put you not only above material privations, but also above the rest of mankind." In other words, the script is a shrewd method of promoting adjustment to humiliating conditions by presenting them as objectively comical and by giving a picture of a person who experiences even her own inadequate position as an object of fun apparently free of any resentment. (pp. 166–67)

A "light show," presented as "simple entertainment," seems at first to suggest an individual's ability to resist authority. But instead, Adorno argues, it implicitly tells us that our anti-authoritarian feelings are "enough," that we don't need to try to change an unfair system because we know we're better than it. No matter how poorly teachers are paid, they don't need to strike for higher wages, because, with the "right attitude," they can be happy. This is the effect of the culture industry: "don't worry; be happy."

Resisting Television

One might be tempted to point out, contrary to Adorno's example of the TV comedy, that some popular culture, including television, seems to resist dominant ideologies: that there are rebellious shows that seem to "fight the power." The theorists, however, would reply that even—or especially—when a product of the culture industry seems to be rebellious or "anti-authoritarian," it will tend to reinforce a totalitarian and conservative mindset. When the rebel police officer Dirty Harry (Clint Eastwood)—in the series of films based on that character—refuses to follow his police chief's orders, he is doing so because he believes even more strongly in the notions of force and justice that support police authority in the real world. When Bella, from the *Twilight* series, turns her back on the human world to embrace Edward's "rebellious" vampire identity, she only reinforces the patriarchal structures that subordinate young women. When Rick Mercer and *This Hour Has 22 Minutes* poke fun at Canadian politicians, they nonetheless reinforce the idea that the currently dominant political parties are our primary vehicles for political action. Finally, although *Dexter* (see Chapter 6) seems to be the ultimate in "anti-social" television, since it invites us to identify with a serial killer, the show can be said to reinforce heteronormative ideals: Dexter wants the "perfect" family and is most sympathetically portrayed when he struggles to feel "normal" emotions relating to traditional middle-class values. In these cases, what Adorno and Horkheimer call the "overt" messages of these shows (their anti-totalitarianism) are less important than the "hidden" message (which is in fact a very conservative, authoritarian message). In turn, because mass culture is so prevalent, because we are constantly inundated with its images and messages, it begins to shape our very psyches and behaviours, as we discussed in Chapter 6.

The worst part of the culture industry, Adorno and Horkheimer say, is that there is no way to escape it. We may feel superior to television shows like the ones they describe or the ones discussed in the "Resisting Television" box, and we may even create an "anti-advertising" or "anti-culture industry" identity as in the case study at the end of the chapter. But we can only turn to other products of the culture industry to show that superiority:

> Marked differentiations such as those of A and B films, or of stories in magazines in different price ranges, depend not so much on subject matter as on classifying, organising, and labelling consumers. Something is provided for all so that none may escape; the distinctions are emphasized and extended. . . . Everybody must behave (as if spontaneously) in accordance with his previously determined and indexed level, and choose the category of mass product turned out for his type. Consumers appear as statistics on research organization charts, and are divided by income groups into red, green, and blue areas; the technique is that used for any type of propaganda. (Adorno & Horkheimer, 1994, p. 123)

People who say they don't watch "Hollywood films" or own a television but instead buy only classical music and watch "art films" are not thus evading the "culture industry"; they are participating in its economics by identifying themselves merely as a certain *type* of consumer, no better or worse (in the eyes of the culture industry) than any other consumer. And the ideal type of consumer for the culture industry is a passive one: a spectator who consumes the same products again and again rather than actively participating in the culture.

In this way, the culture industry regulates both group and individual behaviour. Even those critics who analyze the culture industry aren't immune: "The triumph of advertising in the culture industry is that consumers feel compelled to buy and use its products even though they see through them" (p. 167). Consumer passivity and the flattening of culture are all-pervasive, making these the primary vehicle for hegemonic ideas.

Contemporary Hollywood trends can provide a good example of the flattening and homogenization of culture that Adorno and Horkheimer discuss: the endless "reboots" of film franchises (from *Star Trek* and *Star Wars* to superhero movies—themselves "reboots" of comic books), and their often predictable plotlines, can be seen to show a lack of originality, a focus on consumerism, and a reproduction of certain hegemonic visions of violence, war, masculinity, and so on. Nor is this flattening new: the plethora of *Tarzan* films from the 1930s to 1960s, the continual production of gangster films, and so on all point to the homogenizing structures of the culture industry and to the passive audience that, Adorno and Horkheimer would say, is the ultimate "product" of that industry.

Aura and Mechanical Reproduction: Walter Benjamin

Walter Benjamin (1892–1940), another member of the Frankfurt School, agrees with Adorno and Horkheimer that how contemporary cultural products are produced profoundly changes our experience of those products. Unlike Adorno and Horkheimer, though, Benjamin is interested in describing what he sees as the complexity of our relationship to these products, and in so doing he lays the groundwork for later popular culture studies.

In his essay "The Work of Art in the Age of Mechanical Reproduction," Benjamin attempts to come to grips with how the experience of viewing art has changed in the modern period, when new technologies—photography, film, and others—mean that specific works of art can be reproduced time and again. Although "[i]n principle a work of art has always been reproducible," the "[m]echanical reproduction of a work of art . . . represents something new" (Benjamin, 1969, p. 218). For Benjamin, works of art before the age of mechanical reproduction were largely tied to a specific time and place. If you wanted to see the *Mona Lisa* or Haida poles, you would have to physically go to where they were, to share the same space with that work of art, what Benjamin calls "its unique existence at the place where it happens to be" (p. 220). The work of art in this situation is invested with a uniqueness: it is a specific object in a specific place, and nothing else can replicate its existence. The unique nature of a work of art is thus tied to its originality and authenticity. If the *Mona Lisa* is reproduced as a postcard you take home from the Louvre, you know it's not the "real" *Mona Lisa*, and if someone tried to sell you *the Mona Lisa*, you would know that it was likely a forgery, a fake. The original piece of art is, for Benjamin, invested with a certain authority and authenticity that lends to the viewing experience a quality that is lacking from these copies.

Benjamin uses the term **aura** to define this experience, and he connects the aura of a work of art to the aura one experiences in nature:

> We define the aura of [natural objects] as the unique phenomenon of a distance, however close it may be. If, while resting on a summer afternoon, you follow with your eyes a mountain range on the horizon or a branch which casts its shadow over you, you experience the aura of those mountains, of that branch. (pp. 222–23)

Benjamin's aura is the feeling one gets when witnessing a beautiful object in its necessary and specific location, and recognizing that that object and the experience of seeing it is a singular one. For Benjamin, this aura lends a feeling of "[u]niqueness and permanence" to that beautiful object (p. 223): nothing else in the world is like it, and its beauty is intrinsically part of its identity and cannot be removed from it.

While a natural object derives this aura simply from its relation to the viewer within its natural surroundings—that is, from the uniqueness of that particular natural object within the larger context of the surrounding natural world—the artistic, human-made object must derive its uniqueness in another way. How can you tell that a work of art is unique to begin with, and not derivative of something else? Benjamin says that our knowledge of the uniqueness of a cultural object is inseparable from our knowledge of its place in a larger cultural tradition. It doesn't matter *what* tradition the object is placed in, so long as it's placed within a larger cultural context: "An ancient statue of Venus, for example, stood in a different traditional context with the Greeks, who made it an object of veneration, than with the clerics of the Middle Ages, who viewed it as an ominous idol. Both of them, however, were equally confronted with its uniqueness, that is, its aura" (p. 223). The uniqueness and aura of the object is tied to its role within a specific ritual, whether that ritual is religious, political, aesthetic, or more generally cultural. Placing the artistic object within such a tradition, and recognizing its importance, provides it with both a purpose and place within the larger social order of which we are a part.

The technological ability of a machine to exactly reproduce a work of art, however, effectively eradicates the uniqueness of such an object, and hence its aura. Anticipating and laying the foundation for Jean Baudrillard's theory of the postmodern simulacrum (see Chapter 10), Benjamin writes,

> [F]or the first time in world history, mechanical reproduction emancipates the work of art from its parasitical dependence on ritual. To an ever greater degree the work of art reproduced becomes the work of art designed for reproducibility. From a photographic negative, for example, one can make any number of prints; to ask for the "authentic" print makes no sense. (p. 224)

Adorno and Horkheimer make a similar point, writing that "Real life is becoming indistinguishable from the movies" (Horkheimer & Adorno, 1994, p. 126). Because of its complete lack of uniqueness, the modern, mass-produced and reproduced cultural object loses any sense of traditional aura. The "distance" that Benjamin discusses in relation to natural aura is replaced with an ever-accessible closeness. No longer do we need to go to the Louvre to see the *Mona Lisa*: we can buy prints of it to hang in our living rooms. More importantly, for Benjamin, contemporary cultural forms like photography no longer have an original at all, nor do they have that specific location in time and place—in tradition—that aura derives from. If "[u]niqueness and permanence" are tied to that natural scene and the traditional form of art, then "transitoriness and reproducibility" are tied to the mechanical arts (p. 223). The act of "pry[ing] an object from its shell" in turn "destroy[s] its aura" (p. 223): when any art object can be reproduced and moved anywhere, Benjamin argues, the uniqueness of the experience of artistic beauty is slowly destroyed.

But what is left in the place of this experience? For Benjamin, the aura of the experience of the beautiful object embedded in a particular tradition and context—a "ritual"—is replaced by politics (p. 224). Like Adorno and Horkheimer, he sees contemporary culture as shrinking the distance between art and reality. However, where the former theorists see this fact as leading to an inability of culture to give us the space necessary to examine our lives fully, Benjamin sees the potential for a democratizing effect. Contemporary cultural forms—and especially, Benjamin says, film—can awaken us to the processes that govern our daily lives and put us in a position to critically assess them:

> By close-ups of the things around us, by focusing on hidden details of familiar objects, by exploring commonplace milieus under the ingenious guidance of the camera, the film, on the one hand, extends our comprehension of the necessities which rule our lives; on the other hand, it manages to assure us of an immense and unexpected field of action. Our taverns and our metropolitan streets, our offices and furnished rooms, our railroad stations and our factories appeared to have us locked up hopelessly. Then came the film and burst this prison-world asunder by the dynamite of the tenth of a second. . . . The camera introduces us to unconscious optics as does psychoanalysis to unconscious impulses. (pp. 236–37)

While the destruction of aura may strike Adorno as leading to the death of artistic meaning, for Benjamin it "burst[s] . . . asunder" previous assumptions about the world, and so can lead to a new politicization of culture that can be used to combat movements like Fascism (Hitler had already come to power by the time Benjamin wrote this essay).

However, there is still some significant space in Benjamin's essay to see this loss of aura as a political and cultural problem. He does write, after all, that film places "the public in the position of the critic," and yet "at the movies this position requires no attention. The public is an examiner, but an absent-minded one" (pp. 240–41). This has led to some divided opinions of Benjamin's relationship with modern culture. As one source puts it, "On the one hand, with regard to some of his writings, Benjamin's concept of aura has been accused of fostering a nostalgic, purely negative sense of modernity as loss—loss of unity both with nature and in community. . . . On the other hand, in the work on film, Benjamin appears to adopt an affirmative technological modernism, which celebrates the consequences of the decline" (Osborne & Charles, 2011).

The Aura of *The Maltese Falcon* (1941)

The Maltese Falcon (1930), Dashiell Hammett's famed hard-boiled detective novel, was made into an equally famous film that can be read as a meditation on aura and political revelation, the very concepts that characterize the divergent readings of Benjamin's theories. In the film (as in the novel), a group of people are trying to hunt down the famed Maltese Falcon, a supposedly jewel-encrusted, immensely valuable sculpture. As in most film noir and hard-boiled narratives, much murder and mayhem surround these attempts, with private detective Sam Spade (Humphrey Bogart) being almost indistinguishable from the criminals he tries to—and eventually does—catch. In the end, the Falcon (at least the one that's found) turns out to be nothing but a plain statue, of no intrinsic worth whatsoever.

What's interesting for our purposes is the way the Falcon "itself" comments on questions of the market and aura. The criminals searching for the Falcon have lengthy tales about its place in world history and its singularity, treating it as an object of not just great material value but also of great historical worth. In other words, it has aura. But it turns out to be a "fake," and at the end of the film we're left questioning whether there's any such thing as the real Falcon, even as the criminals vow to keep searching. In this way the film shows how aura itself can be "sold" as a marketable item.

And yet the film does critique this marketing, perhaps operating, as Benjamin argues, to expose the "unconscious impulses" of capitalist society: here, those impulses are figured as the pointless obsession of criminals.

Photo 7.1   The Maltese Falcon, as it appeared in the 1941 film.
Source: AF Archive/Alamy

THE MEDIUM IS THE MESSAGE: MARSHALL MCLUHAN

The divided reaction to his work helps to place Benjamin as a bridge between Adorno and Horkheimer's negative readings of the culture industry and the Birmingham School's view of popular culture as a potential space of active political and social involvement. This bridging space is inhabited by another theorist, though, one who is much closer in time to the Birmingham School and who also helped create the field of popular culture studies: media theorist Marshall McLuhan (1911–1980). Born in Edmonton and educated at the University of Manitoba and Cambridge University, McLuhan is Canada's best known cultural and media theorist. He's famous for coining the phrase "the medium is the message," which is both the title of a chapter in his work *Understanding Media* (McLuhan, 1964) and a pithy summary of that work's main point. This phrase has become so popular as to become part of popular culture itself. (In fact, McLuhan had a way with coining such phrases: he's credited with "the global village" as well.)

"The medium is the message" also summarizes McLuhan's methodology. Much like the formalist literary critics who were writing at this time, McLuhan was primarily interested in analyzing the forms culture took. Specifically, he argued that the content of contemporary mass culture was less important than the way in which it was transmitted to its consumer or viewer. Like Benjamin, McLuhan saw the rise of mass communications technology as significantly altering our relationship with culture. However, Benjamin, as well as Adorno and Horkheimer, focused on the difference these technologies created between traditional forms of art or culture and the new mass culture; McLuhan, conversely, was interested in the specific nature of these new media forms, their difference from each other, and what effect they had on the culture consumer.

For McLuhan, the effect of the medium doesn't change depending on what's shown through that medium: a television comedy and a television documentary share the same medium, and for McLuhan that commonality is more important that any difference in content.

He uses the examples of the lightbulb and the train to explain this position:

> The electric light is pure information. It is a medium without a message, as it were, unless it is used to spell out some verbal ad or name. This fact, characteristic of all media, means that the "content" of any medium is always another medium. The content of writing is speech, just as the written word is the content of print, and print is the content of the telegraph. If it is asked, "What is the content of speech?," it is necessary to say, "It is an actual process of thought, which is in itself nonverbal." An abstract painting represents direct manifestation of creative thought processes as they might appear in computer designs. What we are considering here, however, are the psychic and social consequences of the designs or patterns as they amplify or accelerate existing processes. For the "message" of any medium or technology is the change of scale or pace or pattern that it introduces into human affairs. The railway did not introduce movement or transportation or wheel or road into human society, but it accelerated and enlarged the scale of previous human functions, creating totally new kinds of cities and new kinds of work and leisure. (pp. 23–24)

The train may share the basic purpose and goal—the same content—as a horse-drawn buggy, but the form that that content takes—it can move faster, stop less regularly, and traverse greater distances in less time—transformed the economies of the world. Likewise, the airplane, and its increasing popularity, helped to usher in the age of globalization. A lightbulb may share the same purpose as a candle, but since it gives off more light and can be harnessed in greater numbers more safely, it can transform the types of life a society can have after dark.

Similarly, McLuhan argues, while the content of culture remains relatively static across media, the form that media takes transforms culture. Benjamin makes a similar point, of course, when he argues that mass reproduction—and hence the technological media that allow that reproduction—alter our relationship with a piece of art.

Hot Media and Cold Media

McLuhan's analysis is much more specific, however, when he draws distinctions between types of mass media. He contends that contemporary media can be divided into two groups: hot media and cold. **Hot media**, he argues, are "high definition" media that fully engage one or more of our senses, making us passive receivers of its images, sounds, and so on (p. 36). **Cold media**, conversely, are "low definition," forcing us to fill in gaps in the transmission, making us more active readers/viewers/listeners or consumers more generally (p. 36). So, a photograph, which reproduces an event with clarity and precision, is "hot" because it doesn't require us to pay close attention to figure out what's going on. A cartoon or comic, because it is much less precise and clear in its visual depiction of a scene, requires us to work more actively to understand it.

Importantly, for McLuhan, television is an example of a cold medium—writing in 1963, the televisions McLuhan knew were generally much smaller, had poorer reception, were black and white, had small speakers, and so on. So, televisions required work on behalf of the viewer to understand what was happening.

It's tempting to see the distinction between hot and cold media, between the passive and active viewer, as also a distinction between being a "subject" of media and an "agent" in relation to it. McLuhan didn't see it this way, however: he saw the difference between hot and cold as one that transforms the very ways people engage in the world. Because cold media, like older television, require so much involvement of their audience, they transform the ways in which that audience engages with the world: "The young people who have experienced a decade of TV have naturally imbibed an urge toward involvement in depth that makes all the remote visualized goals of usual culture seem not only unreal but irrelevant" (p. 292).

This involvement in the unreality of television (something that theorist Jean Baudrillard explores further, as discussed in Chapter 10) creates a paradoxical desire to be deeply involved in life, and an inability to "see ahead," because the television viewer wants immediate satisfaction. "TV makes for myopia," McLuhan writes, but also creates a longing for "involvement." Instead of a "job" the "TV child" wants a *"role"* (p. 292).

McLuhan was writing a half-century ago, and clearly some of his distinctions between hot and cold media can be troubled now: television can be high-definition and can be paused, rewound, etc., and people can have well-constructed home theatres that mimic the theatre-going experience, minimizing the need for the viewer to "fill in" information. Likewise, many new forms of media have been created since McLuhan wrote: the internet was barely conceived of before he died, and the idea of a largely interactive media technology—such as that used by Facebook, Twitter, or Instagram, for instance—would have been almost inconceivable (though some science fiction texts and early gaming technology did look forward to it).

So can McLuhan's categories be applied to such new social media? At first glance, as the descriptor "social" implies, these media would seem to fit into the "cold" category: they require direct action on behalf of an "audience" that can no longer even be characterized as simple "viewers," since they must generate as well as watch the content.

And yet some aspects of social media are distinctly "hot": not only are images often presented in clear high-definition, but Facebook, for example, is inundated with ads that directly target their audience: Facebook users' very activity on the site directs certain ads their way, creating the perfect situation for a passive, or "hot," reception of the capitalist message. Likewise, depending on your circle of friends or followers, social media can have the effect of simply reinforcing already held opinions, with you and your friends sharing ideas and beliefs without challenging each other to think in new ways. In this way, social media would seem to function as a very hot media.

Perhaps then, social media—and maybe all advanced media technology—functions as a blend of hot and cold media, in just the way McLuhan describes them.

Clearly, this new way of being in the world is problematic for McLuhan, but he still sees that longing for involvement and depth as a potential source of "pedagogical richness," provided it's not left "[u]nbridled" (p. 292). As with Benjamin, then, we are left in a tense space, where these new media do create new forms of engagement and activity in the world but can also lead to new forms of passivity and emptiness. In the next section we discuss theorists who likewise see this tense positioning, but fall firmly on the side of agency, rather than subjection, in relation to people's engagement with popular culture.

THE BIRMINGHAM SCHOOL

Whereas the Frankfurt School looked upon the social and cultural roles of popular culture with suspicion, and in some cases outright hostility, the later **Birmingham School** is often seen as championing their radical possibilities. Of course, as we saw in the discussion of Walter Benjamin, the Frankfurt School wasn't so monolithic in its approach, and the same can be said for the Birmingham theorists. Still, these theorists offer a much more positive vision of popular culture, specifically in terms of people's engagement with it.

Like the term *Frankfurt School*, *Birmingham School* refers both to a group of loosely associated theorists and critics and to a general critical paradigm based on their work. The "school" is the Centre for Contemporary Cultural Studies, founded at the University of Birmingham in 1964. It is largely credited with popularizing the term *cultural studies* and with framing the study of popular culture as a legitimate academic discipline. In fact, when people use the term *cultural studies*, they're often referring directly to the Birmingham School's vision of the discipline, which is sometimes referred to as **British Cultural Studies**.

The Centre for Contemporary Cultural Studies was founded in part to encourage the widening of the scope of university study—to move away from traditional social science and humanities methodologies as well as to challenge the traditional object choices of those studies. The analysts at the Centre thus studied British working-class culture, various subcultures, and popular cultural objects, including popular music, television, and other material. In many ways, then, this tradition of cultural studies is responsible for this book and for the classes you're studying it in.

Importantly, the Centre also explicitly challenged the disciplinary divisions that constitute traditional university studies. So, while people in English and in sociology departments, for example, didn't traditionally teach together or engage in collaborative research, the Centre encouraged communication and research sharing between these disciplinary "silos," as they came to be called. Tied to this interdisciplinary practice, and in part because of it, the conventional objects and methodologies of study within these disciplines were also challenged. To use our two examples again, while English professors had traditionally studied the canon of literature using what were, by 1964, standard formal analyses of patterns of metaphor, imagery, and so on, Birmingham-inflected cultural studies had them turning to such spheres as history, sociological studies of reception, and studies of race and gender, making the study of English more material and social-scientific in some ways; likewise, rather than sociologists engaging in empirical studies of the material practices of a given group, they began to focus on the cultural aspects of that society in order to examine its more aesthetic elements, often incorporating techniques used in humanities disciplines, such as close textual analysis. This transformation is often referred to as the **cultural turn**, echoing the **linguistic turn** we discussed in Chapter 5.

Taken together, then, these practices begin to break down the traditional barriers between academic disciplines and to open up both the material and the methods of the study of culture. Part of this project also broke down the biases surrounding what constituted "good" or "high" culture, and also questioned traditional assumptions about the value of popular culture.

In the remainder of this chapter we discuss some of the specific theoretical and critical methods developed by some of the major thinkers of the Birmingham School. Like many of the theorists we've already examined, including those from the Frankfurt School, Birmingham School theorists were greatly influenced by Marxist thought, although they developed it very differently from the Frankfurt School.

Working Cultures

One of the primary theoretical advancements of the Birmingham School is the idea that people don't simply consume culture passively but are instead active **agents** with respect to cultural products and the use thereof. While Adorno and Horkheimer see the consumers of the "culture industry" as passive vessels that get filled up by the dominant ideological messages embedded in popular culture, the Birmingham School thinkers see the relationship between dominant ideologies, cultural products, and their reception as much more complex. In this section we'll trace two of the significant deployments of this premise, in the works of E. P. Thompson (1924–1993) and Stuart Hall (1932–).

E. P. Thompson's book, *The Making of the English Working Class* (Thompson, 1963), is often cited as being foundational to the new cultural studies. The first lines of its preface make clear both what Thompson sees as the problems of early sociological histories and how his new study will differ from them: "This book has a clumsy title," he writes, "but it is one which meets its purpose. *Making*, because it is a study in an active process, which owes as much to agency as to conditioning. The working class did not rise like the sun at an appointed time. It was present at its own making" (p. 9). Building on Marx's prescription that one must look to how people actually live their lives in order to understand their society, Thompson goes further, noting that within their "lived experience" people actually respond to and interpret their social surroundings and what happens around them. To use the terminology we've been employing, and which Thompson uses similarly here, he sees people as *agents* rather than just *subjects* in their own lives.

Just as importantly, his study of class changes traditional approaches as well. Rather than *assuming* both the makeup and importance of class as a social structure, one that seemingly pre-exists and shapes people's interactions with each other, he sees class as a *process* that happens when people interact. For Thompson, class isn't a "structure" or "category" but instead a dynamic, relational action that occurs between people and that allows them to "feel and articulate the identity of their interests as between themselves, and as against other men whose interests are different from (and usually opposed to) theirs" (p. 9). Thus, although people's "class experience is largely determined by the productive relations into which men are born," the ways they react to those conditions as a group, their "[c]lass-consciousness," is not so directly determined, as a more simplistic or linear Marxism would have it (pp. 9–10). Thompson argues that there is "a *logic* in the responses of similar occupational groups undergoing similar experiences" that can be discussed and analyzed (p. 10), but that this is different from saying those responses—and so those people— are fully determined by those experiences. Therefore, he writes, class must be understood "as a *social* and *cultural* formation" (p. 11; emphasis added).

Thompson is quite clear that he's attempting to transform historical and sociological study in such a way as to recognize in "working people" a conscious, agential relationship to their world. He states outright that he realizes he is

> writing against the weight of prevailing orthodoxies. There is the Fabian orthodoxy, in which the great majority of working people are seen as passive victims of *laissez faire*,

with the exception of a handful of far-sighted organisers. . . . There is the orthodoxy of the empirical economic historians, in which working people are seen as a labour force, as migrants, or as the data for statistical series. (p. 12)

Thompson challenges these two orthodoxies, along with a third that sees earlier periods as important only insofar as they predict our period. The first two narratives, he says, "tend to obscure the agency of working people, the degree to which they contributed, by conscious efforts, to the making of history," while the third twists history into part of our moment, ignoring how "in fact it occurred" (p. 12). Thompson thus sees class identity as an identity that is in flux and changes as people interact. This basic premise forms the foundation of later popular cultural studies of identity, as we will discuss in Part IV.

Thompson's eight-hundred-page opus presents, in minute detail, many of the cultural and social aspects of the development of the working class in England, offering, ultimately, a very focused history, the specifics of which aren't necessarily useful for us. But the idea that history was necessarily specific to a particular people or region is itself an important development: rather than pointing to a universal history, Thompson's argument about the agency of specific people necessitates a close and focused analysis. This laser-sharp focus on particularities became a feature of Birmingham School criticism as well as of some of its later offshoots (such as New Historicism, discussed in Chapter 8).

Cultural Agents

But while this specificity of focus means it can be difficult to present an overarching methodology for the various studies that constitute the Birmingham School, some of its members did attempt to provide wider theoretical models for the study of particular cultural objects. Among these, Stuart Hall's study of television and its audiences stands out.

Like Thompson, Hall was invested in reading the consuming audience as active rather than passive in the creation of meaning. His best known meditation on this relationship is in his essay "Encoding/Decoding" (Hall, 1980). Focusing on communication technologies and specifically on television, Hall, like Thompson, begins his piece by explaining how this new approach differs from more conventional studies:

Traditionally, mass-communications research has conceptualized the process of communication in terms of a circulation circuit or loop. This model has been criticized for its linearity—sender/message/receiver—for its concentration on the level of message exchange and for the absence of a structured conception of the different moments as a complex structure of relations. (p. 128)

In this earlier model, there is no room for misunderstanding or misinterpretation. But for Hall, this misses the primary method of communication that television (and other forms of mass communication) employ: what he calls **discourse**, a term that will become increasingly significant in cultural studies. *Discourse* refers to the entire range of signifying practices in a society, composed not only of language but also of the codes that structure our daily practice, production, use, and interpretation of media. As such, *discourse* is too multifaceted for its meanings to be completely determined by the culture producer, as in the more simplistic model above. To put it simply, clearly different readings, some often counter to the producer's intent, do occur. Hall is interested, in part, in what this fact means to a larger theory of reception and communication.

Given that messages don't always move smoothly and linearly from producer to receiver, Hall spells out another model to explain the production of meaning within this relationship. Any element of mass communication must be made within discourse, or more generally within "language," he argues, and as such it is within the slippery realm of language (as we defined it in Chapter 5) that meaning is created. This makes it difficult, if not impossible, to control the meaning from the "production" end of culture:

> [I]t is in the *discursive* form that the circulation of the product takes place, as well as its distribution to different audiences. Once accomplished, the discourse must then be translated—transformed, again—into social practices if the circuit is to be both completed and effective. If no "meaning" is taken, there can be no "consumption." (p. 128)

In other words, meaning is never controlled by just one party in the dialogue; the meaning of a text or television show isn't fully contained within that object, just waiting to be discovered by the viewer. Instead, when a statement is created, the producer may "encode" meanings in it, but the receiver must still "decode" the message, and those two processes may not arrive at the same meaning.

But why don't they? Is it because we are all individuals and so have essential, in-born differences that lead us to different conclusions? Hall would say no, that instead both the production and the reception of a work are acts that are engaged in a variety of discursive practices, each of which helps to shape the meanings that both sides see in the work. Hall uses the diagram in Figure 7.1 to explain how meanings are determined on both sides of the production/reception circuit.

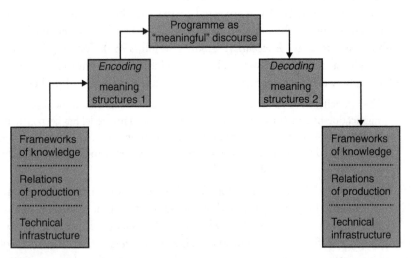

Figure 7.1 Encoding/Decoding

Source: Hall, Stuart, et al., eds. *Culture, Media, Language: Working Papers in Cultural Studies, 1972–79*, p. 130.

Important to note is that Hall, building on Marx but also on other theorists we've studied in Part III, does not see meaning and interpretation as completely free or constructed by an individual's free response. He views us as subjects and agents, not as individuals. Thus, on the left-hand side of the diagram, the producer of a text must create meaning within a set of structures that work to predetermine that meaning to one degree or another, whether owing to the technical limitations of a television studio's equipment or the larger social class structure within which the studio exists (including which "demographic" it's trying to reach). Likewise, viewers are determined by their own positions within these structures: Does the viewer have a large-screen HD television or a small black-and-white? What is the viewer's relative class and social position?

Encoding/Decoding   Within these structures, Hall focuses on the significance of the top category, the "frameworks of knowledge." These are the "the discursive rules of language" (p. 130), those semiotic structures discussed in Chapter 5 without which words would be meaningless. But because the producer and receiver of the television show or other communication are in differently determined positions within society—different **subject positions**—their relationships to these frameworks will also be different. Because of this difference, Hall writes,

> Clearly, what we have labelled in the diagram "meaning structures 1" and "meaning structures 2" may not be the same. . . . The codes of encoding and decoding may not be perfectly symmetrical. The degrees of symmetry—that is, the degrees of "understanding" and "misunderstanding" in the communicative exchange—depend on . . . the structural differences of relation and position between broadcasters and audiences. (p. 131)

Different groups are determined in different ways, and so read and interpret examples of discourse differently. Therefore, in order to offer a scholarly analysis of television, Hall says we have to pay attention not only to its content and the technical conditions of its production and reception (its form, generally speaking), but also to the ways both interact within larger codes of discourse, which also vary depending on which particular audience is viewing the program.

Still within this complex interpretational matrix, Hall says we can see three general positions from which people interpret a television show. These are the "dominant-hegemonic position," the "negotiated code or position," and the "oppositional code" or position (see pp. 136–38). In the production of television (or film, or any cultural work that requires a great deal of money and resources), the "encoded" message (on the left side of Figure 7.1) is in all likelihood going to ideologically support the status quo. Viewers in the first position, above, will agree with this message: as Hall writes, "When the viewer takes the connoted meaning from, say, a television newscast or current affairs programme full and straight, and decodes the message in terms of the reference code in which it has been encoded, we might say that the viewer is *operating inside the dominant code*" (p. 136). However, some people are aware of these codes, but because they are operating in a

Encoding/Decoding *Kony 2012*

In a clear example of Hall's theory of the differing decoding practices of different groups, some relatively well-to-do white Westerners made a video, *Kony 2012*, in an attempt to highlight the abuse of child soldiers by Joseph Kony during conflict in the area around the Democratic Republic of the Congo. The video went viral on social media when many more well-to-do Westerners (and others) viewed and shared the video in order to raise awareness of the situation and of Kony himself. However, when the film was shown in Uganda to Ugandans, some of whom had been Kony's victims, they had a completely different reaction: they pointed to errors and misrepresentations in the film and worried that it might negatively impact people's vision of Uganda, which Kony had left years before. The clearly opposed, radically different "frameworks of knowledge" in these two audiences led to diametrically opposed interpretations of the film.

See Flock, Elizabeth, "Kony 2012 Screening in Uganda Met with Anger, Rocks Thrown at Screen," *Washington Post* (15 March 2012). Online.

completely different "framework," they will read the message in a completely oppositional way, the third position Hall discusses:

> [I]t is possible for a viewer . . . to decode the message in a *globally* contrary way. He/she detotalizes the message in the preferred code in order to retotalize the message within some alternative framework of reference. This is the case of the viewer who listens to a debate on the need to limit wages but "reads" every mention of the "national interest" as "class interest." He/she is operating with what we must call an *oppositional code*. (pp. 137–38)

These two positions, the first and third in Hall's list, coincide with my reading of the two opposed reactions to the *Kony 2012* video. One group bought into the creators' emotional plea for awareness, but the other saw in that same message a statement that conveyed ignorance and misinformation about Africa, ignorance and misinformation that generally characterize dominant Western narratives of Africa. So, even though the creators and "dominant code" viewers saw themselves as doing something noble to help Ugandans (and Africans more generally), the "oppositional" viewers saw the creators as actually doing the exact opposite.

The third group, which contains those following a "negotiated code," falls between the other two positions. In this group, Hall argues, viewers *generally* accept the dominant position, but are likely to reinterpret it somewhat, or apply that position differently to their own personal or specific-group interests:

> Negotiated codes operate through what we might call particular or situated logics: and these logics are sustained by their differential and unequal relation to the discourses and logics of power. The simplest example of a negotiated code is that which governs

the response of a worker to the notion of an Industrial Relations Bill limiting the right to strike or to arguments for a wages freeze. At the level of the "national interest" economic debate the decoder may adopt the hegemonic definition, agreeing that "we must all pay ourselves less in order to combat inflation." This, however, may have little or no relation to his/her willingness to go on strike for better pay and conditions or to oppose the Industrial Relations Bill at the level of shop-floor or union organization. (p. 137)

In short, then, the "negotiated code" is one that can support the status quo at the macro but not the personal level. This can lead to people working against their own stated beliefs in their daily lives (for example, those who believe in the dictates of the Catholic Church but nonetheless use birth control). It may also lead people to work against their own interests (for example, those who vote to cut federal spending on social programs like food stamps or unemployment insurance, even as they or their family, friends, and co-workers rely on those programs).

For Hall, the meaning of any given text can never be found through critics simply examining that text at their desk. Instead, the several *meanings* that can be ascribed to the text are the product of a matrix of social, cultural, linguistic, and other frames of reference that are constantly shifting depending on the multiple positions of producers, viewers, and texts. Any critical analysis of a given text or situation, then, has to carefully situate its own position in this matrix even as it carefully delineates the position of all those other actors. This critical practice makes Birmingham School interpretations very specific and detailed, as we'll see in the next section.

Subcultures

Thus far we have focused on popular culture as a phenomenon encountered by the population *en masse*, so to speak. We've discussed the relationship between popular culture and ideology, hegemony, myth, and other ways of framing dominant belief systems, whether as methods used by the dominant class to maintain the status quo or as a reflection of a society's larger beliefs and/or practices. As Hall's formulation of oppositional and negotiated codes of interpretation makes clear, though, not everyone responds to cultural objects or practices in the same way. But these multiple positions are not solely—or always visibly—due to such macro-social group distinctions as class, gender, race, or sexuality. There are also divisions of region, age, body type, and so on, as well as explicitly cultural distinctions even within a generally coherent group. For example, although any particular group of teenagers in a high school may share most or even all the characteristics listed above, they may still break into different cliques or groups that see themselves as radically opposed: in addition to the generally dominant groups in school, there are emo kids and goths, punks and posers, and so on. These can all be referred to as **subcultures**, and many cultural theorists have used the practices of these subcultural groups to understand larger social and cultural dynamics.

The major statement on subcultures was made by Birmingham School theorist Dick Hebdige (1951–). In his book *Subculture: The Meaning of Style* (Hebdige, 1988), he makes it clear that overly general discussions of "dominant ideology" fail to meet the purposes of cultural studies because they don't offer detailed enough analyses to be valuable. He argues that "in highly complex societies like ours, which function through a finely graded system of divided (i.e. specialized) labour, the crucial question has to do with which specific ideologies, representing the interests of which specific groups and classes will prevail at any given moment, in any given situation" (p. 14). In other words, as with Hall's theories, Hebdige argues that we must analyze very specific situations and moments, since large or sweeping statements will fail to capture the social nuance of any particular cultural moment and thus misunderstand "how power is distributed in our society" (p. 14).

To explain this approach further, Hebdige turns to Antonio Gramsci's theory of hegemony, which we discussed in Chapter 3. Because hegemony is a functional union of ideologies across the whole range of a given society, and because this union must therefore function through consent and not just coercion, it is, Hebdige notes, unstable at best. If the dominant classes are to maintain power, then popular commodities, from television shows to safety pins, must help to gain consent from a variety of non-dominant groups. But because these groups' interests can differ, there is no way for the dominant classes to fully control the "messages" these commodities contain. This is the basic conclusion that Hall comes to as well in his theories of "encoding" and "decoding."

Hebdige takes this instability of meaning a little further: "forms cannot be permanently normalized," he writes. "They can always be deconstructed, demystified" by cultural critics, but "commodities" can also be "symbolically 'repossessed' in everyday life, and endowed with implicitly oppositional meanings, by the very groups who originally produced them" and by the groups who use them (p. 16). In this way, he writes, the dominant ideologies of a society "can be prised open. The consensus can be fractured, challenged, over-ruled, and resistance to the groups in dominance cannot always be lightly dismissed or automatically incorporated" (pp. 16–17). Again as for Hall, but unlike the conclusions drawn by Adorno and Horkheimer, Hebdige sees in everyday culture (the way in which people produce and use cultural items in their daily lives, including items of popular culture) a space not only for ideological control, but also for resistance to the dominant way of seeing things. In other words, although popular culture is produced and disseminated within the hegemonic functions of the market, it's possible to rewrite or respond to those hegemonic codes in the ways people use that popular culture as part of their everyday lives.

It is this space of resistance—albeit one that *can* be co-opted by the dominant culture—that Hebdige sees in youth countercultures. Writing in the late 1970s in England, the most obviously resistant of these subcultures for Hebdige were the punks. Situating punk within a white, working-class cultural matrix, and tying it to the simultaneous rise of the popularity of reggae in black British youth culture, Hebdige paints a picture of self-contradictory youth subcultures that nonetheless allow for a critical entry point into working-class resistances to the upper-class, white hegemony of England and the larger

British Isles. He argues that punk, by appropriating the styles of reggae and Jamaican culture even as it attempts to situate a "white" ethnic identity, articulates a resistance to the dominant culture that challenges what Hall would call the "dominant-hegemonic" code of cultural interpretation.

From a detailed discussion of the particular histories, traditions, music, and dress of these subcultures, Hebdige concludes that "[s]ubcultures represent 'noise' (as opposed to sound): interference in the orderly sequence which leads from real events and phenomena to their representation in the media" (p. 90). Instead of a linear narrative, which would tend to support dominant interests, subcultures exploit "spectacle" in order to use the media against the dominant culture that controls it. To do this, punks, and subcultures in general, use certain styles that directly challenge hegemonic norms. "Style in subculture," he writes, citing Roland Barthes's notion of "myth," is "pregnant with significance. Its transformations go 'against nature,' interrupting the process of 'normalization.' As such, they are gestures, movements towards a speech which offends the 'silent majority,' which challenges the principle of unity and cohesion, which contradicts the myth of consensus" (p. 18). Whereas the dominant group uses the "myth" of cohesion to frame national, racial, gendered, sexual, economic, or other ideologies, saying, in effect, that "we are all in this together, so don't rock the boat," subcultures rock the boat in ways that people can't ignore, in effect showing people that things weren't that stable to begin with.

Bricolage   One of the ways in which subcultures both embody and represent this instability is through the use of **bricolage**. Taken from Claude Lévi-Strauss's work (see Chapter 5), the term *bricolage* is used to refer to the use of material objects in people's immediate surroundings "to 'think' their own world" (Hebdige, 1988, p. 103). In other words, the objects one uses in daily life are seen to be complexly interconnected in ways that help explain the world. For Lévi-Strauss, in so-called "primitive" and magical world views, the **bricoleur** uses the limited objects that surround him in his life in order to explain those aspects of his environment that he cannot "properly" understand: thus, famine or natural disaster could be attributed to gods who appear in the form of animals that the *bricoleur* sees every day.

Hebdige and other subcultural theorists appropriate this (somewhat condescending) notion of *bricolage* to explain how subcultures express themselves. Important to remember, Hebdige says, is the fact that "subcultures are not privileged forms; they do not stand outside . . . of the social totality"; in other words, while they may be resistant to one degree or another, subcultures are still part of the larger society (pp. 85–86). In the case of punk and reggae, Hebdige notes, these subcultures still express themselves through the dominant social mode of "conspicuous consumption": i.e., through purchasing and using commodities (pp. 102–03), but they turn that consumption against the dominant forms expressly encouraged by hegemonic forces: "It is basically the way in which commodities are *used* in subculture which mark[s] the subculture off from more orthodox

Photo 7.2 Punk style.

Source: Janette Beckman/Getty Images

cultural formations" (p. 103). *Bricolage* in the contemporary sense thus involves the redeployment of everyday objects in new ways in order to challenge (consciously or not) hegemonic assumptions.

In the case of punk, certain objects associated with the working classes, and with normative domesticity, are deployed in ways that explicitly challenge the hegemonic post-war narratives of British cohesion and success. Safety pins—most commonly used in diapers at the time and so representative of British family values, the future of the next generation, and so on—are redeployed in seemingly "unsafe" ways, as clothing accessories and body piercings. By combining these with garbage bags as clothing, and with collage- and graffiti-style artistic expressions, punks' very style served to undermine the dominant narrative in which each of these items has a particular place. "The punk subculture, then, signified chaos at every level" (p. 113). Instead of just resisting the dominant culture, punks reordered the signifying practices of that culture even as they refused to participate in it.

Of course, 1970s punk gave way to other subcultural forms in music and fashion, which in turn gave way to others. What happens to the resistance embodied by these forms? Well, you can likely answer this for yourself: if you type "punk fashion" into an internet search engine, many of the top hits you'll see are for clothing stores or high-end fashion shows. Punk, in other words, has in many ways gone mainstream, as have other subcultures. How does this happen? *Bricolage* again offers an answer here: these subcultures use items of the *dominant culture* to make their statements. This makes them susceptible to being reappropriated by the dominant culture. As Hebdige argues, "Cut ups and collages, no matter how bizarre, do not change so much as rearrange things, and needless to say, the 'explosive junction' never occurs: no amount of stylistic incantation can alter the oppressive mode in which the commodities used in subculture have been produced" (p. 130). In the cult film *Withnail & I*, which is set at the end of the 1960s, Danny, subcultural guru and philosopher (and drug dealer), bemoans this fact, saying, "They're selling hippie wigs in Woolworth's, man." Subcultural resistance is necessarily fleeting. But still, Hebdige writes, these forms of stylistic resistance do "have [their] moment" (p. 130) and can offer entry points to struggles to resist hegemonic control.

Adbusters

Can one turn to clearly resistant examples of popular culture—examples that critique popular culture itself—to find the space of resistance that Adorno and Horkheimer seem to say is impossible but that the Birmingham School suggests *is* possible? To answer this, let's turn to two Canadian examples: the Adbusters movement and political theorist Naomi Klein's analysis thereof in her well-known work *No Logo* (1999).

Adbusters, a collective founded in Vancouver, is best known for their "culture jamming" magazine of the same name. In this magazine, the group publishes revised versions of popular corporate advertisements that are designed to expose the ideologies lying behind the originals. One campaign, targeting tobacco ads, features a version of the Camel cigarette mascot, Joe Camel, revised as "Joe Chemo," showing the familiar character dying in a hospital. The ads not only highlight the health effects of cigarette smoking but also expose the fact that tobacco companies profit from making people ill. Adbusters was also instrumental in the early days of the Occupy Wall Street movement.

In her book, Naomi Klein discusses the usefulness of such anti-consumerist activity as a way of disrupting the ideological apathy generated by popular (capitalist) culture and awakening people's political will and thought. Klein and others see Adbusters as using the tools of the culture industry against itself in a way that rejects the more pessimistic of Adorno and Horkheimer's statements. Part of the way they do this is through *bricolage*, pasting different images together in unusual contexts, creating something new and challenging of the dominant order.

But even as Adbusters resists dominant ideologies, it can get folded back into them (just as the TV shows discussed in the "Resisting Television" box, and as Hebdige discusses with subcultures). Indeed, some of Adbusters's campaigns and strategies have been critiqued. After all, although they're a not-for-profit group they still sell their magazine, and have developed a certain "brand identity" among, especially, counter-cultural youth in ways that mimic the demographic targeting of the very ads they critique. This is especially true of their "Blackspot Shoes" campaign, in which they teamed with Canadian shoemaker John Fluevog to create "brandless" shoes—in a very branded way. To their detractors, this move into product marketing seemed to transform Adbusters into the very thing they critiqued. Adbusters's website (www.adbusters.org) even includes a "culture shop" from which you can purchase items. In this way, rather than "jamming" the dominant culture, Adbusters could be read as in fact reinforcing the very aspects of advertising culture they critique: they are constructing a type of consumer, and positioning themselves as a brand. Klein refers to this critique as a form of "purism" that's much like the critiques "lobbed at every punk band that signs a record deal" (Klein, 2000, p. 296), but still, this kind of "selling out" does cause a philosophical problem for such movements. What starts off as an attempt to create a "cold" media intervention, in McLuhan's terms, becomes too "hot"; what exactly the "encoded" and "decoded" messages are becomes unclear or confused.

Moreover, mass media and the culture industry have in a way desensitized us to culture jamming. Klein writes that "In these information-numb times, we are beyond being abruptly awakened by a startling image, a sharp juxtaposition or even a fabulously clever détournement" (p. 296) (*détournement*, as defined by a French group of artists known as the Situationists, means to transform dominant media tools or images against themselves). Contemporary advertising can be seen to employ the very methods of culture jamming, even if to the opposite effect. For example, consider an ad released by the company E*Trade for its stock-trading website. In this commercial, a man is watching another commercial for a (fictional) drug called Nozulla; following the pattern of such commercials, a voiceover lists the possible side effects, which include "children born with the head of a golden retriever," "the condition known as hot-dog finger," and "seeing the dead." This commercial effectively "jammed" commercials marketing drugs to non-specialists, but did so only in order to sell another product—the E*Trade website (many copies of this commercial are available on the internet).

Photo 7.3 The "Joe Chemo" campaign.

Source: Elaine Thompson/AP Images

Discussion Questions

1. Adorno and Horkheimer argue that the culture industry is designed solely to generate consent to the status quo and create consumers. How do you think they would respond to Stuart Hall's assertion that one can create an "oppositional" reading of an item of popular culture?

2. McLuhan saw TV as a medium that makes its viewers long for depth in their lives and yet also makes them incapable of looking forward because they want *immediate* "involvement." Does this sound like present-day critiques of video games and gamers' engagement with them? If so, does that similarity tell us anything about gaming? Or does it open up a critique of McLuhan?

3. We discussed above whether social media is a "hot" or "cold" form, following McLuhan's definitions. But McLuhan also says that the "medium is the message": how does social

media shape what people say or think through them? Do online videos shape their messages in ways that differ from those of television and film?

4. In the "Resisting Television" box we discuss how Rick Mercer's rants, and television political satire in general, can reinforce hegemonic political beliefs and structures. Can you find examples that challenge this reading? Can your examples both challenge *and* reinforce dominant beliefs?

5. One of the primary conclusions of Hebdige's study of subcultures is that although subcultures originally set themselves against the dominant culture, they are often reappropriated by it. Can you think of recent examples of this process? How do you know when a subculture has been reappropriated?

Further Reading

Fiske, John. *Television Culture*. 1987. London: Routledge, 2006.

Jay, Martin. *The Dialectical Imagination: A History of the Frankfurt School and the Institute of Social Research, 1923–1950*. 1973. Berkeley: U of California P, 1996.

Turner, Graeme. *British Cultural Studies: An Introduction*. 3rd ed. London: Routledge, 2003.

Chapter 8

History, Power, Discourse

INTRODUCTION

Having focused on the development of the discipline of cultural studies in Chapters 6 and 7, the remainder of Part III will demonstrate how some of those broad theoretical foundations have developed somewhat more recently, and how they've been used to study both culture and society. In this chapter we discuss how concepts of power have come to hold a central place in cultural studies. Coming out of our discussions of Marxism, these later studies focus on how power is distributed throughout society in both overt and more subtle ways, and on the role popular culture plays in the processes of power. Moving beyond the economic concerns of the Marxists, in part by turning to psychoanalysis and other practices, these later theorists expand the discussion of power to other social categories and identities, laying the groundwork for our discussion of identities in Part IV.

Important to this chapter, as it was to Chapter 7, is the concept of discourse. As we learned in Chapter 7, *discourse* refers to the entire range of signifying practices in a society; it comprises not only language but the codes that structure daily practice, including the production, use, and interpretation of media. We can also refer to specific types of discourse: there are institutional and professional discourses (the sets of language used by the military or medical professionals, for example, that are specific to their practices) as well as discourses relating to certain populations or groups in a society (for example, gendered language and the discursive elements of certain subcultures). Important to remember, then, is that we are all expert in a wide range of discourses, some of which we share with most people in our society and some that are more specific to a smaller group. We may also move through different discourses at different points in our lives: right now you likely use the discourse of education, including not just specific terms like *midterms* and *syllabus* but also certain behaviours, some of which many students engage in, others less so. Similarly, different groups can share specific aspects of a discourse but relate to it differently based on their position in relation to the discourse, especially in terms of power: your professors will use much of the same discursive structures and practices as you do, but given their subject positions within the university system, they may view them very differently.

The theorists we analyze in this chapter are primarily interested in how such wide varieties of discourses interact with each other and alter our understanding and interpretations of given events and texts. They are all especially interested in how these relations affect our readings of history.

HISTORY, CULTURE, MEANING

Whereas such "schools" of criticism as the Frankfurt School and the Birmingham School were defined more by a set of common concerns (and an actual physical school) than a specifically defined methodology, other forms of cultural criticism in the latter half of the twentieth century were defined by a particular approach or limited set of approaches, often consciously structured to solve what critics saw as certain problems in the academic study of culture. One of the more influential of these schools, especially for humanities disciplines, is **New Historicism**. The New Historicists, who came to prominence in the 1980s and 1990s, were primarily interested in interpreting literature within its historical context. But this task isn't as easy as it may seem, since many of these critics argue, as did thinkers from the Birmingham School, that "historical context" is not a stable site of meaning. Instead, history and literature are both unstable sources of meanings, as the postmodern theorists, to whom we turn in Chapter 9, have pointed out. This means that the New Historicists develop theories about history and culture that place both of those within the unstable realm of language.

Defining New Historicism

Probably the clearest definition of the practices of New Historicism comes from Louis Montrose. In his essay "Professing the Renaissance: The Poetics and Politics of Culture" (Montrose, 1989), he defines New Historicism by comparing it directly with older literary and historical methodologies, and to the postmodern theories of Jacques Derrida (see Chapter 9). Montrose's discussion of New Historicism echoes many of the issues we analyzed in relation to the Birmingham and Frankfurt schools, specifically in terms of the role of criticism itself: he sees criticism as a cultural product that in turn needs to be analyzed and theorized.

Montrose sums up this position very neatly, and while he does so specifically within a discussion of historical, literary, and political analysis, we could rework his essay to equally address psychological or other forms of cultural study. Montrose writes:

> The writing and reading of texts, as well as the processes by which they are circulated and categorized, analyzed and taught, are being reconstrued as historically determined and determining modes of cultural work; apparently autonomous aesthetic and academic issues are being reunderstood as inextricably linked to other discourses and practices—such linkages constituting the social networks within which individual subjectivities and collective structures are mutually and continuously shaped. (p. 15)

Montrose sees in the emergence of New Historicism what we have seen in our discussion of the shift from theories of the **individual** to those of the **subject**: it is a shift from an understanding of texts, people, history, and so on as unified, stable, and isolated (as individuals) to an understanding of these things as decentred, multiple, and always mediated. That is, we never see an object "in itself" but only representations of it, or only in relation to specific contexts.

So, there is no final, unalterable meaning to Shakespeare's play *Hamlet*, nor to other items of popular culture. Instead, there are several always tentative and in-formation interpretations of popular culture, all of which are tied to a variety of other issues, texts, and discourses. And, following such writers as Freud and Louis Althusser, Montrose says that it is within this complex interplay of "structures" that meaning is shaped.

Moreover, a historical approach to the text of *Hamlet* will, following Montrose's discussion of New Historicism, point to the fact that there is no "singular" object called *Hamlet* but instead a series of versions, reworkings, and performances. Just as Stuart Hall says that a television viewer can "decode" a meaning from a program that's completely different from the one the producer thought was being "encoded," so too is every viewing of *Hamlet* actually a viewing of a different play.

Contexts are thus vastly important, given that a text—whether it's a work of art, a building, or an advertisement—is always engaged in a variety of discussions with other texts. The job of the theories we've discussed to this point is to offer us a framework for understanding how those works interact to create meaning, and what our own role is in that meaning.

What is only gestured to in most of these theories, however, is that this "context" is itself a series of texts or set of discourses that need to be analyzed. There is no final ground on which we can rest our meaning; we are always in Plato's cave, seeing a multitude of indistinct shadows behind which there is no reality we can easily access (see Chapter 2). Building on such writers as Ferdinand de Saussure and, later, Jacques Derrida, the New Historicists would point out that no matter what we're discussing, it is, at the very least, filtered through language: we are always operating at the level of the signifier.

It is precisely this dual emphasis on text and context that Montrose discusses. He writes that this New Historical approach

> may be characterized chiastically, as a reciprocal concern with the historicity of texts and the textuality of history. By *the historicity of texts*, I mean to suggest the cultural specificity, the social embedment, of all modes of writing—not only the texts that critics study, but also the texts in which we study them. By *the textuality of history*, I mean to suggest, firstly, that we can have no access to a full and authentic past . . . unmediated by the surviving textual traces of the society in question . . . and, secondly, that those textual traces are themselves subject to subsequent textual mediations. (p. 20)

As he notes, Montrose is here using the literary device known as a *chiasmus*: "a sequence of two phrases or clauses which are parallel in syntax, but reverse the order of the corresponding words" (Abrams, 1999, p. 272). This chiasmus—"historicity of texts"/"textuality of history"—could be, in some ways, a thesis statement not only for New Historicism but for much of popular cultural studies. Montrose is saying, first, that texts are part of the history surrounding them—they are affected and informed by the discourses and ideologies in which they are created and received. And so they aren't simply objective, untouchable statements of Beauty or Truth, but can be read much more specifically than that and tied to their contexts. Second, he's arguing that history can be read like a text—that is, it's open to interpretation and multiple readings, and is *not* simply an uninvolved, objective

Historical Fact, Historical Narrative

If we take Montrose's chiasmus—"historicity of text, textuality of history"—at face value, does it mean we're unable to say that there are historical facts we can agree on? Taken together, the "historicity of text" and the "textuality of history" mean that a critical approach to any text or historical moment must analyze both the text or object at hand and its context, because neither can be taken as "pure fact," so to speak. There are historical facts, of course: we know that John Cabot explored the east coast of what is now Canada in 1497, and that before him the Norse landed at what is now Newfoundland. But when we look back at the actual accounts of Cabot's explorations, or even examine discussions of them in history textbooks, those facts are added to a layer of cultural and social contexts that we must analyze and interpret. Every event in human history takes place within a vast network of narratives, power exchanges, and social structures, making any simple "fact" just one piece of a much larger discursive puzzle. Culture is part of history, but history is also composed of the slippery objects and practices of culture, which means that, yes, there are facts about history, but they're never "simple," and they rarely tell us the whole story.

statement of fact. This chiasmus is something we'll see come into play in many of our later discussions of culture and identity.

Montrose also takes one other step in the passage above, one that has become significant in recent cultural analysis: the analysis of criticism and theory itself. If the critical chiasmus Montrose addresses has as one of its poles the historicity of texts, then certainly critical and theoretical texts also fit into this schema—the "texts in which we study" history and culture. He writes, "In such terms, our professional practice, like our subject matter, is a production of ideology: By this I mean not merely that it bears the traces of the professor's values, beliefs, and experiences—his or her socially constructed subjectivity—but also that it actively instantiates those values, beliefs and experiences" (p. 16). All our critical acts are engaged in and arise from the historical conditions surrounding us, and can reflect our engagements—conscious or unconscious—with those surroundings. And this leads to what Montrose refers to as the "heightened . . . reflexivity" (p. 16) of recent theory and criticism. That is, if our critical acts are part of the cultural problems we're analyzing, then we need to analyze those critical acts as we are enacting them. This self-reflexive criticism was especially popular in the 1980s and 1990s, but it still has a significant place in cultural analysis.

And yet Montrose says that this reflexivity is "necessarily limited" (p. 16)— excessive reflection would reproduce a focus on the centrality of the critic/dominant position; it would become almost narcissistic and get one nowhere. (Even such a statement as that is open to analysis and critique—and so on, and so on. . . .) New Historical analysis is not only very detailed work; it also takes a lot of critical self-awareness. In the next two sections we'll look at examples of theorists from each of the two sides of Montrose's chiasmus.

"The Historicity of Texts"

One of the critics most closely associated with New Historicism is the literary scholar Stephen Greenblatt (1943–). Whereas Montrose offers a general definition of New Historicism, Greenblatt offers a new historical methodology through which to study literature, one that can be expanded for a wide variety of other cultural materials.

Greenblatt sets New Historicism directly against earlier forms of literary study, specifically formalism and what is called New Criticism. These schools focus on the form of literature, and see each work of literature as a unified whole—what New Critic Cleanth Brooks, echoing John Keats, referred to as a "well-wrought urn." A poem was, for these earlier critics, like the individual: it was self-contained, and one did not have to look beyond the poem itself to discover its essential meaning.

In his edited collection of essays, *The Power of Forms in the English Renaissance* (Greenblatt, 1982), Greenblatt also defines New Historicism against old historicism, or the way history and literature were studied together before New Criticism and formalism took hold in the academy. So, he rejects both formalism and what came before it, and he incorporates the political and historical context of a work into our understanding of its meaning and its production.

A brief discussion of these earlier schools is thus in order. The formalists focus on artistic form alone, removing the work of literature from any other context—if you analyze solely the form of a particular work or genre, you're not that interested in the historical context of the creation of that work. For Greenblatt and critics like him (including most of the theorists discussed in this book), such a methodology turns the study of literature and culture into a very insular, ivory-tower kind of study; literary study doesn't need to know history, philosophy, sociology, or anything else, and vice versa. Each discipline becomes self-centred.

But one of the things that formalism tried to do was move away from studies of literature that just "plunked" it into history, reading Shakespeare, say, only in terms of the macro-political structures of his day; the formalists saw this as undermining the value of literature and culture. As we've seen, however, from Mikhail Bakhtin forward, many theorists have argued that meaning is always social, and that literature or art or film cannot be seen as isolated aesthetic objects. Every statement, every utterance—whether it's a lecture, a conversation with friends at the bar, a novel, or whatever—is always engaged in a social moment.

Discussing the difference between a historian's account of Elizabeth I's response to Shakespeare's *Richard II* and actual accounts from the time (the modern historian, Dover Wilson, seeing the play as positive toward the Queen's power, while Elizabeth viewed it as feeding into a sense of threat toward her reign), Greenblatt asks:

> How can we account for the discrepancy between Dover Wilson's historical reconstruction and the anxious response of the figures whose history he purports to have accurately reconstructed? The answer lies at least in part in the difference between a conception of art that has no respect whatsoever for the integrity of the text . . . and one

that hopes to find, through historical research, a stable core of meaning within the text, a core that unites disparate and even contradictory parts into an organic whole. . . . Dover Wilson is not a New Critic: he does not conceive of the text as an iconic object whose meaning is perfectly contained within its own formal structure. Yet for him historical research has the effect of conferring autonomy and fixity upon the text, and it is precisely this fixity that is denied by Elizabeth's response. (pp. 4–5)

There are a lot of specific details here, but there is, basically, one overall critical move that is significant for our purposes: Greenblatt is distinguishing New Historicism from **essentialist** theories. He shows that formalism and what comes before it are alike in that they are essentialist. So, while the formalists rejected earlier historical criticism because it was too subjective and set literature up as being subordinate to history, the formalists and these earlier critics, according to Greenblatt, are both essentialist—they both see meaning as being stable and ultimately discoverable, they just differ in where they put the meaning.

Greenblatt and the other New Historicists don't think this way—they build on Derrida and other postmodern critics, who argue that meaning is never stable, that we can never discover an ultimate Truth or source of meaning. Making arguments similar to Bakhtin's, these critics contend that texts, politics, and all other forms of discourse are constantly unstable and moving. So when someone says "In the fifteenth century, people believed X," they're really engaged in a shorthand, because in every time period there are a variety of beliefs, structures, and systems, all of which work against or for each other in a multitude of different ways. When people say that the present day is "the information age," or the "electronic age," you know that that's not completely true—many people in North America and the rest of the world don't have access to the internet, and a good number of people in Canada and elsewhere actively work against a society predicated on technology. Studies of history, literature, and culture, among other topics, that make large pronouncements like these are working monologically, a Bakhtinian term that Greenblatt himself uses: "The earlier historicism tends to be monological; that is, it is concerned with discovering a single political vision, usually identical to that said to be held by the entire literate class or indeed the entire population. . . . This vision, most often presumed to be internally coherent and consistent . . . has the status of an historical fact" (p. 5).

This type of monologic discourse, as we learned from Bakhtin, has certain political ramifications, too. Greenblatt writes, "Protected then from interpretation and conflict, this vision can serve as a stable point of reference, beyond contingency, to which literary interpretation can securely refer. Literature is conceived to mirror the period's beliefs, but to mirror them, as it were, from a safe distance" (p. 5). This attempt to be monologic goes hand in hand with claims that literature, culture, and the criticism thereof is above or beyond politics, a claim that we know, from Althusser, is often simply a function of ideology, masking the ideological work being done by both the cultural object and the criticism thereof.

New Historicism, though, starts with the assumption that there are so many conflicting positions and viewpoints at any given moment in history that it's impossible, or at least naive, to say that one can completely understand it, and so conclusions themselves are always tenuous. This isn't to say that New Historicism doesn't make conclusions. New

Historicists do detailed archival research—finding and examining old journals, newspapers, history books, legal documents, and literature, among a huge number of other material—in order to develop very detailed arguments about a text or a moment in time. But these arguments don't settle onto a necessarily unified conclusion: instead, they often point to the contradictions that exist in any moment of time and text, the "places of dissension and shifting interests, occasions for the jostling of orthodox and subversive impulses," as Greenblatt calls them (p. 6). And these studies tend to be very narrow in their focus because they do see so much going on in any given moment: each and every text or cultural object is "link[ed] . . . to the complex network of institutions, practices, and beliefs that constitute the culture as a whole" (p. 6). For New Historicists, history is a very dynamic interplay of all different kinds of voices—it is heteroglossic and dialogic, to use Bakhtin's terms again.

Still, we have to remember not to fall into the trap of thinking that all of these pieces can be fit together into one solid picture that contains one meaning. Instead, a New Historical approach (and a generally postmodern approach, as we'll see in Chapter 9) must be open to recognizing and discussing the contradictions in a text or in a cultural moment. And this means that the New Historicists are also self-reflexive, showing how their own writings are involved in these dynamic forces.

Reading New Historicism New Historically

Interestingly, one could take a New Historical approach to the rise of New Historicism itself: Why did it appear when it did? What larger cultural and social dynamics did it interact with? Well, New Historicism began in the 1980s and 90s, when there were many more people getting PhDs in English than there were teaching and research jobs for them. Thus, New Historicism could be read—new historically—as coming out of a time when people needed to justify the amount of work being done on, say, Shakespeare. So to say that there's an endless number of contexts that Shakespeare fits into, all of which need to be analyzed, is very much a defence of having that many people in university studying English literature. And yet, by attacking traditional scholarship, New Historicists made the nature of literary study very suspect, which meant that a lot of people who were doing this kind of work fell between the cracks: they weren't quite historians and they weren't quite literary scholars.

Here lies a contradiction—New Historicism, analyzed in its cultural context, both reinforces and undermines the value of literary study. This contradiction itself serves as an example of the instability and disunity that New Historicists themselves often see in literature and history.

To support these claims and thereby make such an argument effectively, however, one would have to look back to detailed records of the numbers of PhDs being produced, the number being hired academically, and the representations of academics in professional publications, in popular culture, in the media, and so on. It would be necessary to conduct historical, archival research; literary, filmic, and other cultural analysis; and possibly demographic and sociological data interpretation. As we've discussed, New Historicist work does indeed require an intense attention to detail, to the historical record, and a careful, close reading of texts in order to develop a solid analysis.

"The Textuality of History"

Both Greenblatt and Montrose are discussing primarily an approach to the study of literature, one that moves away from the notion of literature as a special, asocial, decontextual-
ized form of knowledge, as the formalists would like to have it. For many formalists, poetry
may be historically situated, but only to a degree—because for them, literature, and often
specifically poetry, transcends the historic moment and can last forever. In formalism,
poetry is historically informed only in that it becomes the purest, most essential example
of the Truth of a culture, and if you analyze a poem using formalism's supposedly scientific, objective analysis you will be able to fully understand and appreciate that truth. The
New Historicists, by contrast, say that any notion of *the* Truth of a culture or historical
moment, or the idea that a text can capture it, is impossible. This is because all knowledge
is mediated by language, and language is unstable, and because our access to the historical
moment is available only through an impossibly huge number of texts and context—so all
we can do is attempt to discuss the interplay of certain texts and contexts. Both Greenblatt
and Montrose, then, turn to history, itself a site of unequal power distribution and struggle,
in order to explain the contradictory meanings they see in literature.

Hayden White (1928–), conversely, is a historian who turns to the field of literary
study in order to explain what he sees as the form the study of history takes. White makes
similar sorts of claims about the non-unity of history and the impossibility of a fully objective, fully elaborated, fully contained textual meaning, but he's coming from the other
side of the issue. Rather than the literary critic turning to the object of historical study, we
see the historian turning to the object of literary study.

This approach is most clearly laid out in his essay "The Historical Text as Literary
Artifact" (White, 1985), where he sets up what he sees as traditional historical study, and
then immediately questions its value. He calls this process of questioning **metahistory**.
A "meta" analysis is one that studies its own methodologies or approaches. "Metafiction,"
for example, is a form of fiction that calls attention to its own production as an object: a
play that shows its own backstage and a film that references itself as a fiction (such as the
end of *Monty Python and the Holy Grail*) are forms of metafiction. So "metahistory" is a
form of history that calls into question and analyzes its own assumptions and processes.

White writes,

> In order to write the history of any given scholarly discipline or even of a science, one
> must be prepared to ask questions *about* it of a sort that do not have to be asked in the
> practice *of* it. . . . This is what metahistory seeks to do. It addresses itself to such ques-
> tions as, What is the structure of a peculiarly *historical* consciousness? What is the
> epistemological status of historical *explanations*, as compared with other kinds of
> explanations that might be offered to account for the materials with which historians
> ordinarily deal? What are the possible *forms* of historical representation and what are
> their bases? (p. 81)

White is asking what it is that makes the study of history special as a discipline, and what
differentiates it from other kinds of study. How, exactly, does a historian describe and

understand a diary from an early European settler of Canada, and how is that different from the way a literature scholar or a sociologist or even an environmental scientist would look at it? He then asks, "What authority can historical accounts claim as contributions to a secured knowledge of reality in general and to the human sciences in general?" (p. 81). Lying behind this question, of course, is the fact that people *usually* assume that the study of history provides a contribution to "a secured knowledge," and that this is so because history is tied to a scientific form of knowledge. So, the traditional form of historical study can be roughly compared to the traditional formalist study of literature—the objects are stable and fully understandable to the critic who approaches them objectively and scientifically.

This is the approach that White wants to question. He begins his critique by noting that most historical studies, like many literary works, are narrative in form: they tell a story. But this fact is most often ignored: "[I]n general there has been a reluctance to consider historical narratives as what they most manifestly are: verbal fictions, the contents of which are as much *invented as found* and the forms of which have more in common with their counterparts in literature than they have with those in the sciences" (p. 82). Basically, White's starting point is to examine the similarities that the study of history has to the study of literature, and, specifically, to look at the ways in which the structure of historical texts is similar to the structure of literary ones.

In order to define what historical narrative consists of, White first lists what history is not. He writes that history is not a listing of facts, nor an uninvested, unmediated discussion of past events. Instead, he says that history is a narrativization of facts, and he uses the theories of Canadian formalist literary critic Northrop Frye to analyze these narratives. He begins by quoting Frye's analysis of historical study: "'The historian works inductively,' [Frye] says, 'collecting his facts and trying to avoid any informing patterns except those he sees, or is honestly convinced he sees, in the facts themselves'" (p. 82). So, for Frye, the historian's job is to assemble facts, to piece them together as the facts themselves tell you they should be put together: the narrative is part of the essential truth embedded directly within the facts. This is the traditional sense of historical study. For Frye, the historian just transcribes facts in the way that the facts dictate, and any error is the historian's fault.

White critiques this traditional view of historical study by turning to Frye's literary theory—in other words, he plays one part of Frye's theory off against another. As mentioned above, Frye is very much a formalist literary critic—he sees meaning as being derived, in part, from a certain number of pre-existing literary forms, such as the tragedy, the comedy, the romance, and so on. Frye situates these forms in relation to the history of Western literature and religion. All literature, for Frye, can be understood once you figure out which form is being used. Summarizing Frye's theory, White writes, "The fundamental meanings of all fictions, their thematic content, consist, in Frye's view, of the 'pre-generic plot-structures' or *mythoi* derived from the corpora of Classical and Judaeo-Christian religious literature. According to this theory, we understand *why* a particular story has 'turned out' as it has when we have identified the archetypal myth, or pregeneric plot structure, of which the story is an exemplification" (p. 83). For Frye, this generic element is what makes literature literature: historical narrative, on the other hand, moves away from this "fictional element," the "mythic plot structure" (p. 83). Objectively finding the structure of this literariness is what the analysis of literature should be all about, Frye says.

Much can be said to critique this model of literary study, from its focus on Judeo-Christian structures at the expense of others to its relatively narrow definition of literature. But important for our purposes here isn't the application of the theory to literature, as Frye intended, but White's application of it to history. White turns Frye's theory on its head, applying this formalist theory to what Frye saw as the exact opposite of literature—the study of history. White says that the supposed facts of history are organized just as literature is, and that the study of history isn't simply the study of facts, but rather, like literary study, the study of generic form. So, even though White employs a formalist literary analysis, he does so to show that "facts" and "Truth" are impossible to ultimately find. He argues that "Historical situations are not *inherently* tragic, comic, or romantic. . . . All the historian needs to do to transform a tragic into a comic situation is to shift his point of view or change the scope of his perceptions. Anyway, we only think of situations as tragic or comic because these concepts are part of our generally cultural and specifically literary heritage" (p. 85). Thus, historical "truth" is culturally constructed. Because we are culturally accustomed to certain types of narratives, a series of historical facts will get organized into these narratives. This conclusion doesn't mean, as a traditional historian would say, that the Truth of the events organizes itself in certain ways, but rather that the historian, through a conscious or unconscious choice, organizes the facts into a narrative.

White uses this formalist notion of stories and plot to analyze history in another way as well. In our discussion of psychoanalysis in Chapters 4 and 6, we looked at the ways in which the ideal ego, and so one's sense of self, gets constructed in part from social and cultural influences. Similarly, Althusser argues that our identities are formed unconsciously, for the most part, by the ideological apparatuses of society. White in turn says a very similar thing about narrative structures. Traditional narrative forms function ideologically to make us see historical occurrences according to those models: "As a symbolic structure, the historical narrative does not *reproduce* the events it describes; it tells us in what direction to think about the events and charges our thought about the events with different emotional valences" (p. 91). Thus, the narrative structure into which certain facts are placed can shape or alter our opinion of those facts, making history not a mimetic representation of reality, but instead a mediated and ideological form.

Basically, then, White says that in order to organize historical data into a history, the historian needs to rely on culturally acceptable narrative forms. He compares this process to that of psychoanalysis: "The therapist's problem . . . is not to hold up before the patient the 'real facts' of the matter, the 'truth' as against the 'fantasy' that obsesses him. . . . The problem is to get the patient to 'reemplot' his whole life history in such a way as to change the *meaning* of those events for him and their *significance* for the economy of the whole set of events that make up his life" (p. 87). Likewise, the historian (re)emplots events into a history, and this is dependent on cultural expectations regarding plot.

Part of this process of emplotment requires that a lot of data and facts get left out of any historical narrative. What ends up defining a set of historical narratives is precisely what does not get narrated—thus, from the traditional historian's assumption that history is an ordering of facts in the way that the facts themselves dictate, we end with White's argument that the narrative forms dictate which "facts" get looked at and which facts get dropped by the wayside.

History is formed not according to facts, but rather the facts are tailored according to the needs of narrative. This is Montrose's "textuality of history." What we thought were simply recitations of fact are instead complex narratives that, in their very form, shape how we interpret those facts, and even dictate which facts we see and which we don't.

All of this discussion of history as narrative may make it sound as if White is arguing that historians, if they understand how they're using narrative forms, can then purposefully set out to shape the way we think about certain events. But he denies this position, writing that "it may be observed that if historians were to recognize the fictive element in their narratives, this would not mean the degradation of historiography to the status of ideology or propaganda. In fact, this recognition would serve as a potent antidote to the tendency of historians to become captive of ideological preconceptions which they do not recognize as such but honor as the 'correct' perception of 'the way things *really* are'" (p. 99). White goes on to say that, once we recognize this *literary* structure of historical narratives, we can be better equipped to see the gaps and ideological presuppositions behind those narratives.

White emphasizes the immense complexities of context, and the ways in which context shapes our reading of culture. History, literature, culture, social mores, economics, and other forms of discourse are all involved in a complex play, one that is wrapped up in the power differentials of society. In the next section we look at Michel Foucault's theoretical formulation of these relations. Whereas White sees the realization of this system of relations as one way to resist being controlled or interpellated by these forms, Foucault argues that we can never simply resist the dominant discourses in our culture.

History and Textuality in Heritage Minutes

New Historicists would say that any cultural object participates in both a historical and narrative project, and that the two are in fact inseparable. That said, there are certain examples that make the "textuality of history" especially apparent, among which are so-called popular histories, those works designed to educate the populace about history through the means of popular culture. In Canada, the best known of these popular histories are the so-called "Heritage Minutes," which air on Canadian television and at film screenings as well as being available online. In these minute-long pieces, particular moments in Canadian history—especially those moments that are perceived as transformative—are portrayed with a combination of reenactments and seemingly factual, unbiased voiceover. As Emily West argues, these and other examples of popular history can serve as attempts to solidify a unified notion of Canadian identity. But, as she notes, the "Heritage Minutes" do spend some time presenting moments of discord and "stories of dissent and injustice . . . such as the story of famed rebel Louis Riel" (West, 2006, p. 69). Still, these stories "ultimately reside within a progressive narrative of the current state of the nation as the endpoint of the various dramas and sacrifices that went before it" (p. 69). In other words, history is presented as the occasionally flawed foundation against which we can see how advanced and evolved contemporary Canada is.

Following Hayden White's application of literary analysis to historical narrative, we could say that the Heritage Minutes present a comic narrative of history. This doesn't mean they're funny, but rather that they present a story in which everything turns out well, just as a traditional comic play or novel ends: all the heroes are rewarded and the villains are punished. In the context of presenting Canadian history, such a narrative implies that all of Canada's "bad times" are in the past, and the future is only bright and harmonious.

One particular example, focusing on Agnes MacPhail, Canada's first woman member of Parliament (as the voiceover tells us), can specify this process for us. Opening inside Kingston Penitentiary in 1935, the piece shows Agnes MacPhail witnessing the torture of prisoners. Cut to the House of Commons, where MacPhail raises the issue of prison conditions, asking, "How can such a society be called 'civilized'?" A male member of Parliament then stands and suggests that because she's a woman she doesn't understand the conditions in prison.

Shouting "Is this normal?," MacPhail slams down one of the torture implements on her desk. The voiceover then tells us that MacPhail's "courage would lead to the overhaul of the entire Canadian penal system."

The story thus presented is one that, on its surface, presents serious social problems in Canadian history: sexism, the abuse of prisoners, and a general lack of concern for human rights. But, the story continues, such problems have been dealt with because of the courage of one woman. What are the implications, then? Certainly that sexism and torture are bad, but also that they lie in the past: after all, MacPhail was, the voiceover tells us, only the "first" of many women MPs, and the "penal system" was "overhauled," so such torture is now abolished. While both of these statements are correct, the idea that sexism no longer exists (or, indeed, that the number of women in Parliament is representative of the population) is untrue, as is the idea that prisons are now "overhauled" to the point that there is no longer any abuse—indeed, Kingston Penitentiary was still operational in 2013, and in 1994 news broke of women prisoners being systematically abused in it.

While this Heritage Minute thus does give us accurate facts about history, its comedic narrative structure serves to present the past as "other," as something we have moved beyond, thus potentially misleading viewers into thinking that such things as sexism or prisoner abuse are themselves "in the past," an assumption that could help allow them to continue today.

For examples of the Heritage Minutes, see www.historicacanada.ca.

DISCOURSE AND POWER

Important to both Greenblatt and White are the ways in which narrative structures are embedded within larger social contexts and, therefore, within social power structures. Michel Foucault (1926–1984), whose work we discuss at greater length in Chapter 11, is often associated with the New Historicists because he was interested in rewriting received historical knowledge, specifically in order to examine the way discourse frames that knowledge. Most of Foucault's books fit into a large project designed to challenge assumptions about the history of the West, and in particular the history of Western institutions. From the history of science to the prison and to mental health institutions, sexuality, and government, Foucault examined not so much official institutional histories but the debates surrounding those institutions: his work analyzes how people talk about those institutions, how they're framed within other public discussions, and generally how they fit into the discourses of the time. These analyses often point to contradictions or disruptions in the official histories, something we'll see especially when we turn to Foucault's discussion of sexuality in Chapter 12.

One of Foucault's central topics in all these analyses, however, is power and its functions in society—or, phrased more properly, power's functions *as* society. This discussion of power is very much connected to Marxism, specifically the ways it frames concepts of dominance and being dominated as well as its notion that resistance is necessarily formed within or against ideological discourse. Foucault's analysis of power and domination both arises from and critiques that Marxist formula, in part by incorporating analyses of the "textuality of history" and the "historicity of text."

In *The History of Sexuality*, Vol.1, Foucault offers his most significant and specific discussion of power. He goes to great lengths to point out precisely how his definition of *power* differs from previous definitions. First, he explains how he is *not* using the term *power*, making explicit connections to some of the theoretical concepts we discussed earlier in this chapter and in previous chapters. He says that he doesn't mean the violent or physical power exercised by the state through what Althusser calls the **Repressive State Apparatuses**. Second, he differentiates his notion of power from the **Ideological State Apparatus**. Third, he doesn't mean **hegemony**, which both Antonio Gramsci and, following him, the Birmingham School see as a set of ideological mechanisms that "pervade the entire social body" (Foucault, 1990, p. 92). Foucault is thus quite explicitly removing his use of the word *power* from Marxist usage, in which it is roughly equated to the "power to exercise domination" in various forms. This is a radical departure from the definitions of power and control given by many of the other theories we've analyzed. Foucault says, on the contrary, that these forms of domination are only the limit cases, or end points, of the exercise of power.

Foucault takes the concept of power out of a simplistic hierarchical structure of dominance and domination. But where does he "put" power? The answer may seem frustrating: everywhere and nowhere. That is, power is everywhere because Foucault sees it as functioning in every social situation: power is a function of discourse, of the relations between people within society. But it's also nowhere: in Foucault's use of the term, no one person or group can "hold" power in any final or ultimate sense because power is inseparable from discourse, and therefore inseparable from how we make meaning in our lives. Power, Foucault says, is the very medium in which we act, and through which everything functions. He writes that power can be defined as "the multiplicity of force relations" in any given situation; he then clarifies that power "is the moving substrate of force relations" in any situation where people hold unequal positions in relation to each other, which means that such power dynamics "are always local and unstable" (pp. 92, 93). Unlike Gramsci's notion of hegemony or Althusser's discussions of ideology, but similar to Greenblatt's and Montrose's emphasis on contradictions in history, Foucault here is saying that the exercise of power is by definition part of a specific context. That is, it doesn't belong to one overarching structure, and can't be exercised with any form of uniformity.

This emphasis on the "local and unstable" exercise of power doesn't mean, for Foucault, that there are no larger groupings of power or that no dominance is being exercised. Remember, he says that larger groupings are the limit cases of the exercise of power. But for Foucault, any attempt to understand the effects of these larger groupings must begin at a local level—it's a kind of "think globally, act locally" theory except that the "global," the large structure, is even more intimately tied to the local than in this environmentalist phrase.

Because power operates primarily at the local level in his theory, Foucault has sometimes been accused of not truly accounting for massive uprisings or revolutions in which the exercise of power takes on a larger, more "global" character. But Foucault does address this issue, saying that such massive, transformational events do obviously take place, but that they are also very rare; the cultural critic is more often going to encounter "mobile and transitory points of resistance, producing cleavages in a society that shift about, fracturing unities and effecting regroupings" (p. 96). Foucault is here talking about revolution—what is usually seen as the overthrow of the dominant by the dominated—and he says that yes, these binaries do exist, and yes, these revolutions can occur, but *generally* speaking, resistance—and dominance—are exercised at a local level.

But we have still not come to his definition of power. He goes into great detail about this definition in Volume 1 of *History of Sexuality*, but again reverts to defining what power is not. Power is "not something that is acquired . . . [or] something that one holds onto" (p. 94), and there is "no binary and all-encompassing opposition between rulers and ruled at the root of power relations" (p. 94). Perhaps most importantly, however, he says that "Power comes from below" and that "Where there is power, there is resistance, and yet, or rather consequently, this resistance is never in a position of exteriority in relation to power" (pp. 94, 95). That "power comes from below" and is "not something . . . one holds onto" is significant because it means that power is never stable, and so society can never be fully controlled by one dominant or powerful group. "Hence," he continues, "there is no single locus of great Refusal, no soul of revolt, source of all rebellions. . . . Instead there is a plurality of resistances, each of them a special case" (pp. 95–96). In other words, for each exercise of power there is an embedded action of resistance, and vice versa: the two mutually imply and create each other in every level. Even though there isn't, for Foucault, an overall and complete structure of power of which everything is a part (like, say, hegemonic control of class), there are larger and smaller strategies of power, each of which enables the other.

Sex, Morality, and the Production Code

Foucault's discussion of power is made in the context of a larger discussion of sexuality, which we turn to in Chapter 11. But part of his overall analysis of discourse has to do with the relationship between institutions and restrictions on speech, and how those restrictions shape people's sense of self, often in paradoxically generative ways. Analyzing the prison and the discourses of criminality and justice (in *Discipline and Punish*), the asylum and medical discourse (in *Madness and Civilization*), and the concept of truth and scientific discourse (in *The Order of Things*), Foucault's body of work demonstrates that our systems of knowledge about the world and about ourselves are intimately shaped by—and in turn help to shape—our social institutions and relations of power. Thus, rather than just study "the history of science" or the "history of prisons," Foucault instead studies the development of the discourses surrounding these institutions: that is, he wants to know how we talk about things, and how that language shapes our knowledge.

There are also institutions of popular culture that develop their own discourses and ways of understanding themselves: one can think of the gaming industry, or social media, or Hollywood film, to cite only a few examples. But, these institutions and discourses aren't isolated from each other; just as medical discourse affects the prison system, so too does Hollywood language affect gaming, and vice versa.

In one particularly telling moment in the history of popular culture, the relations between sexual discourse, discourses of religion and morality, and the institutions of Hollywood came even more visibly to the surface than usual, and helped change the ways in which people understood both film and sex. In 1934 the organization in charge of distributing Hollywood films to theatres began enforcing the so-called Production Code. Instigated by certain religious leaders and groups, the Production Code was designed to protect supposedly vulnerable audiences from the negative moral effects of seeing inappropriate behaviour on screen. To do so, the Production Code prohibited certain acts and images from being shown. If a film were to violate the Code it wouldn't be distributed, and hence was effectively censored and kept from theatres.

Among those things to be kept from the screen were "sexual perversion" (meaning any representation of homosexuality or sex outside of marriage), "profanity," drugs, and genitalia. By keeping these things off the screen, the Production Code was intended to help stem their existence (or "misuse") in the real world.

In a non-Foucauldian reading, the Production Code would represent a simple exercise of power by a dominant group who held that power, silencing other groups (including gays, lesbians, sexually active women in general, and so on). According to Foucault, however, no exercise of power ever functions purely in that one direction. Any such attempt to silence people leads to a form of resistance, and thus to the creation of new forms of discourse and new subject positions to go with them.

In the case of the Production Code, film creators and audiences alike became much more adept at certain forms of close interpretation—at reading certain coded representations of things no longer allowed to appear explicitly on screen. Thus, while the (little known) pre-Code 1931 film version of *The Maltese Falcon* can more or less directly state one character's homosexuality, the post-Code 1941 version (the famous one, starring Humphrey Bogart) must only hint at it, using certain coded images and language that developed around the notion of alternative sexualities. Recognizing a certain style of clothing or a certain reference to the colour lavender, audiences could read more into—and possibly identify with—behaviours and identities that weren't explicitly represented. Thus, the very identifications that the Production Code was supposed to stop through its exercise of power were in fact extended, as the audience was given the freedom to interpret and "read into" certain representations all kinds of new possibilities. We will return to this aspect of Foucault's theory in Chapter 11.

Foucault's theory of power is thus inherently connected to a New Historical approach. If each and every instance of discourse is involved in numerous exchanges of power at the local and global level, exchanges that can complement or contradict each other, then how can one possibly come up with a unified history of a nation, a culture, or even a particular event? These theorists and critics suggest that any rigorous interpretation needs to analyze the specifics of a given piece of discourse and its interaction with other moments and discourses. Unlike, for example, the hegemonic approach of the Birmingham School, such an analysis may inevitably point only to contradiction and more questions, indicating that any given text or moment is cut through with conflicting positions and meanings. Performing a New Historical or Foucauldian discursive analysis thus isn't as simple as saying that you can examine a newspaper ad to understand the larger capitalist structures. For Foucault and New Historicism, that one text could also show and provide moments of discord—and such discord leads us back to a discussion of agency. As Foucault writes, "[T]here can exist different and even contradictory discourses within the same strategy" (p. 102). A car commercial, for example, can employ an environmentalist discourse (showing the car in a pristine wilderness, for example) even as it talks about the car's powerful engine (which runs on fossil fuels), or a political leader can apply an anti-intellectual, anti-education discourse even while holding several university degrees and employing a clearly knowledgeable, educated rhetoric about the economy. These are straightforward examples, but they point to the ways a given discursive moment can employ several contradictory elements.

This emphasis on instability and contradiction rather than totality or unity of argument leads directly into Chapter 9, where we look at theories whose explicit focus is our always contingent and incomplete ability to interpret texts, culture, and even ourselves.

Case Study

History, Power, and Discourse in Canadian Textbooks

The theories and critics studied in this chapter have all focused on one conclusion: that "history" as a concept is never simply a static set of facts but instead a series of competing interests and texts that separately and together form a complex, unstable set of social meanings.

Moreover, these facts, texts, and meanings are all embroiled in the specifics of power relations and discourses at both the moment they happen and the moment they're studied (since, after all, historians and popular culture critics bring with them their own time, location, and set of discursive assumptions).

Perhaps one of the best sets of texts through which to understand the application and importance of these theories is the public school history textbook. Generally depicted as containing unbiased facts, following a scientific discourse that demands objectivity, textbooks in fact often disguise the functioning of power as objectivity, thus presenting a particular perspective on history as undeniable fact. Textbooks therefore engage in the form of ideological work discussed in previous chapters.

But it's the manner in which these books do so—the specific discourses and power struggles in which they engage—that matters to someone using the tools mapped out in this chapter. We can't trace all of these here, but we can look at a few, specifically the discourses of progress, rights, and gender and race.

In his analysis of history textbooks used in Ontario in the 1960s and after 2000, Ken Montgomery indicates the ways in which they present a specific—and specifically biased—vision of Canada. Citing a published lecture by Foucault, Montgomery writes that "textbooks function as 'knowledge apparatuses' that are 'formed, organized, and put into circulation' to constitute the legitimate knowledge of the nation, but also to legitimize the existence and rule of the state as normal, natural, and unproblematic" (Montgomery, 2005, p. 427). In other words, textbooks don't just give us facts, or even tell us particular versions of the facts; instead, they tell us how to think about those facts, and what does and does not constitute a legitimate fact about Canadian history.

Montgomery notes that "the representation of racism in Canadian history textbooks configures Canada as a good and tolerant space (or one becoming progressively good and tolerant) in which racism is imagined to be the exception and fighting against racism the norm" (p. 438). Thus, newer textbooks can include the fact that the Canadian government and its dominant white population has engaged in racist acts, but can do so in such a way that the nation looks even less racist given that such acts were fought against. The fact that actual racism still exists, and the possibility that the history of racism in Canada is not one of a continual improvement, are swept away.

Likewise, Penney Clark discusses the representation of women—and those areas where there's a lack of representation—in B.C.-approved history textbooks. She notes that while women's role in the nation is recognized in more recent textbooks, it often takes the form of what's called "filler feminism": "Women are highlighted in boxes separated from the ongoing narrative of the textbook. While this has the effect of increasing the number of women listed in the book's index (useful when provincial and school district textbook selection committees count), it conveys the message that women are peripheral to the core narrative" (Clark, 2005, p. 257). So while these more recent textbooks offer more discussion of women's roles, the general patriarchal narrative of Canada's history remains intact.

In both of these examples, seemingly progressive or liberal political ideologies (anti-racism and feminism) are put in the service of the dominant or hegemonic narrative (racist and sexist political or narrative structures). This is why, Foucault would say, we need to look beyond the superficial narratives of power and resistance, since what seems like resistance may in fact serve the interest of the dominant group, and—as in the example of the Production Code—vice versa.

Discussion Questions

1. Bring in a set of advertisements to class. Can you identify different sets of discourses in them? How do you think the advertisers are using them? Do you see any possible contradictions between these discourses?

2. Bring in a history textbook and try to identify moments when the author uses the literary genre of tragedy to describe an event. What does that do to your reading of the facts?

3. Find an example of an official document—a government commercial for the energy sector, for example—and examine it closely to decide on its overall "argument" or position, and then discuss whether it uses any discursive elements that work against its main thrust.

Further Reading

Gallagher, Catherine, and Stephen Greenblatt. *Practicing New Historicism*. Chicago: U of Chicago P, 2000.

Greenblatt, Stephen. *Renaissance Self-Fashioning: From More to Shakespeare*. Chicago: U of Chicago P, 1980.

Foucault, Michel. *Discipline and Punish*. Trans. Alan Sheridan. New York: Vintage, 1995.

——. *History of Madness*. Trans. Jonathan Murphy and Jean Khafla. Ed. Jean Khafla. New York: Routledge, 2006.

Vesser, H. Aram, ed. *The New Historicism*. New York: Routledge, 1989.

White, Hayden. *Figural Realism: Studies in the Mimesis Effect*. Baltimore: Johns Hopkins UP, 1999.

Chapter 9
Postmodernism and Poststructuralism

INTRODUCTION

The theoretical approaches to popular culture, including structuralism, that arose in the late nineteenth century through to the mid to late twentieth century were established during a span that's often referred to in critical studies as the modern period. In cultural fields, such as art and literature, this period also gave rise to a loosely defined artistic and cultural tradition known as **modernism**. Theories that have arisen out of the latter part of the twentieth and into the twenty-first century explicitly build on and challenge the assumptions of modernism and structuralism. This period has come to be known—somewhat uninventively—as the **postmodern** period, which is often seen as going hand in hand with **poststructuralist** cultural theories. In this chapter we first summarize some of the principles of modernism and then move into our primary discussion of the major postmodern and poststructuralist theories.

FROM MODERN TO POSTMODERN

As we learned earlier, the advent of the twentieth century brought with it many social transformations that disrupted people's sense of place in the world. There were different artistic and cultural responses to these changes, many of which involved radical experimentation with the form and content of traditional cultural objects. In painting, poetry, art, architecture, and many other fields, distinctly "modern" styles were created that were seen to both reflect and respond to the massive social and technological changes gripping much of the world.

The experimentation in cultural forms expanded between World Wars I and II, during the period that is known in some critical traditions as High Modernism. During this period, such literary authors as T. S. Eliot and James Joyce, artists including Picasso and Salvador Dalí, and architects and designers like Frank Lloyd Wright and the Bauhaus school, among others, were radically changing the foundational principles of their art in ways that mirrored the transformations in the world. It's important to recognize, of course, that the changes and large-scale developments in social structure and culture were matched by changes in daily lives: from the women's enfranchisement and other civil rights movements to the move toward large urban centres, developments in transportation technologies, the expansion in the use of electricity, and countless other "smaller" changes in everyday life, the world of the "average" person was changing dramatically.

One part of these changes was the development of a mass popular culture through such media as radio, television, and the pulp press. People across the globe were becoming "consumers" of culture, and often of the same cultural products across countries and even continents. But along with this burgeoning cultural globalization came a sense of a "fracturing" of culture: no longer, it seemed, were there central social institutions and conventions that gave a larger, more universal meaning to life, meanings that people could share. (As we know, of course, such "universal" understandings are more often ideological assertions than they are accurate visions of the world.) Even belief in the self-control of the individual was, as we've seen, giving way in the light of new developments in psychology and economics that gestured to new visions of subjectivity and meaning.

We can see aspects of this vision of the world in some of the theories we've already examined. In structuralist theory, discussed in Chapter 5, we have a very modernist sense that meaning is arbitrary, but that there are still overarching, universal structures that we can strive to understand. Ferdinand de Saussure argued that individual signifiers are arbitrary in relation to their signified concept, but that meaning is created once we understand that each sign is part of a larger whole called language. Similarly, Claude Lévi-Strauss argued that individual mythological stories may seem relatively meaningless, but when we trace images, motifs, and figures that occur in a larger number of myths (what he called "mythemes") we can grasp something universal about the human condition. While Saussure and Lévi-Strauss wouldn't think so, some later writers see this division—between the arbitrariness of the individual sign and the longing for a larger universalism of an overall structure of meaning—as a tension at the heart of structuralism and of modernism writ large.

Modernist Superman

Many cultural products reflected the modernist feeling of fragmentation—consider Picasso's wildly out of shape faces, or the fragmented images of cartoons and comic strips—but many also longed nostalgically for the unity of older world views. Superman, that icon of the comic book world and the first true "superhero," enacts both of these moves. Alienated from his world (he is, literally, an alien) and never able to reveal the "true" identity that lurks beneath the surface of his false one (one that looks remarkably like the "average Joe"), Superman nevertheless champions the supposedly "universal" values of truth and justice (even as he engages in a modern form of nationalism—something we discuss in Chapter 13—by championing the "American way," despite being created in part by a Canadian). Living a fragmented and alienated life (he is two people, neither of whom is complete or whole) even as he struggles to regain and support those earlier, "universal" values that seem to be disappearing in the modern world, Superman embodies the tensions of the modern world even more clearly than Picasso's fragmented portraits.

According to some thinkers, we're still living within the tension of this modern moment. Other theorists, however, say that, especially in the years following World War II and moving into the digital age of the 1980s and beyond, we have entered a new period: a period that follows on from the sense of fragmentation in the modernist period, but explodes it into something even more radically unstable, something that is *post*modern. Still others see this radical instability as something that already existed in the modernist period (and, indeed, in other periods); they argue that structuralists and other modernist thinkers allowed us to see this instability, but that they weren't willing to take into account its full implications. In the next few sections we'll discuss theories of culture and meaning that emphasize this fragmentation—the "little narrative[s]," to use Jean-François Lyotard's term (Lyotard, 1984, p. 60), that make up our lives as opposed to the universal stories to which earlier thinkers clung.

Postmodern Language: Deconstruction

From the 1960s forward into the 1980s, the primacy of structuralist interpretations of language was being challenged. Among the foremost critics and philosophers to take up the challenge was Jacques Derrida (1930–2004), with his theory and critical practice known as deconstruction.

Derrida's writings are often held up as being among the most difficult in contemporary theory. His early works are composed of close readings of philosophical and literary texts, with his primary techniques being related to those of literary study: he examines the metaphors, metonyms, and other literary devices in a text in order to support or lead to his philosophical arguments. For example, one of his best-known works, *Of Grammatology* (1967), offers a series of close readings of works by different authors, including works by Saussure and Lévi-Strauss. Derrida's primary goal was to demonstrate how the logical arguments these writers present ultimately end up contradicting each other, pointing, for Derrida, to the inherent slipperiness of language itself.

Before we turn to his actual text, it's useful to briefly explain the term **deconstruction**: it has been defined as part of a methodology that is "aimed at showing how a text always subverts or exceeds the author's intended meaning . . . owing to an unperceived linguistic instability" (Rabaté, 2005, p. 257). In other words, any given text is never fully circumscribed by an author's intentions, and in fact the text can often present meanings that seem to directly contradict those intentions. While Freud might argue that this contradiction results from the author's unconscious desires finding expression, even against the author's conscious wishes, Derrida argues that this slippage between the intended meaning and the various other meanings is due to what Mikhail Bakhtin called **heteroglossia**. As we discussed in Chapter 5, Bakhtin says that every word always brings with it the various meanings it has had in the past—that meaning isn't stable because of shifting contexts. Derrida picks up on a similar strain of thought, and says that texts always contain meanings that undermine their intended or obvious aims because language itself is unstable. Like Bakhtin, he stresses that "one must speak several languages and produce several texts at once" (Derrida, 1982, p. 135; also qtd. in Rabaté, 2005, p. 257)—that is, every time you write something there will be several ways of interpreting it, given the slipperiness of language, the impact of context, and so on.

In *Of Grammatology*, Derrida critically analyzes Jean-Jacques Rousseau's autobiography, *The Confessions* (1782), often seen as the first and prime example of modern autobiography. The topic of Derrida's analysis is Rousseau's use of the word *supplement*, which in French means both "substitute" and "addition." Derrida performs an extremely close reading of Rousseau's use of this one word in order to make larger claims about how language and criticism function.

Discussing this work by Rousseau, Derrida states, "[T]he writer writes *in* a language and *in* a logic whose proper system, laws and life his discourse by definition cannot dominate absolutely. He uses them only by letting himself, after a fashion and up to a point, be governed by the system" (Derrida, 1974, p. 158). In other words, any given writer cannot absolutely control the meaning of his text owing to heteroglossia, to use Bakhtin's word again. When Rousseau uses the word *supplement* to mean "addition," it always also carries with it the meaning "substitute," and the slippage between the two causes some problems for Rousseau's text, making its meaning not as clear as he might have thought. But, as the second part of this quotation says, in order to communicate, we have to allow this to happen—if we were constantly trying to write the completely clear, unambiguous sentence we'd never be done, and so would communicate nothing. Whenever we write something, we both determine some of its meaning but in turn allow ourselves to be determined by some of its other meanings. There is always a chance that we'll be misunderstood, but if we didn't ignore that possibility, we'd never say anything.

This continuous heteroglossia results, for Derrida, in the idea "that no single 'plane of discourse' can be established, that the metaphors always clash violently and, fundamentally, that any writer" who tries to create a unified and self-evident meaning is "attempt[ing] to achieve the impossible" (Rabaté, 2005, p. 258). This description should recall to us our discussions of the formalists in Chapter 5, who said that the study of language and literature was a science, that texts do contain a solid and definite meaning, and that a proper form of criticism should be geared toward finding that meaning. This type of criticism is, for Derrida, impossible.

But, at the same time, we still function as if it is possible. The goal of deconstructive criticism, for Derrida, is to show where meaning breaks down in order to help us have a continual dialogue, to show that no one meaning ever takes dominance. This constant play of meanings, he says, is "a task of reading" (Derrida, 1974, p. 158). He writes,

> To produce this signifying structure obviously cannot consist of reproducing, by the effaced and respectful doubling of commentary, the conscious, voluntary, intentional relationship that the writer institutes in his exchanges with the history to which he belongs thanks to the element of language. This moment of doubling commentary should no doubt have its place in a critical reading. To recognize and respect all its classical exigencies is not easy and requires all the instruments of traditional criticism. Without this recognition and respect, critical production would risk developing in any

direction at all and authorize itself to say almost anything. But this indispensable guardrail has always only *protected*, it has never *opened*, a reading.

Yet if reading must not be content with doubling the text, it cannot legitimately transgress the text toward something other than it, toward a referent (a reality that is metaphysical, historical, psychobiographical, etc.) or toward a signified outside the text whose content could take place, could have taken place outside of language . . . *There is nothing outside the text.* (p. 158)

Obviously, Derrida's writing is difficult! But this is one of the clearer statements of his critical principles. Basically, just before this, Derrida says that criticism needs to be geared toward showing where notions of unified meaning break down—where monoglossia is shown to be fake and heteroglossia asserts itself. But in this passage, Derrida is definitely *not* saying that meaning is impossible or that we can say whatever we want about a text. Derrida says that the goal of criticism is not to "reproduce" or simply explain the author's intentions, nor to replace those intentions with the critic's. Instead, the goal of criticism is to point toward the system of meaning in which the author is functioning. Like Saussure, then, Derrida sees language as a self-contained structure, but, unlike Saussure, he sees it as a structure that is constantly breaking down around itself: hence, he is a "poststructuralist."

Deconstructing Boiling Water

To illustrate how deconstruction works, let's take a slightly misleading but memorable example: you've been asked to do a chemistry experiment to show that the boiling temperature of water is 100 degrees Celsius. But you quickly discover that it takes a certain system, including a certain air pressure, a certain purity of the water, etc., for water to boil at exactly 100 degrees. So in order to prove the "fact" that water boils at 100 degrees you'd need to devise a series of experiments in which water did not boil at 100 degrees.

If Derrida were "reading" this experiment, he'd say that the only way to prove water boils at 100 degrees is to prove that it *doesn't* boil at 100 degrees in order to show where that idea breaks down. This experiment—and its "failure"—tell you something about the system of science: it isn't about absolutely proving something, but about constantly proving and disproving in a never-ending dialogue. This doesn't mean you can say that water never boils, or that water never boils at 100 degrees; you still need to stick to the text of your experiment. But once you've looked at the wide range of variables, the focus of that experiment is different: you set out to show that water boils at 100 degrees, but to do this you show the exact opposite—that in some conditions water doesn't boil at 100 degrees. What this tells you is that measuring boiling temperature with this scale isn't a rigid, completely stable thing, but rather part of a larger, constantly shifting and unstable "system" of boiling in which each instance of boiling is defined by its difference from other such moments.

This example is useful, but only to a point. To a degree (pun intended), this example merely illustrates the scientific method, which involves rigorous attempts to disprove certain hypotheses, along with repetition of experiments in order to validate their findings. In a traditional understanding, this method brings about a knowledge of real, unassailable facts. But the example is nonetheless useful because it shows precisely how unstable those "facts" can be, pointing to the possibility that our belief in them is, at least to a point, simply conditioned by the dominance of a scientific world view in contemporary culture. Not many of us understand the mathematics and extrapolation involved in current theoretical astrophysics, for example, but we still tend to believe Stephen Hawking or Neil deGrasse Tyson when they're on TV. Deconstruction, as an analytical technique and as a philosophy, can allow us to see where those world views break down, and thus allow us to recognize when "truths" are merely repetitions of certain assumptions. When we discuss Jean-François Lyotard below, we'll see a similar postmodern approach to scientific discourse.

For Derrida, criticism isn't simply an explanation of a pre-existing idea or of a self-contained, always true notion; instead, criticism sets out to show precisely where meaning is destabilized, and this allows the critic to say something about how meaning is produced. The process still requires that the critic pay a lot of attention to the text itself in order to show precisely how meaning becomes unstable. A little later in *Of Grammatology* Derrida writes, "Although it is not commentary, our reading must be intrinsic and remain within the text" (p. 159). Every text, however, always contains a series of competing "differences" within itself. Deconstructive readings always show that language and individual words are, to use Bakhtin's terminology, both centripetal and centrifugal at the same time. And this means that criticism itself is never stable, but must constantly argue separate points: a word in a text does "X," but it also does "Y," and so on and so on.

Fundamentally, deconstructive readings often follow a general methodology: such an analysis "focuses on binary oppositions within a text, first, to show how those oppositions are structured hierarchically; second, to overturn that hierarchy temporarily . . .; and third, to displace and reassert both terms of the opposition within a nonhierarchical relationship of 'difference'" (Kneale, 2005, p. 235).

Many cultural studies theorists and critics have faulted Derridean theory for its focus on the text, and its seeming denial of the importance of social context, but this mistakes a basic principle of Derridean readings. For Derrida, the statement "there is nothing outside the text" and his insistence on close readings apply just as much to what we can uncritically call "context" as they do to whatever primary cultural object we're reading at a given moment. What Derrida tells us, as we discussed in Chapter 8, is that "context" isn't just a collection of facts but instead a collection of "texts," each of which embodies and carries with it various contradictions and varieties of meanings. Like Saussure, Derrida denies us anything outside of language, but he does so in order to point out that we are always making assumptions, and always interpreting things, and that we must always question those assumptions and interpretations. This conclusion has obvious implications for politically and historically invested readings.

Deconstructing Hollywood Horror: *The Cabin in the Woods*

Traditional Hollywood horror film—from the classic films of the 1930s through to the slasher flicks of the 1970s and 80s and up to recent "found-footage"–style horror like *Paranormal Activity* (2007)—thrive on the construction of binaries, relying on them to present often conservative gender and/or sexual moral lessons or to generally uphold a hegemonic set of values. *Scream* (1996) actually analyzes some of these binary tropes in its discussion of the "rules" of horror films. The typical slasher film, such as *Friday the 13th*, for example, focuses on a group of teenagers who briefly escape the confines of civilization on a weekend trip to a cabin, campground, or some other remote, isolated spot. Often while there they will "experiment," as the phrase goes, with sex, drugs, crime, or some other activity deemed "anti-social" or "immoral" in the larger society (at least as it's presented in the film). At the height of their debauchery, the teenagers will start being murdered, generally by a monstrous figure, often portrayed as someone who was himself (almost always "him" self) a victim of some form of social misdeed: Jason, in the original *Friday the 13th* (1980), was supposedly a drowning victim whose mother becomes a killer, but in the sequels it is revealed that he was traumatized by seeing his mother killed; Freddy Krueger in *Nightmare on Elm Street* was a child murderer, but was himself murdered by his parents after he was released from prison. In many cases, those teenagers who are the most "immoral" will die first, until we're left only with the "good kid" or kids who survive until the end and defeat the monster. Generally virgins, or somehow otherwise innocent, these figures represent the "proper" teenage behaviour. Thus, the films present an archetypal narrative: teenagers will rebel, but they must be brought back into line in order for society to continue in peace. When that narrative is combined with the monster's representation as somehow "abnormal"—often sexually—and with the

films' often vaguely racist narrative (the "black person dying first" is a common trope in Hollywood horror), we can read these narratives as presenting a set of hierarchical binaries: male/female; chaste/sexual; white/black, and ultimately, good/bad. The subordinate part of the binary is silenced, allowing for the dominant side to triumph.

In a traditional deconstruction of such a narrative, the critic would look for a moment when a particular binary is inverted, or becomes its opposite. For example, the hero of such a film almost always has to use violence, and even murder, to survive. Likewise, the "monster" is often presented somewhat sympathetically. Taken together, these can be read to mean that murder is, in fact, a laudatory act. Thus, the morality of the entire film falls apart.

A more contextually based deconstruction could look at the film's advertising, or why an audience goes to such a film. Generally speaking, it is the monster who is advertised, the figure who stands opposed to traditional values, and in sequels, it is the monster who most often returns. This emphasis on the figure of the monster highlights a tension at the heart of binaries that horror films propagate: good must triumph, but evil always has to take precedence over good.

It is this tension that the film *The Cabin in the Woods* (2012) exploits. Like the *Scream* series, *The Cabin in the Woods* plays with horror film convention: here, the cabin turns out to be run by a secretive organization that uses it to make sacrifices to the demons that would otherwise destroy the planet. Working very much like Hollywood producers, this organization follows certain rules of sacrifice (the teenagers killed must be immoral, for example, though there is leeway as to whether or not the virgin dies). The supposedly moral message of Hollywood horror is here flipped: the reason why the "evil" children are punished is not to allow "good" to triumph but instead to serve an even greater evil—in this case the insatiable consumerism of the audience, represented here by the demon itself. Unlike in the traditional horror film, the lines between good and evil become indistinguishable, following the methodology of deconstruction outlined above. And, in the end, the two remaining teenagers prove that this deconstruction opens up new possibilities: as they smoke a joint, they let the demon destroy the world.

THE MEANINGS OF POSTMODERNISM

Derrida's theories of the impossibility of getting "outside the text" and of the inherent contradictions in language point to a transformation in the study of culture. From the universalisms of older interpretations of the world (whether religious, scientific, or Platonic) to structuralism's simultaneous assertion of the arbitrariness and universalizing structures of meaning, we come now to an inherently fragmented, impossibly complex view of the world. We can illustrate the difference with the example of the nursery rhyme "Humpty Dumpty" (which Lewis Carroll also used to illustrate language games in his 1872 novel, *Through the Looking Glass*): "Humpty Dumpty sat on a wall / Humpty Dumpty had a great fall / All the king's horses and all the king's men / Couldn't put Humpty together again." From a traditional, universalist perspective, Humpty Dumpty would be a symbol for meaning itself, and it's the advent of the modern world that "breaks" or fractures Humpty Dumpty. But the structuralists and modernists would think that, through careful analysis or experimentation, they could—possibly—find a way to put "Humpty together again." Postmodernists and poststructuralists, however, would say that there is no way to reattach the various fragments of shell—of meaning—and indeed that Humpty was always a bit cracked. So we are left with a pile of incompatible, fragmented visions of the world, each of which is self-contradictory and none of which perfectly fit together again.

One of the implications of Derrida's reading of language—as of Saussure's before it—is that there really is no ground outside of language itself to legitimize meaning. Saussure tries to transfer this ground to both the overarching structure of language and the community of speakers of a given language, saying that it is common agreement and the relationship of sign to sign that lend meaning to specific utterances. Derrida, however, points out that this assumption still relies on an ability to communicate one's intent perfectly, and that this is never fully possible given the inherent contradictions in language itself. Thus, if one follows Derrida's argument, it seems that there is no stable ground on which to legitimize meaning.

If Derrida is interested in the specifically linguistic elements of this lack of legitimization, other theorists point to the way in which it is expressed by and reflected in the larger culture, and they often do so by discussing what is now known as postmodernism.

The Postmodern Condition

Many people saw this "new" lack of a foundation to meaning (which Derrida would argue isn't "new" at all) as a significant problem for the world. Expanding on the modernist sense of loss and fragmentation, this radical undermining of the ground of meaning seemed terrifying. As Frederic Jameson, to whom we'll return later, writes, "legitimation becomes visible as a problem and an object of study only at the point in which it is called into question" (Jameson, in Lyotard, 1984, p. viii). But other people saw this new questioning of legitimation as a profoundly freeing idea. Jean-François Lyotard (1924–1998), for one, saw this supposed "crisis," as Jameson explains, as permitting a "disalienating excitement of the new and 'unknown' . . . as well as of adventure" (p. xx).

Lyotard's major statement of this position is *The Postmodern Condition: A Report on Knowledge*. This book, which was originally written as a report for the Quebec government's Conseil des Universités, analyzes developments primarily in science, but also in aesthetics, in order to understand the postmodern period's radical undermining not only of *traditional* belief systems (or myths, to use Barthes's and Lévi-Strauss's term) but of *all* systems that purport to offer complete and true world views. Lyotard's term for such systems is **metanarratives**: a narrative that legitimates a particular world view. So, for example, one metanarrative is the idea that all science is purely objective, and that any two people, if they examine a situation or experiment in a rational and dispassionate way, will *necessarily* come to the same conclusion, with the parallel belief that discovering such scientific truths is a good in and of itself that makes the world a continually better place. This metanarrative legitimates science as a proper and true way of understanding the world: "this is the Enlightenment narrative," Lyotard writes, "in which the hero of knowledge works toward the good ethico-political end—universal peace" (pp. xxiii–xxiv). Any number of science fiction movies, where the scientist battles against a corrupt military or an equally corrupt corporation, reinforces this metanarrative: science itself is always good because it's always true, and it stands outside petty individual concerns.

Lyotard argues that in the postmodern period, however, because of the profound transformations in the world and the speed with which they happened, people began to question these metanarratives. As with Derrida's reading of language, for Lyotard the world is too complex and contradictory for any one world view to be absolutely True (what we can call "capital-T Truth"). Like Bakhtin, again, Lyotard thinks that people who want to claim that a singular Truth is to be found in the world are acting monologically—they are trying to force that truth onto the world rather than discovering one that actually exists. Instead, he says, there are any number of smaller, non-universal "truths" that co-exist in the world and that are contingent on their context.

This denial of the universal claims that philosophy had long made, and of the quest for Truth that underlines the scientific endeavours of modernity, was seen as very threatening by some people. Lyotard, somewhat sarcastically, lists several of the complaints made against postmodernism:

> I have read from the pen of a reputable historian that writers and thinkers of the 1960 and 1970 avant-gardes spread a reign of terror in the use of language, and that the conditions for a fruitful exchange must be restored by imposing on the intellectuals a common way of speaking, that of the historians. . . . I have read a talented theatrologist for whom postmodernism, with its games and fantasies, carries very little weight in front of political authority, especially when a worried public opinion encourages authority to a politics of totalitarian surveillance in the face of nuclear warfare threats. (pp. 71–72)

Listing several of these complaints against the lack of "authority" and "common way[s] of speaking" that postmodernism describes, Lyotard points to the concern that the fragmentation of postmodernism leads to chaos. "[I]n the diverse invitations to suspend artistic experimentation," he writes, "there is an identical call for order, a desire for unity, for identity, for security, or popularity" (p. 73). Postmodernism denies the possibility of such "order" and "unity."

But, Lyotard argues, such a modernist longing for Truth brings with it its own sense of terror: "the attack on artistic experimentation is specifically reactionary: aesthetic judgment would only be required to decide whether such or such work is in conformity with the established rules of the beautiful" (p. 75). In other words, if we believe that there is a capital-T Truth or capital B-Beauty in the world, as Plato did for example, then there is no room for true innovation or change. Art and culture would become, under such a regime, static and univocal.

Postmodernism instead recognizes that freeing art and meaning from a desire for *the* Truth allows for an explosion of new and previously unheard voices. Lyotard, speaking of science, calls such unheard voices examples of the "little narrative" or "petit-récit." He sees them as the only source for "imaginative invention," setting them against the metanarrative that stifles anything new or challenging (p. 60): we can call these the "small-t truths," where the plural indicates the possibility of several competing, even contradictory "truths" all at once. Lyotard says that the postmodern is merely the extension of modernism's experimental aspects, freed from the desire for unity and from a nostalgia for a simpler world where everyone knew what the Truth was:

> The postmodern would be that which, in the modern, puts forward the unpresentable in presentation itself; that which denies itself the solace of good forms, the consensus of a taste which would make it possible to share collectively the nostalgia for the unattainable. . . . The artist and the writer, then, are working without rules. . . . (p. 81)

For Lyotard, any desire for an easily understood, unifying meaning to culture, or to the social world itself, is actually a call for a silencing of the many different and contradictory voices that make up the world. He sees postmodernism as the ability to live with an unfettered heteroglossia.

This call for a world in which traditional rules for art and traditional forms of culture are no longer seen as the *only* or *best* way of looking at the world lies at the heart of the study of popular culture. After all, only a few decades ago, there wouldn't have been university courses in comic books offered alongside courses in Shakespeare. We have, in many ways, embraced the postmodernity that Lyotard examines.

Postmodern Culture

But culture itself, and specific examples within it, also changed in the postmodern world. The style and content of paintings, novels, and other more "traditional" forms changed. Likewise, while many works of popular culture still argue for a more "conservative" view of the world (one of "common values," for example), still others embrace the fragmentation that Lyotard discusses.

Canadian cultural critic and theorist Linda Hutcheon (1947–) has defined "postmodern culture" in an especially clear way. In *A Poetics of Postmodernism: History, Theory, Fiction* (1988), she sets out to first define the concept of the postmodern and then offer examples of postmodern culture. Employing a blend of Derrida's and Lyotard's theories, she defines postmodernism as a questioning of the "concepts that have come to be associated with what we conveniently label as liberal humanism: autonomy, transcendence, certainty, authority, unity, totalization, system, universalization, center, continuity, teleology, closure, hierarchy, homogeneity, uniqueness, origin" (Hutcheon, 1988, p. 57). But, she notes, "to put these concepts into question is not to deny them—only to interrogate their relation to experience" (p. 57). Hutcheon argues, in other words, that postmodern culture calls into question the myths, in Barthes's sense, or metanarratives, to use Lyotard's term, through which the modern world makes sense of itself. As with Barthes's myths, however, she says that questioning these ideas doesn't necessarily mean throwing them out altogether, but does require that we force ourselves to question our assumptions.

Hutcheon goes on to discuss how particular works of culture present this questioning. Her central focus is literature, but much of what she writes can be applied to visual and oral cultures, cultural practices, and popular cultures in general. She argues that, of all the postmodern cultural challenges to modernity and humanism, "[o]ne of the major" ones

> has been to the notion of center, in all its forms. . . . If the center will not hold, then, as one of the Merry Pranksters (in Tom Wolfe's *The Electric Kool-Aid Acid Test*) put it, "Hail to the Edges!" The move to rethink margins and borders is clearly a move away from centralization with its associated concerns of origin, oneness . . . and monumentality . . . that work to link the concept of center to those of the eternal and universal. The local, the regional, the non-totalizing . . . are reasserted as the center becomes a fiction—necessary, desired, but a fiction nonetheless. (p. 58)

For Hutcheon, as for Lyotard, exposing supposedly universal Truths as myths allows for an increase in the number of "truths" we can listen to. Postmodernism, for these theorists, expands our ability to hear those voices previously pushed to the margins. Rather than terror at the notion that "the center," or Truth, "will not hold" (a line Hutcheon borrows from William Butler Yeats's modernist poem "Second Coming"), we celebrate the "Edges." In practice, this has meant increasing attention to issues and people who have been silenced by the dominant culture's myths. (In Part IV we'll discuss theorists who build on these postmodern and poststructural thinkers, examining works and concepts relating to race and racism, queer sexualities, and other topics and identities that had been left largely unexamined or subjected to a systemic silencing and bias.)

In postmodern literary fiction, the decentring that Hutcheon discusses is presented in several ways: parody and intertextuality are two of the central techniques. In postmodern literature, the text (whether it's a poem or a novel or a comic book) is never "self-contained." That is, the work does not present a singular meaning but rather opens itself

One of the best recent examples of postmodern parody is the TV comedy news show *The Colbert Report*. Performing a parody of right-wing television political pundits, the star, Stephen Colbert, reproduces their style and rhetoric even as he undermines the political assertions they make. It doesn't end at that simple parody, however (after all, parody existed long before postmodernism). In 2011, Colbert also founded Colbert SuperPAC, a political fundraising committee. In keeping with his larger political parody, he did so to critique the very fundraising laws in the United States that allowed him to establish this campaign. We can't ignore the real-world fact of this campaign, though; Colbert had an actual political machine with which to try to affect the American election. He ran commercials in contested districts, and even testified before the Federal Election Commission.

Where does the parody end and real-life political action begin? What is there to *believe* in as "truth" here (or are we just left with a sense of Colbert himself calls "truthiness")? Is Colbert a real political power, or a fake one? These fundamental questions about what we can consider "real" or not are the questions that our postmodern world forces us to ask. Although some theorists of the postmodern (notably Baudrillard, discussed below) would view the conscious decision to be parodic as reinforcing a notion of stability, parody like Colbert's (unlike the more direct satire of Jon Stewart on *The Daily Show*) does have the ability to endlessly trouble the boundaries between the "real" and the "unreal," as Linda Hutcheon argues.

up to several, contradictory readings, explicitly and implicitly relying on other texts and contexts to make its point. Parody highlights this contradiction by walking the fine line between echoing something as an authority and simultaneously making fun of that authority. In this way, parody presents a "centre" or an "origin" to its meaning (the original text it's making fun of) and so *needs* that text to make its point, while it also goes beyond that origin, not allowing itself to be easily pinned down.

SIMULATION AND THE MARKET

It's one thing to talk about questioning truth or reality through a work of fiction, or even something as complex as *The Colbert Report*, but isn't it taking things too far to move these questions into the "real world" as such—don't these become empty philosophical questions in the face of such grim realities as war and famine? Certainly many critics would say so, but other writers identified loosely as "postmodernists" do approach this kind of radical questioning of the world around us—or, more accurately, of our perceptions of the world around us. As we saw in our discussions of Marshall McLuhan in Chapter 7 and Hayden White in Chapter 8, many contemporary theorists focus on how our perceptions of the world are mediated by our contexts—whether that context is, to take a few examples, personal, technological, literary, or historical. One person's vision of an event could well be radically different from that of another who witnessed the very same event, even when they're basing their accounts on the same facts. What does that mean for the "reality" of such an event? Can we say that one event actually occurred, or must we say that two similar but still different events occurred?

Simulacra

The questions raised by the concept of mediation—the way our perception of certain events is determined at least in part by the medium or the filters through which we view it—are central not only to McLuhan but also to Jean Baudrillard (1929–2007), who arguably takes his answers to these questions further than any other theorist. Building explicitly on McLuhan, Baudrillard contends that the sheer amount of, and increasing media technologies for, "simulations" of reality has led to an undermining of the very notion of reality in this postmodern age. He argues that we tend to think of simulations as having a relation to the real: like signifiers, they're supposed to refer to an actual concept or object. So, a map, he writes, is a simulation of the landscape it represents, and should make sense only in relation to that landscape. But our world has become so inundated with simulations that they've taken on a life of their own: they no longer have a direct connection to any reality; we can no longer distinguish between the simulated and the real.

Discussing science fiction, advertising, literature, and film, Baudrillard argues that we live in an age in which we can no longer directly experience reality but only the simulation of reality. And because we experience only that simulation, we can say that reality itself no longer exists for us. We live in an age so saturated by media that we no longer even perceive it as media—that is, as something that *mediates* our experience of the world. Baudrillard writes, "The medium itself is no longer identifiable as such, and the confusion of the medium and the message (McLuhan) is the first great formula of this new era. There is no longer a medium in the literal sense: it is now intangible, diffused, and diffracted in the real" (Baudrillard, 1994, p. 30). Baudrillard is saying that, in a world where there are screens everywhere, where advertising appears in every room, and where we don't just watch our technology but it also watches us back, we can no longer access the "real." In this world, things that "simulate" the real become our only point of reference, what Baudrillard calls **simulacra**: simulations that we treat as if they were reality. Baudrillard argues that because of the proliferation of simulacra, we don't experience reality anymore; we experience only the **hyperreal**: a vision of reality that is inseparable from the technologies and media used to (re)present it.

Baudrillard traces out what he calls the "successive phases of the image," or the (historical) development toward postmodern culture:

> it is the reflection of a profound reality;
>
> it masks and denatures a profound reality;
>
> it masks the *absence* of a profound reality;
>
> it has no relation to any reality whatsoever: it is its own pure simulacrum. (p. 6)

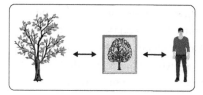

Phases 1 and 2: Realism and Idealism

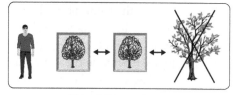

Phase 3: Mass Production

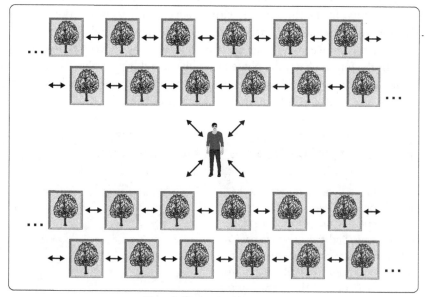

Phase 4: Simulacra and Hyperreality

Figure 9.1 Baudrillard's Phases of the Image

We can explain these phases as follows. First, in what we can call the "traditional" meaning and use of simulations, such tools directly represented a particular real object. So, a painting of a particular landscape can be said to "reflect" the "reality" of that land-scape. In the second phase, however, are those images that cover over the reality of a given situation, presenting one that is, for example, more ideal. So, a painting of a land-scape that shows predators and prey lying down together, or a technologically advanced society in perfect harmony with that landscape, with no pollution presented, wouldn't so much present reality as "mask" the reality of animals eating each other or of pollution. In the third phase we enter the modern era of mass reproduction, where the relationship between image and reality starts to fall apart. Rather than reflect reality—either as it is or as one would want it to be, as in the first two phases—the image covers over the fact that the world is missing something "profound." In this phase of mass reproduction, everyone is buying the "same" simulation of something to the point that the "original" being repro-duced stops mattering so much.

It's the fourth phase, however, that Baudrillard is most interested in, and that he says characterizes the period we've been calling postmodernity. In this phase the image or the media actually takes the place of reality: reality itself no longer lies behind the image at all, and people treat the image as the primary or "pure" object. This is what Baudrillard calls hyperreality: the moment when the real itself ceases to be referenced, and we are surrounded with only simulations that have no connection to the real at all. (Figure 9.1 maps out these phases.)

In the first two phases, the "profound reality" of the actual tree takes precedence; the image may reflect or "mask" that reality, but the viewer sees the image as being secondary to that reality. In the third phase, with its advent of mass production, the viewer's relationship with the simulated image takes precedence; while a relation to reality is assumed, it is at such a remove from the image or product that the viewer has no direct relationship to it. In the fourth phase, the phase of simulacra and hyperreality, only the image is left; reality has disappeared behind the image such that the viewer's only relationship to the concept of a "tree" comes from simulated images of "trees."

Disneyland, Tourism, Status Updates, and the Postmodern

Baudrillard sees Disneyland as "a perfect model" of hyperreality. On one level, he writes, Disneyland is a second-phase representation of America itself: "[E]verywhere in Disneyland the objective profile of America, down to the morphology of individuals and of the crowd, is drawn. All its values are exalted by the miniature and the comic strip. Embalmed and pacified . . .: digest of the American way of life, panegyric of American values, idealized transposition of a contradictory reality" (p. 12). On this level, Disneyland is a Barthesian myth of America: it presents an ideological ideal that the reality of America, or of any nation state, doesn't match on an everyday basis. But Baudrillard goes beyond this ideological analysis. Rather than Disneyland trying to (mis)represent the real America, he says, America is itself trying to simulate Disneyland: "Disneyland exists in order to hide that it is the 'real' country, all of 'real' America that *is* Disneyland. . . . Disneyland is presented as imaginary in order to make us believe that the rest is real" (p. 12). In modern America, and the industrialized West as a whole, we are constantly in contact not with the actual world but only representations. When we first see the CN Tower

Simulacra: Do we ever see the Eiffel Tower, or do we only see pictures of the Eiffel Tower?
Source: Ekaterina Pokrovsky/Fotolia

or Niagara Falls, we no longer experience it as it is because we've already seen countless pictures of it. Our experience of that "reality" always comes second to its representation. In this way, Baudrillard says, there is no reality in the postmodern world: images have superseded it. Any trip to a museum, or to any place with a lot of tourists and cameras, demonstrates this: How many people do you see who are looking at the landscape, or the painting, or the artifact, only through the screen of their digital camera? Are they thinking about the reality in front of them or about the picture they'll eventually look at? And are they taking a picture of, say, the Mona Lisa only because it's already a famously reproduced image? Likewise, how many times have you been in the middle of a situation while thinking about how you'll describe it on Twitter or on your Facebook status? Are you living in the real at that moment or in hyperreality, thinking only of your digital reproduction of the moment? For Baudrillard, this is the triumph of the simulacrum over the real. This is what he means when he says that "the map . . . precedes the territory" (p. 1). The real has ceased to exist as a fully fleshed out space because we can only experience the simulations that surround it. This is why Baudrillard (and The Matrix, following him) discuss "The desert of the real itself" (p. 1): compared with the vibrant pictures and colours of virtual reality, actual reality in the postmodern world has become such a barren, empty space that we can't even imagine "the real."

Postmodernism and Capitalism

Baudrillard's work, then, is primarily a critique of postmodernism, which he sees as a triumph of the surface or the image over depth. This analysis is taken further by Fredric Jameson (1934–), an American writer who offers a Marxist perspective on the postmodern. Explicitly disagreeing with Lyotard, Jameson sees postmodernism not as a period characterized by a philosophical and practical break from previous metanarratives, but as a symptom of the economic structures of what he calls "late-stage capitalism." For Jameson, postmodernism is what happens when every aspect of life, and every discourse, is subsumed by the discourse of commodification. In the postmodern period, Jameson says, *everything* has become a commodity, and those commodities matter only in relation to one's own present moment. Whereas Lyotard sees in the postmodern a collapse of the old metanarratives that functioned to silence alternative voices or perspectives, Jameson sees a world that has become a supermarket, where all voices become simply advertisements for more and more products. For Jameson, Lyotard's lauding of the political possibilities of postmodernism is a failure to place the postmodern in its historical and economic context: "[E]very position on postmodernism in culture— whether apologia or stigmatization—is also at one and the same time, and *necessarily*, an implicitly or explicitly political stance on the nature of multinational capitalism today" (Jameson, 1991, p. 3). Postmodernism is a function of capitalism, Jameson argues, not a way to critique it.

To make this argument, Jameson defines modernism and postmodernism in structuralist terms. While both the modernist and postmodernist periods are fascinated by change and experimentation, "the moderns," he writes, "were interested in what was likely to come of such changes and their general tendency: they thought about the thing itself, substantively, in Utopian or essential fashion" (p. ix). Jameson is here alluding to the modernist poet William Carlos Williams, who once famously wrote that there are "no ideas but in things" ("A Sort of a Song"). Postmodernism, on the contrary, "only clocks the variations themselves, and knows only too well that the contents are just more images. In modernism . . . some residual zones of 'nature' or 'being' of the old, the older, the archaic, still subsist; culture can still do something to that nature and work at transforming that 'referent.' Postmodernism is what you have when the modernization process is complete and nature is gone for good" (p. ix). In other words, the modernists still believed in—or hoped for—the possibility of a connection between signified and signifier. Even if that connection was arbitrary it

Postmodern Capitalism, Poster Sales, and Art

Think of the massive poster sales that happen on so many Canadian university campuses. One poster that appears at most of the sales is a reproduction of Gustav Klimt's painting, *The Kiss*: Does it matter that Klimt's original painting, which he completed in 1908, is currently hanging in an art gallery in Vienna? Do people know if they're purchasing an exact reproduction or not? Or are they simply taking part in a commodity culture, where they're identifying themselves as "romantics" or art connoisseurs through this reproduced image without having to know anything about the artist or the original painting? Indeed, an episode of the often analyzed television series *Buffy the Vampire Slayer* pokes fun at university students for buying this poster for precisely that reason. Baudrillard calls this the "[p]anic-stricken production of the real and of the referential" (Baudrillard, 1994, p. 7): as we move deeper into a mass-market and mass-reproduction world, people keep wanting to connect to things they identify as "real"—but this only leads to more and more reproduction, to the endless replacement of the real with simulation, to more and more poster sales and fewer and fewer original artworks.

A reproduction of Gustav Klimt's *The Kiss*.
Source: Liliya Kulianionak/Shutterstock

The commodification and meaninglessness of contemporary culture is perhaps best indicated by the difference Jameson notes between a Picasso painting of a woman's face and an Andy Warhol silkscreen of a Campbell's soup can. Picasso's painting may be vastly different from a classical portrait, but it's still an attempt to create an artwork that is unique and stands apart from the mass reproductions one sees in the marketplace. Warhol's silkscreen, which itself could be reproduced again and again, is indistinguishable in many ways from an advertisement for the soup. Art and consumerism become one (it's possible, of course, to read Warhol's work as critique, but it still serves to point to the indistinguishability of "culture" from "consumer item"). If, in the modernist period and earlier, "culture" could to a certain degree stand apart from capitalism in that it could still critique certain ideological positions and not just reproduce them, in the postmodern world "culture" and "economics" have become the same thing (Jameson, 1991, p. xxi).

could still generate meaning in a larger social structure, since the arbitrariness led to the possibility for change, not to meaninglessness. Postmodernism, however, occurs when all culture becomes a consumer item, or a commodity: there is no meaning beyond the surface of the object itself.

In this chapter we've seen very different representations of the period and theoretical perspective known as the postmodern. For simplicity's sake, we can call these the "positive" and "negative" views (recognizing, of course, that the actual theories are more complex than this). In the "positive" camp, the postmodern move away from "origins" and metanarratives means that other stories and other voices that may have been silenced in the past now have the potential opportunity to speak with as much authority as previously dominant voices; the hierarchical binaries, in Derrida's terms, have been overthrown for a system of difference. In the "negative" camp, we see not only the potential chaos of a lack of centred truth but also a supremacy of the marketplace that makes the artificial and the simulated more important than reality. We become just commodities, our lives an effect of those simulations rather than something we conduct intentionally and with purpose. It's not the goal of this textbook to unify such theoretical disagreements, but it's important to remember that both "camps," so to speak, see the postmodern period as one that's defined by its fragmentation and its lack of a unified vision of what is real. Reality, for postmodernists, has become a "story," and often whoever is seen to have power is seen to be able to dictate what "reality" really is. This is why, for Baudrillard and Jameson especially but for other theorists of the postmodern as well, science fiction becomes so important—it is, after all, a genre of fiction that explicitly presents flights of fantasy (faster-than-light travel, for instance) as if they were "real." For Baudrillard and others, we are living in a science fiction world. In the case study that follows, we discuss how one such science fiction work is itself an attempt to explain postmodern theory.

Case Study

The Matrix

In their film *The Matrix* (1999), the Wachowski siblings were relying on a long tradition in science fiction texts, especially those that come from the so-called subgenre of cyberpunk, made famous by Canadian author William Gibson. These works often deal with notions of virtual reality, the relationship between media and identity, and many of the issues discussed in this chapter. Likewise, in *The Matrix* and its two sequels, the Wachowskis explicitly explore the themes of postmodern theory and its social ramifications. The first film follows a relatively simple plot: the world as we know it is actually a computer simulation, designed to keep the human population docile so that computers can run the real world. In other words, everything we perceive as "real" is in fact a simulation that covers over the reality of humanity's exploitation. The goal of the hero, Neo, in the first movie seems to be to destroy the computers so that people can "wake up" and recognize reality.

But, in fact, he doesn't do this: at the end of the first movie, the computer simulation is still running, and Neo flies away. In the sequels, it becomes clear that Neo is himself a function of the computer systems, one that forces them to change and adapt so as not to become obsolete.

Why would the films present such an ambiguous storyline? The answer may lie in the theoretical underpinnings of the trilogy. In an early scene in the first film, Neo (then in his "everyday" identity as Thomas Anderson) picks up a copy of Baudrillard's *Simulacra and Simulation* from his bookshelf. Opening it, he reveals a book that has had its inside carved out and replaced with a selection of illegal software and other material that Neo wants to hide, presumably from

the police and thieves. This not-so-subtle joke, in which Baudrillard's book itself becomes a simulation—one that covers the "reality" (more on that later) that is Neo's illegal activity—points to the ways in which the film purposively plays with the very postmodern theories we've learned about in this chapter. Likewise, when Morpheus, the leader of a resistance group, starts to train Neo in how to exploit the software of the Matrix in order to fight against the computers' agents, he takes Neo to a blank, all-white room, with an old chair and a television in it. On the television, Morpheus shows Neo the "actual" world: a post-apocalyptic landscape with no life in it. Quoting Baudrillard, Morpheus refers to this as "the desert of the real."

The film, then, serves as an extended allegory for the ways in which our lives are constantly and fully mediated by technology, by computers, television, and other simulations of the "real," to the point that we can no longer access the real: Neo and Morpheus only "see" the "desert of the real" on a simulated television inside yet another computer simulation. And, in keeping with this theory, the Matrix isn't destroyed at the end of the last film, but merely changed: we can no longer escape our postmodern world, and even the "hero" is just another function to keep us locked in the system.

The *Matrix* films thus seem to follow what we called the "negative" view of postmodernism, which holds that our lives have been rendered permanently hollow and superficial by the marketplace, that we, like Neo, are no more than "copper-top" batteries that keep the system of simulated life running.

But the ending of the first film also points to the more "positive" aspects of postmodernism.

When Neo has (temporarily) defeated Agent Smith, the Matrix's lead "enforcer," Neo calls the Matrix directly, and says to it, "You're afraid of change. I don't know the future. I didn't come here to tell you how this is going to end. I came here to tell you how it's going to begin. I'm going to hang up this phone, and then I'm going to show these people what you don't want them to see. I'm going to show them a world without you. A world without rules and controls, without borders or boundaries, a world where anything is possible. Where we go from there is a choice I leave to you." He then flies away, showing that he leaves the Matrix functioning. Rather than simply end the simulation, Neo wants to find a way in which more people, more voices, can make use of it—to create a world "without borders or boundaries," a postmodern world that denies the limits set on it by earlier metanarratives of control. The *Matrix* films, as allegory, show us the two-sided coin of postmodernism, both its promises and its potential failings.

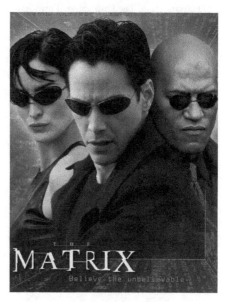

An ad for *The Matrix,* featuring the three main characters surrounded by the computer code of their simulated world.

Source: ROADSHOW FILM LIMITED/Album/Newscom

Discussion Questions

1. Social media, including Facebook and Twitter, are often said to be a way to connect with people. Can you think of ways in which they actually serve to distance people from communication with each other? Do they *mediate* our relationships in such a way as to fundamentally alter them?

2. Baudrillard argues that our perceptions of the real world are always mediated by simulations of that world, so that people's visions of "America" are informed more by media about "America" than by the real thing (which, he says, we can no longer even access). Are there "simulations" of Canada that shape how we view it?

Further Reading

Anderson, Perry. *The Origins of Postmodernity.* London: Verso, 1998.

Haslam, Jason. "Coded Discourse: Romancing the (Electronic) Shadow in *The Matrix.*" *College Literature* 32.3 (2005): 92–115.

Hassan, Ihab. *The Postmodern Turn: Essays in Postmodern Theory and Culture.* Columbus: Ohio State UP, 1987.

Huyssen, Andreas. *After the Great Divide: Modernism, Mass Culture, Postmodernism.* Bloomington: Indiana UP, 1986.

Rosenau, Pauline Marie. *Post-Modernism and the Social Sciences: Insights, Inroads, and Intrusion.* Princeton: Princeton UP, 1991.

Taylor, Victor E., and Charles E. Winquist, eds. *Encyclopedia of Postmodernism.* London: Routledge, 2001.

Part IV
Cultural Theories: Identities

Chapter 10
Feminism and Gender Studies

INTRODUCTION

Foundational approaches to the theoretical study of popular culture feature two recurring themes: 1) that there are ways in which culture can help to construct identity (following an anti-essentialist logic); and 2) that in any given society there are certain social institutions and structures that inform who holds power. Joining these themes together, we can see that constructions of identity and social power are intertwined. Popular culture can reflect, reinforce, and sometimes challenge the ways power functions in a society, in part by hiding or making visible, reinforcing or questioning those ideologies that define certain social structures, and certain notions of human identity, as being "natural" or "normal."

Part IV of this book is dedicated to exploring the ways in which categories of identity are informed, constructed, and defined by popular culture, and in turn how different groups can manipulate popular culture in attempts to reinforce or even alter their social power. We've already discussed some of these issues in relation to economic **class** in Chapters 3 and 6, but in Part IV we'll discuss other identity categories, specifically gender, race, sexuality, and nationality.

These categories are often cited in discussions of social power and the political movements related to the differentials of that power. Cultural studies theories and critics have used their analyses to engage with those political movements, as we saw in our discussions of Marxism, class struggle, and related forms of popular culture analysis. So Part IV will discuss popular culture in relation to the mechanisms of power affecting the identity categories listed above. It will also point to the ways in which cultural analysis has engaged in political debates and actions regarding the social distribution of power.

Although for ease of critical summary and discussion we address these categories of identity separately, of course that's not how they work—or how we experience them—in our daily lives. Gender and race inform and impact each other, as do sexuality and nationality, as do any combination of these. Many of the theorists discussed in these chapters explicitly deal with such interrelations of identity; you could, then, read sections of these chapters in combination rather than separately.

This chapter analyzes the ways in which gender is culturally constructed, and the roles that popular culture plays in that process. We also examine the theories and methodologies of popular cultural study, and the ways they have been influenced by, and in turn help to inform, the disparate political movements now known by the general term *feminism*.

SEX VS. GENDER

Before we discuss the various forms of feminist theory and political action, one distinction might be useful to keep in mind. While there are clear differences in approach between feminist theorists from, say, the 1970s and those from the 1990s or 2000s, there are many continuities as well. Important for many contemporary feminist theories, for example, is the distinction between sex and gender. This distinction is often seen as being introduced to feminist thought by Simone de Beauvoir (1908–1986) in *The Second Sex* (1949), in which she writes that "One is not born, but rather becomes, a woman" (de Beauvoir, 2011, p. 283). The basic distinction is one between biology and social behaviour: **sex** is often used to refer to a person's biological sexual makeup, while **gender** is used to refer to social expectations and codes of conduct, ranging from what clothing one wears to, in many cases, what jobs one can hold.

This key distinction informs much of the discussion in this chapter, and looks back to our distinction between **essentialist** and **anti-essentialist**, or social constructivist, theories of identity. Traditional, often patriarchal, social structures and practices would claim that there is a correlation between one's biological sex and one's social gender: someone born female would "naturally" act feminine, while someone born male would act in a masculine manner. Contemporary gender theory and feminism trouble the ease of this correlation, however, pointing out that what are considered to be "natural" gender behaviours and practices change over time and between societies and cultures, and that such gender expectations often serve to reinforce sexist social structures. The theorists discussed below all take as their ground the idea that gendered behaviour is in fact a mutable social construction and not a natural, biological, essential fact. The political and theoretical challenges offered by this division are in turn important for the recognition that human gender identity is multiple, and not constrained by the binary of "male/masculine" and "female/feminine," as we will see in our concluding discussion of female masculinity, and as evidenced by transgender and intersex identities.

This foundational claim regarding the divisions and multiple relations of sex and gender, based on much of the theories of identity discussed in earlier chapters, has profound implications for anti-essentialist arguments about other identity formations that have been or are often still associated with biological essences, such as those of sexuality and race, as we will discuss in subsequent chapters.

The complicated divisions and interconnections of sex and gender thus focus attention on the ways in which gendered behaviour, and by extension gendered identity, are socially constructed, in part by representations in popular culture of gendered bodies and behaviours. These representations serve not only to reflect dominant beliefs and expectations about gender but also to reinforce (and challenge) those beliefs.

FEMINISM: WAVES OF HISTORY

As with the subjects of the other chapters in Part IV, the term *feminism* is used to identify both certain theoretical positions that inform cultural criticism and specific political activities, in this case those oriented toward improving the social condition and political recognition of women. As with our discussion of Marxism, it is, to say the least, difficult to separate theory from practice. Before discussing contemporary feminist cultural theories, therefore, it's important to briefly address the history of feminist struggles that inform and are in turn informed by those theories.

In the history of Western democracies, women have been legally considered fully participating citizens, as holding full rights and responsibilities as sovereign individuals, for a relatively short period of time. However, while those rights have been legally recognized in much of the world, it is also true that even where their rights are so recognized, women still fight for equal treatment under the law and in society more generally. Facts concerning Canadian women's unequal pay and unequal representation in government and business, along with statistics concerning relative rates of domestic abuse against women and violent crime more generally, are all too easily found. The status of women in Canadian and many other societies and public life has changed over the past few centuries, but the struggle for full equality continues, as it does in many parts of the world.

As with our discussion of essentialist cultural theories in Chapter 2, the history of feminism sketched below is decidedly **Eurocentric** in its focus. Non-Western feminisms have varied histories that both connect to and radically vary from the history offered here. As with those earlier cultural theories, however, some knowledge of this history is important in the study of popular culture, especially in North America, in whose popular culture the history of Euro-American feminisms plays a significant part. However, because of the incompleteness of this history, many of the theorists we examine in the latter part of this chapter focus on critiquing this Eurocentric approach to feminism. A quick sketch of this history therefore seems in order, even as we must recognize its partial nature. The changing social position and roles of women are reflected in the history of feminist political action and thought. While we can identify these Eurocentric and other problems with the following generalized summary, many studies of feminism divide this history into three periods, also known as the **three waves of feminism**.

First Wave: Personhood and the Vote

The first wave of feminism was the period when women were fighting to be fully enfranchised—that is, to be recognized as citizens who have the right to vote. While many Canadians now take for granted the notion that each individual over the age of eighteen has the right to vote, that situation (known as the universal franchise) has existed in this country only since the latter half of the twentieth century, with other Western democracies having similar timelines. In Canada, the last group of adults to achieve the vote were those First Nations members identified in the Indian Act as "Status Indians," who were finally given the unfettered right to vote in 1960 (see www.ournellie. com, a site dedicated to Canadian suffragette Nellie McClung, for an excellent timeline of women's rights and the status of groups' right to vote). The United States has a similar history, with women being granted the right to vote in 1920 and earlier laws recognizing the rights of African Americans to vote being more fully enforced and recognized in the

1965 Voting Rights Act (although there are still cases in which the right of certain groups to vote is infringed or violated, and aspects of the Act were struck down by the U.S. Supreme Court in 2013). Unlike in Canada, in certain American states people who have been convicted of crimes are rendered ineligible to vote, either for a certain period of time or for life.

Voting is both a right and responsibility that adheres only to those people who are considered citizens of the nation: that is, those who constitute the body politic of a democracy. This recognition, in turn, is tied to **Enlightenment** notions of the rational, self-regulated, and sovereign **individual**.

In the histories of many peoples and democracies, however, women, along with other socially subordinated groups, were not so recognized. Women were seen as fundamentally irrational, as being controlled by their emotions and their bodies and thus incapable of taking part in the rational control of society. As feminist theorist Sidonie Smith has forcefully argued, in the history of definitions of subjectivity, patriarchal philosophers, scientists, and culture producers have "locate[d] man's selfhood somewhere between the ears," whereas a woman's identity is positioned "between her thighs" (Smith, 1993, p. 12). Tied to this sexist philosophy were legal restrictions: until well into the twentieth century, women were legally subordinate to their husbands, fathers, and even brothers and adult male children; the right of women to hold their own property was restricted, as were their forms of employment and remuneration.

Building on the Age of Enlightenment and its many democratic revolutions, several previously disenfranchised groups, including working-class men, various racial and ethnic groups, and women, began to fight for their right to vote. These campaigns were known as suffrage movements. Starting in the late eighteenth century and moving through the nineteenth and into the twentieth century, many women and some men began to fight for women's right to vote. Several women's suffrage organizations were formed, with the most active period (in, for example, England, Canada, and the United States) being in the early part of the twentieth century. While many of these groups tried to win the vote through peaceful and legal means, some of the most famous women's suffrage organizations and leaders—including the British organization the Women's Social and Political Union (WSPU) led by Emmeline Pankhurst—took more militant steps, among which were the interruption of Parliament and elections, the smashing of windows, other vandalism, and, when they were arrested and treated as common criminals, hunger strikes, which led to some of the more famous moments of the international campaigns. These more militant women's suffrage campaigners were called **suffragettes**, originally a derogatory term that was then appropriated by the women themselves. Of particular importance for our topic is the way in which the women's suffrage movement used popular culture and the media (in the form of **print culture** and performance) to further their goals (see the "Canadian Suffragettes" box and the accompanying image).

The women's suffrage movement achieved success at different times in different places: women in some nations are still denied the vote. In Canada, women over the age of twenty-one gained the federal vote in 1918 (some ten years earlier than their British counterparts).

Canadian Suffragettes and Popular Culture: Women's Parliament

The height of the women's suffrage movement in such nations as the United Kingdom, the United States, and Canada came in the opening decades of the twentieth century. Working both in tandem with each other and apart, women's groups in these nations fought to have their right to vote recognized on the same basis as that of men, while many also fought for the rights of women more generally.

In their struggles to gain the franchise, many of the suffrage groups engaged heavily in cultural production. Writing and publishing newspapers and journals, holding demonstrations and performances in theatres, writing autobiographies, novels, and other literary works, and ensuring that their marches and militant acts would be covered in the mainstream press were all acts regularly and effectively used.

In Canada, perhaps the best known popular cultural act engaged in by suffragettes was the Women's Parliament. Organized by writer and activist Nellie McClung (1873–1951), the Women's Parliament was a stage performance that capped an evening of singing and other theatre acts, held at Winnipeg's Walker Theatre on 28 January 1914. Having recently engaged in an argument with Manitoba's Conservative premier, Sir Rodmond Roblin, McClung staged a satirical vision of a Parliament run by women wherein she rejected the pleas of disenfranchised men who were petitioning for the vote, thereby inverting the arguments used against women.

Playing the part of the premier, McClung is reported to have said, in part, "We wish to compliment this delegation on their splendid gentlemanly appearance. If, without exercising the vote, such splendid specimens of manhood can be produced, such a system of affairs should not be interfered with....Another trouble is that if men start to vote they will vote too much. Politics unsettles men, and unsettled men mean unsettled bills—broken furniture, broken vows and divorce" (Cleverdon, 1974, p. 59). Also satirizing Roblin's dismissal of charges of corruption in his government,

McClung's performance, and the Women's Parliament as a whole, was thereafter staged in other theatres. In fact, it was so popular that it's often credited not only with converting many people to the suffragettes' cause but also with helping to topple Roblin's government and bringing in a new government more friendly to the women's cause, and thus hastening the achievement of the franchise.

This use of popular culture, and specifically satire, for propaganda purposes has long been a staple of political life, but the suffragettes' use of it was both politically adept and effective, and its influence can still, arguably, be seen in Canadian political satire today.

A Mock Parliament TO WIN THE VOTE FOR **WOMEN** Walker Theatre January 1914

Une parodie de parlement POUR LE VOTE DES **FEMMES** Théâtre Walker Janvier 1914

Reproduction of an ad for the Women's Parliament.
Source: Parks Canada

The history of the movement to recognize women's right to vote is not a linear one in Canada, however. Women with property in Quebec had the right to vote through much of the first half of the nineteenth century, but were denied that vote starting in 1849. At the moment of Confederation in 1867, women were explicitly denied the federal and provincial vote (as was everyone else except for male, natural-born British subjects over the age of twenty-one). The first bill to allow some propertied women the vote was introduced, but defeated, in 1883. The year 1916 was a significant one in Canadian women's history: it saw the enfranchisement of women in Manitoba, Saskatchewan, and Alberta, with other provinces following suit over the course of the next decade (see ournellie.com).

Second Wave: Equality, Representation, and Radicalism

Whereas *first-wave feminism* denotes women's fight for the right to vote, *second-wave feminism* refers to the struggle for social and legal equality with men on the one hand, and a radical sense of a feminist and women's identity—one completely separate from patriarchal and masculine visions of women—on the other. A **patriarchy** is a social system in which men are given, by virtue of being men, more social privilege and power than women; it refers to those social systems that legally demarcate more power for men or that do so through social convention and tradition, or both. Rights-based second-wave feminist political action focused on issues of equality in the workplace (women's access to certain careers, advancement within their chosen careers, and equal pay with men), equality in treatment under the law, and violence against women (such as sexual violence and domestic abuse). Radical feminist action shared some of these goals, but also argued that patriarchal structures pervade society and culture to such a degree that the only way to end sexism was to bring about an entirely new social order.

Giving precise dates for second-wave feminism is impossible, since many of these struggles continue and some of the philosophical claims of second-wave feminism are still current among many feminists. That said, the height of second-wave feminism in North America is usually dated as occurring between the 1960s and the 1980s.

Much of the cultural work of second-wave feminists was intended to critique the ways in which a variety of cultural forms—including those of popular culture—reflected and reinforced the **ideological** and material dominance of men. The structures of male dominance in a society, generally referred to as the *patriarchy* or *patriarchal forces*, were shown to be prevalent throughout culture—as seen in everything from film to literature, to fashion and art, to the ways in which those subjects were taught in schools and universities, and to the whole range of society—as a **hegemonic** force. Much of the cultural criticism and theoretical models that arise out of second-wave feminism, as we will see below, are geared to exposing the patriarchal bias in and structures of social and cultural institutions and objects. These works also often focus on the representation of women within culture, and the ways in which such representations can reinforce patriarchal beliefs, especially through the **objectification** of women and women's bodies.

Second-Wave Feminism and the University

As part of their critique of patriarchal knowledge systems, which were seen to limit the possibilities for women's very state of being, second-wave feminists worked toward creating new and positive social roles and cultural representations of women as well as new forms of knowledge production and critical thought. Part of this work has helped shape the teaching of culture and cultural studies, both in universities and in public schools; in various disciplines, courses were created that focused on women and women's cultural work (such as women's literature, women's roles in business, and feminist theory, to name a few). In addition, universities formed women's studies departments that offered (and still offer) interdisciplinary approaches to academic study, especially but not solely within the humanities and social sciences. This educational work was also tied to increasing the presence of women—as students, professors, and administrators—within the university system itself. In many ways, then, second-wave feminism is responsible for much of the opening up of academic study that led to cultural studies and the study of popular culture.

However, it's important to recognize that such departments often face problems from both within and outside their universities, with people questioning the necessity for their existence (as any quick internet search will show): this is one example of why it's necessary not to fall into the trap of seeing the "waves" history as a linear and consistently progressive one.

Women's liberation march in Washington, D.C., 1970. (Note the prominent George Washington University banner, stating an alliance of "Students Employees Faculty Wives Neighbors.")
Source: Library of Congress Prints and Photographs Division Washington

Writing, Patriarchy, Resistance, and Popular Literature

Among the central feminist theoretical and critical concepts to arise in the 1970s were the related ideas of phallogocentrism and écriture féminine, developed by Jacques Derrida and Hélène Cixous, respectively. **Phallogocentrism** is the combination of two terms: *logocentrism* and *phallocentrism*. *Logocentrism* describes a system of thought or belief in which a particular form of rational, linearly structured, binary thinking is seen as the only proper way to view the world, and that this vision is encoded in language itself (such as in English, with its many concepts structured around binary oppositions, such as black/white, right/wrong, and so on). *Phallocentrism* refers to a social system that is structured primarily to benefit men (symbolically represented by the phallus). So, a patriarchal society is necessarily phallocentric.

Combining these two concepts, Derrida defines *phallogocentrism* as a patriarchal ideology that positions men on the positive side of a hierarchical binary, a binary that is encoded into language. A simple example of this is the way in which the singular, third-person pronoun used in English to refer to people is generally divided by gender into *he* and *she* (with *it* generally not referring to people). Furthermore, until recently (and still in some publications), *he* was taken to be a "universal" pronoun that could refer to any person in general. Thus, we have a gendered binary in language (*he/she*) that is hierarchical (*he* is the norm): a phallogocentric structure.

The culture of France (where Derrida was writing), and of the larger Global North could certainly be read as phallogocentric, where the very language people used encoded patriarchal ideas. How does one fight a political system that exists at the very level of language (and therefore thought)?

To answer this question, Hélène Cixous developed the radical theory and practice of **écriture feminine**. More than simply "women's writing," Cixous envisioned écriture feminine as a new form of language use altogether, through which a feminist-centric world view could be expressed. This practice would aim to undermine the binary and linear forms of logocentrism, which is intimately tied to patriarchal thinking, as described above. Cixous writes, "Woman must write her self: must write about women and bring women to writing, from which they have been driven away as violently as from their bodies.... Woman must put herself into the text—as into the world and into history—by her own movement" (Cixous, 1976, p. 875). Cixous argues that this feminist agency, connected to women's physical, emotional, and intellectual experience of the world, would inevitably lead to a radically new form of writing and new forms of being in the world—even to new forms of love. She contends that a form of "Other love" (both love for the "other" and a different, or other, form of love) could thus be created: "Other love.—In the beginning are our differences. The new love dares for the other, wants the other, makes dizzying, precipitous flights between knowledge and invention. The woman arriving over and over again does not stand still; she's everywhere, she exchanges, she is the desire-that-gives" (p. 893). Cixous's own writing style here mimics that which she envisions for écriture feminine: non-linear, focused on women, and accepting of multiple visions of truth that aren't limited to the "right/wrong" binaries of phallogocentrism.

While this theory challenges certain second-wave feminist assumptions (insofar as it challenges binary oppositions) and opens up feminist thought to the notion of radical difference that we'll explore in the "third-wave" section below, the notion of écriture feminine can also help explore the role of a particular woman-centric feminism in popular culture. The question we need to raise is, Can such a practice be possible in popular culture?

Laura Mulvey, whose work we discuss below, argued that popular cinema denies women's agency, but that new forms of cinema can be created that do not do so. Many popular women authors also took up this challenge. Two examples come from the popular form of science fiction: Margaret Atwood's *Handmaid's Tale* (1985) and Suzette Haden Elgin's *Native Tongue* (1984). Both works present a dystopian future in which contemporary patriarchal structures are expanded to the point that women become the equivalent of slaves and servants. Both texts also show women subverting the logics of their societies in order to gain some power.

Elgin's novel is most interesting on this point, because in it women create their own language, one that exists outside of the rigid, logical, binary form used by the patriarchy (in the novel, linguists basically run the world...another dystopian vision, perhaps). With this language, the women form a separate political community and resistance movement and eventually break largely free of men's control. Moreover, Elgin herself developed the language, known as Láadan, and published a dictionary and grammar for it (much as, on the other side of the spectrum, *Star Trek* fans developed Klingon into a full language). Elgin also, in non-fiction works, stresses the role that language can play in reducing violence.

On Láadan, see www.laadanlanguage.org.

One form of second-wave feminism is often self-identified as radical feminism. Radical feminism asserts, both theoretically and politically, that patriarchal social structures frame knowledge—and even language itself—in terms of a hierarchical divide between men and women, and argues that any true feminist politics must therefore critique or move beyond traditional philosophical and social forms of knowing. In other words, just as anti-racist and postcolonial activists and theorists (see Chapter 13) argue that the structures of Global North societies deny the experiences, knowledge, perspectives, and human rights of colonized peoples and people of colour, so too do second-wave (and other) feminists argue that the structures of any patriarchal society deny the experiences, knowledge, perspectives, and human rights of women. Thus, not only do patriarchal social and political institutions deny women's participation, such thinkers argue, but patriarchal epistemologies also deny the validity of women's thought.

Third Wave: Women, Difference, and Gender

Despite the clear social gains made by second-wave feminists and the continued usefulness of some of their theoretical and analytical models (particularly for the study of patriarchal images in popular culture), many feminists, especially from the early 1990s forward, began to critique some of its practices and assumptions. Specifically, some second-wave feminist theories and practices were critiqued for offering a supposedly universal voice for women, a voice that in fact arose from the limited position of white middle- and upper-class heterosexual women. Note how, for example, Cixous uses the singular form *woman* as an all-encompassing term for all women, no matter how different. Such an ideological universalizing of a dominant class of women was seen to either ignore or silence other women (among them women of colour, working and poor women, lesbians, and transgendered women). Likewise, the emphasis on the patriarchal objectification of women, especially in the form of pornography, was seen by some to take a too general approach to the topic of sex, and to deny the sexual identities and pleasures of women that could exist in opposition to, or outside of, patriarchal objectification. Finally, it was argued that the sole focus on patriarchy ignored, if only through omission, other forms of social and cultural violence, such as class oppression and racism.

This bias toward a dominant subset of women was therefore perceived by some, as we discuss below, to replicate or reinforce patriarchal power by participating in the larger hegemonic structures of the ruling classes. Thus, feminist activism and practices took on less universalizing roles, focusing on the particular needs of specific groups of women, often in conjunction with anti-racist, queer, or other activists in attempts to transform social practice. The theories associated with this plural form of feminisms are often referred to by the collective term *third-wave feminism*, though such a generalization does, in some ways, work against the aims of these disparate practices. Indeed, feminist theorists interested in difference between and among women have also questioned the Eurocentric vision of feminism set out in the history of feminism offered above, and assert the strengths in looking to feminist activisms and theories in non-Western cultures, outside the "waves" history.

Feminism, Religion, Culture: The Quebec Charter of Values and #lifeofamuslimfeminist

So-called "third-wave" feminist arguments and activisms are intersectional in focus, looking for the ways in which feminist activism and theory can support and be supported by anti-racist, queer, immigrant, and other political voices. Such an approach necessarily involves a questioning of one's own position, and an attempt to recognize when the political aims and goals of one group might negatively or positively affect those of another. We can see one example of such a discussion taking place in relation to choices of traditional dress by some Muslim women, the attempt to ban such dress under the guise of feminism, and the responses to that attempt—in the last category, the social-media platform Twitter was the site of a few prolonged, global discussions of feminism, religion, cultural practice, and their intersections.

In September 2013 the Quebec government proposed a bill that was commonly referred to in English as the Charter of Values (a bill that subsequently died with the Parti Québécois government's electoral defeat). This bill proposed to change the Quebec Charter of Human Rights and Freedoms by banning the display of some religious icons and images by government and public employees. Part of the stated reason for this move was to "promote equality between women and men." As such, certain religiously or culturally prescribed forms of dress, such as the niqab and hijab, worn by some Muslim women, would be banned.

Critics of the Charter noted that Christian symbols, such as the cross in the provincial legislature, would still be allowed, which pointed to the legislation's biased approach. Moreover, others argued that proscribing some women's dress—by not allowing them a choice as to what to wear—could be seen as working against a feminist argument for equality.

As debates over the Charter continued a Twitter conversation began, not in response to the Charter but nonetheless picking up on the issues of feminism and bias surrounding it, even as the conversation highlighted some of the ways in which women's experiences, and therefore forms of feminism, differ. Started by Noorulann Shahid in January 2014, #lifeofamuslimfeminist soon went viral. As Shahid wrote in a subsequent article, she was "attempting to explain . . . the difficulties I'd faced as someone who identifies as both Muslim and Feminist." Seeing Islam as "an inherently feminist religion," she still wished to talk about the need to fight "patriarchy and misogyny within both the Muslim community and society as a whole." But non-Muslim feminists insisted that her choice to wear the hijab was inherently misogynist. She writes that "I had Muslims telling me I did not need feminism and mainstream feminists wanting to 'liberate me,'" meaning that she was unable to find a place within what she calls "mainstream feminism."

The hashtag, however, became a site for other Muslim feminists to engage and discuss these and other issues. It also became a space to openly challenge patriarchy of various forms and the biases of that "mainstream" feminism. Intersectionalities of feminist action and religious belief, as well as codes of behaviour and personal choice, were introduced into this wide-ranging and multi-voiced public discussion. Part of the discussion, then, demonstrated the simple fact that, in Shahid's words, Muslim women "are women with a variety of interests—from football to pop music to politics to science" and shouldn't be represented just by "the way that we choose to dress." This public, popular forum thus became a means to complicate and reject what many saw as the overly simplistic focus of political gestures like the Quebec Charter, opening up new forms of political and feminist solidarity that recognized the differences between and multiplicity of women, and therefore the multiplicity of forms of feminist action.

Shahid, Noorulann. "Why I Created the #LifeOfAMuslimFeminist Hashtag." Huffpost Students. *Huffington Post United Kingdom.* huffingtonpost.co.uk. 06 February 2014. Web. 18 February. 2014.

In other words, whereas second-wave feminism emphasized the critique of the hierarchical binary that positioned "man" as having power over "woman" in various ways in society, such that male/female was the equivalent of active/passive, mind/body, and other binary formulations we will discuss below, third-wave feminism focuses on the ways in which power operates across the social field: different men would be positioned in different ways, as would women, and in relation to each other. That isn't to say that third-wave feminists have abandoned the notion that society functions in patriarchal terms; their critiques of the patriarchy are, however, expanded and added to analyses of racial, class, sexual, and other differences. In terms of academic study and political practice, this move is echoed by one that saw some women's studies departments and programs transition to gender studies programs, which include the analyses of various gender identities and structures.

FEMINIST THEORIES AND POPULAR CULTURE

The foregoing history of feminism's "waves" is intended to briefly trace the goals and aims of the different forms of European and North American feminist activism. It's clear, however, that each of these "waves" of history is tied to a particular set of critical and theoretical understandings of society, culture, and women's roles therein, and that these understandings and contexts overlap in complex ways. While this manner of approaching the history of feminism seems to describe a linear and progressive history, all of these forms intersect and are complicated by each other to a certain degree (especially for the so-called second and third waves).

For the purposes of studying popular culture, the critical theories associated with second- and third-wave feminisms are especially significant. Below, we trace out some of the central themes of and arguments relating to these theories, especially as they apply to the analysis of popular culture forms and practices. While there are some important theorists from the first wave of feminism, or who bridge the first and second waves (Simone de Beauvoir especially comes to mind), we'll focus on the more contemporary theories, which are more widely used in popular culture studies. Again, it's important to recognize that the division between these "waves" isn't clear cut, and that the connection between a theory and a particular "wave" is likewise sometimes more complex than an introductory text can explore.

Representing Women

A significant aspect of second-wave feminism was its emphasis on the importance of the cultural representation of women. Following the general outlines of arguments made by earlier cultural critics, many feminist analysts argued that women's social disempowerment is furthered by popular representations of women as passive objects who existed primarily for the pleasure and use of men.

Film and the Male Gaze   One of the most influential cultural critiques of the representation of women was the essay "Visual Pleasure and Narrative Cinema," by film theorist Laura Mulvey (1941–). Building on psychoanalytic theory, Mulvey argues that film is composed centrally around the gaze—that is, around how the viewer looks at the film and how the film itself presents the gaze through the perspective of particular characters and through the camera lens. Mulvey traces out specific types of gazes and discusses the ways they relate to dominant gender paradigms. For Mulvey, film helps to position the viewer, and therefore helps to reproduce ideological subject positions for the viewer. The general audience, meanwhile, comes to expect and demand certain forms of film that play into the reproduction of these positions, following much the same argument about the creation of the subject that Louis Althusser offers (see Chapter 6).

Relying on psychoanalytic theory, Mulvey sees these ideological constructions as playing themselves out in unconscious structures, specifically in the formation of the **ego** and the **ideal ego** (see Chapter 4) and their relationship to exterior objects. Transforming this into a gendered argument, Mulvey contends that patriarchal culture offers models of behaviour that help to reproduce particular, unconscious ideals for both men and women. What we see in Mulvey's essay is a psychoanalytic rendering of second-wave feminist arguments: woman is, within a patriarchal system, always already constructed as the absolute other against which man defines himself. Within this system, then, women are constructed as silent and passive—as incapable of making their own meaning. In other words, women are constructed as lacking **agency**. "Woman then stands in patriarchal culture," Mulvey writes, "as bearer, not maker, of meaning" (Mulvey, 2009, p. 15).

Why is this the case? Mulvey argues that, because the category "woman" is constructed as the absolute other of "man," the concept of "woman," and therefore specific, actual women, can become a threat to the patriarchal order. She begins by pointing out that, in psychoanalytic theory, the male child's mother comes to symbolize castration and the fear of it, because the mother does not have a penis. Meanwhile, Mulvey also draws on the theory of penis envy, discussing how, in this construct, the mother desires a phallus—or the agency that the penis represents within a patriarchal **symbolic order**. In other words, we can read the notions of castration fear and penis envy as metaphors that gain meaning within the specific—in this case patriarchal—matrix from which they arise. If men are powerful and women aren't, then the patriarchal logic would say that women must want to take men's power from them.

In order for the patriarchy to reinforce itself, this threat that women embody must be silenced. There are two central ways in which patriarchal culture does this, and both, Mulvey argues, can be defined as acts of looking, specifically as gazing at something for pleasure. First, the act of men looking for sexual pleasure at images of women reduces the threat that women embody: "The argument must return again to the psychoanalytic background: women in representation can signify castration, and activate voyeuristic or fetishistic mechanisms to circumvent this threat" (pp. 25–26). Mulvey, relying on Freud, uses the term **scopophilia** to refer to the voyeuristic "pleasure in looking at another person as an erotic object" (p. 25). The second form of pleasure she discusses is related to the ideal ego: men can watch the film and identify with the ideal ego presented by the hero, who overcomes the female threat and/or retains the woman's passivity. The hero in popular film, Mulvey states, often "has all the attributes of the patriarchal superego" (p. 25). These two main processes are, of course, tied to the various stereotypes of women in popular film and popular culture more generally, which basically fall into the threatening/nonthreatening categories—the innocent virgin or the threatening whore.

Both of these identification processes, for Mulvey, are enabled by the ways in which film presents itself as "real" by erasing any visible signs of the filming process, making the actual hardware and work behind the film invisible—very much as ideology makes itself invisible as such. She writes,

> There are three different looks associated with cinema: that of the camera as it records the pro-filmic event, that of the audience as it watches the final product, and that of the characters at each other within the screen illusion. The conventions of narrative film deny the first two and subordinate them to the third, the conscious aim being always to eliminate intrusive camera presence and prevent a distancing awareness in the audience. (p. 26)

Mulvey and Hitchcock

While Laura Mulvey's theories are generally used to expose the patriarchal functions of the gaze in cinema, there are ways of using her analyses to highlight how traditional filmic representations of women and men can cut through the supposed realism of the film itself. Using an example from Alfred Hitchcock's famous and often cited 1958 film *Vertigo*, Mulvey argues that identification with the male hero can disrupt the safety of the (male) audience's gaze. The hero has "all the attributes of the patriarchal superego," and so "the spectator, lulled into a false sense of security by the apparent legality of his surrogate, sees through his look and finds himself exposed as complicit, caught in the moral ambiguity of looking" (p. 25). But Hitchcock's film can recognize the dynamics of the gaze that Mulvey discusses, and so it undermines the patriarchal power of the gaze by calling attention to it. Something similar happens in Hitchcock's *Psycho*

(1960) when the camera makes the audience see through the eyes of Norman Bates, a serial killer, as he peeps on a woman he is about to murder. The erotic gaze of scopophilia is potentially exposed to the audience as a violently patriarchal one.

Mulvey expands on Hitchcock's representation of voyeurism, and the way it can work against misogynistic ideologies, in a 2010 lecture for the British Film Institute on Hitchcock's "blondes": she contends that Hitchcock represents an ambiguity about these women's "subordination" to men within the "happy ending." Hitchcock actually uses these figures to point out the "artificiality" of "cinema itself" in a way that can disrupt the audience's relationship to the events shown on the screen—a disruption that, Mulvey argues in her more famous essay, must be made. See "Laura Mulvey on the Blonde" (*BFI Live*. British Film Institute. Bfi.org.uk).

Film presents itself as real, as believable, striving not to "distance" the audience from the experiences on the screen; the audience should not, when watching a traditional narrative film, be reminded that what they are watching is an artifice. This dynamic permits the reproduction of patriarchal ideology through the two types of pleasure we discussed above. By identifying with the hero, by taking pleasure in participating in the erotic gaze that presents women as sexual objects, and by seeing these as "real" relations, the audience of a popular film is aiding in the reproduction of patriarchal subject positions.

In general, the pleasure that an audience takes in identifying with the seemingly realistic portrayals on the screen leads to the reproduction of sexist identity models that position men as being in control of the gaze, as active and as "creator[s] of meaning," and women's bodies as the passive object of the gaze, and therefore only the "bearer[s]" of patriarchal meaning.

Mulvey ends her essay by calling for a new kind of film that would disrupt the pleasure and power of the gaze. She argues that creating films that disrupt the audience's ability to identify with the characters on screen, and that highlight the artificiality of film's images, would help to show people that these supposedly "real" and "natural" representations of active men and passive women are merely patriarchal fictions that can be disrupted not only on screen but also in material life.

The Body and Representation   If for Mulvey the representation of women's bodies as objects of visual pleasure leads to a psychological reinforcement of the patriarchy, for other feminist theorists the representation of particular forms of women's bodies plays an equally problematic role. Susan Bordo (1947–) discusses the ways in which patriarchal gender ideals can affect women's self-perception and their relation to their own bodies. Like Mulvey, however, although perhaps more controversially, she demonstrates how, within this patriarchal construction of women's bodies, some women's own extreme extensions of these body images can actually be read as a form of unconscious critique of patriarchal expectations, a critique that highlights the biases of **normative** gender constructs.

Mulvey's assertion that popular film is ideological and serves to further entrench the patriarchy may not seem like that much of a radical argument today, at least not as much as it did in the mid-1970s, when it was published. The idea that popular culture is a medium with political implications is fairly well accepted, as we have seen. But Bordo takes this debate in another direction, and analyzes the ways our very bodies are also sites of political contestation and debate. Her argument goes beyond analyzing the portrayal of body image in the media; instead she argues that we must understand our very bodies within this larger cultural and political context: "The body—what we eat, how we dress, the daily rituals through which we attend to the body—is a medium of culture. The body . . . is a powerful symbolic form, a surface on which the central rules, hierarchies, and even metaphysical commitments of a culture are inscribed. . . . The body is not only a *text* of culture. It is also . . . a *practical*, direct locus of social control" (Bordo, 2005, p. 165). So, as with film and other cultural media, bodies, our physical beings, are spaces on which interpretations are placed and contested—and, as we know from all the theories we've been studying, these interpretations are themselves determined in part by our political, social surroundings rather than the other way around.

Bordo, writing more from a third-wave perspective, argues that all bodies, male or female, can be read in this way: all identity categories (gender, race, class, and so on) rely on bodies being read and constructed in particular ways. But her focus is on gender, and specifically on the ways in which the "normative" feminine body is constructed:

> Through the pursuit of an ever-changing, homogenizing, elusive ideal of femininity— a pursuit without terminus, requiring that women constantly attend to minute and often whimsical changes in fashion—female bodies become docile bodies—bodies whose forces and energies are habituated to external regulation, subjection, transformation, "improvement" . . . At the farthest extremes, the practices of femininity may lead us to utter demoralization, debilitation, and death. (p. 166)

In other words, bodies are regulated by the types of narratives surrounding them. These narratives are what subject us to having certain types of value judgments attached to our bodies, and this judgment leads in turn to a construction of certain constraining definitions of ourselves.

But Bordo says that these definitions are not just constraining, but enabling. As with our earlier definition of *agency*, she argues that when we are constrained we are enabled—if we were completely self-contained individuals, we would have no framework within which to function or understand ourselves. Bordo, encapsulating a particular form of third-wave response to second-wave feminist politics, writes that, to develop a critical language capable of understanding the "pathways of modern social control," feminist theory must

> reconstruct... the feminist paradigm of the late 1960s and early 1970s, with its political categories of oppressor and oppressed, villains and victims.... Following Foucault, we must first abandon the idea of power as something possessed by one group and leveled against another; we must instead think of the network of practices, institutions, and technologies that sustain positions of dominance and subordination in a particular domain. Second, we need an analytics adequate to describe a power whose central mechanisms are not repressive, but *constitutive* ...; for example, of the mechanisms that shape and proliferate—rather than repress—desire, generate and focus our energies, construct our conceptions of normalcy and deviance. (p. 167)

As in our discussions of Foucault (see Chapters 8 and 11), Bordo argues that the social field is more complex than a simple binary opposition of men/women, power/subjugation would allow. She builds on this foundation to argue that certain psychological diagnoses and diseases, both historical and from the contemporary period, highlight the ways in which women's bodies are culturally inscribed. Such conditions as hysteria, agoraphobia, and anorexia can be seen as hyper-extensions of the very conditions that ideological notions of femininity place on women's bodies: "Working within this framework, we see that whether we look at hysteria, agoraphobia, or anorexia, we find the body of the sufferer deeply inscribed with an ideological construction of femininity emblematic of the period in question" (p. 168). Thus, "[t]he bodies of disordered women in this way offer themselves as an aggressively graphic text for the interpreter—a text that insists, actually demands, that it be read as a cultural statement, a statement about gender" (p. 169).

To specify this general argument, we can say that women are told that they must constrain their physical actions to the home and the domestic sphere. This is similar to the psychological disorder agoraphobia, wherein the woman will not leave the house. This condition can be read as an ultimate form of oppression by patriarchal interpellation: a woman internalizes the dictates that she must be the "domestic goddess" to the point that she cannot function in public at all. But for Bordo the argument doesn't stop there: this agoraphobic behaviour is "abnormal" behaviour—it takes the oppressive definitions of women to the extreme and, in so doing, it highlights the oppressive structures and disrupts them, showing them for what they are: "In agoraphobia and, even more dramatically, in anorexia, the disorder presents itself as a virtual, though tragic, parody of twentieth-century constructions of femininity" (p. 170).

Importantly, of course, one should not gloss over the suffering of the person in this form of cultural critique. Bordo isn't saying that these disorders constitute a viable form of social rebellion, but rather an unconscious one; she's also saying that these patterns

Lady Gaga, the Gaze, and the Body

As we've seen, certain forms of feminist cultural analysis focus on the representation of women and their bodies, especially the ways in which they are objectified to and by a patriarchal male gaze, one that often renders women solely into objects of sexual desire. Such representations are also analyzed in relation to the effects popular culture may have on women's views of and practices concerning their own bodies. Other cultural analyses focus on the ways particular works of or moments in popular culture participate in the larger cultural construction of normative gender identities. Still others look to popular cultural material that resists such gender formations, or that aids in the construction of alternative or resistant gender identities (we'll discuss this last form in relation to Judith Butler's discussion of drag in Chapter 11).

One example from contemporary popular music and media culture proves especially fruitful—and complicated—in relation to all these forms of cultural analysis: Lady Gaga, and specifically her music videos.

In many ways, Gaga's presentation in her music videos, like those of many women pop stars, repeats the presentation of the female body within the scopophilic gaze that Laura Mulvey discusses. In the video for "Telephone," for example, Gaga appears nearly nude in several scenes in a prison, consciously echoing the "women in prison" exploitation film genre. With the camera often focusing on specific body parts, Gaga seems to fulfill the objectified, passive role of "object of the gaze" that Mulvey critiques.

However, Mulvey's argument was itself critiqued for its denial of the possible pleasurable roles that the gaze and film might hold for women, with some later feminists arguing that there is a role for women-centric pleasures in popular culture. The video's visual and narrative references to Ridley Scott's 1991 film *Thelma and Louise* may indicate a generally feminist or anti-patriarchal narrative being put forward, while the references to

Quentin Tarantino's *Kill Bill, Vol. 1* (2003) may point to a more general sensationalizing of revenge and violence. Is it possible that Gaga's videos represent a woman in powerful control of her sexuality rather than as a passive object? Or is this possibility actually silenced in the video under a generally sensationalist and patriarchal gaze?

Those questions may be difficult to answer in any simplistic or final way, but the idea that Gaga's performance seems to do something more complicated than reproduce the sexual objectification of women is one that some critics hold. Canadian cultural critic Karen E. Macfarlane, for example, argues in part that Gaga presents herself as a monstrous figure, one that challenges heteronormative significations. With her body and her dancers' bodies choreographed to appear as "glamorized versions of the appearance of the monster in horror movies," Macfarlane argues, Gaga's "monstrous iconicity positions her own body as an unstable, indeterminate referent," one that can frustrate a simplistic patriarchal scopophilic gaze (Macfarlane, 2012, pp. 122, 123). Her explicit use of this "monstrous" body, even as she "glamorize[s]" it, echoes Bordo's discussion of women's resistant hyper-extension of patriarchal body expectations. This interruption of the domineering gaze can also be seen, Macfarlane continues, in the persistent rumours that Lady Gaga might have a penis, rumours that Gaga also calls attention to in the video for "Telephone," only to again frustrate an assertive camera gaze by blurring the region when it is on screen.

If Lady Gaga both fulfills and frustrates a patriarchal scopophilia, she is more direct in her vision of the network of activisms that are part of her political persona: linking women's power, LGBTQ rights, animal rights, and media performance, Gaga could be seen to embody Haraway's cyborg (see below) politically as well as imagistically, given her often science fiction–influenced costuming (all framed, as Macfarlane demonstrates, within the monstrous Gothic).

of illness and diagnosis can be analyzed to show the biased functioning of the dominant cultural discourse and practice. "In hysteria, agoraphobia, and anorexia, then, the woman's body may be viewed as a surface on which conventional constructions of femininity are exposed starkly to view, through their inscription in extreme or hyperliteral form" (pp. 174–75).

Bordo's overall point is that the body is a site where all these cultural discourses mesh and fight with each other, and so representations of the gendered body, in popular culture for example, become explicitly political texts that can—even must—be interpreted in order to understand the effects of gendered representations in relation to the exercise of social power. Doing so can help frame a resistance to such restrictive gender codes. She writes that she "view[s] our bodies as a site of struggle, where we must *work* to keep our daily practices in the service of resistance to gender domination, not in the service of docility and gender normalization" (p. 184).

Women, Difference, and the Digital

While second-wave and related theories tend to focus on the patriarchal representations of women, their effects on women's lived experience, and the need to resist those discourses to form a basis of social equality for women, much of third-wave feminist theory focuses on what it sees as the "problems" within feminist discourses themselves and the ways they can unwittingly reproduce some of the biases that shore up a patriarchal hegemony. Specifically, many theorists associated with the third wave critique how earlier forms of feminism assume a universal and essential femininity, pointing to the ways this essentialism masks a bias that favours a certain subset of women, in particular straight, white, middle- and upper-class women. In the name of fighting the patriarchy, such theories serve to silence women who may differ from this norm (lesbians, women of colour, transgendered women, working women, and others).

Fight the Powers   One particularly strong articulation of this approach comes from American feminist and cultural critic Audre Lorde (1934–1992), in her essay "The Master's Tools Will Never Dismantle the Master's House." Written in response to the Second Sex Conference in New York in 1979, in which Lorde participated, the essay tackles the problematic relationship between the dominant forms of feminist academic work and the structures of racism. Coming out of what could generally be seen as second-wave theories, Lorde nonetheless becomes important to the third-wave in recognizing the connection between sexism and racism, and specifically between patriarchy and white supremacy. Lorde points out that, to combat one of these oppressive structures, the other must be fought as well. Feminism and anti-racist practices and cultural criticism must intertwine, Lorde argues.

Lorde defines her political and critical methodology by stating that its main focus must be on the concept of difference itself, "difference of race, sexuality, class, and age" (Lorde, 1984, p. 110). Whereas second-wave feminism focuses on defining what is essentially the same in women or in women's experiences of the patriarchy, Lorde's essay focuses on the extant ideological and lived differences of one group of women from another, seeing this as a necessary step in any kind of political action against the bigoted practices of the dominant culture. This emphasis on difference isn't simply a matter of celebrating different cultural traditions, but of noting how oppression and privilege function differently across society, and therefore necessarily lead to both profound and subtle differences in how people experience the world. She writes that "Advocating the mere tolerance of difference between women is the grossest reformism. It is a total denial of the creative function of difference in our lives. Difference must be not merely tolerated, but seen as a fund of necessary polarities between which our creativity can spark like a dialectic" (p. 111). It is the very idea of differences between people that leads to discussion, debate, and progress.

The first step of Lorde's essay thus discusses the value of difference and of interdependency in society. A more functional society, she argues, would be built not on notions of power and social hierarchy, but on **interdependence**—that is, on the recognition of the fact that we all need each other (and our differences) in order for society to function properly. "Only then," she writes, "does the necessity for interdependency become unthreatening. Only within that interdependency of different strengths, acknowledged and equal, can the power to seek new ways of being in the world generate, as well as the courage and sustenance to act where there are no charters" (p. 111). A recognition of differences can be a positive thing socially, but only if it's not tied to hierarchical determinations of social power in relation to race, gender, sexuality, age, and so on. Recognizing society as an interdependent structure also leads to a sense that people need each other—our different skills, our different perspectives, our different backgrounds—in order for all of us to function to our fullest capacities.

The second step of her article deals with the political ramifications of this interdependence when it is tied to an analysis and understanding of oppression. So, in a society like that of the United States or Canada, where the people in positions of power—in government, economic institutions, large corporations, and so on—are by and large white men, what are the consequences for people who want to fight against the various forms of oppression in that society? One of the answers, in Lorde's view, is to see how these political fights are tied together, how they are, again, interdependent. Struggles to ensure equal rights for women should be tied, she argues, to struggles for equal treatment for people of colour, for gays and lesbians, for the poor, and for other marginalized groups, since ignoring the ways in which these oppressions are interrelated can simply lead to further oppression. As she writes early in the essay:

> It is a particular academic arrogance to assume any discussion of feminist theory without examining our many differences, and without a significant input from poor women, Black and Third World women, and lesbians. And yet, I stand here as a Black lesbian feminist, having been invited to comment within the only panel at this conference where the input of Black feminists and lesbians is represented. What this says about the vision of this conference is sad, in a country where racism, sexism, and homophobia are inseparable. (p. 110)

For Lorde, a conference about feminism, about empowering women, becomes less than effective when it all but silences the differences between women of race, class, and sexuality, among other ways in which women may self-identify or be identified by the society around them. "In our world," she writes, "divide and conquer must become define and empower" (p. 112). Whereas second-wave feminists saw a unified, linear fight against the patriarchy, with women speaking as one voice, Lorde argues that such a univocality further silences both women and members of other oppressed groups.

This argument is neatly contained in the title of her essay: "The Master's Tools Will Never Dismantle the Master's House." Invoking both sexist and racist oppression (in the gendering of *master* and the echoes of the language of slavery), this statement implies that feminists cannot fight against sexism if they use the same racist language and practices that dominant white male culture does.

Significantly, Lorde argues that people can never be simply identified in an uncomplicated, essentialist way with one group they happen to be part of: not all women are the same, nor do they occupy similar places in relation to social power structures; a working-class man likewise occupies a different position from an independently wealthy man of colour. But the working-class white man may still experience certain privileges that the wealthy man of colour does not, while the latter may experience forms of bigotry and oppression. One cannot assume, she implies, that one knows or can speak on behalf of an entire group, for the simple reason that no group is monolithic.

She ends her essay by noting, basically, that it's everyone's job to educate themselves—that people who are discriminated against should not have to argue for their own worth to people who occupy positions of social power. That kind of work takes away from the time needed to spend on the larger struggles. She argues that, if one is in a position of power, then trying to force people without power to explain their importance is just another level of oppression. The information is out there, says Lorde; people just need to learn how to educate themselves, to learn that we are all interdependent, and that one form of oppression—racism or sexism or classism, for example—is intricately tied to others, just as we all are as people.

The Powers of Difference   Audre Lorde can be thus seen as laying some of the most important theoretical and practical groundwork for a recognition of the differences within feminism; this work is then built upon by many others. One of these thinkers, bell hooks (1952–), significantly develops the notion of a feminist political and cultural theory built around the concept of difference, and she explicitly analyzes popular culture from this perspective.

In her work *Feminist Theory: From Margin to Center* (1984), hooks explains the impetus behind her theory and activism, writing that "Much feminist theory emerges from privileged women who live at the center, whose perspectives on reality rarely include knowledge and awareness of the lives of women and men who live on the margin. As a consequence, feminist theory lacks wholeness, lacks the broad analysis that could encompass a variety of human experiences" (hooks, 1984, p. x). Feminism here widens out from the particular, wanting not a narrow approach to the problems of specific women in a specific relation to power in society, but instead a more "global" theory that addresses the oppression and liberation of men and women in a variety of social positions.

But is there a danger in this widening of feminist concerns? Might it read almost as a desire for a universalist approach that can address everyone? As we've seen in our discussions of ideology and **mythology**, such universalizing moves are often masking their own relations to power.

hooks avoids this danger by insisting on the particularity of experiences of different people. In other words, this is not a universalizing gesture, but a gesture of interdependence, of allying the concerns of particular groups and individuals with others. Her theory describes feminism as a network of relations (a metaphor we'll explore further below) rather than a universalizing singular voice. Feminist politics must therefore be open to self-critique, to the recognition that some feminist practices from what hooks calls the "center"—privileged white women—have worked to silence voices from the margins. The relatively privileged perspective of these women prevented them, hooks argues, from developing an even stronger base of support.

One example hooks uses speaks to the role of popular culture in patriarchy, and in feminist struggle in particular. Writing that "Class biases led women organizing [the] feminist movement to simply assume that feminist theory and strategy would be best disseminated to masses of women via written materials. The focus on written material actually prohibits many women from learning about feminism" (p. 108). For this reason, she argues, feminist activism must make education one of its pillars. She writes that without such activities as literacy programs, and because "Many theorists do not even intend their ideas to reach a mass public," feminists "must take some responsibility for the superficial and perverted versions of feminist ideas that end up in the public imagination, via tv for example" (p. 108). Whereas much feminist work emphasized higher education (such as the creation of women's studies programs, discussed earlier), hooks argues that it's literacy programs that should be seen as primary feminist activities, since they can help "illiterate women from all classes" and can also help women "with learning how to think critically and analytically" (p. 108).

As part of this critical and analytical project, hooks turned, in much of her early work, to the analysis of popular culture. One of her better known arguments, from her *Black Looks: Race and Representation* (1992), focuses on Madonna. Discussing how many analyses of Madonna in the 1980s and 90s featured her expression of "sexual agency" as a form of resistance to the "white patriarchy," hooks notes that, to do so, Madonna appropriates African American culture and uses black men as images of a certain sexual freedom and power (hooks, 1992, p. 161). As hooks goes on to argue, not only does this repeat racist stereotypes of black men, it also ignores how charges of sexual licentiousness are used as a white supremacist and patriarchal tool against black women. Far from a superficial "feminism" tied to sexual agency, then, Madonna's performance can be read as part of a white supremacist and patriarchal rhetoric that works against some women's rights. For hooks, the true promise of feminism comes from recognizing the problems with privilege, and the simple fact that people from privileged positions have "perspectives on reality [that] rarely include knowledge" of those "who live on the margin" (hooks, 1984, p. x). That realization should mean, hooks argues, giving a central place within feminism to women who are on the margins of society and who "have knowledge of both margin and center" because they can see the functions of oppression operating in several ways in their own lives.

Rewiring the Power　　The notion of interdependence and the need for recognition of a multiplicity of voices are clearly significant themes in much of third-wave and poststructuralist feminist theory. Another way of approaching the issue is articulated by Donna Haraway (1944–), who focuses on the relationship between gender, class, and modern technology. Haraway directly confronts what she sees as some of the mythologies of second-wave feminism, and points to their continuation of particular patriarchal myths. To combat these ideological narratives, she tries to revise feminism by appropriating the figure of the cyborg from robotics, technology research, and science fiction. Importantly, though, she goes to great lengths to say that this "cyborg feminism" is not a purely positive and uncomplicated political narrative on its own: she uses the figure, she writes, precisely because it's always a complicated one, moving between superhuman hero and monster (Haraway, 1991).

Haraway's argument has influenced much work that came after, not only in feminist studies but also in science fiction literature, technology studies, and elsewhere. One of the best summaries of Haraway's work comes in the form of an interview with her by Hari Kunzru in the tech magazine *Wired*. This piece begins by echoing the villainous Borg from *Star Trek: The Next Generation*: "For Donna Haraway, we are already assimilated" (Kunzru, 1997, p. 1). It continues with a very useful summary of Haraway's cyborg theories:

> [T]he cyborg—a fusion of animal and machine—trashes the big oppositions between nature and culture, self and world that run through so much of our thought. . . . [W]hen people describe something as natural, they're saying . . . we can't change it. Women for generations were told that they were "naturally" weak, submissive, overemotional, and incapable of abstract thought. That it was "in their nature" to be mothers rather than corporate raiders, to prefer parlor games to particle physics. If all these things are natural, they're unchangeable. (p. 3)

These are the same ideologically reproduced stereotypes that Mulvey analyzes. The flip side of these stereotypes is that when women act against these types, they're labelled as "monstrous," "evil," or "unnatural" and therefore even further marginalized and vilified by society. However, the article continues, if genders "are constructed, like a cyborg," then it's possible for them to be "*reconstructed*"; in other words, we can challenge and alter those ideologically enforced subject positions: "With the hard-won recognition of their social and historical constitution, gender, race, and class cannot provide the basis for belief in 'essential' unity. There is nothing about being 'female' that naturally binds women. There is not even such a state as 'being' female, itself a highly complex category constructed in contested sexual scientific discourses and other social practices" (Haraway, 1991, p. 155). As we'll see below, however, this is only one aspect of Haraway's cyborg theory.

Before moving on to the more troubling aspects of cyborg identity that Haraway investigates, we have to ask the question: Why would Haraway revise feminism through the image of the cyborg? In so-called second-wave feminism, domination and power were seen to function primarily in one particular direction—from the dominant male class onto the subordinated, oppressed female class. This view meant that resistance was, in a way, uncomplicated—to combat sexism, women could act together as women to reject or fight against the patriarchy. But, as Lorde demonstrates in her essay, what this vision led to was a kind of unspoken assumption that all women were alike, and that all women were oppressed in the same way—that there was something essential about being a woman that made all women alike. Echoing Lorde, Haraway discusses the problems with this essentialist logic, writing that she thinks dominant forms of feminism, and even resistant forms such as those practised by "socialist feminists," are "guilty of producing essentialist theory that suppressed women's particularity and contradictory interests," if only "through unreflective participation in the logics, languages, and practices of white humanism and through searching for a single ground of domination to secure our revolutionary voice" (p. 160).

Like Lorde, then, Haraway wants to combat the silencing of non-white women, working-class women, lesbians, and other non-dominant voices with feminism. The idea is to create a more pluralistic feminism that recognizes not only similarities but also the differences between women, and that seeks what Mikhail Bakhtin would call a more **dialogic** discussion within feminist movements. And this is where Haraway and the cyborg fit in.

Whereas the earlier essentialist and universalizing rhetoric was often tied to a myth of the "Earth Mother" or "Goddess"—a natural, essentialized figure of feminine power— Haraway offers the myth of the cyborg as an image of interdependent difference. The cyborg can't be pinned down to an essence: "[T]he cyborg has no origin story in the Western sense.... An origin story in the 'Western,' humanist sense depends on the myth of original unity, fullness, bliss and terror.... The cyborg skips the step of original unity, of identification with nature in the Western sense" (pp. 150–51). The cyborg, as a myth, escapes the notion of essentialism—the cyborg is never an individual, but always a subject, subservient to the mechanical apparatus that keeps it alive and driven by multiple power sources. Moreover, because it's created out of different parts, the cyborg is dialogic, with different bits and pieces "talking" to each other in order for the whole to function.

But, for Haraway, this "cyborg" isn't just a metaphor. In the postmodern world, everyone *is* a cyborg. We use technology to produce a sense of who we are, and to perform our daily functions: whether it takes the form of a manufactured drug to maintain a proper blood pressure; radiators to keep us warm in winter; the genetic manipulation done on plants to protect them from disease (and to make them patentable), plants which are then harvested by machine, flash frozen by machine, and shipped around the world, to be identified with a bar code at the cash register where we pay for them with a bank card; or the fact that many of us interact with friends only online through social media, our lives are intimately and constantly mediated by technology.

Our daily lives are thus all about networks of other people, technologies, and the material world. Haraway builds on Lacanian notions of identity (discussed in Chapter 6) in which the self exists only in relation to others. She takes this to an extreme, saying that we exist only as people within complex networks of other people, of nature, and of technology—and that we are constantly crossing the borders between these different categories. This vision leads her to say that we have "fractured identities" (p. 155). We can't really separate our "personal" concerns from the larger system of connections we have to other people and other systems in the world, be they biological or mechanical, or more often than not, a complex interweaving of the two.

Cyborg politics is all about crossing boundaries—we can't be isolated individuals; we are instead subjects who are engaged in constant negotiations. Each person has an infinite number of subject positions that are always in connection with a wide range of social networks. That means basically that one occupies a lot of different **subject positions**, and none of them are stable.

Importantly, this interconnection is both a positive and a negative force in Haraway's theory. On the positive side, she makes an argument similar to Lorde's, writing that "There are grounds for hope in the emerging bases for new kinds of unity across race, gender, and class, as these elementary units of socialist-feminist analysis themselves suffer protean transformations" (p. 173)—the changing aspects of modern identity, in other words, open up the possibilities for wider political action of the sort Lorde describes. Tying this to contemporary science fiction writers, she argues that "Cyborg writing," and by extension, cyborg feminism, "must not be about the Fall, the imagination of a once-upon-a-time wholeness.…Cyborg writing is about the power to survive, not on the basis of original innocence, but on the basis of seizing the tools to mark the world that marked them as other" (p. 175). Instead of using "the master's tools," Haraway argues that feminists and others must hack the master's network, to make it function for them rather than against them.

But some aspects of this cyborg politics are problematic. The idea of networks and difference can also be used by the dominant culture as a form of domination and oppression: "'Networking' is both a feminist practice and a multinational corporate strategy," she writes (p. 170). Likewise, "Among the many transformations of reproductive situations is the medical one, where women's bodies have boundaries newly permeable to both 'visualization' and 'intervention'" (p. 169). Although these new technologies can be sources of possible power through the interconnection of such "oppositional" politics as antiracism and feminism, they can be used by the dominant culture to further oppress women and other groups. We have the power to alter ourselves, to negotiate networks and allow all kinds of voices to speak, but, at the same time, the technology used to create this network is at the heart of contemporary economic exploitation and war. The ability to deny the essence of different groups is also the power to silence them.

Haraway's cyborg discourse is thus a constant negotiation between finding ways of joining voices together for positive action and the danger of the network also being used to silence people. As we saw with Mikhail Bakhtin's writings from nearly a century earlier (see Chapter 5), Haraway views language and social life as a **dialogic heteroglossia**, where disparate voices can be connected together but also be split apart and silenced. But, for Haraway as for Bordo, this structure goes beyond language and is taken to the level of our very bodies.

What all of this means for Haraway is that we have to take active responsibility for our actions and our place in the social network—that we have a responsibility to ensure we don't engage in totalizing or universalizing theory that denies people the right to negotiate spaces for themselves in the network as best they can. "Weaving," she writes, "is for oppositional cyborgs" (p. 170). She summarizes these arguments on the final page of her essay: "Cyborg imagery can suggest a way out of the maze of dualisms in which we have explained our bodies and our tools to ourselves," such that we develop more complex notions of gender identity, beyond male/female, masculine/feminine, and so on. She continues, directly referencing Bakhtin,

> This is a dream not of a common language, but of a powerful infidel heteroglossia. It is an imagination of a feminist speaking in tongues to strike fear into the circuits of the super-savers of the new right. It means both building and destroying machines, identities, categories, relationships, space stories. Though both are bound in the spiral dance, I would rather be a cyborg than a goddess. (p. 181)

Gender Studies and Masculinity

As we've seen in our discussion of Haraway's cyborg feminism, much third-wave feminist theory expands the discussion of feminism beyond a critique of the patriarchy and into an analysis of the social construction of gender. Much more could be said on this subject, especially with reference to noted theorist Judith Butler, whose theories of gender performance and performativity are very important to the analysis of gender. However, since those discussions are taken up in Chapter 11 on the subject of sexuality (which is intimately connected to discussions of gender), the remainder of this chapter will explore a relatively recent development in feminist and gender studies: the study of the social construction of masculinity. Just as particular notions of femininity develop historically in relation to patriarchal social and other identity structures (as Haraway and Lorde point out), so too can we see masculinity not as an essential expression of the male sex, but as a historically contingent set of behaviours and identities that are variously expressed and challenged by people within society.

Male Masculinities   Perhaps the best known study of masculinity is sociologist R. W. Connell's book, *Masculinities*. Connell's aim is to "present a theory of masculinities, embedded in a social theory of gender" (Connell, 2005, p. xi). As this statement and the title suggests, Connell (1944–) argues that, rather than being a singular expression of a biological male essence, masculine gender behaviours are culturally prescribed, and necessarily multiple. Masculine identities, as all gender identities, Connell states, "come into existence at particular times and places, and are always subject to change" (p. 185). Thus, what is considered as particularly masculine behaviour among, for example, heterosexual, white, urban and working-class men and women in contemporary Canada may differ radically from that of the seventeenth-century English aristocracy; masculinities may even, in the same historical moment, differ in certain ways regionally across the country, or between communities and neighbourhoods within a city.

For Connell, gender identities, and forms of masculinity specifically, are thus a product of specific social conditions. Using ethnographic studies of specific populations and analyses of historical documents, she develops a complex vision of the ways different forms of masculinity coincide and can serve to reinforce, or challenge, dominant social gender paradigms and structures. Perhaps the best known aspect of Connell's work is her categorization of different forms of masculinity and their interrelations. Masculinities can be grouped, she argues, into hegemonic, subordinate, complicit, and marginalized identities.

Relying on Antonio Gramsci's notion of hegemony, she defines **hegemonic masculinity** as that form of masculine identity which is granted, and works to maintain, "a leading position in social life" (p. 77). Within patriarchal societies, "[h]egemonic masculinity can be defined as the configuration of gender practice which embodies the currently accepted answer to the problem of the legitimacy of the patriarchy, which guarantees (or is taken to guarantee) the dominant position of men and the subordination of women" (p. 77). Figures of hegemonic masculinity "may be exemplars, such as film actors, or even fantasy figures, such as film characters" (p. 77), but they will always represent a direct and supposedly "normal" or "natural" connection between a form of masculine identity and social power. One can think here of the holders of the "gaze" in Mulvey's analysis of film, those men who are the "creators" of meaning. Important to remember in this definition is that Connell does not see one type of masculine figure (the hockey player, or James Bond, or the corporate raider) as *the* example of hegemonic masculinity across all time: these are historically contingent figures. Moreover, building on Gramsci's use of hegemony as a way of referring to a collection of different groups in power working to maintain the status quo of a given society, Connell sees hegemonic masculinity as a set of different masculine types (and the men who exemplify them) that work together, as it were, to maintain patriarchal dominance over women. Thus, the mostly male Canadian Parliament, the mostly male Canadian business CEOs, and the mostly male professional sports stars and movie action heroes are all part of hegemonic masculinity, but hegemonic masculinity is not reducible to any one of those figures.

Connell introduces the idea of **complicit masculinities** to define those men who may not exemplify the hegemonic ideal but who still serve, in their masculine performance, to reinforce the domination of women. Thus, "[m]arriage, fatherhood and community life often involve extensive compromises with women rather than naked domination or an uncontested display of authority"; such men will "respect their wives and mothers" and never be "violent towards women," but still these men will "draw the patriarchal dividend" of social privilege, and may argue against feminist practices or challenges to what they see as the "normal" pattern of domestic and social life (pp. 79–80).

Subordinate masculinities, conversely, are those forms of masculinity that are directly oppressed by, or denied access to, the forms of social power allotted to hegemonic masculine behaviour. This subordination takes place within a hierarchical vision of "types" of masculinity, what Connell refers to as "specific gender relations of dominance and subordination between groups of men" (p. 78). Both historically and currently, the most clearly subordinate form of masculinity involves homosexuality or other forms of queer masculinity. "This is much more," Connell writes, "than a cultural stigmatization of homosexuality or gay identity. Gay men are subordinated to straight men by an array of quite material practices" (p. 78).

Finally, echoing Lorde's analysis of the interconnections of racial, class-based, sexual, and gender identities, Connell defines **marginalized masculinities** as those that are defined in relation to other forms of social marginalization or oppression, such as race or class, since the "interplay of gender with other [identity] structures...creates further relationships between masculinities" (p. 80). Connell turns to the U.S. for her example, writing that "[i]n a white supremacist context, black masculinities play symbolic roles for white gender construction. For instance, black sporting stars become exemplars of masculine toughness, while the fantasy figure of the black rapist plays an important role in sexual politics among whites, a role much exploited by right-wing politics in the United States" (p. 80).

Connell's categorization of masculinities takes place in an overall feminist critique of the patriarchy. To examine the cultural constructs of masculinity outside of the context of the patriarchal subordination of women in contemporary society would be to miss the forest of gender relations for its individual trees.

Female Masculinities   Whereas Connell's work focuses on the multiplicity of masculinities, her focus is primarily on the masculinities experienced and exhibited by those who are identified as biologically male. But if masculinity, and gender in general, are socially constructed, and if there exists (as we will see in Chapter 11) what Eve Kosofsky Sedgwick calls a "nonce taxonomy" of gender and sexual identities, then is masculinity necessarily limited to, or only experienced by, those with particular bodily forms?

In *Female Masculinity*, Jack Halberstam works to answer this very question. Discussing identity categories ranging from the tomboy to the stone butch, to drag kings, to transgendered and transsexual persons, and studying cultural material from Radclyffe Hall's 1928 novel *The Well of Loneliness* to James Bond films to the gendered space of the airport bathroom, this work analyzes the complex ways in which gender categories are continually recognized as fluid and multiple, even as ideological and repressive apparatuses strive to "police" a rigid binary in which masculinity is the "natural" expression of an unchangeable biological maleness, and femininity similarly the "natural" expression of physical femaleness.

One of the primary examples used in *Female Masculinity* is what Halberstam calls the "bathroom problem." Recognizing that "sex-segregated bathrooms" are necessary in a patriarchal society in which the violent abuse of women is common, Halberstam notes that the bathroom, and especially the airport bathroom, is nonetheless a site of gender policing, especially for those who identify as, or are identified as, women. Female-born people whose gender appears "ambiguous" are often confronted about being "in the 'wrong' bathroom" (Halberstam, 1998, p. 20), and are thus labelled as the "not-woman" and "not-man" who exists not just "in-between" but outside the normative gender categories, as the "gender deviant" (p. 21). This problem indicates a need, Halberstam says, for "[e]ither...open-access...or multigendered bathrooms, or...wider parameters for gender identification" (p. 24).

The expression of masculinity by female persons is, in itself, a multifaceted set of identities for Halberstam; this expression exists in a series of relationships to what Connell would call hegemonic masculinity, which Halberstam associates explicitly with a white, heterosexual male masculinity. Heterosexual female masculinity, for example, might "[menace]...gender conformity" on occasion, "but all too often it represents an acceptable degree of female masculinity" that reinforces both heterosexual hegemony and patriarchy (p. 28). The "excessive masculinity of the dyke," conversely, is explicitly threatening to that order (p. 28).

Turning to popular culture, Halberstam argues, for example, that the female masculinity associated with Sigourney Weaver in *Alien Resurrection* (1997) becomes "far more threatening and indeed 'alien'" when she "combines her hard body with some light flirtation with co-star Winona Ryder" (p. 28). Thus, one must "not simply create another binary in which masculinity always signifies power; in alternative models of gender variation, female masculinity is not simply the opposite of female femininity, nor is it a female version of male masculinity" (pp. 28–29). In this way, the subtitles in this section raise the very problems that Halberstam is addressing: by subtitling the discussions "Male Masculinities" and "Female Masculinities," the text might seem to be challenging gender binaries (by referencing multiple forms of identification), but by resorting to "male" and "female" as the qualifiers, it could still reinforce the binary structure of gender normativity. There are, instead, a multiplicity of gender identities that operate against and outside of traditional binary forms: one must not just add a third or even fourth category, but recognize that the categories are multiplicitous and changing.

Indeed, the recognition of a variety of gender identifications, long recognized within queer theory, politics, communities, and cultures, is also becoming more recognized in so-called mainstream popular culture: in February 2014, acting on this recognition of multiple and fluid gender categories, Facebook added over fifty new gender categories with which users could self-identify. This critique—one is tempted to say explosion—of the binary categories of gender, sex, and sexual identities will also be a focus of Chapter 11 on sexuality and queer theory.

Case Study

Splice: Anti-Feminism, Female Masculinity, Technology, and the Distorted Body

Splice (2009), a Canadian horror film, tells the story of a pair of genetic scientists, Elsa and Clive, who are also a romantic couple, and who create a new life form by combining human and animal genetic material. First creating two new creatures—one male and one female, nicknamed Fred and Ginger—for medical experimentation, they then create a human-animal hybrid named Dren. After Ginger undergoes a spontaneous sex change, leading to Fred and Ginger killing each other in a form of competitive, alpha-male behaviour, Elsa and Clive smuggle Dren out of the research laboratory and raise her as their child. From there, the film quickly turns disturbingly violent and arguably horribly misogynist.

Dren ages very rapidly, and quickly becomes dangerous. Elsa at one point ties Dren up and cuts off part of her tail for research purposes; after this, Clive has sex with Dren. Eventually, Dren escapes from the barn where they have her held; Dren seems to die, but then, like Ginger, transforms into a male. He rapes Elsa, and when Clive tries to stop him, he kills Clive with his (newly regrown) stinger. Elsa manages to kill him. We then see her back at work—pregnant—at the end of the film.

Hailed for its creature effects and acting—Dren is especially realistic throughout—the film asks questions about scientific ethics in a way not too different from Mary Shelley's nineteenth-century novel *Frankenstein*, which clearly inspired aspects of the film. But equally obviously, the film foregrounds issues of gender and sexuality. Where it offers a coherent message, it suggests a radically anti-feminist, potentially violent misogynist one, which some reviewers noticed shortly after its release; see, for example, the strong—and very funny—review of the film by "XY Marla" on the blog "Danny Isn't Here, Mrs. Torrance" (listed in Further Reading), which makes points that are similar to a few below.

As the film progresses, we learn a little about the backgrounds of the characters. Elsa was raised by a woman portrayed, explicitly, as a second-wave feminist concerned about the representation of women: she forced Elsa to give up her Barbie doll when she was young. Becoming a scientist, Elsa would seem to follow in her mother's footsteps. However, she continually laments her life, wanting to return to more "traditional" role as a mother. Moreover, when Dren is an adolescent she compares herself to a Barbie doll, at which point Elsa teaches her how to put on makeup. After Elsa says "My mother wouldn't let me wear makeup. She said that it 'debased women,'" she rhetorically asks, "Who doesn't want to be debased once in a while?" Primarily the creation of Elsa, designed to fulfill her longing for a child, Dren is thus represented as the end point of a "malformed" womanhood. It's easy to read a clearly anti-feminist argument here, one that uses transphobic representations to support its position: Elsa's feminist upbringing and scientific work are presented as "corrupting" her natural instincts, leading to Dren, who is monstrous in large part because of being both female and male. Likewise, Clive's hegemonic masculinity is represented as being stifled

throughout, leading to his "need" to have sex with Dren. The final rape and murder scene, then, can be read as a particularly violent, horrifically misogynist "correction" of Elsa's and Clive's alternative gender performances.

In some ways, this film can be read as a reactionary—and particularly blunt—misogynist and gender-normative response to the theories discussed in this chapter. Elsa's mother's concern that her daughter not be subjected to the objectification of women (as discussed by Mulvey) leads to Elsa's "divided" nature. Clive's inability to function as a representative of hegemonic masculinity leads to his death. As "nerds" (their company is, after all, named Nucleic Exchange Research and Development), neither fits traditional gender paradigms: Elsa is too intellectual to be the traditionally "embodied" woman (as Sidonie Smith describes), and Clive isn't physically "manly" enough or in control. The fact that Clive and Elsa are named after characters in James Whale's 1935 film *Bride of Frankenstein* adds to this reading, as that film is widely seen as having a distinctly queer subtext.

In short, Dren (typographically the opposite of "nerd") is presented as the end result of Elsa and Clive's gender non-conformity: Dren's body, both the grotesque body discussed by Bordo and the cyborg body discussed by Haraway, is presented as that which destroys the natural order of things, and which must be destroyed if that order is to be reestablished.

But it is through this final figure that we can offer a counter reading of the film. As Haraway says, the cyborg is both a tool of oppressive power and a way of rebelling against that structure, just as anorexia is, for Bordo, a means of both control and (problematic) resistance. So too can we read Dren: a vilified figure who stands outside of traditional sexual and gender roles, Dren's power can be read—to a point—as a resistant power, one that denies the constrictive definitions both Elsa and Clive try to force on her/him. But again, this is a counter-textual reading, one that is, on the surface of the film, silenced by its overarching conservative narrative.

Discussion Questions

1. Find two advertisements, either in print or video: one that you think is directed primarily at women, and one that you think is directed primarily at men. Which people in the ad do you identify with, and why? Whose perspective do you see through? What do these ads imply about men and women?

2. Lorde, Haraway, Connell, and Halberstam all, in different ways, note that it's impossible to discuss gender identity without discussing other forms of identity discussed in this textbook (sexuality, race, and class being the usual examples). Can you think of an example from popular culture that deals with multiple forms of identification and/or social oppression based on identity? Do you think it's successful in its attempt to pair these representations? Why or why not?

3. In the "Lady Gaga, the Gaze, and the Body" box, it's argued that Gaga interrupts or frustrates the scopophilic gaze, and that she also embodies Haraway's image of the cyborg. Do you agree? Why or why not? Does Lady Gaga's self-imaging differ from that of other pop stars? How so? Gaga is, after all, part of what Theodor Adorno and Max Horkheimer call the **culture industry**: Is there a way in which she reproduces the hegemonic functions of gender and patriarchy? Are there other women celebrities who connect more strongly to any of the arguments presented by the theorists discussed in this chapter, or is modern celebrity itself complicit in patriarchal structures?

Further Reading

Butler, Judith. *Gender Trouble: Feminism and the Subversion of Identity*. New York: Routledge, 1990.

De Lauretis, Teresa. *Alice Doesn't: Feminism, Semiotics, Cinema*. Bloomington: Indiana UP, 1984.

Friedan, Betty. *The Feminine Mystique*. 1963. New York: Norton, 1997.

Gilbert, Sandra, and Susan Gubar. *The Madwoman in the Attic: The Woman Writer and the Nineteenth-Century Literary Imagination*. New Haven: Yale UP, 1979.

Greer, Germaine. *The Female Eunuch*. 1970. New York: HarperCollins, 2009.

Halberstam, Judith. *Female Masculinity*. Durham: Duke UP, 1998.

hooks, bell. *Feminist Theory: From Margin to Center*. 1984. 2nd ed. London: Pluto Press, 2000.

Irigaray, Luce. *This Sex Which Is Not One*. Trans. Catherine Porter. Ithaca: Cornell UP, 1985.

Martin, Emily. "The Egg and the Sperm: How Science Has Constructed a Romance Based on Stereotypical Male-Female Roles." *Signs* 16.3 (1991): 485–501.

Silverman, Kaja. *The Acoustic Mirror: The Female Voice in Psychoanalysis and Cinema*. Bloomington: Indiana UP, 1988.

Wollstonecraft, Mary. *A Vindication of the Rights of Women*. 1792. Ed. Deidre Shauna Lynch. 3rd ed. New York: Norton, 2009.

XY Marla (pseud.). Rev. of *Splice. Danny Isn't Here, Mrs. Torrance*. 9 June 2010. http://dannyisn-theremrstorrance.wordpress.com. 29 August 2013.

Chapter 11
Sexuality and Queer Theory

INTRODUCTION

Sex surrounds us. Sex is beautiful. Sex burns calories. Sex is enjoyable. Sex is a vehicle for violence and oppression. Sex is biological. Sex is cultural. Sex is a subject unlike any other. Sex is a subject that connects to many others.

These often contradictory statements have all been believed to be true by a number of people, and yet none of them fully describes what it is that we call sex. Like the study of gender in Chapter 10, the study of sex and sexuality is rendered complex by the various ways in which sex is part of our daily social and cultural lives. The study of sexuality, like that of all the identity categories we examine in Part IV, cuts across different fields, including biology, psychology, sociology, and cultural studies. Questions about sex and sexuality also get to the heart of such "big picture" issues as "nature vs. nurture" and the relationships between theory and practice, morality and politics, and pleasure and power, among other issues. One has only to look at the debates over marriage and adoption rights, for example, or at the fact that "any man who has [had] sex with another man, even once, since 1977" was, until May 2013, barred from giving blood to the Canadian Red Cross (www.blood.ca; now, men must have been abstinent from sex with other men for at least five years) to see that sexuality is an area of heated social debate. Both popular and high culture, of course, have long been fixated on sexuality. Whether in terms of portrayals of sex acts themselves, of sexual ideals or morals, or of courtship rituals and their various frustrations, popular culture without sex is . . . well, it is simply unimaginable.

In this chapter we'll discuss the various modern theories of human sexuality, from the so-called sexologists of the nineteenth century through to contemporary cultural theories, especially those from the field of queer studies, a field that challenges the assumptions of the supposedly essential nature of sexuality. Like the other theories we've examined, **queer theory** emphasizes the social construction of identity, and is thus a commonly used critical resource when studying the representation of and role that sexuality plays in popular culture. Of course, our discussion of sexuality is directly tied to that of gender in Chapter 10, and our subsequent studies of race, nationalism, and postcolonialism also relate in complex ways to each other and to gender and sexuality. As you read Part IV, ask yourself how these categories relate to and affect each other.

LET'S TALK ABOUT SEX

While the ostensible focus of this book is modern and contemporary popular culture from the late nineteenth century forward, in the case of the culture(s) of sex, it will help to give some larger historical background. Doing so is important because the topic of sex, tied as it is to morality, law, politics, and even our very sense of self, can often seem deceptively transparent. We all know what sex is, after all.

Or do we? As we discovered in Chapter 10, the term *sex* is a complex one. Referring at once to an individual's biological structure and sometimes to the social and cultural reflection of that structure (what most theorists call *gender*), *sex* also means different kinds of physical acts, and can as well refer to a set of personal and group identifications that one makes, what will here be called sexuality. Sex, then, like all the other identity categories we've discussed, is a complex network of sometimes complementary, often contradictory, meanings.

That said, given the proper context, we do know what we mean when we talk about sex. Generally, in the senses that the terms *sex* and *sexuality* are used in this chapter (as opposed to the biological sex/gender discussion in Chapter 10), most of us will recognize that we are talking about certain kinds of physical—often genital—pleasure and acts, as well as identities (straight, gay, bisexual, transsexual, and so on). We also tend to separate these terms from other activities in our daily lives: generally speaking, national political debate isn't regarded as sex, nor is mowing the lawn, no matter how often we hear about politicians' sex lives on the news or how many episodes of *Desperate Housewives* we've watched. Sex, then, is *a* part of our lives, one that may be more or less important to us as individuals at any given moment, and one that differs from other aspects of our lives.

This understanding of sex—as an act, as genital pleasure, and/or as an identity that we can (even should) keep separate from other parts of our lives, especially from our public lives—is, however, a relatively new concept. If we are to follow the traditional **Eurocentric** history, we can start in classical Greece. In the ancient world, sex was, to use Robert A. Nye's term, very much "embedded" in daily life as a way of understanding and encouraging crop production, for example. Moreover, the right kind of sexual desire and energy (that of an older male citizen for a younger male) was seen, according to Socrates via Plato, as "the first step on a heavenly ladder to wisdom" (Clark, 2008, p. 24). Obviously, sex in the contemporary West, owing to the influence of Christianity and other religions along with various modern sciences, is, in many ways, dramatically different. Simply stated, this proves that the cultural roles and understandings of sex and sexuality *change*. They are *malleable*. Therefore, one can't approach the cultural study of sexuality with one's own assumptions about sex (whatever they are) remaining unquestioned. The goal here is to think critically about the role that sex plays in popular culture. And to do that fully, we must be aware that sex isn't a pre-existing or singular concept, but one that is tied to the **ideologies** of specific times and places. Perhaps the best way to begin, then, is with the "invention" of modern sexuality, which is usually situated in the nineteenth century.

Modern Sex

Tracing the movement in the West from the ancient and classical periods through to Christian visions of sex, as many historians have done, allows one to see the transformations of sexual morality and forms, a widening division between physicality and spirituality, and an increasing emphasis on the private and procreative as the only "proper" kind of sex. This history is not without its variations, however. Moving into the modern era—beginning with the nineteenth century—we can see these visions of what constitutes "proper" and "improper" sexual behaviour and their relation to specific forms of morality and decency. The general understanding of the Victorian period's vision of sexuality is that it was a very repressive one, when sexual behaviour was heavily regulated by what Louis Althusser would call various repressive and ideological apparatuses, including the courts, the family, the church, and so on. Peter N. Stearns outlines some of the dominant features of the Victorian approach to sexuality:

> Familiar components included a deep belief that sexual activity should be confined to marriage and that young people's impulses needed to be controlled. . . . Even within marriage, sexual pleasure must be moderated by appropriate standards of restraint. Marital fidelity was vital. Decorum must also surround the public culture, so that sexuality would not be irresponsibly encouraged or vulgarities find the light of day. (Stearns, 2009, p. 90)

There are a number of facts and stories used to support this history of Victorian prudery—from behavioural manuals for young women to the oft-repeated legend that little coverings were created for furniture legs so that the "ankles" of couches couldn't be seen (because they were too risqué . . .).

Victorian science was used to support the notion that sex had to be regulated in order for society to function smoothly and productively. And it is here that our earlier discussions of Marx, Freud, and others can be recalled, as well as our division of the **individual** and the **subject**. As noted in Chapter 3, in the Victorian period the definition of humanity started to change: no longer seen as primarily spiritual and rational individuals in control of their own actions, humans were now subject to scientific study, as subjects who are both acted on and affected more by their surroundings or by economic forces out of their control. Something similar happened when Victorian scientists began to analyze the subject of sex. Well before Freud, Richard von Krafft-Ebing was analyzing what he saw as pathological behaviours that stemmed from the "sex instinct." In order to do this, though, Krafft-Ebing and other so-called "sexologists" had to be willing to see humans, and their sex lives, as the proper objects of scientific study. Moving sex into the realm of science, Krafft-Ebing, like Freud after him, argued that in some cases people could not be seen as "responsible" for their actions, actions that may have been caused by psychological pathology. Sexuality becomes not an expression of the person; instead the person becomes an expression of sexuality.

Indeed, for Krafft-Ebing, culture itself becomes a product of human sexual drive: "Sexual influence is . . . potent in the awakening of aesthetic sentiments. What other foundation is there for the plastic art or poetry? From (sensual) love arises that warmth of fancy which alone can inspire the creative mind, and the fire of sensual feeling kindles and preserves the glow and fervor of art" (von Krafft-Ebing, 1965, p. 39). While Krafft-Ebing may wax poetic on the cultural role of sex, he, like other sexologists, saw the sex drive as a determining factor of an individual's life. Many sexologists were thus concerned with controlling pathological behaviour in order to ensure a "healthy" society. All kinds of "aberrant" sexual behaviour—masturbation, homosexuality (or "inversion"), prostitution—were seen to cause illness to those involved and to the society of which they were a part; they thus had to be properly controlled and regulated, and, if possible, stopped altogether (although, it needs to be said, Krafft-Ebing himself did not view homosexuality as a mental illness or psychological problem, as Freud would, but instead as often being caused by a transformation in the brain that happened before birth). One of the most famous examples of Victorian sexual repression appears at the very end of the nineteenth century, when Oscar Wilde, the famous playwright, poet, and novelist, was put on trial for committing acts of "gross indecency," in this case having sexual relations with young men. Wilde was found guilty and sentenced to two years of hard labour in prison.

The Oscar Wilde Trials

Oscar Wilde (1854–1900) was an Anglo-Irish playwright, poet, novelist, and critic who came to fame in Victorian England and subsequently around the world. His plays, including *The Importance of Being Ernest* (1895) and *A Woman of No Importance* (1893), were extremely popular (and are still regularly staged and adapted to film). They generally fit into the "comedy of manners" genre, which often pokes fun at the upper classes. Wilde engaged in a speaking tour across Canada and the United States in 1882.

Beyond his literary work, Wilde was best known as a member of the loosely termed "aesthetic movement," or "aestheticism," a school of art, literature, and criticism that placed value on the aesthetics or beauty of life over so-called moral values.

Wilde, who was married and had children, also had sexual relationships with men; and because homosexual acts were illegal in Victorian England, he was eventually imprisoned. Wilde had a lengthy relationship with Lord Alfred Douglas, the son of the Marquess of Queensberry (best known for the "Queensberry rules" in boxing). Queensberry

heard of Wilde's relationship with his son, and left a (misspelled) note for Wilde at one of the latter's clubs, addressed to "Oscar Wilde, posing somdomite." Douglas convinced Wilde to take his father to court for libel. In order to defend Queensberry against the suit, the marquess's lawyers set out to prove that Wilde had had sexual affairs with young men.

Wilde lost the trial, and was thereafter arrested for committing "acts of gross indecency" and sent back to court, this time as the defendant. The first criminal trial ended with the jury unable to reach a verdict, but in a subsequent trial Wilde was found guilty and sentenced to hard labour in prison. While there, he wrote a lengthy letter to Douglas, since published as *De Profundis*. Upon his release he left England and wrote the poem *The Ballad of Reading Gaol* (originally published in 1898 as being written by prisoner "C.33"). Wilde's health was weakened by his time in prison, and he died in 1900, three years after his release, at the age of forty-six. Later in the chapter we'll return to an analysis of his trials.

Following the nineteenth-century sexologists, modern psychiatry, especially as defined and influenced by Freud, saw the sex drive as one of the primary forces of human life. Much of this material is covered in Chapters 4 and 6, and so only a portion will be repeated here. In general terms, Freud understood much of an individual's psyche as being framed by the way the child's relationship to its parents developed, a relationship he framed in largely sexual terms. For example, the male child's desire to be like his father, to gain that position of control and power, becomes expressed through an Oedipal desire to possess the mother and kill the father, to take the father's place in society, in effect. Freud, and later Jacques Lacan, viewed this as an important stage in the development of the child's sense of self. For Freud and later psychoanalytic thinkers, then, sex becomes even more a centre of life. The **repression** or **sublimation** of our sexual urges is necessary for us to function in society, Freud argued (thus aligning himself to a degree with his Victorian times), but too much repression, or too strong an urge, can lead to psychological conflicts that can be resolved only by discovering the source of the problem through the "talking cure"—through openly discussing those desires that should, the Victorians would say, be kept hidden.

QUEER THEORIES

As Michel Foucault points out, however, there is obviously a paradox in this Victorian repression and its relation to our Freudian heritage. At the very point that Victorian society was supposedly becoming increasingly repressive in terms of sexuality, more and more scientists, psychologists, and the like were actively studying human sexuality, publishing books about it, and detailing all the many and varied acts of sexual pleasure—including such sexual "pathologies" as sado-masochism, "inversion," and so on. Weren't these the things that were supposed to be silenced or, at best, ignored in the Victorian world? How do we account for this paradox, this very loud silencing of sex? Foucault's answer to this in the late 1970s helps to instantiate the loose theoretical school known as queer theory.

Defining Queer Theory

Before continuing the summary of Foucault's foundational work, it will be useful to discuss in general terms what queer theory is. The best place to start is with the word *queer* itself. In its etymological origins, dating to the sixteenth century, *queer* meant simply "odd" or "strange," but by the end of the nineteenth century it was beginning to be used as an epithet for gay men. The term gained in popularity in that offensive sense throughout the twentieth century. However, by the early 1990s, some gay and lesbian activist groups and academics began to use it as a positive term, as a way for the community to refer to itself.

The use of the term *queer* in queer theory signals the attempt to destabilize any easy, essentialist assumptions, no matter from which position those assumptions come. Likewise, the acronyms now associated with queer activism—such as LGBTTIQQ2s, discussed in the "Gay Rights, Queer Activism" box—highlight that there is no "natural" political

Gay Rights, Queer Activism, Queer Theory

While gay rights advocates have existed since at least the nineteenth century, the contemporary movement is usually seen as beginning in 1969, after a group of gay men and lesbians fought back against a violent police raid at the Stonewall Inn in New York (an event often referred to now as simply "Stonewall"). By 1990, the activist group Queer Nation was formed. Unlike some other gay and lesbian rights organizations, Queer Nation's mandate was to explicitly and vocally confront homophobia and the silencing of queer voices by the dominant society. Their most famous slogan, "We're here! We're queer! Get used to it!," embodies this approach. Queer Nation's politics were thus about visibility and direct confrontation, and the term *queer* took on the connotation of a confrontational sexual politics.

Born out of the AIDS activism of the group ACT UP, Queer Nation, as Jonathan Katz writes, "sought to reinvent gay activism along the lines of guerrilla politics and street theater, choosing a name that was deliberately provocative and antiassimilationist" (Katz, 2000, p. 725). Similarly, *queer*, as a self-identifying term, served to break down political barriers between different groups in the gay, lesbian, bi- and transsexual, and other gender and sexually non-normative communities, allowing for a somewhat unified response to homophobia that nonetheless sought not to marginalize any voices from within this disparate community (hence the abbreviations LGBTQ and, more recently and especially in Canada, LGBTTIQQ2s, standing for Lesbian, Gay, Bisexual, Transgender, Transsexual, Intersex, Queer, Questioning, and 2 Spirited, where the last is a term used predominantly by peoples of the First Nations). At the same time, a group of literary and cultural theorists began to challenge homophobia in the academy as well as the **heteronormative** assumptions that

lay behind much literary theory and philosophy; these analyses came to be grouped together under the rubrics of queer theory and queer studies. While there had been many studies of sexuality in literary and cultural criticism before this period, queer theory, like Queer Nation, focused on tearing down the homophobic assumptions of many earlier theoretical and critical positions. Queer theory tends to use philosophical analyses and cultural criticism to explode any notion of stable categories of sexual—and other—identities.

A June 1990 Queer Nation demonstration against homophobic violence in New York. The banner reads "Queers Take Back the Night."

Source: Ed Bailey/AP Images

group that shares a political struggle (an essentialist politics we discussed in relation to second-wave feminism in Chapter 10), but rather several coalitions of groups with similar interests who can work together to institute political change. Queer theory thus often crosses the line between theory and activism, just as it also often moves beyond discussions of sexuality to point to how sexual, classed, racial, and gendered oppressions are interlinked. Often, people will refer to such destabilizing theoretical moves and cultural criticism as working to "queer" the status quo.

A good example of these points comes from Judith Butler, whose early contributions to queer theory are discussed below. At a Christopher Street Day event (a LGBTQ Pride event named in honour of the location of the Stonewall Riots) in Berlin, Germany, on 19 June 2010, Butler refused to accept a "civil courage award" from the organizers. She accused the event of being used to help perpetuate racism against immigrants and so to create a double discrimination against queer immigrants. In other words, she argued that the event—which was supposedly fighting discrimination—was actually perpetuating it. Butler could thus be said to have "queered" an event that was, on its surface, supporting the LGBTQ communities, by openly confronting what she saw as that event's collaboration with other forms of oppression.

While the term *queer theory* began to be applied to this form of intervention in theoretical and cultural analyses only in the 1990s, it is often said to begin with Michel Foucault (1926–1984), specifically his book *History of Sexuality*, Volume 1, published in French in 1976 and translated into English in 1978. It is with this highly influential text that we begin a more detailed discussion of queer theory.

Michel Foucault's *History of Sexuality*

According to traditional histories of sexuality, the twentieth century, especially its second half, was focused on trying to move away from Victorian prudery in order to allow ourselves to become "sexually liberated" in ways that the Victorians were not. This supposed move away from a cultural and personal repression can be said to begin with Freud and the psychoanalytic "talking cure," in which, as we've seen, a repressed trauma is brought to consciousness through a process of analysis and discussion between the patient and the psychoanalyst. Once the trauma was consciously recognized, and so no longer repressed, the patient's symptoms would begin to fade. The end of the Victorian period and of Victorian repression thus seem to be signalled by the rise, at the beginning of the twentieth century, of a Freudian conception of the psyche and the psychoanalytic process.

Foucault, however, aimed to show that it was the Victorians themselves who gave us the tools to talk about sex in the way that we do. Foucault's project, the three-volume *History of Sexuality* (a fourth was largely written before Foucault died, but not published), is informed by the understanding that there are more than two groups (the dominant and dominated), or more than two vested interests, in any given debate, and that this includes debates over sexuality. Also informing Foucault's analysis is the understanding that discussions concerning sexuality end up focusing on these binaries (repressed vs. liberated, straight vs. gay, men vs. women, and so on). Foucault and queer theory in general aim to explode those binaries.

Let's begin by situating the category of Foucault's study, focusing primarily on Volume 1. Ostensibly, it's a history text—it's called, after all, *The History of Sexuality*. But this isn't a book that details events and occurrences, focuses on dates, or creates a chronological narrative of supposedly "objective" or "true" facts and events. Foucault's work is instead a study of the history of a particular kind of discourse. So, rather than give us a history *of sexuality*, Foucault gives us a history *of how people have talked about and defined sexuality*. In other words, instead of focusing on portraying facts, he focuses on portraying how certain things came to be seen as facts: he's giving us a history of the histories of sexuality (see Figure 11.1).

Some examples from the text will clarify this structure. Foucault begins *History of Sexuality* by writing,

> For a long time, *so the story goes*, we supported a Victorian regime, and we continue to be dominated by it even today. Thus, the image of the imperial prude is emblazoned on our restrained, mute, and hypocritical sexuality.
>
> At the beginning of the seventeenth century a certain frankness was still common, *it would seem*. (Foucault, 1990, p. 3; added emphasis)

Foucault goes on to write, "But have we not liberated ourselves from those two long centuries in which the history of sexuality must be seen first as the chronicle of an increasing repression? Only to a slight extent, *we are told*" (p. 5; added emphasis). It seems (note that phrase) that Foucault is offering a quick summary of the narrative provided above, in which the Victorian period serves as the locus of a sexual repression that Western society has been combatting ever since. But look again at the phrases italicized in these quotations: "so the story goes"; "it would seem"; "we are told." These qualifications point to the fact that Foucault is setting up this particular "history of sexuality" as itself a story—a fiction—that serves particular purposes.

So, a general history of sexuality holds that in the Victorian period open discussions of sexuality became taboo and sex itself came to be seen as something that should only be engaged in for procreation, be limited to husbands and wives, kept "productive," and so

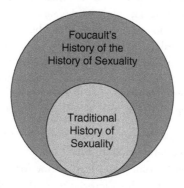

Figure 11.1 Foucault's History of the Histories of Sexuality

on, as discussed above. This history of sexuality is the still common and often accepted one—that the Victorian period saw a rise in the repression of sexual expression, and that we are still suffering from this repression today. But for Foucault, this history—like *all forms of discourse*—is itself functioning within a social framework of power dynamics, as we learned in Chapter 8. This history is therefore not an objective truth about sex, but merely *one of the discourses of sexuality that it purports to explain.*

What Foucault wanted to do is analyze this history to see if the way it's told and propagated serves any function in relation to sex. One of the results of this construction of a history of repression—what he calls the **repressive hypothesis**—is that it makes any discussion of sex seem to be, in and of itself, a daring and transgressive act, one that gives us a feeling of freedom:

> [F]or decades now, we have found it difficult to speak on the subject of sex without striking a different pose: we are conscious of defying established power, our tone of voice shows that we know we are being subversive. . . . Something that smacks of revolt, of promised freedom, of the coming age of a different law, slips easily into this discourse on sexual oppression. Some of the ancient functions of prophecy are reactivated therein. Tomorrow sex will be good again. (pp. 6–7).

But, sadly, it won't. For Foucault, this discourse of sexual freedom, of the sexual revolution, is only possible if it in fact maintains the discourse of repression—if we don't have repression, we can't have this feeling of transgressive freedom when we discuss sex. Think about the first time you talked about sex in a classroom—in a health class, or maybe in the class you're reading this book for: there were likely some giggles, your embarrassed professor may have been blushing, and things seemed briefly somewhere between awkward, awful, and perhaps exciting.

For Foucault, the discourse of repression, and the feelings of transgression that necessarily accompany it, thus serve particular purposes. He writes,

> Briefly, my aim is to examine the case of a society which has been loudly castigating itself for its hypocrisy for more than a century, which speaks verbosely of its own silence, takes great pains to relate in detail the things it does not say, denounces the powers it exercises, and promises to liberate itself from the very laws that have made it function. I would like to explore not only these discourses but also the will that sustains them and the strategic intention that supports them. The question I would like to pose is not, Why are we repressed? but rather, Why do we say, with so much passion and so much resentment against our most recent past, against our present, and against ourselves, that we are repressed? By what spiral did we come to affirm that sex is negated? What led us to show, ostentatiously, that sex is something we hide, to say it is something we silence? (pp. 8–9)

Foucault lays out three doubts as to the legitimacy and purposes of this notion that sexuality was repressed in the Victorian period and into our own (when, for Foucault, people seem to constantly talk about "sexual liberation" of one form or another). First, he wonders if sex was actually repressed in the Victorian period—if there really is a strong case for it. Second, he wonders if theories of repression are really the best way in which to understand the power dynamics invested in sex. Remember, repression plays a huge role in Freudian and other psychoanalytic theories, so Foucault is really questioning, or at least reformulating, some of the foundational theories we've examined (as he does with Marxist theory through his reformulation of the way in which power works, as we saw in Chapter 8). This questioning of these ideas becomes his third doubt or place of analysis: Do the critical discourses and theories that supposedly explain and deal with the "problem" of repression in fact only help to reproduce and support repression?

Foucault does not wish to prove that the traditional history is wrong, but instead to place these critical discourses *into* a history of sexuality themselves. He shows that critical theories of repression and sexuality don't stand above their subject matter and explain it, but are in fact part of that very subject matter, and arise from it. Foucault completely revises the role of sexual discourse in society and culture:

> A first survey made from this viewpoint seems to indicate that since the end of the sixteenth century, the "putting into discourse of sex," far from undergoing a process of restriction, on the contrary has been subjected to a mechanism of increasing incitement; that the techniques of power exercised over sex have not obeyed a principle of rigorous selection, but rather one of dissemination and implantation of polymorphous sexualities; and that the will to knowledge has not come to a halt in the face of a taboo that must be lifted, but has persisted in constituting . . . a science of sexuality. (pp. 12–13)

In other words, the discourses of repression don't isolate or silence sexuality, but instead allow for its increasing centrality to life. More than that, the sciences of sex in the nineteenth century, those that "pathologized" various non-normative sexual behaviours like homosexuality, fetishism, sadism, and so on, did not in fact marginalize or "cure" those problems but instead opened up new possibilities for sexual identities.

Wilde's Trials II: The Construction of Male Homosexuality

As Ed Cohen argues in *Talk on the Wilde Side*, Oscar Wilde's trials were immensely popular subjects—his case was the "Trial of the Century" of its day (Cohen, 1993). People learned about the trial primarily through the reports in newspapers, which took the proof of aberrant acts out of the act itself and placed it on a "type" of person, a process that helped to further the repressive ends of Victorian society. Cohen goes to great lengths to show how Wilde is constructed through various newspaper reports as "extra-ordinary," "extravagant," "indecent," "immoral," and various other terms that position Wilde's character in opposition to "normal" behaviours or identities.

As I have discussed elsewhere (see the Haslam entry in Further Reading), the *Times* newspaper, in defending the witnesses accused of being involved with Wilde, declared, "But let those who were inclined to condemn these men for allowing themselves to be dominated, misled, and corrupted by Mr. Oscar Wilde remember the relative position of the parties, and remember that they were men who had been more sinned against than sinning." Later in the same column, the witnesses were further described:

> There were general observations applicable to all the cases; there was, in point of fact, a startling similarity between each of them on his own

admission which must lead the jury to draw most painful conclusions. There was the fact that in no one of these cases were the parties on an equality in any way with Mr. Wilde; they were none of them educated parties with whom he would naturally associate, and they were not his equal in years. The jury would have observed a curious similarity in the ages of each of them. Mr. Wilde had said that there was something beautiful, something charming about youth which led him to adopt the course he did. It was absurd; his excuse in the witness box was only a travesty of the facts. ("Central Criminal Court, May 1," *The Times*, 2 May 1895)

These descriptions indicate that Wilde is domineering and active in his approach to "sin" (a term used possibly to rejoin notions of "gross indecency" with the religious creed against sodomy, as discussed by Cohen), that his reasons for associating with young men cannot be defended by his "excuses," and that the "unnatural" "course" he "adopted" was one that would be "painful" to the

moral sense of the jury, which, like both the *Times* and its readers, is capable of discerning the "facts" behind Wilde's defence.

Thus, as Cohen discusses, Wilde is constructed as the antithesis to the sexual identity of the so-called normal male—a construction portrayed in explicitly moral terms. Cohen argues, however, that this typing inadvertently helps to construct an identity for people engaging in certain kinds of (homo)sexual acts. In other words, these newspaper reports were unambiguous in their condemnation of Wilde and his "type," but the fact that they focused so much on Wilde's character, even more than on his acts, opened up new possibilities for male sexualities. Following Foucault's argument, Victorian repression here ends up not silencing non-normative sexualities, but in fact helping to codify them as sexual identities and therefore allowing them to flourish.

Critics have challenged Foucault's history, pointing out that there were identity categories for varying sexualities before the Victorian period, but Foucault's analysis nonetheless opens up a new way to analyze the representation of—and silences surrounding—sex in popular culture. That repression can be *productive of* rather than *silencing of* different sexual identities is a significant insight that informs much subsequent queer theory and cultural analysis. In these analyses, discourse and popular culture are seen as primary sites for the creation of identity (and thus take an anti-essentialist view). As we'll see at the end of this chapter, even a text as supposedly "straight" as L. M. Montgomery's much-beloved Canadian classic *Anne of Green Gables* can be read through this lens.

Performative Identities: Judith Butler

Many people picked up on Foucault's insight regarding the way in which discourse can generate identities (sexual and otherwise). This anti-essentialist, constructivist vision doesn't say that people don't "feel" a certain way, or that we can all wake up one day and consciously decide to change our sexual identity. Instead, these discourses give us sites or locations with which we can identify. But for some theorists, even the way we "feel on the inside," so to speak, is generated by our cultural surroundings, just as we saw with the "ideal I" in Lacan and interpellation in Althusser.

Of the queer theorists who followed Foucault, arguably no one has had as significant an impact as Judith Butler (1956–). Butler's theories of identity construction, developing both

Foucault's and Lacan's earlier work, have had a profound influence on cultural studies. This is especially true of her development of the theory of **performativity**—a term she takes from linguistics—in relation to identity. (As we'll discuss later, this term is often confused—even by some academics—with the concept of simple performance, such as acting. But what she means by *performativity*, while related to certain kinds of performance, is radically different.) Her most extended study of gender performativity is found in her book *Gender Trouble*, but it is more succinctly laid out in her 1991 essay "Imitation and Gender Insubordination" (Butler, 2004), which will be the focus of this section. First, we'll discuss Butler's decentring of origins—that is, her attempt to call into question the idea that there are natural sexual identities that are "normal," from which any deviance is "abnormal." We'll then expand on this foundation to look at her notion of the performativity of identity.

With Butler's work, however, we also have an approach to cultural analysis that crosses the borders between theory, practice, and activism. Butler discusses how theory and activism are inseparable, or at least should be. One of her projects is, explicitly, not to "theorize" political practice or activism, but to show how "theory," as she practises it, is inextricably bound to her political activism. In a sense, then, her essay is a theoretical polemic about the polemical nature of theory. This relationship was a major concern in the late 1980s and early 1990s when the essay was written, when so-called "high theory" was being brought into the realm of popular cultural studies, which of course was heavily invested in political debates and battles. Butler points to this debate in one of her footnotes, where she describes how she responded "too strongly" (p. 135) to a questioner during an event at which she was speaking. She details the question and the reply at length in the note, and then writes, "Curiously, this incident was invoked at a CLAGS (Centre for Lesbian and Gay Studies) meeting at CUNY sometime in December of 1989 and, according to those who told me about it, my angry denunciation of the social worker was taken to be symptomatic of the political insensitivity of a 'theorist' in dealing with someone who is actively engaged in AIDS work. That attribution implies that I do not do AIDS work, that I am not politically engaged, and that the social worker in question does not read theory" (p. 136)[†]. She thus points to the ideological assumptions people make regarding the relationship between "theory" and "practice," the academy and the "real world." On an everyday level, her note is also an attempt to fix some misunderstandings, but the very fact that we can talk about an "everyday level," that Butler brings in an apology and an autobiographical discussion, as she does throughout the article, points to the blurriness of the boundaries between daily life, activism, and theory.

This connection between theory and activism might seem like a minor issue, but it's tied to one of Butler's central arguments, one that comes very much out of a Foucauldian understanding of power and identity. Butler writes, "[I]dentity categories tend to be instruments of regulatory regimes, whether as the normalizing categories of oppressive structures or as the rallying points for a liberatory contestation of that very oppression" (p. 121). In other words, **hegemonic** power relations get reinforced and challenged through and by discourse,

---

[†]Source: Butler, Judith. "Imitation and Gender Insubordination." In The Judith Butler Reader, Wiley/Blackwell, pg. 119–137. Copyright (c) 2003. Reprinted by permission of the Copyright Clearance Center.

and part of these relations involve the creation of identity categories: straight and gay, black and white, academic and activist, and so on. And, obviously, there are issues of domination and oppression involved in these categories and relations. As we discussed in Chapter 8, Foucault adds another level to this by saying that the relation between dominator and dominated isn't a unidirectional one, and that even apparently liberatory discourses can be engaged in the very oppression they are attempting to fight—and so for Foucault, discussions of "sexual liberation" are very much part of the "repressive hypothesis." Butler likewise states explicitly that all forms of identifying practices "tend to be" functions of "regulatory regimes"—that is, practices that regulate and control behaviour in various forms.

Obviously, however, these categories exist and people identify with them in a variety of ways. Her essay, then, is not about doing away with identity categories, since that would be part of the problematic "liberatory" rhetoric that Foucault says is invested in the "repressive hypothesis." Butler wants to examine how the process of classification, especially in terms of gender and sexuality, is a constantly problematic one, and one that, in the end, does not fall into a stable or unidirectional exercise of power and domination, but is instead destructured, decentred, and dynamic.

What remains, then, is to discuss the ways in which Butler proves that identity categories are unstable and not tied to an ultimately defining structure of essential difference. Butler analyzes this process of definition, whereby the dominant subject, which says it is the "true," or the "essential" subject, in fact defines itself against various others. Butler argues that in dominant Western discourse, heterosexual identity is set up as the original and natural identity, with other sexualities therefore described as improper copies or unnatural imitations of that identity. In this dominant narrative, one's biological sex is "naturally" related to and reflected in one's gender, which is then "naturally" related to one's sexuality (so that someone who is biologically male is "naturally" masculine and attracted to women). Any variation or change in this narrative is then represented as "abnormal," or as a form of "perversion" of that norm. We can see this happening in the Wilde trials, and in nineteenth-century sexual discourse in general. When science began to look at the issue of homosexuality in the nineteenth century—turning it into an object of study—one of the dominant ways of perceiving homosexuality was, as we've seen, what was called "inversion," where, in part, the "natural" desire of one sex for another is "inverted" onto the same sex.

But what Butler points out is that the "natural" or "original" or "universal" sexuality still defines itself by what it isn't, leading into her main theoretical argument:

> Logically, this notion of an "origin" is suspect, for how can something operate as an origin if there are no secondary consequences which retrospectively confirm the originality of that origin? The origin requires its derivations in order to affirm itself as an origin, for origins only make sense to the extent that they are differentiated from that which they produce as derivatives. Hence, if it were not for the notion of the homosexual *as* copy, there would be no construct of heterosexuality *as* origin. Heterosexuality here presupposes homosexuality. And if the homosexual *as* copy *precedes* the heterosexual as *origin*, then it seems only fair to concede that the copy comes before the origin, and that homosexuality is thus the origin, and heterosexuality the copy. (p. 128)

The logical argument that Butler sets up here can be explained simply: Butler is saying that the only time one needs to define something as "original" is after someone has made a copy. There was no need to call Coca-Cola's recipe the "original" or "classic" recipe until after they invented "New Coke," after all. So, Butler *seems* (note that word, because Butler will come back to critique this point) to be creating a counter-discourse, polemically inverting heterosexuality's claims to dominance in order to make a political point about the legitimacy of queer identities. And to a degree, the history of sexual discourse supports this conclusion. As Eve Kosofsky Sedgwick (discussed below) has noted, the popularization of "the word 'homosexual' . . . preced[ed], as it happens, even that of the word 'heterosexual'" (Sedgwick, 2008, p. 2).

However, for Butler, a flipping of the hierarchical relation of these two categories only *seems* to be the case: she informs us (while possibly punning on the nineteenth-century meaning of *inversion*) that "simple inversions are not really possible. For it is only *as* a copy that homosexuality can be argued to *precede* heterosexuality as the origin. In other words, the entire framework of copy and origin proves radically unstable as each position inverts into the other and confounds the possibility of any stable way to locate the temporal or logical priority of either term" (p. 128). Following the typical model of a Derridean deconstruction (see Chapter 9), Butler exposes the hierarchical binary of the cultural representation of sexuality, and then reverses the binary in order to expose its untenability (see Figure 11.2).

For Butler, then, sexual identity categories, whatever they are, are unstable. Just as for Foucault no one holds power, for Butler no one contains or is contained by a stable sexuality. And this theory about the instability of sexual identity goes against a lot of liberatory gay and lesbian (as opposed to queer) theory and activism, wherein it is claimed that homosexuality is natural and part of one's stable identity. Some activists still feel that arguments such as Butler's are politically problematic, because they seem to work against naturalizing the legitimacy of queer identities. Butler acknowledges this point in order to

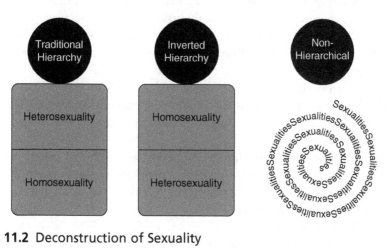

Figure 11.2 Deconstruction of Sexuality

critique it: "But *politically*, we might argue, isn't it quite crucial to insist on lesbian and gay identities precisely because they are being threatened with erasure and obliteration from homophobic quarters? . . . There is no question that gays and lesbians are threatened by the violence of public erasure, but the decision to counter that violence must be careful not to reinstall another in its place" (p. 125). She's arguing precisely what Foucault does—that to a certain extent, liberatory discourses that are engaged in a binary with oppressive discourses can in fact be part of the same hegemonic structure and help to reproduce it, if that rhetoric (re)produces its own "regulatory regimes."

Butler argues against such binaries, saying instead that sexual (and all) identity is open, unstable, and constantly redefinable, which leads into her discussion of performance and performativity. As we've seen, Butler dismantles any rigid hierarchical binary between homo- and heterosexuality. What we're left with is the idea that sexual identity is a constant play of imitation, but with no original that is being imitated. Or, if someone were to define queer identities as only imitations of heterosexuality, they could be only an "imitation of an imitation," because the notion of heterosexuality as origin collapses in on itself (p. 129). This radically empties out, for Butler, the homophobic claims lying behind the notion of homosexuality as an imitation or "fake" identity. We're caught here in a dynamic play of identity in which all identity categories as such can be seen only as constantly under threat of "exposure" as "fakes."

One of the conclusions of this argument, then, is to emphasize the "performance" over the "essence" of gender. Butler argues that gender identity isn't centred on a core, that it isn't derived from some essential, inside part of our minds or our bodies. Gender identity is only the surface, the play of identity, and heterosexuality is the sexual identity that performs itself as an origin—but isn't. All gender performance is, to a degree, a drag performance, Butler says: it is a putting on of an identity not one's own, because gender and sexual identity belong to no one in an essential way. So does this mean that we can all just switch genders at will, or that our self-identification as a particular gender or sexuality is unimportant or always feels fake? Obviously not, and Butler deals with this fact: "Although I have concentrated . . . on the reality-effects of gender practices, performances, repetitions, and mimes, I do not mean to suggest that drag is a 'role' that can be taken on or taken off at will. There is no volitional subject behind the mime who decides, as it were, which gender it will be today. On the contrary, the very possibility of becoming a viable subject requires that a certain gender mime be already underway" (p. 130). This concept should be familiar to us, as it picks up on Althusser's ideology, or on the "public opinion" that Freud says helps to form our ego ideal. Our *being* in gender can exist only if the play of gender is "always already" underway.

Butler uses the term **performative** to explain this always existing "gender mime." The term *performative* comes out of speech-act theory, specifically the writings of J. L. Austin. Austin describes the performative category of speech as those parts of language that literally create something through the act of speaking: Austin's most famous example is someone saying "I do" at a wedding ceremony (Austin, 1975, p. 5). When a couple says that phrase in front of a minister, a justice of the peace, a captain of a ship, or certain Elvis impersonators in Las Vegas, that couple is, simply by saying it, becoming married. Butler uses this idea to define the ways in which she thinks gender and sexual identities work in the world. Gender and sexuality are performative because it is in the act of playing an identity that that identity comes into being. In other words, we don't act out a pre-existing biological or other essence when we act as "men" or "women," but rather in the act of "being" those categories, they actually come into existence.

Before elaborating on this argument, one of the things we should keep in mind is that there is a difference between the words *performance* and *performative*. A performance is just that: the act of fulfilling a role. Performative acts are ones that create something. So, in Butler's essay, performing a gender role is a performative act that creates that very feeling or category of gender.

But within this understanding of performance and performativity, we need to remember that, as noted above, "the very possibility of becoming a viable subject requires that a certain gender mime be already underway" (p. 130). The performative nature of gender is something that, for Butler, is always already in place, and our coming into "being" as social *subjects* is dependent on this pre-existing performative act; there is no "individual" making decisions behind the scenes, so to speak. She builds on the foundational psychoanalytic theories we have already examined, where for Lacan, to take one example, the self or the "I" is formed only in relation to others, so the "I" (what we feel ourselves to be "inside") comes into to being only in relation some "Other" (something "outside"). Let's look at precisely how Butler uses this decentring of identity: "the self only becomes a self on the condition that it has suffered a separation . . ., a loss which is suspended and provisionally resolved through a melancholic incorporation of some 'Other'" (p. 133). But remember, this "Other" is also always implicated in another "Other"—our coming into being is always tied to a coming into performance and imitation with no origin. So even though we develop a sense of internalized identity, we develop it within a performative symbolic matrix.

Butler explains her theory through popular culture, analyzing Aretha Franklin singing "You make me feel like a natural woman" (p. 133). In her song, the (woman) singer is only made to *feel like* a "natural" woman through the actions and gaze of someone else. "Natural" femininity here is at several removes from the person "feeling" it. Butler then asks, "But what if Aretha were singing to me? Or what if she were singing to a drag queen whose performance somehow confirmed her own?" (p. 134). Butler answers these questions by arguing that, "If gender is drag, and if it is an imitation that regularly produces the ideal it attempts to approximate, then gender is a performance that *produces* the illusion of an inner sex or essence" (p. 134). So, if our psychological identity is formed through a connection with an "other" as both Freud and later Lacan would argue, and if this is itself taking place within a symbolic matrix where there is no stability or essential core *anywhere*, then our very psyche, our unconscious being which is formed in this process, is a destabilizing agent that can disrupt our sense of self, our identity. It is not the core that gives our lives meaning or determines us, it is our lives that determine our "core."

Performing Heteronormativity: The Case of the Pregnant Barbie

Gender representation in Mattel's line of Barbie dolls has long been a source of controversy. Indeed, most toys and children's clothing, along with their marketing, are heavily gendered. Walking through a children's section in a mall, one can see the switch from a "boys' aisle" to a "girls' aisle" by the transformation from generally darker colours to almost nothing but pink.

While much could be said of this aspect of children's culture in relation to the feminist theories we discussed in Chapter 10, the gender implications here also touch on issues of sexuality. Specifically, girls' toys often reproduce dominant ideological forms of heteronormativity, positioning girls as "naturally" interested in domesticity (think Easy Bake Oven) and child rearing.

On this last point, one particularly interesting product is Midge, Barbie's "best friend," and specifically her short-lived pregnant version. In 2002, Midge, her husband, Alan, and their children were sold as the "Happy Family line": Midge was sold visibly pregnant, with a removable magnetic stomach, from which one could "deliver" her baby, Nikki.

These dolls were explicitly marketed, in part, as "educational" aids. As one report on the dolls notes, "An article on Mattel's Barbie.com Web site says the 'Happy Family' dolls . . . can be 'a wonderful prop for parents to use with their children to role-play family situations—especially in families anticipating the arrival of a new sibling.'" The article, by University of Southern California psychology professor Jo Ann M. Farver, says the series "provides a way to talk about pregnancy without elaborating on the details a child can't fully comprehend" ("Pregnant Doll"). What such a statement belies, however, is that in taking out specific, reliable facts about sex, pregnancy, and birth, the only "message" the dolls can send relates to the "naturalness" of a particular family structure (after all, teaching children that their mother's stomach is magnetically removable is likely not the point . . .). This "family" play thus takes an explicitly artificial scene and endows it with the weight of cultural authority, transforming the "performance" of role-playing with dolls into a performative structure that serves only to reinforce a heteronormative structure.

Unfortunately for Mattel, the dolls were also seen to reproduce a non-normative family structure: since pregnant Midge was "sold separately," and since her wedding ring wasn't visible, conservative groups thought the doll was promoting teen pregnancy; the dolls were removed from the shelves. Here, perhaps, we can see the slippery nature of performative identities, which, as Butler states, can sometimes highlight their own constructedness.

Source: "Pregnant Doll Pulled from Wal-Mart After Customers Complain." *USA Today*. 24 December 2002. usatoday30. usatoday.com. 07 September 2013.

Nonce Taxonomies: Eve Kosofsky Sedgwick

The same year that Butler's *Gender Trouble* was published, Eve Kosofsky Sedgwick (1950–2009) published another landmark work in queer theory: *Epistemology of the Closet.* Whereas Foucault wanted to analyze how sexuality is formed as an object of discourse and Butler wrote about the formation and perpetuation of sexual identity structures, Sedgwick was interested in the ways the very systems of knowledge in the Western world have been structured by a division between (male) homo- and heterosexuality.

Like other queer and poststructuralist theorists, then, Sedgwick was interested in showing the inherent problems with binary thinking. Rather than focus on how those binaries break down in specific terms, she was primarily interested in the ways these false binaries of sexuality have shaped Western consciousness. Building explicitly on Foucault, Sedgwick argues that, following the end of the nineteenth century and moving forward to our own time, "it becomes truer and truer that the language of sexuality not only intersects with but transforms the other languages and relations by which we know" (Sedgwick, 2008, p. 3).

"Epistemology" is the branch of philosophy that is primarily concerned with questions of how we know things, and what can and can't be known in any given situation. Sedgwick's "epistemology of the closet" holds that Western society's knowledge is limited by the framework of binary sexual opposition. The fact that we posit a division between homo- and heterosexuality, for Sedgwick, frames specific kinds of knowledge of the world for us. It can put blinders on our world view that limit our politics, science, literature, self-awareness, and so on, and not just in relation to sexuality per se. Sedgwick is interested, though, in the way the figure of the "closet," or being closeted, has functioned in and around queer culture. In her book's introduction she proposes several "axioms" that attempt to reframe the obvious assumptions of Western epistemology in order to expose the "open secrets" that lie beneath.

Going through the details of all these axioms would take too much space here, but it's useful to look at the first axiom she proposes, which is, as she says, the most apparently obvious: "People are different from each other" (p. 22). Sedgwick reads this obvious statement to show how the simplistic and over-large categories into which we try to force people are too general to function effectively in the real world. She also shows how current academic analyses (including studies of sexuality) are, rather than "liberatory," actually just as unwieldy in their definitions of people's lived experiences. Of the phrase "people are different," she writes,

> It is astonishing how few respectable conceptual tools we have for dealing with this self-evident fact. A tiny number of inconceivably coarse axes of categorization have been painstakingly inscribed in current critical and political thought: gender, race, class, nationality, sexual orientation are pretty much the available distinctions. They, with the associated demonstrations of the mechanisms by which they are constructed and reproduced, are indispensable, and they may indeed override all or some other forms of difference and similarity. But the sister or brother, the best friend, the classmate, the parent, the child, the lover, the ex-: our families, loves, and enmities alike, not to mention the strange relations of our work, play, and activism, prove that even people who share all or most of our own positionings along these crude axes may still be different enough from us, and from each other, to seem like all but different species. (p. 22)

Sedgwick is pointing out that while, in academic work, we tend to use large categories in order to make claims about groups and individuals, those categories cannot possibly be refined enough to explain those people—or ourselves—in any meaningful way. She goes on, however, to argue that all people, in their daily lives, have "reasonably rich, unsystematic resources of nonce taxonomy for mapping out the possibilities, dangers, and stimulations of their human social landscape" (p. 23). For Sedgwick, it is these "nonce"—meaning particular and temporary—categories of organization, and not the "blunt" instruments she lists above, that need to be the focus of epistemological research.

If one does use a "nonce taxonomy" for understanding sexuality, for example, then one must move beyond the binaries of "straight/gay" and "men/women" to recognize a variety of different practices and identifications that exist within and beyond those categories. Sedgwick lists a number of different actions and identifications—many sounding very similar to the hyper-categorization of the nineteenth-century sexologists—which, she writes, as "most of us know . . . can differentiate even people of identical gender, race, nationality, class, and 'sexual orientation'—each one of which, however, if taken seriously as pure *difference*, retains the unaccounted-for potential to disrupt many forms of the available thinking about sexuality" (pp. 24–25). In the varied but obviously not exhaustive list of these categories, she includes the facts that "Some people like to have a lot of sex, others little or none," "Some people like spontaneous sexual scenes, others like highly scripted ones, others like spontaneous-sounding ones that are nonetheless totally predictable," "Some people's sexual orientation is intensely marked by autoerotic pleasures and histories," and "some people, homo-, hetero-, and bisexual, experience their sexuality as deeply embedded in a matrix of gender meanings and gender differentials" while "Others of each sexuality do not" (pp. 25–26). We all may recognize ourselves or others in this list, Sedgwick says, but if we see any of these items as a *primary* sexual identification (as we do with "gay" or "straight"), then they disrupt our traditional modes of thought about sexuality. Moving beyond sexuality into those other "coarse axes" of identification, we can do the same thing. Whereas Butler's essay deconstructs the binaries of sexuality, Sedgwick attempts to write about the world beyond those binaries, offering yet another queer destabilization of theory and practice.

Queering Queer Theory

As with the other chapters of *Thinking Popular Culture*, this one risks making it sound as if relatively few figures are representative of a wide and constantly developing field. In this case, Foucault's, Butler's, and Sedgwick's works, while foundational, have been expanded on, analyzed, and greatly revised. After all, these texts were written before the term *queer theory* had been popularized: Sedgwick's text, as she notes in a new preface to a later edition, doesn't even use the term. Queer theory as a field is one that is committed to constantly unsettling any received or traditional concepts that risk becoming reflexive ideologies, and queer theory itself isn't immune to this unsettling. One more example, before turning to a case study, will point to another direction one can take within this rich and exciting area of theory.

Building on the destabilizing practices of the theorists discussed above, cultural critic Lee Edelman (1953–) proposes a vision of queer theory and queerness itself as that which stands radically opposed to many of the foundational principles of Western thought.

Edelman turns away from liberal approaches to queer theory and activism, a liberalism that would reject the "ascription of negativity to the queer" and work to incorporate multiple sexual subjects into the body politic (one can think here of the fight for recognition of same-sex marriage rights as an example). Instead, Edelman writes, "[W]e might . . . do better to consider accepting and even embracing" the negative associations ascribed to queerness (Edelman, 2004, p. 4). In this way, Edelman wants not to gesture toward some perfect world (a utopian impulse he associates with liberal social programs) but instead to deploy queerness as an ever-present challenge to the status quo. He writes, "[S]uch queerness proposes, in place of the good, something I want to call 'better,' though it promises, in more than one sense of the phrase, absolutely nothing" (p. 5). Edelman thus rejects the teleological, or future- and goal-oriented, epistemology of much of Western thought, while also rejecting the liberal rhetoric that would place queer subjects into that epistemology. Just as the term *queer* in queer theory functions as a reappropriation of a homophobic epithet, Edelman wants to reappropriate homophobic statements that place queerness as the opposite of "Western civilization."

Not content to invert, explode, or otherwise undermine the binaries of sexuality, as the other theorists we've examined have done, Edelman shows how the binary of "straight" and "queer" figures another one: that of "productive future" or "civilization" vs. "death" or "disorder." Reading these figures through Lacan and Freud, Edelman sees "queerness" (which is both identified with and functions beyond people who are "stigmatized for failing to comply with heteronormative mandates") as a sign that can "*figure* the undoing of civil society, the death drive of the dominant order," and thus can expose the biases that that order tries to silence. And so, for Edelman, "queerness can never define an identity; it can only ever disturb one" (p. 17).

Case Study

Queering *Anne of Green Gables*

Queer analyses of popular culture are as varied as the theoretical texts we've discussed in this chapter. Queer readings of popular culture can focus on how a creative work challenges heteronormative assumptions—that is, the assumption that heterosexuality is the "natural" and "original" sexuality—or they can point to the endless play of gender and sexual performances in a given text or historical moment, or they can show how sexual identity is tied to other such identity performances and constructions as race, class, nationality, and so on.

One rich form of queer analysis is the "queering" of a supposedly "straight" item of popular culture.

Such readings often take a deconstructive approach in order to demonstrate how the "straight" reading of the text is always already implicated in its own undoing, that the very heteronormativity the work or cultural moment seems to espouse is in fact always undoing itself. In Canadian academic circles, probably the most famous of these analyses is Laura Robinson's queer reading of L. M. Montgomery's *Anne of Green Gables*. Anne is, of course, a significant figure in Canadian popular culture: Montgomery's novel has remained one of the most consistently popular works of fiction in Canada ever since it was published in 1908 (in the United States). Beyond the original novels, Montgomery's creation has since been transformed for the stage, film, and popular television programs, and has been the centre of many tourism campaigns.

Robinson first presented her paper at the annual meeting of the Association of Canadian College and University Teachers of English in spring 2000, but the paper was the subject of controversy even before she read it. A version of it was published as "Bosom Friends: Lesbian Desire in L. M. Montgomery's Anne Books," and the controversy itself has been discussed in numerous forums, including Cecily Devereux's "Anatomy of a 'National Icon': *Anne of Green Gables* and the 'Bosom Friends' Affair." Robinson analyzes how the novel performs a heteronormative silencing of same-sex desire between Anne and other girls in the novel. Her argument builds on Adrienne Rich's concept of **compulsory heterosexuality**, according to which a patriarchal society explicitly denies women the experience of their own sexual lives, subordinating women to a heterosexual framework in which men are always in the active and dominating position. What Rich calls a "lesbian existence" functions to deny the compulsory nature of this patriarchal existence, allowing women to experience their own lives, separate from such domination.

For Robinson, "intense female friendships" are "central to every book" in Montgomery's Anne series. Reading Montgomery's references to (and strong negative reaction to) lesbian desire in her journals, Robinson demonstrates that "Montgomery was patently aware that these friendships could suggest other possibilities, such as same-sex desire" (Robinson, 2004, p. 13). She develops these and other points to analyze how, "[b]y constructing a world where women's love for each other is a source of power and fulfilment, and then emphasizing the inevitability of marriage, Montgomery's novels underscore the fact that, at the turn of the twentieth century, heterosexuality was compulsory. At the same time, by exposing the operations of compulsory heterosexuality, Montgomery's Anne books subtly challenge the patriarchal traditions

that intervene in women's relationships with each other" (p. 13). In other words, Robinson's essay points to the ways the Anne books *silence*, through marriage, the very possibility of the fulfillment of lesbian sexual desire, despite the fact that Anne's relationships with girls and women are so central, and are often described in physical terms (hugging, kissing, and so on), while her relationship with boys are not. Because the novels continually lead or gesture to the goal of straight marriage, but always revert to Anne's relationships with girls and women, they are constantly invoking the very possibility of a "lesbian existence" that they seem to work to repress.

Robinson's argument thus picks up on the base laid out by the queer theorists discussed in this chapter, pointing to the ways in which a supposedly "normal" or "essential" heterosexuality is actually built on the un-solid foundation of performative sexual and gender roles that are always, as Butler argues, comparing themselves to what they are not. Nor was Robinson the first or only scholar to make such an argument. As she details in the published version of the paper, numerous literary critics, historians, and others have pointed to the erotic language used between girls and women in the Anne novels, and the ways these relationships "displace[d] and disrupt[ed] heterosexual conventions" (p. 15).

But the controversy sparked by the sensationalist reporting on the paper is as informative for our purposes as the original paper is. This controversy, importantly, began even *before* Robinson had uttered one word of her argument. Devereux writes,

> Tom Spears, a reporter at the *Ottawa Citizen*, "broke" the story of Robinson's reading of "lesbian desire" in *Anne of Green Gables* prior to the presentation of the paper. . . . Spears's report, which was based on a reading of the paper Robinson had sent him . . . set the tone in establishing what the paper was "about": it was "about" the singular discovery by an English professor that English Canada's best-loved literary heroine *was* a lesbian. (Devereux, 2002, p. 34)

The story went on "to become front-page news," news reports in which "Robinson would be attacked and ridiculed." Many "letters to the editor" to different newspapers followed, suggesting, as Devereux quotes one letter-writer saying, that academics were "destroying these classics by 'queering' them" (pp. 36–37).

How then to read this reaction to a paper that, at the time, only a very few people had heard, and no one but Robinson herself and one reporter actually had in front of them? Well, using the theoretical tools we've discussed, we can see it in the following ways, which aren't exhaustive of the queer approaches that could be taken to either the texts or the situation. One could follow Foucault's argument concerning the repressive hypothesis and note that the sensation of someone speaking about *Anne of Green Gables* and sexuality, specifically in terms of the repressive nature of compulsory heterosexuality, functions to lull us into feeling that we're moving beyond that repression. But the immediately negative and, yes, repressive reaction to the argument points us in another direction. We could instead read the vehement reaction against Robinson's reading as a form of repression that, like some of the more pathologizing nineteenth-century sexologists, doesn't *silence* the potential queerness of Anne but instead helps to promulgate that reading. In other words, like Robinson's reading itself of the Montgomery books, every time someone felt the need to speak against the potential queerness of Anne, that person had to mention the queerness of Anne: the reader who vilified Robinson, and by extension other academics, for "queering" texts thereby admits to the possibility of such readings of "classics." As Foucault writes, such a response "speaks verbosely of its own silence [and] takes great pains to relate in detail the things it does not say" (p. 8)—that is, in many ways these responses in fact prove Robinson's point about compulsory heterosexuality and its silencing of the various forms of female love relationships.

The reaction against Robinson's article—especially as that reaction was based on very little information about the actual argument—can also be read through Butler's piece. Specifically, the vociferous

denial of the possibility of Anne's homosexuality (even though that wasn't what Robinson was arguing) and the equally loud condemnations of such queer readings can, perhaps obviously, point to both the performed and performative nature of heterosexuality. As Butler argues, drag performances (and, one could say, queer analyses of popular culture) work "to expose heterosexuality as an incessant and *panicked* imitation of its own naturalized idealization. That heterosexuality is always in the act of elaborating itself is evidence that it is perpetually at risk, that is, that it 'knows' its own possibility of becoming undone: hence, its compulsion to repeat which is at once a foreclosure of that which threatens its coherence" (Butler, 2004, p. 129). That the very mention of homosexuality in relation to *Anne of Green Gables* would inspire such a heated response, and that that response actually made the argument better known across the country (and even globally) than it otherwise would have been, points not only to the "panicked" defence of heterosexuality but also to its constant need to invoke homosexuality as a ground against which heterosexuality is defined. Once again, the response to the then-unheard paper proves the paper's very point. Likewise, through becoming a "figure" of queerness in Edelman's sense, this "queer Anne" can threaten the very future (seen in the youth of Anne and her always deferred future) of dominant society's sexual binaries, and even of the society itself, leading to this sense of panic.

Finally, the response to Robinson's work also points to how the "nonce taxonomies" of sexuality that Sedgwick details are denied by a binary epistemology that grants the status of "identity" to only a homo/hetero pairing. The logic of the panicked response to Robinson's paper would seem to claim that if a paper argues that the novels point to a level of sexual desire between women, then that paper must be arguing that Anne (and by extension her creator) is gay. These reactionary responses would say that because Montgomery wasn't gay (and was, indeed, hostile toward expressions of physical attraction between women), therefore Anne can't be gay, therefore these expressions of love between women and girls in the novels don't express "lesbian desire." Nowhere in the anti-Robinson response is there a notion that sexuality can exist along a spectrum of different desires, that lesbian or same-sex desire can be expressed to varying degrees even among people who do not identify as "gay," or that the novels may in fact be an attempt to repress or expunge that desire. The lack of an understanding of a "nonce" sexual system leads to the inability to analyze or express desires that may go beyond that binary system.

Discussion Questions

1. Can you think of other examples, in addition to *Anne of Green Gables*, that appear on the surface to be "straight" examples of popular culture, but if read closely might undermine their own heteronormative assumptions? Are there particular characters in popular culture that have both "straight" and "queer" connotations?

2. In 1954, Fredric Wertham, a psychologist, published a book called *Seduction of the Innocent*, in which he wrote that superhero comics, specifically Batman and Robin stories, presented "a subtle atmosphere of homoerotism [*sic*]" (Wertham, 1954, p. 190). Wertham saw these comic books as therefore being harmful to children, because children could be influenced by this "atmosphere" and thus drawn away from what he saw as a "normal" life. Does Wertham's theory fit into Foucault's "repressive hypothesis"? If it does, what implications does that have for analyzing Wertham's reading of Batman and Robin?

3. Judith Butler argues that drag performances highlight the performative notion of gender and sexuality; that is, a drag queen or drag king points to the ways our society "tells" us how to act out gender, and in so doing highlights that gender is just that: a set of social codes or acts. Can you think of any other examples of popular culture that highlight the performative role of gender? What about Madonna's, Marilyn Manson's, or Lady Gaga's videos: Do they highlight the "acting out" of gender, or do they reinforce certain gender or sexual roles? Can they do both?

Further Reading

Creekmur, Corey K., and Alexander Doty, eds. *Out in Culture: Gay, Lesbian, and Queer Essays on Popular Culture*. Durham: Duke UP, 1995.

Delany, Samuel R. *Times Square Red, Times Square Blue*. New York: New York UP, 1999.

glbtq: *The Online Encyclopedia of Gay, Lesbian, Bisexual, Transgender, and Queer Culture*. <http://www.glbtq.com>.

Goldie, Terry, ed. *In a Queer Country: Gay and Lesbian Studies in the Canadian Context*. Vancouver: Arsenal, 2001.

Haslam, Jason. *Fitting Sentences: Identity in 19th- and 20th-Century Prison Narratives*. Toronto: U of Toronto P, 2005.

Holland, Merlin. *The Real Trial of Oscar Wilde: The First Uncensored Transcript of the Trial of Oscar Wilde vs. John Douglas (Marquess of Queensberry), 1895.* New York: HarperCollins, 2003.

Kinsman, Gary. *The Regulation of Desire: Sexuality in Canada.* Montreal: Black Rose Books, 1987.

Kuefler, Mathew, ed. *The History of Sexuality Sourcebook.* Peterborough: Broadview, 2007.

Peele, Thomas, ed. *Queer Popular Culture: Literature, Media, Film, and Television.* New York: Palgrave, 2007.

Phillips, Kim M., and Barry Reay, eds. *Sexualities in History: A Reader.* New York: Routledge, 2002.

Chapter 12

Race, "Race," and Racism

INTRODUCTION

In Chapters 10 and 11 we focused on identity categories—gender and sexuality—that are assumed by many to be expressions of a biological essence, but that we discussed as social constructions. This chapter continues that **anti-essentialist** discussion in the context of the identity category of **race**.

We'll discuss the origins of the modern notion of race, and then move into contemporary cultural theories concerning race, racial identity, and racism, along with the relationship between cultural theory, popular culture, and anti-racist activism. As with our discussions of feminism and sexuality, important to keep in mind here is that this is an introduction to an increasingly complex, constantly developing field. The history that follows again begins with **Eurocentric** definitions of race and the concomitant practices of racism (the former, in many ways, inventing the latter), and then moves on to the many direct challenges to those definitions and practices offered by anti-racist and rights activists and theorists. These challenges were most directly occasioned by the anti-racist struggles during civil rights movements in North America and elsewhere, from their origins in the late nineteenth century through to their heights in the 1960s and up to today. Particularly influential in the development of cultural studies analyses of race were several critics coming out of African American and other black diasporic traditions. It is out of these material struggles by oppressed peoples to have their rights recognized that several theories of race and anti-racist cultural practices developed.

Added to these theories, of course, are works concerning other racialized groups and contexts. We'll discuss, for example, the representation of Indigenous peoples in Canada, a discussion that will take us directly into the theories of nationalism and postcolonialism discussed in Chapter 13, which are intricately tied to those of race. Also connected in this context is Canadian "multiculturalism," which we also discuss in Chapter 13. As with the identities discussed in the preceding chapters, it's important to remember that discussions of race, gender, sexuality, class, nationality, and other categories don't exist in isolation but are always braided together, in popular culture and elsewhere.

THE MAKING OF RACE

While human beings have often found ways of differentiating one group of people from others, the notion that there are specific, biological subsets of the human species called races—distinguished largely by phenotypical variations (in skin tone, notably, but also hair colour and type and other physical features)—has a relatively brief history. Indeed, the term *race* has itself been used in several different ways, not only to distinguish human beings physically but also by geography, language, cultural practices, and other aspects of human life. As we discuss in Chapter 13, the terms *race* and *nation* were interchangeable at different moments in Western history.

The use of race as a way of biologically or culturally differentiating people from each other is an unscientific one. Human beings are all members of the same species—we are all *Homo sapiens*, primates within a specific biological family, genus, and species; and so, biologically speaking, the differences between us are merely minor physical variations. People whose recent ancestry traces back to particular regions or populations may tend to have one sort of skin tone, while those whose ancestors come from a different region or population could well have a different skin tone, and of course other minor physical variations exist. But although we can distinguish certain physical differences or traits that may or may not relate to genetic heritage, the concept of race extends far beyond the cataloguing of such differences, and is historically connected to power and social hierarchies.

Race, like gender and sexuality, is thus often represented as a "biological" and essential fact, but in reality it has a particular discursive history that derives from what we would now call pseudo-science, and that is inseparable from the histories of imperialism, conquest, slavery, and other violent forms of global social interaction, as well as resistance to them. Before moving on to contemporary cultural theories of race and its representation in popular culture, then, we need to trace the origin of race as a category of identification by going back to the Enlightenment and Romantic periods and their "scientific" studies of humanity.

The Modern Categories of Race

The categories of race as we understand them find their origins in the early days of global exploration and contact between different human populations, specifically in the form of European expansion and colonization. Phenotypical and cultural differences were often seen as being related, and were explained according to whatever world view or ideology dominated at the time. One early form of the division of humanity took shape through the religious notion of the Great Chain of Being, through which all elements of life were said to be ordered on a chain that had its pinnacle at God.

It was during the eighteenth and nineteenth centuries, when European scientists began to turn a categorizing gaze onto humanity itself, that the modern taxonomy of race was solidified. Perhaps the most influential of these "racial" thinkers was the German scientist J. F. Blumenbach. Often regarded as a founder of anthropology, Blumenbach was especially interested in the physical differences of peoples from different parts of the world. In the third edition of his most famous study, *On the Natural Varieties of Mankind* (1795), Blumenbach divided the human species into five "varieties," or races, based on their physiognomy, including skull shape. Blumenbach referred to these varieties as "*Caucasian, Mongolian, Ethiopian, American*, and *Malay*" (Blumenbach, 1969, p. 264). While most of these terms—with the exception of *Caucasian* for white or northern European people— have fallen out of use as racial categories, the basic outlines of modern racial divisions are visible here.

Blumenbach believed that all species had a more perfect variety, one that held true to its original form and from which all other varieties had "degenerated" into their current form. Within human varieties, Blumenbach decided that the Caucasian, or northern European type, was the "primeval" or original one. What was his "scientific" evidence for this claim? That this "variety" has, he writes, "that kind of appearance which, according to our opinion of symmetry, we consider the most handsome and becoming," and which has "the most beautiful form of the skull" (pp. 265, 269).

Unlike other racial scientists of his day, Blumenbach did not divide humanity into different sub-species, instead seeing in these "varieties" one overarching type of humanity. But within this larger category he did posit a hierarchy, ranging from the more "original" and "beautiful" form of the Caucasian group to the more "degenerate" forms of other groups, thus paving the way for a pseudo-scientific racism that remains a social problem today. We can already see the difficulty with viewing race as being a currently scientifically meaningful category: the term *Caucasian* is still used, after all, even though it was popularized almost three centuries ago by a man who, based on a small collection of skulls, decided which he thought to be the most beautiful. Clearly, there is more of the social and ideological to the formation and maintenance of racial categories than there is the scientific.

National Characteristics

In addition to Blumenbach's relatively arbitrary division of humanity, what we now think of as race was inexorably tied to discussions of nationality. As we discuss in Chapter 13, from the mid-eighteenth century through to the nineteenth, the **nation** wasn't necessarily completely coterminous with the idea of a **nation state**, a political entity with specific, legally demarcated borders. While it might include such a definition, the nation was also tied to notions of the "spirit" of a people settled in a particular geographical region, sharing such cultural behaviours as religion, dress, and music. *Nation* in this period therefore often collapsed the distinction between people living under a certain political structure and within specific borders, and what we would now call ethnicity or cultural identity.

Similarly, though, *nation* also demarcated those elements of biology and hereditary origins that we often now associate with race. All of these categories were wrapped up in the definition of what was called **national character**, a category of identity defined by such nationalist thinkers as Johann Herder (see Chapter 13), but also by rationalist, empiricist, and scientific philosophers, including Immanuel Kant (1724–1804).

For Kant and similar thinkers, people from different parts of the world had distinct, essential identities that differentiated them from people in other parts of the world. These included cultural variances of religion and art, but all such particularities were seen to arise from essential, immutable differences between groups of people. Thus, for Kant, even within Europe the Italians, the French, the English, the Dutch, and so on all had distinctly different forms of aesthetic appreciation and scientific capabilities, which in turn related to distinctions of temper and "spirit" such that these peoples were distinct from each other in ways that could be proven through observation. He writes, for example, that "The characters of mind of the peoples are most evident in that in them which is moral. . . . The Spaniard is serious, taciturn, and truthful. . . . The Italian seems to have a feeling which mixes that of a Spaniard and that of a Frenchman. . . . The Frenchman has a dominant feeling for the morally beautiful. . . . The Englishman is at the beginning of every acquaintance cold and indifferent toward a stranger" (Kant, 2011, pp. 51–54). It is a list that continues on and on.

Significantly, Kant didn't think he was offering mere opinion here; he believed that what he was saying was true and could be proven through empirical evidence. Therefore, while these descriptions may seem to be archaic and bigoted nationalist **stereotypes**, some of Kant's opinions (he would call them observations) point to pernicious nationalist and racist claims that have informed public policy and social biases well into the contemporary period, and even today. After all, Kant and others didn't just say there were differences between these various peoples; they also placed these groups in hierarchical relations to each other, where some national characters were better than others. In other words, Kant's vision of the "truth" of national character, and similar views held by others, helped to form and produce ideological claims of superiority and inferiority.

Given the imbricated nature of nation and race in this period, Kant's and others' visions of national character thus also helped to reproduce what we would now call racist stereotypes. Indeed, we can say that the very notion of race was invented by their racism. Expanding his study beyond northern Europe, Kant addresses "the Arab," "the Chinese," "the Indians," the "Negroes of Africa," and "the savages . . . of North America," among other groups, making the most grotesquely racist statements regarding intellect, capability, morality, and so on (pp. 58–59).

In short, the very creation of the modern notion of race is inseparable from what we know of as racism. Pseudo-scientific claims about racial identity were used as justifications for the Atlantic slave trade, for example, even as slavery created the material conditions whereby people of African heritage were subjected to systematic racial oppression.

CULTURAL THEORIES OF RACE, "RACE," AND RACISM

In the preceding section we saw that the creation of the category of race in the Western world was coterminous with the social production of racism, and hence that categories of race are based more on cultural and ideological forces than on scientific fact. In other words, while race has in the past been defined as an essential characteristic of individuals and groups, a natural division of humanity, we can now see it as a socially and culturally constructed category that serves to (re)produce certain social relations of power and dominance; i.e., it serves particular **hegemonic** purposes. In order to question racist social structures, then, many (though not all) contemporary cultural critics of race and racism begin with an anti-essentialist argument, much as we saw in our discussions of gender and sexuality. And whereas some of the foundational contemporary cultural theories of race developed out of the civil rights movement and focus especially on African diasporic communities in different parts of the world, many more analyses of race and popular culture expand on these to examine the representation, and the personal and community perspectives, of other racialized groups, especially through the study of minority or politically disenfranchised or underrepresented groups. We'll now trace out some of these anti-essentialist theories as well as their precursors and responses to them.

Race, Representation, and Indigenization

As in studies of gender and culture, analyses of race in relation to popular culture often focus on issues of representation—who is represented and who is not, the manner in which particular groups are represented, and who controls the production of the representations. Generally speaking, following the paradigm of materialist or **Marxist** analysis, the control of the means of production (in this case, the control of media production and distribution) implies an ideological control, or a control of ideas themselves (in this case, the content of films, television, music, and so on). This understanding of cultural production generally implies that, in a society in which certain social hierarchies are maintained based on race—i.e., in a racist social structure—the culture will reproduce those racist hierarchies. Likewise, we could use **structuralist** analyses such as those of Roland Barthes to discuss the **mythologies** of race reproduced in the popular culture of a particular society and time.

Often, such dominant cultural products thus perpetuate certain racist stereotypes. These stereotypes, following the logic of racial essentialism outlined above, ascribe both individual and group behaviour to members of particular races, arguing that such behaviour is both the result of and can define the characteristics of all members of a given racial group. Thus, the behaviour of one person from group X is taken as an example of the behaviour of the entire group, or the behaviour of a specific person is ignored or explained on the basis of its relation to stereotypical, mythical assumptions about the behaviour of the group to which the person belongs. These stereotypes, as a form of myth or hegemonic discourse, ultimately serve to maintain the dominance of a particular racial group (in the Global North, they tend to support a white supremacist, and **patriarchal**, social structure).

One telling North American example of such a stereotyping practice is the representation in popular culture of Aboriginal peoples from both the United States (notably in Hollywood film) and Canada. In their study of the representation of race and diversity in Canadian media, Augie Fleras and Jean Lock Kunz discuss the range of stereotypical

Miss America, Gender, and Race

One does not have to look far to discover myriad forms of racist stereotyping in popular culture. One example points to how racial identification is more dependent on racism itself than the other way around, and how these stereotypes feed into gender, sexual, nationalist, and other forms of identification, as we discuss throughout Part IV.

On 15 September 2013, Nina Davuluri was crowned Miss America. Dating back to the 1920s, Miss America is a beauty pageant that, like other pageants of its kind, is routinely criticized for objectifying women and purveying a standard of beauty that reinforces particular patriarchal and other ideological interests. Moreover, the pageant was for almost fifty years restricted to white women, particularly to young, unmarried white women. In other words, the pageant not only reinforced certain gender codes but also enforced a hierarchy of beauty that placed young white women at the top. Starting in the 1970s, black women and members of other racial minorities were allowed to participate as contestants.

Davuluri is the daughter of Indian immigrants, and her win could thus be said to challenge the racist stereotypes of beauty. Nonetheless, when she won, the power of racist bigotry and stereotyping was made clear. Social media outlets, especially Twitter, witnessed an unleashing of racist invective. Calling Davuluri—an American-born Hindu of Indian-born parents—an "Arab," a "Muslim," and a "terrorist," these tweets unwittingly exposed the vicious power of stereotyping. People associated the colour of her skin, and perhaps her performance of a Bollywood-style dance, with a general **Orientalist** stereotype (to be explored in more detail in Chapter 13). This set of stereotypes is, both before and following the 9/11 attacks, associated with a generalized "Arab" other who is often represented across the popular media as, by definition, non- and anti-American.

While the ignorance of these tweets may be easy for most of us to recognize, their widespread nature demonstrates precisely how powerful popular culture stereotyping of particular "racial" identifiers can be, and how disconnected they are from any form of objective truth. That disconnect, however, makes such stereotypes no less dangerous to those who are subject to them, as these stereotypes provide both support and an outlet for a variety of white supremacist acts of hate.

portrayals of Indigenous people. They list several stereotypes, grouping them into three categories: "primitive savages," "pastoral primitives," and "primitive problem people." In the first, Indigenous people are represented as "wild, defiant and non-deferential, lawless"; in the second as "picturesque, idealized, bucolic, and romantic"; and in the third as "creat[ing] . . . and/or hav[ing] problems" (Fleras & Kunz, 2001, p. 137). As the authors note, some or all of these stereotypes can exist in any given example of dominant media representations of First Nations peoples. "Collectively," though, "these images reinforce the notion of First Nations as peoples from a different time and place, whose histories began with the arrival of the white man and whose reality only makes sense in terms of their interaction with whites" (p. 137). Similarly, such representations often treat all Indigenous peoples—including the disparate populations and practices of the various First Nations, the Métis, and the Inuit—as a homogeneous group: people will often mistakenly use *First Nations* as a collective term for all Indigenous peoples, for example, even though the term refers to specific nations and doesn't include the Métis and Inuit peoples.

Beyond the obviously demeaning and oversimplifying vision of Indigenous peoples such representations offer, they also influence and filter into news media representations of Aboriginal peoples and their interactions with the Canadian government, as Fleras argues elsewhere: "The framing of Aboriginal peoples as model (good) or immoral (bad) compromises the possibility of seeing them as complex personalities with multi-dimensional lives" and instead presents them as "outsiders whose unidimensional lives are defined by their status as pathetic victims, belligerent warriors, and quixotic tree huggers" (Fleras, 2011, p. 219).

Of course, as we've seen, cultural analysis also gives us tools through which to recognize the function of resistant cultural production (for instance, the recognition in Marxist analysis that modern industrial societies always involve competing relations to production that lead to competing visions of society and its people). Other cultural theories, following Foucauldian models of **power**, for example, or **poststructuralist** notions of meaning, allow us to see where those larger structures of domination represented by myth or ideology break down and can be challenged. But we can also see such resistance, when discussing racially othered groups, by analyzing the cultural materials *and* cultural theories that arise from those groups. Against such demeaning, dominant representations of Indigenous people discussed above, as Fleras argues, Indigenous peoples' own media provide other, more complex visions of Indigenous peoples and cultures. Listing several examples of print media owned and operated by Indigenous people, and discussing how Indigenous forms of storytelling have influenced or been represented in recent films, Fleras notes how a recognition of the need to "indigenize" or "aboriginalize" media can help shift not only popular culture representations but also public policy. In some recent cases, resistant voices have arguably broken through the more stereotypical frameworks of traditional media, especially through the medium of social media (see the "Idle No More" box, below). (In Chapter 13 we discuss more issues surrounding Indigenous peoples and Canada in relation to colonial and postcolonial movements and theories.)

The Psychology of Race: Frantz Fanon

As the discussion of Indigenous peoples' representation in North American media makes clear, race, Western imperialism, and colonialism (analyzed in more detail in Chapter 13) are inextricably entwined. Western powers often used racist formulations of other peoples in order to justify their imperial actions, as happened with the European colonization of Africa and the French and English colonization of what is now Canada, for example. Using the essentialist and hierarchical divisions of race discussed earlier, many European powers rationalized their right to colonize, control, and enslave Indigenous populations as the right of the "civilized" society over the "primitive" or "savage" societies. This process is often referred to as **othering**, and it lies at the heart of racist and colonial oppression.

One of the most influential writers to describe the intricacies of the othering process is the Algerian theorist and activist Frantz Fanon (1925–1961). Writing in part from his own experiences as a black man raised in the French colony of Algeria, Fanon, in his 1952

Idle No More and #Ottawapiskat

In fall 2012, Nina Wilson, Sylvia McAdam, Jessica Gordon, and Sheelah McLean founded Idle No More, an activist movement of Indigenous peoples and their allies that focused on resisting Bill C-45. This bill, proposed by the majority Conservative government, was seen by many to jeopardize certain environmental protections and to violate First Nations' and other First Peoples' lands.

In addition to demonstrations, flash mobs, gatherings, and other public events, related protests took place to highlight what is considered to be the government's mishandling of treaties with Indigenous peoples. One of these allied protests was a lengthy hunger strike conducted by Chief Theresa Spence of Attawapiskat First Nation, a community that had experienced a housing crisis a year earlier. Canadian media began covering her hunger strike; new attention was brought to Attawapiskat and its management; and Chief Spence and others were accused of mismanaging the Nation's finances—accusations fuelled by a government audit leaked to the CBC during her strike (see "Timing"). This narrative aligns directly with Fleras's analysis of the representation of Indigenous peoples (Fleras, 2011, p. 219).

News stories surrounding Idle No More, Chief Spence, the audit, and related issues became hot topics for comment threads on news media websites. When many of these threads became heated, exhibiting the forms of racist stereotyping discussed by Fleras and Kunz, the CBC, for one, addressed the issue ("Can Idle No More Comment Threads").

But then something interesting happened. On Twitter, Aaron Paquette started the hashtag discussion topic "Ottawapiskat" (combining Canada's capital city and Attawapiskat), writing "Can we get #Ottawapiskat going? As in, Parliament sure is wasteful in #Ottawapiskat;) just some good natured satire" ("'Ottawapiskat'

Twitter Tag"). In their ensuing replies, people reversed the anti-Indigenous stereotypes we've discussed, transferring them to the federal government and to Prime Minister Stephen Harper in particular. Among the examples were "#Ottawapiskat chief is living in a mansion while many of his people are homeless" and "No accountability from #Ottawapiskat Chief and Council, a pass and permit system should be implemented" ("'Ottawapiskat' Twitter Tag"). Such comments not only reverse the generalizations and stereotypes but also deftly highlight how the actions of white government leaders are rarely analyzed or generalized in the same way as those of Indigenous leaders. Although some (including those cited in the CBC blog article) saw the humour as misguided or counterproductive, it nonetheless highlighted the way in which media coverage and responses thereto had been implicated in the problematic representational politics of race.

Idle No More activists.

Sources: N8n photo/Alamy

"Can Idle No More Comment Threads Be More Constructive?" *YourCommunity Blog.* CBC.ca. 8 January 2013. Web.

"'Ottawapiskat' Twitter Tag Satirizes Idle No More Criticisms," *YourCommunity Blog.* CBC.ca. 14 January 2013. Web.

"Timing of Attawapiskat Audit's Release Is a Ploy to 'Discredit' Me: Theresa Spence," *National Post,* 7 January 2013. Web.

book *Black Skin, White Masks*, analyzes what he sees as the psychological ramifications of the racist othering that goes hand in hand with colonization.

Relying on Freudian and Lacanian psychoanalysis, Fanon argues that black subjects cannot form a direct and uninhibited relationship with the dominant culture around them, and so are necessarily traumatized. Black people in a white-dominated society, he argues, experience an alienation from that society which affects the development of their psyches. This leads to his profoundly unsettling assertion, in the introduction to *Black Skin, White Masks*, that "the black is not a man" (Fanon, 2008, p. 1). This shocking statement means that black people, raised and living in a society dominated by or privileging whites, cannot experience the state of being **individuals**, as we have defined it, nor can they ever even feel as if they can be such individuals. Living in a white world and surrounded by a white cultural **superstructure**, a black person, he writes, "is rooted at the core of a universe from which he must be extricated" (p. 2); that is, black people in white-dominated societies exist in a world that would deny them full existence or independence.

This situation consists of more than a sense of disconnection from one's surrounding world. It is, following psychoanalytic principles, a situation that disrupts the proper formation of the psyche. Remember that, for Sigmund Freud and, following him, Jacques Lacan, a person's sense of self, the **ego**, mediates between the **id**, or instinctual, libidinal desires, and an **ideal ego**, or unconscious ideal sense of self that is formed by social expectations, such as those from the person's parents and the surrounding society. Fanon argues that systemic racism in a society transforms this process into one in which the racialized subject internalizes a lack of self-worth. Why? Because the dominant white culture presents itself, ideologically, as the natural and universal culture, one that the black subject is continually separated from. As he writes, "I believe that the fact of the juxtaposition of the white and black races has created a massive psychoexistential complex"; however, as with the "talking cure" of psychoanalytic treatment, Fanon "hope[s] by analyzing it to destroy it" (p. 5).

Importantly for our purposes, Fanon uses examples from popular culture to explain this socialization process and the psychological damage it inflicts (in a way that looks forward to Fleras's and Kunz's discussions of stereotypes):

> Tarzan stories, the sagas of twelve-year-old explorers, the adventures of Mickey Mouse, and all those "comic books" serve actually as a release for collective aggression. The magazines are put together by white men for little white men. This is the heart of the problem. . . . In the magazines the Wolf, the Devil, the Evil Spirit, the Bad Man, the Savage are always symbolized by Negroes or Indians; since there is always identification with the victor, the little Negro, quite as easily as the little white boy, becomes an explorer, an adventurer, a missionary "who faces the danger of being eaten by the wicked Negroes." (pp. 112–13)

The dominant popular culture has a tradition of representing the colonized or othered populace as primitive or bad, even evil. But because this culture saturates the colonized or racially othered populace as much as it does the colonizer or dominant populace, children—and adults—end up identifying "goodness" with white culture and people and "badness" with black culture and people. Thus, black subjects, Fanon argues, can come to internalize an alienation from their own being.

This is not to say that Fanon believes all black people to be engaged in a process of self-hatred. Indeed, he says that the black person "recognizes the unreality of many of the beliefs that he has adopted with reference to the subjective attitude of the white man" (p. 115). But when they live in a society in which white people have more power and privilege, black people, Fanon argues, are constantly reminded that they don't fully "belong" to the culture in which they live. "[F]or the Negro," he writes (using what was then a progressive or inoffensive term for black people), "there is a myth to be faced. A solidly established myth. The Negro is unaware of it as long as his existence is limited to his own environment; but the first encounter with a white man oppresses him with the whole weight of his blackness" (p. 116). He again uses popular culture to support this claim, challenging potential critics in a note that turns explicitly to the cultural icon Tarzan, to which we return at the end of this chapter:

> I recommend the following experiment to those who are unconvinced: Attend showings of a Tarzan film in the Antilles and in Europe. In the Antilles, the young Negro identifies himself *de facto* with Tarzan against the Negroes. This is much more difficult for him in a European theater, for the rest of the audience, which is white, automatically identifies him with the savages on the screen. It is a conclusive experience. The Negro learns that one is not black without problems. (p. 118)

Thus, for Fanon, the racism of the colonizer's society is reflected in its culture (both **high** and popular) through the form of representation. It's even embedded in the language itself, with words associated with racial otherness (*black*, for example) being associated with negative concepts, while those associated with the dominant group (*white*) take on positive **connotations**. This is why he writes, early in the book, that "what is often called the black soul is a white man's artifact" (p. 6). In order to improve the world, Fanon argues, we must combat such representations and stereotypes, and challenge such mythologies.

Race and "Race"

As noted above, Fanon argues that racism is encoded into language itself. In his foreword to *Black Skin, White Masks*, Ziauddin Sardar builds on Fanon's argument: "The black man speaks with a European language. . . . So, almost immediately, the black man is presented with a problem: how to posit a 'black self' in a language and discourse in which blackness itself is at best a figure of absence, or worse a total reversion?" (p. xv). This question is taken up by later theorists of race and racism, especially in relation to the theoretical topics of essentialism and anti-essentialism. Many of these critics take Fanon's ideas about language in a different direction, in that they touch on how cultural criticism and theory, as a discourse, engages in the forms of identification and oppression that Fanon and others analyze. This is an important step, because it can sometimes seem as if we, as cultural critics, stand above or at a distance from the culture we're analyzing. Such critics remind us that we, too, are part of the very systems we analyze, a realization that is also at the forefront of Fanon's analysis. The theoretical apparatuses we apply are themselves part of the discursive and therefore ideological traditions that we're supposedly analyzing and critiquing.

"Race," Writing, and Anti-Essentialism   Interested primarily in language and literature, Henry Louis Gates, Jr. (1950–), in many of his works, offers a history of black writing in English and discusses the seemingly paradoxical fact that this history begins with its own silencing. This silencing arises from the pseudo-science of the eighteenth and nineteenth centuries discussed earlier, and its categorization of race as a biological determinant. As Gates has pointed out, we still tend to use the term *race* as if it were a given, as if we could easily distinguish between races of people, and it's still often conflated with ethnicity and culture, just as it was conflated with nation in earlier periods.

Gates sees in the events surrounding Phillis Wheatley's poetry (see the "Poetry, Race, and Authority" box) a perfect example of the paradoxical relationship between black creators, and writers especially, and the racist society in which they lived:

> Since the beginning of the seventeenth century, Europeans had wondered aloud whether or not the African "species of men," as they most commonly put it, *could* ever create formal literature, could ever master "the arts and sciences." If they could, the argument ran, then the African variety of humanity and the European variety were fundamentally related. If not, then it seemed clear that the African was destined by nature to be a slave.
>
> Why was the creative writing of the African of such importance to the eighteenth century's debate over slavery? . . . [A]fter René Descartes, *reason* was privileged, or valorized, above all other human characteristics. Writing . . . was taken to be the *visible* sign of reason. Blacks were "reasonable," and hence "men" if—and only if—they demonstrated mastery of "the arts and sciences." (Gates, 1986, p. 8)

Poetry, Race, and Authority: The Case of Phillis Wheatley

In the introduction to the essay collection *"Race," Writing and Difference*, Henry Louis Gates uses African-American poet Phillis Wheatley (1753–1784) as the paradoxical example of the erasure of black writing (Gates, 1986). A slave who was, as she writes in one poem, "brought from Africa to America" in the latter half of the eighteenth century, Wheatley was taught to read and write English by her owners (an unusual act at the time; in some slave-owning states, it was illegal to teach enslaved people to read and write). She became an accomplished poet, writing in the neo-classical form.

Wheatley addressed such topics as the American Revolution, her life story, and other black artists, along with many others. When her owners tried to publish her work, however, no one would believe that a black, female slave could have written the poems, owing in large part to the racist logic, like Kant's, that considered black people not intellectually advanced enough to write. Wheatley was then examined and questioned by a group of educated white men in order to prove she had indeed written the poems; these men included a statement attesting to that fact in her published book.

So, Gates continues, the "presence" or "absence" of writing becomes a **signifier** for the presence or absence of reason, which itself is the defining mark of humanity (p. 8). This brings us back to Kant's racist vision.

Gates goes on to relate that although black people were seen as incapable of writing, in order to ensure that state of things, laws were created to keep them from writing. This presents a paradox for white supremacist society: scientists and philosophers posited that blacks couldn't write—that it was biologically not part of their nature—but people weren't allowed to teach them how to write, a provision that implies they're capable of it. For Gates, this slippage points to the fact that the connection between reason, writing, and race is an ideological one that serves to support certain groups, specifically white upper-class men.

If this supposedly scientific view of race is instead ideological, Gates argues, then the concept of race itself is suspect. Indeed, he writes that "Race, as a meaningful criterion within the biological sciences, has long been recognized to be a fiction" (p. 4). Even if race is biologically meaningless, though, Gates says that "our conversations are replete with usages of race which have their sources" in such figures as Kant and Blumenbach (p. 4). This seeming refusal to acknowledge the fictional nature of biological race leads Gates to suggest that race should always be written as "race," where the so-called "scare-quotes" around the word signal that it can only be used ironically; to write **"race"** is to question it as a stable category of identity.

How, though, does "race" function ideologically, or as a myth, in contemporary culture? Gates argues that "Race is the ultimate trope of difference because it is so very arbitrary in its application. The biological criteria used to determine 'difference' in sex simply do not hold when applied to 'race.' Yet we carelessly use language in such a way as to *will* this sense of *natural* difference into our formulations" (p. 5). Race is an effect of language, Gates argues, and if we are to "assuage or redress" problems surrounding bigotries in society acted out in the name of "race," we must be careful not to reproduce the idea of a naturalized, essential quality to racial identity (p. 5).

In other words, Gates is applying the anti-essentialist theories of both structuralism and poststructuralism (see Chapter 10) to the idea of race. But here arises a central problem that Gates tries to address. Since the tradition of writing he examines is one of the African **diaspora**—that is, the generations of Africans spread all over the world through slavery, colonial displacement, emigration, and so on—and since that tradition is itself written in the oppressor's language and traditions, as Fanon details, then does this tradition in fact reproduce some of the very linguistic dynamics through which black people have been oppressed? Does the cultural tradition of African Americans, for example, repeat the alienation Fanon discusses? As Gates writes, "[H]ow can the black subject posit a full and sufficient self in a language in which blackness is a sign of absence?" (p. 12).

Gates makes the next logical step: If the very act of writing brings with it its own dangers, then what of dominant forms of criticism and theory themselves, which come out of a Euro-American tradition and rely on a foundation of thinking that helped form the very basis of racial differentiation and oppression? Gates proposes a tentative solution to this problem. He argues that anti-racist critics "must analyze the language of contemporary criticism itself, recognizing especially that [such] systems are not universal, color-blind, apolitical, or neutral" (p. 15). In other words, our criticism must be self-reflexive; we must be open to criticizing our own arguments for the way they repeat dominant ideological claims and might silence or write over the cultural acts of people traditionally silenced by that ideology.

Additionally, much along the lines of the "indigenizing" theories discussed earlier, Gates argues that critical theory must look not only to the traditions of European criticism and philosophy, but also to the cultural traditions of oppressed peoples, for example to "the black vernacular tradition." Such vernacular traditions could offer their own methodologies "through which to theorize about the so-called discourse of the Other" (p. 15).

Critiquing and Revising Anti-Essentialism

As is the case with third-wave and poststructuralist feminist theories, however, some people see the anti-essentialist turn as causing as many problems as it solves. Moving from a more essentialist definition of identity in race studies to a more fragmented vision of a multiply constructed subjectivity—with various networked alliances and fractures with other such subjects—can cause a problem of political voice: the first position allows for a unified, rights-based civic activism and theorization, while the second runs the risk of fragmenting a political message and thereby, some would say, rendering any activism arising from it less powerful. bell hooks, for example, while ultimately seeing the necessity of anti-essentialist critiques, writes in her essay "Postmodern Blackness" of concerns about the fragmentation of community implied by anti-essentialism, especially since the "postmodern" theorists who argue for anti-essentialism are predominantly "white male intellectuals and/or academic elites" (hooks, 1990, para. 2). However, she sees in such theories the ability to allow for a coming together of a **heteroglossia** of voices of oppressed people (for example, people of colour, queer people, and women), whereas essentialist theories tend toward silencing groups that don't "belong." "Postmodern culture," she writes, "with its decentered subject can be the space where ties are severed or it can provide the occasion for new and varied forms of bonding" (para. 15). hooks argues that a denial of an essential identity isn't necessarily the denial of a sense of collective identity. In fact, she points toward the idea that talking about an essential identity is actually a way of eliding history—if all women are alike because they have some essential womanness, or if all men are alike because of some essential manliness, or if every member of one race is alike, and so on, then you're saying that you don't have to look to historical events that may have affected a particular group, or that may need addressing or reparation even now (for a longer discussion of hooks's work, see Chapter 10).

In theories of race and their connection to anti-racist activities, however, certain forms of postcolonial and anti-racist activities do take the form of asserting the essential humanity and connectedness of those who were racialized as "other" by the dominant society. One of the most global and well known of these struggles—one that Fanon's and Gates's writings build on—was the struggle for the recognition of the rights of black people throughout the world. Disparate but wide-ranging black communities still shared certain cultural practices as well as material history. This group of societies and communities, known as the African diaspora, is found in those parts of the world populated by black Africans and their descendants, including those throughout the Atlantic region who are descended from Africans who were kidnapped and sold into slavery in Canada, the United States, the Caribbean, and elsewhere. Sharing a past of slavery and racism, many members of this large and diverse group assert an essential sameness that could unite them in their political struggles against oppression and have their human rights recognized. This unity took the form of political and cultural movements known as **pan-Africanism** and **Afrocentrism**, which argue for an essential unity and connection—politically, culturally, and spiritually—between all Africans and the descendants of African peoples (especially those descended from enslaved Africans). Variations on such essentialist theories and movements can also be found in African nationalist and black nationalist movements in Africa, North America, and elsewhere (the most famous of these being perhaps the black nationalism of the Nation of Islam and Malcolm X). This notion of unity provided a powerful political voice for many black people.

But still, as we've seen, the notion of essential racial difference is connected to the history of racism itself, and such essentialist theories can also paper over or ignore other differences, such as those of gender, sexuality, class, and age, between varied groups of people. Moreover, the African diaspora is constituted of a group of people who may share a common past and some cultural traditions founded in that past, but who still live within very different societies, often with different languages, social structures, and their own unique cultural traditions. Asserting essentialist sameness in such cases would seem to ignore those differences as well. However, to focus only on the differences would ignore the cultural similarities that do exist.

Is it possible, though, to figure an analysis of race and of cultural practices connected to race when neither essentialist nor anti-essentialist theories seem to fully function? Two analysts of the cultures of the African diaspora attempt to offer a third way for such an analysis: Paul Gilroy in *The Black Atlantic*, his study of the African diaspora, and Rinaldo Walcott in *Black Like Who*, a study of black cultures and cultural production in Canada. Both theorists focus, in part, on the role music plays in the development of black diasporic cultures.

Black Music, Anti-Anti-Essentialism, and Nomadology

In his groundbreaking study *The Black Atlantic*, Paul Gilroy (1956–) examines "the affinities and affiliations which link the blacks of the West to one of their adoptive, parental cultures: the intellectual heritage of the West since the Enlightenment" (Gilroy, 1993, p. 2). How, in other words, do groups of people who are explicitly defined by the dominant culture as existing outside of the Enlightenment tenets of rationality, civilization, and so on (as discussed earlier) define their existence within that very culture? "[M]odern black political formations," he writes, "stand simultaneously both inside and outside the western culture which has been their peculiar step-parent" (pp. 48–49).

Such a relationship to the dominant white culture allows black Atlantic cultural production, "and, above all, the music," Gilroy argues, to "[overflow] from the containers that the modern nation state provides for them" (p. 40). Thus, an analysis of black musical forms across the black Atlantic allows Gilroy to complicate the traditional Eurocentric binaries of essentialist identities and the perhaps equally Eurocentric critiques offered by anti-essentialist cultural analysis.

Instead, he says, black cultures permit a new form of identity formation in relation to culture, one that recognizes how the material world and our social surroundings construct subjectivity while also allowing for a recognition of a malleable but still cohesive and "authentic" black identity that transcends the particularities of one's nation or specific surroundings. He writes that "Pop culture has been prepared to provide selective endorsements for the premium that some black thinkers wish to place on authenticity" (p. 99). In other words, some black popular culture is presented as more "authentically black" than others.

Of course, as Gilroy notes, this emphasis on authenticity can be read as a particularly cynical form of marketing, one in which "the mass marketing of successive black folk-cultural forms to white audiences" is saturated with a "discourse of authenticity" that's more about "artifice" than the material reality of black experience or culture (p. 99). One can think of how gangsta rap presents as "authentically black" a culture of violence and sexism that is disconnected from much of the realities of inner-city poverty and is in fact relatively foreign to a large portion of the African-American population. Such "authenticity," following a **culture industry** model of analysis, would perpetuate certain forms of racialized stereotypes or myths.

And yet, despite the clear "artifice" of such mass-marketed versions of authenticity, many black thinkers, as Gilroy says, also want to claim a form of authentically black, essential identity. Treating the claims of authenticity on their own terms rather than seeing them merely as the artificial product of the culture industry, Gilroy writes, can help to "break the deadlock" between essentialist and anti-essentialist theories of identity (p. 99).

"Music and its rituals," Gilroy argues, "can be used to create a model whereby identity can be understood neither as a fixed essence nor as a vague and utterly contingent construction to be reinvented by . . . will and whim" (p. 102). Instead, he says, while the notion of an essential black identity may ultimately be a construction of culture, the propagation of certain forms of black music across the black Atlantic region points in a different direction. Rather than a simple multiplicity of different black identities, each constructed by the specific material cultures that surround them in disparate nations, the connections created by music "point towards an anti-anti-essentialism that sees racialised subjectivity as the product of the social practices that supposedly derive from it" (p. 102). Black "soul music," then, isn't the natural outgrowth of an unchanging black essence; instead, that essence is created by the performance and reception of the music itself. The soul might not come first, but that's different from saying it doesn't exist or can be easily changed.

In many ways, Gilroy's "anti-anti-essentialism" echoes Judith Butler's **performative** theory of identity (discussed in Chapter 11), in which our identities are seen as

Cultural Appropriation, Identity, and Miley Cyrus

At the 2013 *MTV Music Video Awards*, pop singer Miley Cyrus caused a minor controversy when she performed a dance piece that involved her stripping down to small two-piece outfit while twerking next to singer Robin Thicke and background dancers dressed as teddy bears. When combined with the controversy over Thicke's video for his song "Blurred Lines," which was deemed sexist by many, Cyrus's act led several people—especially on Twitter, both during and after the performance—to criticize her supposedly overly sexualized performance, while others criticized the critics, calling them out for "slut shaming," or for engaging in a particularly misogynist critique of women who perform an active sexuality. With accusations of sexism flying against both Cyrus and her critics, the controversy made several mainstream news agencies.

As the controversy lingered, though, some cultural critics and public figures began to point out the ways in which Cyrus's performance appropriated aspects of black American culture while simultaneously objectifying and sexualizing black women's bodies. Pieces by "ninjacate" on the feminist blog Jezebel and by Jody Rosen on Vulture pointed out that Cyrus used the African-American background dancers as props, simulating sexual acts on them while calling attention to their bodies, and generally engaged in a form of minstrelsy. As Rosen writes, "For white performers, minstrelsy has always been a means to an end: a shortcut to self-actualization. The archetypal example is in *The Jazz Singer* (1927), in which Al Jolson's immigrant striver puts on the blackface mask to cast off his immigrant Jewish patrimony and remake himself as an all-American pop star. . . . Cyrus is annexing working-class black 'ratchet' culture, the potent sexual symbolism of black female bodies, to the cause of her reinvention: her transformation from

squeaky-clean Disney-pop poster girl to grown-up hipster-provocateur" ("The 2013 VMAs").

But if racial identity is non-essential and culturally constructed, why would Cyrus's performance be considered racist? Several separate but related answers can be made to this question. First, as Rosen and others point out, this performance takes place in the context of a long historical trajectory in which black people have been denied power and black women in particular have been represented as sexual objects for whites. Second, in America, Canada, and elsewhere, race is still part of a hierarchical social framework in which black people are systematically and structurally denied the same degree of access to social power that white people are. In this case, then, Cyrus's performance doesn't further "black" culture but instead participates in the continuing suppression and objectification of black people, allowing her to maintain her (white) position of power while denying it to the black artists whose work she's relying on. Third, to use Paul Gilroy's terms, the culture that Cyrus is appropriating can't be so easily disconnected from the black cultures out of which it grew, in part in response to the very forms of oppression and objectification in which Cyrus's performance participated. Being "anti-essential" may make it seem as if these cultural tropes can be appropriated without question, but, following Gilroy's anti-anti-essentialist framework, we need to recognize the deep-seated connections to the particular cultures and peoples from which these musical and performance traditions arise.

Sources: Rosen, Jody. "The 2013 VMAs Were Dominated by Miley's Minstrel Show." *Vulture*. 26 August 2013. *Vulture.com*. 10 September 2013. Web.

Ninjacate. "Solidarity Is for Miley Cyrus: The Racial Implications of her VMA Performance." *Groupthink*. 26 August 2013. *Jezebel.com*. 10 September 2013.

non-essential and the product of our cultural surroundings but that nonetheless create a feeling of an internal core, a sense of identity and self in relation to others—something that *feels* like an essence even if it's not. Important for Gilroy's analysis of black identity, however, is the fact that this notion of identity formation allows for a communal sense of an in-born identity, one that can be used in a collective politics to combat racist dominant cultures. Equally significant is the fact that this collective identity is nonetheless open to transformation and change. Just as the popular music of black cultures in the black Atlantic (from the blues to jazz, to reggae, to rap, to hip hop, and so on) adapt, alter, and transform each other as well as Eurocentric forms, so too is the notion of an "authentic" black identity both a lived reality and an identity in constant transformation, what Gilroy calls a "changing same."

Cultural critic Rinaldo Walcott (1965–) sees music in relation to black cultures in a very similar way, and uses it to analyze the particular deployments and developments of black identity in Canada. Walcott points out that there is a "dearth of debate concerning ways of thinking blackness in Canada," and attempts to address this critical gap. Turning to popular music, Walcott, like Gilroy, argues that "music remains one of the most complex and significant expressive cultural forms of the black diaspora" (Walcott, 2003, p. 145). Likewise, Walcott sees in black Canadian popular music a participation in a wider black global culture, but notes that there is no singular style that marks this music. Instead, each group or artist chooses a different aspect of "black diasporic expression" with which to engage, and through which to shape, black Canadian and diasporic identities: "The Dream Warriors have returned in their music to a much closer identification with the Caribbean, particularly Jamaica. FreshWes, on the other hand, has clearly identified with America; he has even moved to New York. The migratory practices suggest that avenues for thinking about blackness by black Canadians do not follow a single path" (p. 145).

Walcott borrows the term **nomadology** from theorists Gilles Deleuze and Félix Guattari to describe this cultural practice. Like Gilroy's "changing same," nomadology expresses a cultural identity that is in constant flux but is nonetheless capable of expressing a collective identity: nomadology recognizes identity, and blackness in particular, as a **dialogic** process in which groups can borrow from one another even as they engage in different expressions of self. (Expanding on this discussion, in Chapter 13 we examine the cultural hybridity of hip hop in relation to indigenous youth in Canada.) Thus, Walcott argues, it's not insulting to say "that blackness in Canada is borrowed" from other cultural locations, such as the United States or Jamaica, because "[b]lackness is always borrowed," insofar as a diasporic identity is always in dialogue with various forms of its own expression. He continues:

> [W]hen we theorize black Canadas, diasporic exchanges, dialogues and renewals become a fundamental part of thinking what the politics of blackness might be. . . . To be black and at home in Canada is both to belong and not belong. . . . Nation-centred discourse can only be a trap that prohibits black folks from sharing common feeling, especially when common actions and practices of domination seem to present themselves time and again in different spaces/places/nations. (pp. 146–47)

Whiteness

This chapter has focused its analysis on the cultural construction and self-identification of groups who are racially othered by the dominant white society of Canada and other colonial or racially heterogeneous nations. However, just as masculinity is as constructed a category as femininity within a patriarchal society, so is **whiteness** a racial category that can be analyzed in societies that privilege white people. Indeed, **white privilege**—a social pattern in which white people are accorded certain benefits as a rule, even if done unconsciously—is a concept that has been the subject of cultural analysis (see Further Reading).

But how can we define whiteness, or the representation of whiteness, within popular culture? While all racial categories share an equally suspect scientific background, we've discussed those identities in relation to racism and to communal identities formed in response to, or in the context of, racial oppression. Often, as we saw, popular culture becomes a way for such communities to define themselves and in turn to express a cultural identity against the definitions of them by a racist culture. Does whiteness work similarly?

The answer is both yes and no. Whiteness, because it's tied to the history of Eurocentric imperial power, has its own particular history as a category. This is *not* to say that "whiteness" is an ethnicity with its own heritage and folk identity, as critics have, in different ways, argued with regard to the African diaspora, for example. Indeed, assertions that there is *a* "white culture"—one that needs to be recognized as an ethnic or other form of group identity—tend to arise out of racist discourses (such as those of "white pride"). While on the surface it may seem as if we should be able to discuss "white cultural identity" in the same way that we discuss a black diasporic or Indigenous cultural identity (after all, they're all "racial identities" to some degree), several factors—the material history of racism; assertions of the superiority of Euro-American cultures and whiteness itself with the coterminous history of the domination, exploitation, and genocide of non-white groups; and continuing social inequities in relation to race—make such an assertion deeply problematic, to say the least. If race as an identity category doesn't exist apart from the history of racism, then whiteness as a category doesn't exist apart from its historical positioning as a category of domination and violent oppression around the globe.

However, as we discussed with other racial identities, it is possible to discuss whiteness as a non-essential social construction, and to do so in a way that questions essentialist, racist assertions of white supremacy. One approach to challenging such notions is to examine the history of whiteness as a category: over the past few centuries, the groups who were and were not considered white have actually changed. Noel Ignatiev, for instance, has examined the history of Irish immigrants to America, noting that many considered Irish Catholics not to be white, a category that in the nineteenth century was limited to Anglo-Saxon Protestants (hence the acronym WASP). Over time, however, as social shifts required corresponding shifts in political power, the Irish became more and more identified with the dominant culture in America, and hence "became" white. Whiteness is thus clearly not an essential or biological category, but rather a socio-cultural construct that changes over time. In other words, the supposedly firm boundaries of whiteness have historically been "leaky" (Wander, 1993, p. 15).

One of the ways the social dominance of whiteness has been maintained in the face of its various "leaks" is, ironically, through its erasure as a visible racial category. What does this mean? It means that "whiteness" is taken to be a norm against which other racial identities must be defined. Whiteness is not often flagged in descriptions of people on the news, for example, whereas those from a racial minority may often have their race identified (for a discussion of the representation of race in the media, see Entman and Rojecki in Further Reading). As Jolanta A. Drzewiecka and Kathleen Wong (Lau) point out, the invisibility of whiteness has resulted in its supposed universality (Drzewiecka & Wong, 1999, pp. 198 ff). If it remains hidden and unspoken, any problems in the maintenance of its boundaries will also remain hidden. Whiteness thus comes to be identified not as a specific race but as the norm against which all "other" people must be defined. To be a member of an "invisible" disembodied race is to have access to privilege. As Richard Dyer writes, "There is no more powerful position than that of being 'just' human" (Dyer, 1997, p. 2). Thus, in relation to our earlier discussion of stereotypes, a white person's behaviour (and especially a white man's behaviour) in societies that privilege whiteness will be individualized ("That's just the way *he* is") rather than read in relation to a standard or model of stereotypical "whiteness" ("That's just the way *they* are").

Whiteness, as a racial category within white supremacist or white privileging cultures, is thus often an "invisible" category, in which white people are able to inhabit unquestioningly the role of the individual as we've been defining it. Anti-racist cultural critics and culture producers will therefore often look for moments where they can defamiliarize whiteness in order, in Dyer's words, to make it "strange" and therefore visible (p. 10), such that its power as the "normal" category can be questioned.

Case Study

Tarzan of the Apes and Race

In 1912 Edgar Rice Burroughs published, in the pulp fiction magazine *All-Story*, the novel that would go on to make him famous: *Tarzan of the Apes*. Published two years later in book form, the novel introduces the iconic titular character, Tarzan, a young boy orphaned when his white English parents were stranded on the African coast and killed by a group of giant "anthropoid" apes. Raised in the jungle by those same apes, Tarzan comes of age with no human contact, teaching himself to read and write in English using the books in his parents' cabin. Finally, a native African tribe wanders into the region. Tarzan's ape "mother" is killed, and he proceeds to kill the first other human being he sees in revenge. Eventually meeting other white people (and falling in love with Jane Porter, the first white woman he sees), Tarzan learns the ways of civilization.

This story formed the basis of a massive popular culture franchise, one that has lasted now for over a hundred years. Tarzan has been the subject of other novels as well as film, radio, television, comics, and almost every form of popular culture one can think of.

However, because of its basic premise (a white boy raised in Africa who alternately kills, befriends, and rules over native black Africans, depending on the particular incarnation of the story), Tarzan is also deeply implicated in the popular narratives and

ideologies of race, as Frantz Fanon's discussion of the character (examined earlier) makes clear.

Tarzan also helps to define an "essential" whiteness, a whiteness that is confident in its physical and mental superiority but that oddly must stand apart from "white" civilization, which is presented as decadent and effeminizing. In this narrative, white people (and especially white men) must get back to nature to rediscover their "natural" being, a being that separates them from the "primitiveness" of aboriginal Africans but must also separate itself from a civilization that "weakens" individuals with its many conveniences.

Tarzan dominates much of twentieth-century popular culture, but he's more than a single character; he becomes an icon of "rugged individualism," an American ideal that seems to laud the power of every individual. And yet Tarzan's clear relationship to discourses of race makes this problematic. Tarzan's "individuality" explicitly universalizes his whiteness, seemingly denying the access of non-white people to this universal individuality and making whiteness "invisible" in the way that Richard Dyer and others discuss. Likewise, Tarzan as a character becomes a significant influence on the figure of the superhero as such: What is Superman, after all, but another Tarzan orphaned in a different jungle? Do whiteness and the discourse of racism thus permeate the popular culture figure of the superhero?

Perhaps to an extent, but of course this iconic figure has been reworked: Tarzan is also, for example, a hero of Bollywood film. African-Canadian author Charles Saunders, echoing Fanon, has said that "the Tarzan books made me uncomfortable even as I enjoyed the scope of the author's imagination." Saunders went on to write a fantasy novel, *Imaro* (1981), in which the titular hero was "specifically created as the brother who could kick Tarzan's ass" (Amy Harlib, "Adding to the Gumbo Mix: Charles R. Saunders," *The Zone* zone-sf.com). Resisting the "invisibility" of whiteness and the racist discourses it supports, such refigurations point to how racist narratives of the West's dominant popular culture can be subverted.

Tarzan of the classic films.

Source: M.G.M/Album/Newscom

Discussion Questions

1. In Chapter 11 we discussed how third-wave feminist theorists complicate more traditional feminisms by including the experiences of women of colour, lesbians, working-class women, and others whose perspectives were traditionally left out of feminist discussions. As evidenced by our discussion of bell hooks, such theories could easily have been analyzed in this chapter (and, indeed, in Chapters 11 and 13 as well). In what ways is our understanding of race affected by its intersections with gender? Can you discuss this in relation to the examples studied in this chapter? In what ways do the conclusions of someone like Audre Lorde or bell hooks alter the discussions of anti-racist theory and activism?

2. Do you think superheroes in films or comics tend to reinforce notions of white supremacy in their narratives? Are there particular superhero films that reinforce such notions? That challenge them? Does the medium make a difference?

3. In what ways do news media reproduce certain stereotypical representations of race? Can you find an example in which a person's "whiteness" is rendered invisible in the ways discussed above?

4. Find two articles—one from a mainstream news media organization and the other from an Aboriginal-owned and operated news source—that discuss the same issue relating to Aboriginal Canadians. In what ways do the sources differ (in terms of word choice, the presentation of the situation, who is treated as an authority, and so on)? In what ways are they the same? Do these differences or similarities tell us anything about the political or racial ideologies being relied upon or reproduced?

5. Rinaldo Walcott argues that popular black Canadian musicians find inspiration in, and alter, black musical traditions from other parts of the world (for example, the United States and the Caribbean), and that this practice helps shape "black diasporic expression." Paul Gilroy makes a similar claim in his discussion of the "changing same" of black cultures around the black Atlantic. Can you find other, more recent examples, from Canada or elsewhere, of such a practice? Do they support Walcott's argument?

6. The Disney animated film *Tarzan* (1999) excludes any representation of black African people: Does this make the film less or more implicated in the racialized history of the character? Why or why not?

Further Reading

Delgado, Richard, and Jean Stefancic. *Critical Race Theory: An Introduction*. New York: New York UP, 2012.

Entman, Robert M., and Andrew Rojecki. *The Black Image in the White Mind: Media and Race in America*. Chicago: U of Chicago P, 2000.

Francis, Margot. *Creative Subversions: Whiteness, Indigeneity, and the National Imaginary*. Vancouver: UBC Press, 2011.

Haslam, Jason. "'The Open Sesame of a Pork-Colored Skin': Whiteness and Privilege in *Black No More*." *The "White Problem": The Critical Study of Whiteness in American Literature*. Ed. Patricia Keefe Durso. Spec. Issue of *Modern Language Studies* 32.1 (2002): 15–31.

Hylton, Kevin. *Race and Sport: Critical Race Theory*. New York: Routledge, 2009.

Roediger, David R. *The Wages of Whiteness: Race and the Making of the American Working Class*. New York: Verso, 1991.

Wiegman, Robyn. "Whiteness Studies and the Paradox of Particularity." *boundary 2* 26.3 (1999): 115–50.

Williams, Linda Faye. *The Constraint of Race: Legacies of White Skin Privilege in America*. University Park, PA: Pennsylvania State UP, 2003.

Chapter 13
Nationalism, Imperialism, and (Post)Colonialism

INTRODUCTION

The previous chapters in Part IV focused on what we can call group identities, but they also focused on identities often associated with internal, biological, or psychological states. We have, of course, seen how assertions of the biological nature of race, gender, or sexuality are at least problematic and, in some cases, simply false, and that these identities are framed within, and arguably constructed by, one's surrounding culture. And yet in popular culture, politics, rights movements, and beyond, such identity structures are often treated as an ingrained aspect of human beings, something that's part of them from birth. Even some of the primary proponents of the social construction of identity, from Louis Althusser to Judith Butler, argue that the psychological impact of our surrounding culture is such that the identities it creates for us still feel as if they're "natural."

So the subject of this chapter, national identity, may seem at first blush to be somewhat different from that of gender, sexuality, or race. After all, the formation of the modern nation state is a relatively recent development of human history, and in today's interconnected political and economic world, many people can move between nation states with an ease unknown in earlier times. Can we really discuss nationality as a form of identity structure that's similar to those discussed in previous chapters?

As we'll see, nationality is just as complex an identity structure as those others, and has a similar theoretical history. While the massive global flows of migration would seem to indicate an acceptance of a fluid notion of people's national identity, such movements are wrapped in complex laws and equally complex notions of belonging and exclusion. We'll see how the notion of "nationality" was originally defined within an essentialist logic, as with the other identities we've discussed, and was even seen as a synonym for race at particular times. Recent theoretical developments, as with those other identity categories, have moved toward anti-essentialist theories of national identity. These issues are rendered even more complex when one examines the history of imperialism and colonialism, including how certain groups were oppressed by others even within their own countries or lands, and how they fought back. In these cases, national, ethnic, and racial identities become sites of political, and often violent, contestation. In analyzing the social and cultural structures of such histories and situations, postcolonial studies and theory have had a profound impact not only on academic study, but also on political action and policies.

NATIONALISM AND NATIONAL IDENTITY

Broadly defined, **nationality** or *national identity* as used today refers to the emotional and/or legal connection one has to a particular nation state. **Nationalism** is defined as a both a political position and a personal feeling that emphasizes loyalty or patriotism to that nation state. Such nationalism can be expressed politically (in terms of both internal public policy and external, international relations) and in cultural forms. As we'll see in the case study at the end of this chapter, such international sporting events as the Olympics are often spaces for the cultural exercise of competing nationalist ideologies.

Nation, Nation State, Empire

The terms *nation* and *nation state* are generally seen as interchangeable in common parlance, but this hasn't always been the case: in fact, there are many exceptions to that rule even now (for example, the Québécois are officially recognized as a nation, but one that is part of the larger nation state of Canada). It's important, then, to understand the history of the concept of nation, as well as the history of the political formation of the legal and institutional entity known as the nation state. A **state** in this context means a sovereign governance structure that assumes the right of rule over a certain group of people. A **nation state** is thus a sovereign political entity bound by specific borders. It's often large enough to contain several population centres and smaller jurisdictions that are ceded certain powers under the larger state formation (as with provinces in Canada). It's also generally associated with one or more national languages, and often with specific cultural practices. Thus, as discussed below, a "nation" can refer to a group that identifies itself (ethnically, culturally, politically, or so on) as a people. A nation state can therefore be defined as a sovereign, legal, political formation (the state) of that people (the nation), although contemporary nation states are more complex than this definition would imply.

We're used to thinking of such states in terms of countries. But other state formations exist, and the nation state is relatively new. As with several of the **discourses** we've studied, many historians trace modern notions of the nation and the formation of the modern system of nation states to the eighteenth and nineteenth centuries. In ancient Greece, for example, there were separate city states. A city state, or *polis*, was, as its name suggests, largely limited to a particular city and its surrounding area, and its political structures, customs, and so on could differ entirely from those of its nearest city-state neighbour. Later, and importantly in the centuries leading up the formation of nation states, Europe was dominated by separate **empires**. These imperial states were often extremely large geographically, and their populations therefore varied greatly in terms of language, "race," and cultural traditions. The Roman Empire, for example, at the height of its power included peoples we would now call French, English, Italian, German, Spanish, Egyptian, and more, people with many different religions and cultural practices. Importantly, though, the Romans "exported" their political structure throughout their empire, and exercised legal control over the peoples they conquered.

While different in many of their imperial practices, later empires, such as the Portuguese or the British, stretched over even greater distances, into the "New World" of North and South America, and ruled over several different peoples.

Of course, empires expanded their territories most often through warfare and the violent conquering of other lands and peoples, and many exerted control over these conquered people through physical violence and the suppression of local practices (often using what Louis Althusser would call **Repressive** and **Ideological State Apparatuses**). The people subject to this control often fought against it.

According to many contemporary theorists, nationalism and the concept of a separate nation state arose directly as a response to—and way of acting against—imperial control. But in the eighteenth and nineteenth centuries, these new "nationalists" saw it differently. While they did resist imperial control on the basis of national identity, they saw the latter category as a natural, essential part of their being. We'll first discuss the essentialist origins of nationalist thought, and then move on to contemporary theories of the national identity.

Nationalism Before the Nation

By the beginning of the nineteenth century, what many call the Age of Empires was starting to fade. The American Revolution in 1776 was one of the major instigators of the decline of the largely monarchical empires of the time, but other specifically nationalist revolutions began occurring later into the nineteenth century. What do we mean by "specifically nationalist," though?

The term **nation** has existed in the English language dating from its origins, but rather than being synonymous with *nation state*, it has throughout its history been used to refer to a group of people united by geographical location, language, and/or cultural practices. Thus, within what we would now call the United Kingdom, you can find references dating back at least to the fourteenth and fifteenth centuries to the English nation, the Scottish nation, and so on, even though these were not always nation states in the sense we understand them. The term *nation* also could refer to specific groups within those larger groups; it was not a clearly defined term.

In the eighteenth and nineteenth centuries, though, *nation* began to take on more specific meanings and to be tied to geopolitical concerns. One of the major early philosophers of nationality was Johann Gottfried von Herder (1744–1803). Beginning his career as a linguist, he believed that the separate languages of the world's peoples, when combined with separate cultural practices, including their art, music, and so on, indicated that each of these groups had a separate character. He discusses the famous scientist Linnaeus, who supposedly observed an American bear that had been taken to Sweden; this bear would still wake and sleep following the sunset and sunrise of its homeland. Herder writes that the bear retained

> with his other instincts . . . his native division of time. Is not this remark applicable to others, from different regions of the Earth, from the eastern or southern hemispheres? and if this change hold good with respect to beasts, shall man, notwithstanding his peculiar character, be exempt from it? (Herder, 1800, p. 38)

Herder argues that, like the bear, people from different regions have certain inborn distinctions from those of other regions. Two groups who live farther apart will be more different culturally and linguistically than two groups who live closer together because of the different climate, landscape, and so on. Important to note, though, is that for Herder, moving a population to a different location wouldn't change their character. Following the same logic that led to the development of racial theory at this time by figures like J. S. Blumenbach (as we discussed in Chapter 12), Herder says that the development of separate peoples over time in relation to the land they inhabit has led to inborn, essential characteristics in these groups. As with the bear in the anecdote from Linnaeus, different groups have different "instincts," but in humans these traits are expressed in language, behaviour, and culture.

Herder, like Kant (see Chapter 12), calls these differences **national characteristics**, and each separate group is, for him, a nation. Thus, the German-speaking population of Western Europe, who live within a general region of that continent, form a German nation for Herder, of which he was a part. This German nation is tied to the land that group has inhabited for generations upon generations, Herder would argue; their cultural practices are the natural expression of their essential connection to each other and the land, and hence are the "proper" cultural expressions for that people and that region. And so to express fully one's own nature, one had to engage in a form of nationalism: expressing one's own nature meant fully participating in nationalist culture. Herder refers to this as the expression of the *Volk*, or folk: the spirit of the nation as expressed through its people.

Such an argument has profound political implications, of course, especially in an age dominated by empires that spread themselves and their cultural and political practices across the globe. Relying if not explicitly on Herder, then on similar formations of the nation and nationalism, anti-imperial movements began to take hold, especially in the nineteenth century. Groups known as "Young Ireland," "Young Turkey," "Young Italy," and others expressed a desire for a people to control its own lands, and so fought against British or Ottoman imperial rule, for example. Many nationalist movements were successful. The common form of anti-imperial action took nationalist forms well into the twentieth century, when India and Ireland overthrew British rule, and when black South Africans (in part through nationalist groups like the African *National* Congress) overthrew the settler descendants of Dutch imperialists. (We'll discuss the results of the overthrow of specifically colonial forms of imperialism—when the empire settled members of its central population base in colonies throughout its imperial holdings—in later sections of this chapter.)

But such nationalist movements are not all positive expressions of a people's desire for self-rule. Herderian nationalism, and many European discussions of "national character," such as those by philosophers Immanuel Kant and David Hume, were explicitly **Eurocentric**: that is, they perceived a valued hierarchy of development and civilization within different nations, and they tended to place European civilizations above all others in a manner inherently connected to the racial hierarchies of the time. Combined with the essentialist rhetoric of this form of nationalism, these theories went a long way toward justifying European imperial domination of the world rather than working against it. Herderian German nationalism was arguably transformed, in the twentieth century, into the racist imperial rhetoric of Nazism.

The Nation Before Nationalism: National Identity and Nationalist Ideology

As we've seen in other chapters, such essentialist notions of identity began to be challenged by the theories arising at the end of the nineteenth century and into the twentieth, specifically those of Karl Marx, Sigmund Freud, Simone de Beauvoir, and others. Nationalist identity theory is no different. Building on the theories we studied in Part II, many contemporary theorists of nationalism deny any essentialist elements in "national character," and instead ascribe nationalism to a form of ideology that serves the interest of the governing classes of any given state. In other words, whereas for essentialists like Herder the nation (defined as the identity of the *Volk*) comes before formation of geopolitical structure of the nation state, for many anti-essentialist thinkers, nationalism and/or state policy comes first and helps to form national identity. As Ernest Gellner states, for such theorists, "Nationalism is not the awakening of nations to self-consciousness," as Herder would have it; instead, nationalism "*invents* nations where they do not exist" (qtd. in Anderson, 2006, p. 6).

One influential theory of nationalism, which builds explicitly on Gellner's statement, is provided by Benedict Anderson (1936–), who defines the nation as an **imagined community**. In other words, the nation, that entity supposedly unifying a large group of people living in the same region—including its members' "national characteristics" and their feelings of nationalism—is not a pre-existing essence that is inherently part of those people, a "natural" or essential connection to the geography, climate, or peoples of one's homeland. It is instead an *effect* of their social and cultural existence.

Travel and the Canadian Flag

Why does Benedict Anderson call the nation "imagined"? For the simple reason that "the members of even the smallest nation will never know most of their fellow-members, meet them, or even hear of them, yet in the minds of each lives the image of their communion" (Anderson, 2006, p. 6). Many people have experienced this imagined "communion" while travelling in a different country: if a group of Canadians sees another group wearing Canadian flag pins or hears someone mention a part of Canada, the first group may be more willing to say hello, exchange which region of Canada they're from, and so on. These two groups could have little else in common, but that feeling of community may bring them together, if only briefly. This isn't an effect of any natural similarity between Canadians, as Herder might argue, but instead arises from the cultural signs of a shared imagined community.

Anderson argues that the nation is an "imagined" structure in three separate ways: as a "community," as "inherently limited," and as "sovereign" (p. 6). First, it is imagined as a *community*, he writes, since "regardless of the actual inequality and exploitation that may prevail in each, the nation is always conceived as a deep, horizontal comradeship" (p. 7). Being Canadian, in other words, seemingly cuts across all social classes and divisions between us, and makes us feel—in that imagined way—that those differences don't make us any less "Canadian." This "comradeship" is why, Anderson argues, "so many millions of people" will "willingly . . . die" for their country (p. 7).

Second, the nation is imagined as *limited*, "because even the largest of them . . . has finite, if elastic boundaries, beyond which lie other nations. No nation imagines itself coterminous with mankind" (p. 7). Part of the ideological structure of nationalism requires that we have other nations against which to define ourselves (following, in some ways, the same **performative** structure we saw Judith Butler trace out in relation to sexuality in Chapter 11).

Third, nations are imagined as *sovereign*—as the figure that, in its very being, is necessarily capable of and responsible for ordering and controlling the populace. For nations were born not just at the end of the Age of Empires but also during the Enlightenment, when the notion of "the divinely-ordained, hierarchical dynastic" rule of monarchs was coming to an end (p. 7) and when the notion of the **individual** was born. This period saw an increasing awareness of the multiplicity of different peoples, languages, and customs in the world, several of which were in direct conflict, so the notion of a clearly demarcated, clearly in-charge nation in which people with similar customs were free to pursue their own common goals was clearly an important one.

What these points add up to, for Anderson, is the fact that cultural representations of nationalism create the nation rather than the other way around: nationalism has "cultural roots" (p. 7). Representations of the nation and nationalist icons (like the flag, military statues, and cultural events, as we'll see in the case study) function for imagined national communities very much the way sacred objects and representations of the monarch functioned for religious and monarchic systems, respectively. Less obviously nationalist cultural products—such as newspapers and books—also serve to unite the populace of a nation, and around a specific language (one that differs from the "sacred language" of the religious community's texts, such as Latin). For Herder, culture reflects a nation's identity; for Anderson, culture creates that identity.

POSTCOLONIALISM AND IDENTITY

We've seen how the nation and nationality arose in part in response to the control of imperial forces. Important to consider in this regard is how the experience of being a colony of a larger power influenced and shaped the subjects who lived under that colonial rule, and how that experience was transformed by the overthrow of colonial powers. The transition from imperial to nation states happened throughout the twentieth century (in India, Ireland, the nations of Africa, and elsewhere), but it left countries that are still, in

Tim Hortons and the Imagined Community

Companies often play on nationalist feelings to sell their products, and this is nowhere more evident than in Canada with the Tim Hortons chain of coffee shops. As Patricia Cormack argues (see Further Reading), Tim Hortons—which was founded by and named after a former NHL star, supports other national-identified cultural activities (including hockey and curling), and is affiliated directly and indirectly with the Canadian government and military—is constructed as a site through which Canadians can imagine a unified identity, one that both accepts but overrides differences of cultural heritage, language, race, gender, and other identity categories.

Cormack argues that, in its series of "True Stories" ads focusing on actual Tim Hortons customers, the company presents "common themes" of "endurance, distance, ritual, and even quest"; the ads "involve rugged people, who often endure hardship (self-imposed or otherwise) and find psychological comfort in their rituals involving Tim Hortons" (p. 375). These themes echo those of other nationalist works that traditionally associate Canada with "rugged" nature as opposed to urban centres (of the examples Cormack lists, most are associated with explicitly rural settings). Moreover, she argues, many of these "advertisements are rooted in [the] anxiety and joy of travel and of negotiating the line between friends and strangers while away from home" (p. 377). These ads depict a person who's upset or nervous about being in a "strange" place (a student away from home at university, a soldier in Afghanistan, a recent immigrant to Canada); subsequent images of coming home, recognizing their new setting *as* home, or feeling safe and comfortable are directly tied to buying or being given a cup of Tim Hortons coffee. Whereas Canadian identity is often portrayed as fractured or under threat, Tim Hortons presents a way for all Canadians to literally buy a unified identity. As Cormack notes, in this way Tim Hortons can subtly and not so subtly reinforce a **hegemonic**, "melting pot" Canada as opposed to a multicultural one.

part or in whole, colonized. Add to these the so-called "settler nations," whose colonial project was manifested by the emigration of large numbers of new inhabitants from the colonizing country into the colonized. Canada, with its history of European settlement and its violation of treaties with and displacement and abuse of First Nations peoples, falls into this category.

One of the fields of cultural studies to arise since the 1970s has been postcolonial studies. Focusing on the analysis of and activism in colonial and postcolonial states, this field moves past the discussion of nation to examine the complex, multifaceted identities that exist within the fraught power dynamics of (post)colonial relations.

Orientalism

One of the most important works in postcolonial theory deals more with the discourses of imperialism than with colonial subjects per se, but it's still often credited with establishing the field: *Orientalism* (1978) by Edward Said (1935–2003). Said's study is, in some ways, a history textbook, insofar as it details "Western" and "Eastern" relations during British colonial expansion, a period that runs throughout the nineteenth century and into the beginning of the twentieth. Many history books, as we know them, examine battles, settlements, political events, and so on through a focus on dates and on the biographies of prominent figures (also rendered chronologically). They structure a narrative that focuses on progress, and yet downplay the role narrative plays in their own creation. That is, most history books present themselves as objective statements of fact, not as constructed, limited narratives. As we learned from Hayden White in Chapter 8, this attempt to disguise the textuality, the constructedness of such an object, is often an ideological gesture that paints that history in a particular light. By omitting notions of their own constructedness, these books ideologically reproduce certain dominant relations as "natural."

Said, by contrast, analyzes the ideological forces at work in representations of European interaction with the East. Specifically, he discusses how the imperial powers of the West constructed a notion of the East that they then used as a legitimation of their continued imperial and colonial practices. More specifically, Said examines the history of **Orientalism**: a nineteenth-century subject of study (the practitioners of which were known as "Orientalists") that focused on the history, culture, and languages of the "Orient." This geographical area, described as *the East* or *the Orient* in the period Said examines, basically encompasses everything east of central Europe (including northeastern Africa) and everything west of the New World. Said's primary focus is on the Arab peninsula and what many now call the Middle East, as well as on Western representations of Islam.

Said is thus interested in the discursive traditions of Orientalism and its relationship to historical acts of imperialism. He argues, as do most of the theorists in Part IV, that we can't necessarily have an objective understanding of the world or history because we can't get "outside" of language and are thus constrained by ideological frameworks. But if we examine the history of specific linguistic and discursive practices, then we can understand some of the dynamics—and ideological structures—involved in particular moments and places. This is why his book analyzes

> Orientalism as a Western style for dominating, restructuring, and having authority over the Orient. . . . My contention is that without examining Orientalism as a discourse one cannot possibly understand the enormously systematic discipline by which European culture was able to manage—and even produce—the Orient politically, sociologically, militarily, ideologically, scientifically, and imaginatively during the post-Enlightenment period. . . . In brief, because of Orientalism the Orient was not (and is not) a free subject of thought or action. (Said, 1978, p. 3)

Said argues that the entire shape of Western knowledge and action regarding "the Orient" was in large part determined by the discursive elements of Orientalism. Again, we have a reversal of more traditional notions of cause and effect: whereas traditional historians and anthropologists would say that observation of a time or a region leads to the description of it, Said says that the pre-existing discourse about the East actually shaped people's experience of it. "The point," he argues, "is that . . . the Oriental is *contained* and *represented* by dominating frameworks" (p. 40). This framework isn't completely determining, but it is limiting.

This is a formulation we should be familiar with by now. Out of an ideologically specific discourse, certain groups can benefit: the dominant group who controls certain aspects of discourse can use that control to reproduce and maintain their dominance through that discourse. Said uses this theoretical framework to discuss how world politics has been shaped in part by the dominant discourses of Western imperialism, and how these discourses create certain subject positions for the "non-western," the "other" of the white, male, Euro-American dominant group. He suggests that "European culture gained in strength and identity by setting itself off against the Orient as a sort of surrogate and even underground self" (p. 3). So the Orient, as the dominated, colonized other of Western dominance, is defined and reproduced by a variety of what Althusser would call Ideological and Repressive State Apparatuses (see Figure 13.1).

Said's theory can be applied to a wide variety of cultural objects that engage in particular forms of othering based on a division of West and East, or, as he discusses later in the book, of "developed nation" and "developing nation." Said writes that, from the late eighteenth century forward (during and after the height of European imperialism),

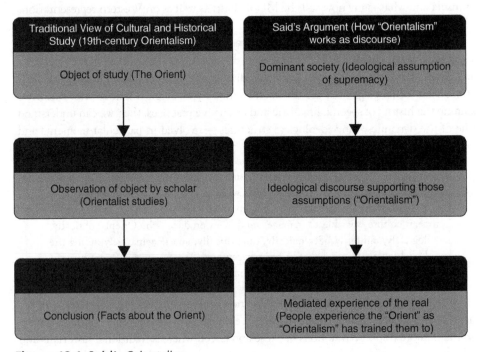

Figure 13.1 Said's *Orientalism*

The Snake Charmer

A typical Orientalist painting, Jean-Léon Gérôme's *The Snake Charmer* (c. 1879), has been read as reinforcing Western portrayals of the "Orient" as "exotic" and "mysterious." This image was also used for the cover of Edward Said's *Orientalism*. As Linda Nochlin details (see Further Reading), the painting captures several elements of Orientalist style and ideology. First, a great deal of attention is spent "realistically" portraying the intricate detail of Eastern dress, art, and other culture, represented in the deep blue tiles and the carpet on which the boy stands. Painted at a time when the Impressionists were at the forefront of the Western art world, Gérôme's more classical attention to detail emphasizes that it's the "Oriental" culture that is meant to mystify and be beautiful here, not the artist's skill itself. Second, as Nochlin argues, the painting presents a combination of primitiveness (represented by the young child's nakedness and the tiles' general state of disrepair) and timelessness—there is nothing in the painting to give you a sense of its specific location in time. Third, the painting toys with a certain sexual licentiousness and ambiguity: the young naked figure could be male or female, and the snake adds a particularly sinful and sexual overtone. In short, the painting presents an Orientalized Eastern culture that's primitive and timeless (and so "immune" to Western civilization) and that stands outside of Western, Christian morality. The Oriental subject is rendered as completely Other.

And yet, as Nochlin argues, picking up on Said, the painting also implicitly positions the Western or Occidental subject in relation to this Orientalized scene: Western subjects are the viewers, who gaze at the snake charmer, the snake holder, and that other audience (the one presented *in* the painting), implicitly defining themselves as a mirrored image of that final group. The Occidental subject is fully defined by not being part of the scene, and yet is still implicated in its performance: "the Westerner is of course always implicitly present in Orientalist paintings like *Snake Charmer*; his is necessarily the controlling gaze, the gaze which brings the Oriental world into being, the gaze for which it is ultimately intended" (p. 37).

The Snake Charmer, by Jean-Léon Gérôme, 1870.
Source: World History Archive/Alamy

Orientalism has taken three forms. The first is an academic form: the departments and scholars in universities that were invested in what was called Orientalist study. The second form, very much tied to the academic, is the creative use of Orientalism: the artistic, literary, or otherwise imaginative constructions of the Orient, in which "poets, novelists, philosophers, political theorists, economists, and imperial administrators, have accepted the basic distinction between East and West as the starting point for elaborate theories, epics, novels, social descriptions, and political accounts concerning the Orient, its people, customs, 'mind,' destiny, and so on" (pp. 2–3; see "The Snake Charmer" box). The third form is the creation of the Orient as a corporate institution. In some ways, contemporary popular culture, insofar as it engages in a contemporary form of Orientalism, falls into the latter two categories.

So the Orient as a subject becomes an object of discussion and debate, something that can be analyzed but must always be contextualized in terms of its relationship to the West. In these comparisons, the West is presented as modern while the East is posited as backward, or as existing in the past. But Said says he's interested not in providing a dogmatic attack on the bigoted constructs of the East (although this is certainly part of the project) but rather in how the discourse of Orientalism sets up a variety of mobile relationships: and in this he explicitly follows Michel Foucault's theories and methodology. In Chapter 8 we learned that for Foucault the exercise of power is first and foremost a local and unstable thing. That is, it doesn't belong to one overarching structure, and can't be exercised with any form of uniformity. However, this emphasis on the "local" and "unstable" exercise of power doesn't mean, for Foucault, that there are no larger groupings of power and no dominance being exercised.

Said sees a similar dynamic at play in the discourses of Orientalism:

> Orientalism is never far from what Denys Hay has called the idea of Europe, a collective notion identifying "us" Europeans as against all "those" non-Europeans, and indeed it can be argued that the major component in European culture is precisely what made that culture hegemonic both in and outside Europe: the idea of European identity as a superior one in comparison with all the non-European peoples and cultures. . . . In a quite constant way, Orientalism depends for its strategy on this flexible *positional* superiority, which puts the Westerner in a whole series of possible relationships with the Orient without ever losing him the relative upper hand. (p. 7)

This closely echoes Foucault's discussion of power. People are in multilayered relationships—as are nations—but there are still large groupings of strategies that work to maintain the status quo.

Said expands on this relationship, arguing that it's a strategy in which the West isn't free to redefine itself, because it must do so in relation to the East:

> [F]or a European or American studying the Orient there can be no disclaiming the main circumstances of *his* actuality: that he comes up against the Orient as a European or American first, as an individual second. And to be a European or an American in such a situation is by no means an inert fact. It meant and means being aware, however dimly, that one belongs to a power with definite interests in the Orient, and more important, that one belongs to a part of the earth with a definite history of involvement in the Orient almost since the time of Homer. (p. 11)

In this inextricable relationship we might be able to see a place where Western dominance breaks down on itself, since it is reliant on this "other" for its own definition of self. This is in part a deconstructionist move, as we discussed in Chapter 9: one that demonstrates how both sides of a binary, of an opposed pair, are reliant on each other for their existence;

When it was released in 2009, *Avatar* (written and directed by Canadian-American filmmaker James Cameron) was heralded primarily for reintroducing the technical marvel of 3-D film. Using a new technology, the film offered audiences a 3-D spectacle unlike any before it.

Avatar was, however, also discussed in relation to the discourses of environmentalism and race. The film has a rather straightforward environmentalist and a seemingly anti-imperialist message: a group of human scientists work on a planet called Pandora, studying the indigenous humanoid population. When human military and corporate interests discover that the rare (and uninventively named) element "unobtainium" is present on Pandora, they proceed to mine it without the indigenous population's permission, resulting in a war in which the indigenous group—led by a human who "goes native"—wins.

Seemingly anti-imperialist and obviously pro-environment, the film was a touchstone for certain political debates in the United States.

These debates were brought to Canada most explicitly when James Cameron was invited by George Poitras, a leader of the Mikisew Cree Nation, to tour Alberta's oil sands. After doing so, Cameron came out strongly against the oil sands projects' environmental impact.

And yet this narrative belies the ways in which Cameron's film engages in a form of othering of indigenous populations that echoes Said's discussion of Orientalism. While many First Nations are deeply and historically invested in protecting the environment (as Poitras's work makes clear), Cameron's allegorical, fantasy representation of such indigenous political involvement risks representing all such groups as primitive, heavily sexualized, and incapable of fighting their own battles without a properly "civilized" man leading them. In this, *Avatar* simply repeats the story of T. E. Lawrence (a.k.a. *Lawrence of Arabia*).

"Oilsands need more regulation: Cameron." CBC News Edmonton. 29 September 2010. Web. 24 August 2014.

---

they are thus not completely opposed as people thought, but caught in a dynamic play. Said makes this explicit, writing that his "real argument is that Orientalism is—and does not simply represent—a considerable dimension of modern political-intellectual culture, and as such has less to do with the Orient than it does with 'our' world" (p. 12).

Mimicry and Hybridity

While Said's text is profoundly important to postcolonial studies, his primary focus is on canonical Western culture and not on the actual cultures of the Middle East or other "non-Western" societies. Later postcolonial theorists and critics focused much more on the indigenous cultures of former Western colonies, and the way in which those cultures were variously suppressed, changed by, and/or resisted the cultures of the colonizers.

Many cultural theorists and critics have analyzed the cultural production of colonized and previously colonized societies and individuals. Two that helped shape this aspect of postcolonial studies are Homi Bhabha (1949–) and Gayatri Chakravorty Spivak (1942–), both of whom generally focus on South Asia and the Indian subcontinent. After discussing some of their better known concepts, we'll turn to postcolonial studies in and of Canada and the First Nations.

Both Bhabha and Spivak rely heavily on the theories of Derrida, discussed in Chapter 9, and both situate their works within larger philosophical, cultural, and critical contexts. As such, students—and advanced researchers—can find their work very difficult to read. But these are thinkers working on precise mechanisms of power and discourse, and so the complexity of their language and thinking is, in some ways, a reflection of the complexities of living within, resisting, and negotiating one's various positions (economic, familial, political, and so on) within a colonial space. Both are thus interested in defining the unstable grounds on which (post)colonial subjects must define themselves (even as they are defined by others).

Both theorists start with the difficulty, in a colonial setting, of the colonized populace finding a voice both within and against the colonial power. In many cases, of course, the colonial power asserts its own "national" language as the language of government and other social institutions: in Canada, Indigenous languages were discouraged by the colonial government, and members of the indigenous population were forced to speak the languages of the European colonizers.

Bhabha is best known now for his theories of mimicry and hybridity. Within a colonial setting, he argues, one of the primary methods through which the colonizer maintains power is to force the indigenous population into enacting a **mimicry** of the colonizer's culture. In making this argument, he relies on Jacques Lacan's use of the term *mimicry*, which Bhabha quotes as an epigraph to his essay, "Of Mimicry and Man: The Ambivalence of Colonial Discourse." Lacan writes, "Mimicry reveals something in so far as it is distinct from what might be called an itself that is behind. The effect of mimicry is camouflage" (qtd. in Bhabha, 1994, p. 85). In other words, when one mimics something else, one is putting forth a surface view that differs from one's supposed essence, which lies underneath this superficial performance.

Bhabha sees the entire site of a colonial space as being run through with a sense of mimicry. The colonial subject, he argues, mimics the dominant, imperial power because the empire has encouraged it. He quotes Sir Edward Cust, a British lord, who wrote to the British Colonial Office in the early nineteenth century about the state of colonial holdings in West Africa. Cust writes,

> It is out of season to question at this time of day, the original policy of conferring on every colony of the British Empire a mimic representation of the British Constitution. But if the creature so endowed has sometimes forgotten its real significance and under the fancied importance of speakers and maces, and all the paraphernalia and ceremonies of the imperial legislature, has dared to defy the mother country, she has to thank herself for the folly of conferring such privileges on a condition of society that has no earthly claim to so exalted a position. (qtd. in Bhabha, p. 85)

For Cust, mimicry is a condition of colonialism insofar as the imperial power imports its culture (its "paraphernalia and ceremonies"). In turn, this situation creates the danger of the colonial state assuming that mimicry is a sign of its own power and not a reflection of the empire's.

Mimicry thus gives the colonial subject a voice through which to exert power, but it also reinforces the power of the imperial rulers, who must be continually mimicked, and so echoed and repeated. This constant exchange of power creates a sense of instability in both colonial and colonizer's identity, and in the exercise of power in the colonial space. Bhabha writes,

> [C]olonial mimicry is the desire for a reformed, recognizable Other, as *a subject of a difference that is almost the same, but not quite*. Which is to say, that the discourse of mimicry is constructed around an *ambivalence*; in order to be effective, mimicry must continually produce its slippage, its excess, its difference. (p. 86)

The colonial power, trying to mimic its own homeland and culture, must always, as Cust does, assert that this place that the colonizers call home is "almost the same" as their "real" home, "but not quite": to acknowledge any reality behind the mimicry (for example, that the colonized subjects have the same rights as English subjects) would be to deny the colonizers' power. But simply not to export their culture, and therefore to live among the indigenous population on their own terms, would likewise deny the supposed supremacy of the colonizers' power. This form of colonial mimicry on behalf of the colonizers both cements their power and undermines it at the same time. Thus, "mimicry" as it is exercised by the colonial or imperial power is "stricken by . . . indeterminacy" (p. 86).

But what of the colonial subjects themselves, who may, in certain circumstances, feel the need to—or be forced to—mimic the speech, politics, or culture of the colonizer in order to gain power? For Bhabha, this is both a powerful and dangerous tool to use; even if it may be necessary, it is, like all forms of mimicry, defined by its own indeterminacy. The colonized subject's mimicking of the dominant culture raises the threat that the rulers of that culture could be replaced, but it also serves to silence or negate the "original" identity of the colonized behind that mimicry. Thus, a member of a colonized group participating in the colonizer's popular culture gains a form of cultural power while being denied access to other forms of cultural and social power outside of that colonial structure.

Mimicry is thus the largely negative result of the colonial situation, reinforcing the colonizer's power; it may be used to undermine that power, but only through the loss of the indigenous subject's own voice. Linked to but radically different from this mimicry is Bhabha's more positive formulation of **hybridity**. Hybridity, for Bhabha, is the condition of the contemporary, **postmodern** world, in which notions of national or other forms of "fixed" identities—identities often associated with earlier conditions of colonial or other dominance—are giving way to more fluid notions of who we are, especially as expressed by those who exist on the margins of dominant society. If mimicry raised the tension of indeterminacy, and thus the potential threat to the colonizer's power, hybridity is a tool to exploit that threat. Relying on an anti-essentialist notion of identity, Bhabha argues that the increasing flow of cultural products and practices around the globe offers people new models of identity that can be combined and deployed in multiple ways in order to resist those dominant forces that would attempt to fix marginalized people into positions of powerlessness. Much like Mikhail Bakhtin's notions of **heteroglossia**, hybridity decentres attempts to restrict discourse, offering new possibilities for agency. The indeterminacy created by colonial mimicry and the othering practices of colonial discourse can function to create this hybrid space: "The ambivalence at the source of traditional discourses on authority enables a form of subversion, founded on . . . undecidability" (p. 112).

Popular culture becomes a site of this undecidability: hybridity doesn't mean that two cultures come together and simply form a "new," third culture, but rather that cultural products highlight the fracture lines and differences between the colonial and colonized,

Cultural Hybridity, Hip Hop, and Indigenous Cultural Production

While hip-hop music and the subculture that surrounds it originated in African-American culture and the larger African diaspora, it has become a global cultural phenomenon. And given its increasing cultural (and economic) significance, it has also become a significant site for cultural analysis.

The expansion of hip hop beyond the African-American community is one area that opens itself up to cultural analysis. The increasing commercialization of rap from the 1990s forward, combined with the popularity of rap and other forms of hip hop among white youth, may point to the ways African-American culture is appropriated and emptied of its specificity—including its politically resistant nature—by the dominant economic structures of the largely white power structure.

However, such an analysis doesn't account for the popularity of hip hop among disenfranchised groups around the world. Following analyses of subcultures by Dick Hebdige (see Chapter 7) and of the interrelated cultures of the African diaspora studied by Paul Gilroy (see Chapter 12), it is clear that people do transform popular subcultural—and even dominant cultural—works for their own ends.

This brings us to the popularity of hip hop among some indigenous youth. In light of the sheer number of hip-hop groups, including many that have reached mainstream popularity, there is growing attention paid to the role that hip-hop culture can play in helping to empower these youth (see Further Reading).

Part of the appeal is the intense hybridity of hip-hop music and culture. Already seen as an adaptation of African forms within a North American context, hip hop has proven especially open to the influence of local traditions. The website "Beat Nation: Hip Hop as Indigenous Culture" explains this hybridity, noting that "Hip hop is giving youth new tools to rediscover First Nations culture. What is most striking about this work is how much of it embraces the traditional within its development" even as it uses contemporary materials of modern music culture (beatnation.org).

In Homi Bhabha's terms, the constant adaptation of hip hop, its continual transformation within new contexts, and its use as a means of empowerment and—as Beat Nation says— "resistance" to the dominant culture are all signs of the power of hybridity.

allowing for the dominant culture to be resisted or redefined. "Culture, as a colonial space," Bhabha writes, "can be transformed by the unpredictable and partial desire of hybridity. Deprived of their full presence, the knowledges of cultural authority may be articulated with forms of 'native' knowledges" (p. 115).

While the notion of hybridity is occasionally critiqued for denying the importance of "original" cultures, Bhabha and others argue that all cultures have changed and developed over time, and notions of "originality" and "fixed" identities are often used only as oppressive strategies to "keep people in their place," so to speak.

The Subaltern

Although Bhabha sees hybridity as a strategy of resistance to stultifying "official" cultures, it can nonetheless be seen as playing into another form of discourse that has been used to oppress indigenous peoples: globalism. In part, it is this problem that Gayatri Chakravorty Spivak analyzes in her famous essay, "Can the Subaltern Speak?," and in her own later revisions to it.

Spivak's essay is in part a response to a research project undertaken by the "Subaltern Studies group." This group takes the key term in their name from Gramsci: a **subaltern** is technically a lower-ranking military figure, but Gramsci used the term to refer to all those who were subordinated to the dominant classes of society. The Subaltern Studies group in turn used the term to reference the subordinated indigenous classes within a colonial state, who were neither members of the colonizing class nor the bourgeois elite of the indigenous population (who are often associated with the nationalist uprisings against the colonizers). The subaltern classes are thus the vast majority of the indigenous population who are, in general, refused a voice in policy, and who, as Ranjit Guha, the group's founding editor, argues, are also ignored by academic studies of nationalism and postcolonial movements (see Spivak, 1999, p. 270).

Spivak sees a problem with this approach, however. If the subaltern is defined as the group that has no voice, then the intellectual risks filling in that voice. Equally problematically, the subaltern becomes defined as a homogenous group, without its own internal differences and variety of voices. The desire to offer *a* voice to this group may seem laudable, but it is another form of colonial silencing. Spivak focuses her essay on a discussion of subaltern women (and the woman *as* subaltern), analyzing the practice of *sati*, in which a Hindu widow immolates herself on her husband's funeral pyre. In Spivak's argument, the woman in this act is always constituted as a silent object, whether from the perspective of the tradition "itself" (something that can no longer be fully accessed without the mediation of the history of colonial intervention) or in the European laws enacted against the practice. In either case, the subaltern woman is left silent; any reasons for her action that might be her own are left unheard. In this case, leaving the postcolonial theorist to speak for the subaltern is simply to write over that subaltern's voice again.

Spivak moves from this analysis to the story of a young woman from Calcutta, Bhubaneswari Bhaduri, who killed herself. Aware, as Spivak writes, that her suicide "would be diagnosed as the outcome of illegitimate passion" (in the belief that she must have been pregnant outside of marriage), she "waited for the onset of menstruation" (p. 307). Without the possibility of this explanation, her suicide was seen only as an act of insanity. However, later it was discovered that "she was a member of one of the many groups involved in the armed struggle for Indian independence" and "had been entrusted with a political assassination." She couldn't go through with the killing, but "aware of the practical need for trust, she killed herself" (p. 307). She waited until she was menstruating so that people would be aware that her actions had another reason.

But, because she was a woman, her reasons weren't properly interpreted or remembered. Asking some of her female relatives about Bhubaneswari, Spivak was asked why she would focus on her instead of her two successful sisters, while Bhubaneswari's nieces replied only that "It appears that it was a case of illicit love" (p. 308). These answers led, in Spivak's first version of her essay, to her declaration that "the subaltern cannot speak!" (p. 308). Hegemonic discourse, whether of the colonial or economically dominant classes (the "successful") or of gender, will deny or overwrite even the more explicitly active subaltern voice. In later revisions, however, Spivak makes it clear that this silencing is not merely the act of "*colonial* authorities," but also of "her own more emancipated granddaughters," who are part of a "new mainstream," or who are, in other words, part of the new, globalized popular culture (p. 309). All such hegemonic structures serve to both construct and silence the subaltern, Spivak writes. The subaltern cannot speak *as* the subaltern, but must first be brought into the mainstream and so become part of the (possibly new form of) hegemony.

Strategic Essentialism

The silencing of the subaltern may seem inescapable, meaning that the most oppressed groups can never be heard. But Spivak's larger point is that the most oppressed groups, the subaltern, are defined as such by their inability to engage in the dominant discourse. This is not to say that members of such groups cannot be spoken to, but that "[w]hen a line of communication is established between a member of subaltern groups and the circuits of citizenship or institutionality, the subaltern has been inserted into the long road to hegemony. Unless we want to be romantic purists or primitivists about 'preserving subalternity' . . . this is absolutely to be desired. . . . Remembering this allows us to take pride in our work without making missionary claims" (p. 310). This may be the moment when a Bhabha-esque hybridity comes into play: the "authentic" subaltern identity is no longer, but that doesn't mean the goal of the postcolonial critic is always to instantiate mimicry or to transform the subaltern subject into a reflection of the elite critic.

But how, then, can an academic critic (necessarily part of what Spivak refers to as the "elite") deal ethically with subaltern subjects? How does one "take pride" in one's analysis while knowing that one is, to one degree or another, overwriting the very people the critic is

World War Z and the Subaltern as Zombie

Based on Max Brooks's novel (although taking very little from it beyond the title and general plot), the 2013 film World War Z is one of a string of so-called "zombie apocalypse" movies and television shows. While the basic concept of the zombie comes from Haitian folklore, and while its entrance into popular culture dates back to the early decades of the twentieth century, the modern zombies of film are usually traced back to George Romero's watershed film Night of the Living Dead (1968) and its sequel Dawn of the Dead (1978). Romero's zombies—reanimated corpses, hungry for human flesh—are often read as satirical critiques of Western consumerism. Mindlessly shuffling through suburban landscapes and shopping malls, Romero's zombies, it is argued, aren't that much different from the average consumer.

The film version of World War Z offers a slightly different allegory, however. Focused on the global outbreak of a zombie virus, the film seems to make an explicit argument for a form of American—or North American—isolationism, one connected to a racial and cultural chauvinism. The film travels through different global regions where the United States has political and military interests, specifically South Korea and Israel. The latter is shown to have been largely protected from the zombie plague by a large wall erected round it—one that explicitly references the actual West Bank barrier. While the American hero, Gerry Lane (Brad Pitt), is there, the wall is opened to allow some Palestinians through. Several Palestinians wave the Palestinian flag and begin to sing and celebrate, and we realize that the noise is attracting the zombie horde from the

other side of the wall. Breaching the wall, Israel is lost—all because of Palestinian noise.

In an earlier scene, as Lane tries to save his family, they're rescued by a Spanish-speaking, non-white, economically disenfranchised family represented as recent immigrants. Only their young son can speak English, and he serves as the translator. Lane attempts to get the family to come with him, but they refuse. The mother and father are almost immediately killed by zombies (becoming zombies themselves), but Lane saves the young boy. At the end of the film Lane returns to his family, safe in what is presented as the fully protected, rugged wilderness of Nova Scotia. Everyone in the concluding scene is white except for the young boy.

Taken as a whole then, the film presents a global narrative in which settler nations are being overrun by a horde of zombies, often represented as the colonized people who "surround" that nation and who speak other languages that sound only like "noise." The only subaltern figure who's saved, and embraced by the white family at the end, is that figure who fully assimilates, learning the language of the supposedly dominant group. Just as Spivak writes, in this film the subaltern cannot speak as the subaltern, gains a voice only within the dominant culture, and is otherwise seen as either mindless and/or as a threat by that dominant culture. And any "weakness" toward the subaltern group by the dominant group (opening up or tearing down walls between the groups, for instance) results in disaster. The film can thus be seen to present a classically imperialist narrative under the guise of a "simple" zombie film.

---

trying to aid, even if by simply exposing their abuse at the hands of power? This question became a central one in postcolonial studies of the 1990s, and it is one that still often haunts postcolonial cultural criticism. Isn't the imposition of the critic's voice simply a version of the cultural imperialism that is so central to the expansion of Western popular culture?

The short answer to that question, for Spivak, is yes. But, as with most answers in cultural theory, it's more complicated than that. The subaltern subject does not, in Spivak's theory, have access to hegemonic forms of representation and critique: by definition, the subaltern figure does not have an agential form of access to dominant forms of discourse. This doesn't mean, however, that we can't work to expose the abuses such groups face under the hegemonic power structure. But in order to do so, we must devise an ethical way of representing these subjects. Spivak's early answer to this need is the concept of **strategic essentialism**. In her essay "Subaltern Studies: Deconstructing Historiography," Spivak defines this "*strategic* use of positivist essentialism" as a means of representing the subaltern subject while attempting to avoid offering an absolute (and hence vaguely "imperialist") definition of that subject (Spivak, 1988, p. 13). In other words, *strategic essentialism* means to deploy an essentialist definition of an oppressed group but to do so always with limited, specifically demarcated political goals in mind. The Subaltern Studies group, for example, attempts to find, between the lines of imperial documents, the "identity" of the indigenous "insurgent," the "rebel consciousness" that imperial forces were acting against (p. 12). This procedure would mean, for example, reading legal, military, and other accounts of colonial activities in India, North America, or other colonial sites for hints about how those accounts (and the actions they describe) are shaped by and respond to interactions with the indigenous populations. These readings necessarily posit an essentialist identity to the indigenous population, but they do so, Spivak argues, for the express purpose of highlighting the fact that European narratives of their own dominance in fact show the opposite. This could have political effects when it comes to asserting the legality of treaties between European colonizers and the First Nations, for example. Even though it involves the critic "speaking for" a subaltern group, it's done for the purpose of exposing fractures in the hegemonic dominance, fractures that may provide new areas for that group to assert its own voices.

Spivak's critical work is clearly complex, and heavily indebted to the philosophical works of Derrida and others. But she reminds us that access to the means of cultural production is largely limited to those who are, to one degree or another, part of a larger economic or social elite. Following the Marxist logic that Spivak relies on, the presentation of colonized groups, and especially of subaltern groups, in popular culture would thus serve to support the dominance of that elite group at the expense of the subaltern group. Understanding the complex dynamics of identity at play can allow for a thoroughgoing critique of such representations (and the social structures they both rely on and support). Furthermore, they can allow for the opening up of culture in such a way that previously silenced voices may begin to be heard.

POSTCOLONIAL STUDIES, POSTCOLONIAL CANADA?

Throughout the preceding discussion have been references to the First Nations, and to the indigenous populations of Canada and North America more generally. As a settler nation, Canada is, of course, part of the history of Western imperialism and colonialism.

Moreover, the history of European and, later, Canadian interaction with the peoples of the First Nations is one that follows the models of oppression and resistance we've discussed in relation to other regions. The terrible history of abuse at residential schools, where First Nations children were taken, forced to abandon their own languages, and, in many cases, physically, sexually, and emotionally abused, is beginning to be more widely reported and understood in the dominant Canadian media and culture. Likewise, there are many reported cases of the violation of treaties between the Canadian government, its European predecessors, and the First Nations, even as First Nations currently fight for self-governance. In this, then, Canada has certainly been a colonial nation, and the question of whether we are yet *postcolonial* is, at most, an open one.

Canadian cultural critics have thus relied on and developed their own approach to postcolonial theory and cultural criticism, especially in relation to the dominant culture's relationship to Indigenous peoples. However, the question of whether postcolonial theory is appropriate in the Canadian context remains. As Laura Moss points out, the definition of Canada within a postcolonial context is not without its critics. Speaking within a literary context, she writes that Canada and its culture

> are often omitted from discussions of postcolonialism . . . on the understanding that you simply cannot compare Canada and Nigeria, for example, because of the vastly different histories, relationships with imperial power, contemporary social and political environments, and current relationships to globalization. . . . Yet, Canada as a colonizing power in relation to the First Nations must bear scrutiny, just as Nigeria needs to be accountable, for instance, in relation to the Ogoni struggle. (Moss, 2003, p. 2)

However, to focus on First Nations peoples in Canada is not the only means of studying Canadian culture through a postcolonial lens. In answering the question "Is Canada postcolonial?" Moss notes that

> even some of the harshest critics of the inclusion of Canada in postcolonial studies will say an emphatic "no," but will follow it shortly with a reference to work by an "exceptional" group: maybe First Nations writers, maybe recent immigrant writers, maybe immigrant writers from other postcolonial locations, maybe nonwhite writers, maybe other marginalized writers, maybe women writers, maybe gay male writers, or maybe writers from religious minorities. The repetition of "maybe" foregrounds the impossibility of a simple answer to the question of Canada's, or even Canadian literature's, relationship with postcolonialism. (p. 8)

One could point to Canada's larger role in globalism, with economic displacement and migrancy that globalism entails, as another way in which Canada and Canadian culture are involved in imperial and colonial forms. As Moss goes on to note, Canada's official policy of multiculturalism can also be a point of analysis in relation to postcolonial criticism and theory. Does multiculturalism serve to protect the rights—including the rights of cultural expression—of minority communities within Canada, or is it a largely economic "marketing" of a particular brand of Canadian nationalism that serves to paper over significant cultural difference and reduce everyone's culture to "folklore," as Rinaldo

Walcott suggests (Moss, p. 13)? We discussed these issues briefly in Chapter 3's "Canadian Multiculturalism and Hegemony" box.

These questions are all significant, but there's no question that Canada is involved in the histories of migrations, diasporas, and colonialism that postcolonial theory takes as its subjects. The forced removal of Indigenous Canadians from their lands and the suppression of their cultures are only the most obvious examples. The cultural productions of the First Nations, their place within and relations to the wider forms of Canadian popular culture (as in the "Cultural Hybridity" box earlier), and their and other minority cultures' deployment within representations of Canadian nationalism are significant and necessary areas of study.

Case Study

The Vancouver Olympics

The modern Olympics are, in obvious ways, moments of cultural nationalism, even as they appear to foster a form of international friendliness. The opening ceremonies of the Olympics are often used by the host nation as a way of representing and even "selling" itself for future tourists.

The opening ceremonies of the 2012 Olympics in Vancouver offer a particular vision of Canada's nationalism, one directly connected to the representation of its relations with the First Nations. The ceremonies began with a set of torches arranged to look like a maple leaf, followed by the singing of the Canadian national anthem. Then came a welcoming by four leaders of the First Nations on whose traditional lands the Olympics were taking place. As the Lil'wat Nation's website tells us, "The Vancouver 2010 Olympic and Paralympic Winter Games are being held within the traditional and shared traditional territories of the Lil'wat, Musqueam, Squamish and Tsleil-Waututh" (www.lilwat.ca). These nations were seen as partners with Canada in hosting the Games.

The opening ceremonies relied heavily on symbols and artifacts from First Nations culture; the First Nations took a prominent role in the "Cultural Olympiad" aspects of the official Games; and many Olympic souvenirs drew on First Nations' culture. The high level of "Aboriginal Participation" is advertised still on the Government of Canada's website (www.canada2010.gc.ca/obj/pa-ap/040201-eng.cfm). The site notes that the Olympic Committee and the "Four Host First Nations Society signed a protocol agreement in November 2005, marking the first time in Olympic history that Aboriginal peoples of Canada have been formal partners with an Olympic organizing committee."

There are many ways to analyze the opening ceremonies and the Olympics as a whole in terms of the participation and representation of Indigenous peoples in Canada. Certainly one way to read this is a positive one, in that there was a clear demonstration of the importance of the First Nations to Canadian culture and society and a recognition of the relationship between the First Nations and Canada as one between equal partners. We can perhaps see an attempt to celebrate cultural difference and to promote political equality between these nations rather than continuing an oppressive colonial relationship that has long marred Canadian interactions with the First Nations. Certainly this is how the official Four Host First Nations represent the events.

There were others who interpreted the events differently, however (see Further Reading). While many lauded the representation and involvement of First Nations, some noted that the use of Indigenous cultural material served Canada's nationalist self-image as a "multicultural society" but only at a superficial level, covering over the inequality that continues to exist in Indigenous communities' general well-being and in their treatment by the justice system and elsewhere. Other Indigenous leaders likewise saw problems with how Indigenous culture was used in the Olympics' marketing campaign: "Chief Stewart Phillip, the president of Union of B.C. Indian Chiefs . . . asserted that '. . . The Disneyesque promotional materials suggests a cosy relationship between aboriginal people of the province with all levels of government and it completely ignores the horrific levels of poverty our people endure on a daily basis'" (qtd. in Toban Black, "An Indigenous Olympics?"; see Further Reading).

Following such arguments, we could say that the participation of First Nations, when read positively, might indicate a certain recognition of the necessity for Canadians to value the hybridity of their national identities, a hybridity that involves a play of differences, all equal, that make up Canada and the First Nations. Likewise, we could see the use of Indigenous cultural material (much of it taken from traditional cultures rather than from contemporary artists) as a performance of a strategic essentialism in an attempt to garner more equal treatment within political negotiations.

Conversely, if we see the opening ceremonies as a form of "marketing" a particular form of Canadian national identity, one that doesn't admit to inequality within the nation's borders, then these ceremonies could be read in terms of colonial mimicry, an assertion that dominant Canadian culture can permit certain forms of Indigenous political involvement but not others.

But given the quotation from Chief Phillip, as well as numerous protests surrounding the Olympics that attempted to highlight the inequality that exists in Canada, we can also analyze these and other forms of postcolonial resistance as using the Olympics for their own ends rather than the other way around.

Part of the opening ceremonies of the 2012 Olympics.

Source: Friso Gentsch/epa/Corbis

Discussion Questions

1. Many companies sell their products as being quintessentially Canadian, or as somehow relating to Canadian identity. Find some examples, and discuss what they tell us about the dominant notions of Canada.

2. Following the discussion of Indigenous hip-hop groups, can you think of other elements of popular culture that speak to a form of cultural hybridity? Do any of them seem to merely use an "othered" cultural figure to sell themselves?

3. While Said's discussion of Orientalism focuses primarily on the eighteenth and nineteenth centuries, aspects of contemporary Western culture still convey Orientalist iconography

and assumptions. In addition to the oft-repeated image of the Arab terrorist in film and television, dating back decades, there are representations of the East as "exotic" and sexualized in ways that may present the West as more active and strong, and all within a global capitalist framework. For example, pop singer Gwen Stefani toured with four "Harajuko girls" who remained silent during interviews. Do you think this was a simple example of Orientalism? Can an argument be made that it was a form of hybridity?

Further Reading

Black, Tobin. "An Indigenous Olympics?" *Sociological Images*. The Society Pages. 15 Feb. 2010. Web. 27 June 2012.

Cormack, Patricia. "'True Stories' of Canada: Tim Hortons and the Branding of National Identity." *Cultural Sociology* 2 (2008): 369–84.

Mitchell, Tony, ed. *Global Noise: Rap and Hip-Hop Outside the USA*. Hanover: Wesleyan UP, 2002.

Moss, Laura, ed. *Is Canada Postcolonial? Unsettling Canadian Literature*. Waterloo: Wilfrid Laurier UP, 2003.

Nochlin, Linda. *The Politics of Vision: Essays on Nineteenth-Century Art and Society*. New York: Harper, 1989.

"Olympic Inukshuk Irks Inuit Leader." *CBCSports*. CBC.ca. 27 April 2005. Web. 27 June 2012.

Phelan, Bryan. "Hip-Hop Activism for First Nations Youth." *Wawatay News Online*. 1 May 2003. Web. 27 June 2012.

Sugars, Cynthia, ed. *Unhomely States: Theorizing English-Canadian Postcolonialism*. Peterborough: Broadview P, 2004.

Watkins, S. Craig. *Hip Hop Matters: Politics, Pop Culture, and the Struggle for the Soul of a Movement*. Boston: Beacon P, 2005.

Yanchyk, Brandy. "Aboriginal Canadians Divided Over Vancouver Olympics." *BBC News*. BBC.co.uk. 1 Jan. 2010. Web. 27 June 2012.

Part V
Writing About Popular Culture

Chapter 14

Writing About Popular Culture Across the Disciplines

INTRODUCTION

As the wide range of topics covered, theories explored, and materials analyzed in the preceding chapters makes clear, the field of popular culture studies is a varied one, in both its methodologies and its objects of analysis. The more specific academic discipline of cultural studies is itself not necessarily unified. While there are university departments called "Cultural Studies" in the U.K., the U.S., and Canada, many of these are interdisciplinary programs, with professors trained in a number of different disciplines in the humanities and social sciences.

Part V is designed, in combination with the case studies and examples throughout the book, to offer students a guide to understanding how their knowledge of the theories discussed in preceding chapters can be used in their own analyses of popular culture. This chapter discusses the different disciplinary approaches to the study of popular culture and how they affect the type of theories and methodologies used in writing assignments. Chapter 15 examines how to distinguish between analysis and opinion in the study of popular culture, and the ways in which theory can be incorporated into certain kinds of written assignments. Chapter 16 contains a selection of sample assignments that students and professors can use as models for course assignments.

Note, however, that Part V isn't intended to replace writing handbooks or discipline-specific writing guides; the kinds of detail available in those resources can't be duplicated here. Instead, Part V offers a way of thinking about the overall goals of written studies of popular culture, a specific sense of why and how one would incorporate the theories we've discussed into those analyses, and some ideas about how to structure particular widely used assignments in an effective manner. Instructors in their particular classes will necessarily add to, change, and even work against some of these models, all of which will help students with their own cultural analyses.

DISCIPLINARY APPROACHES TO POPULAR CULTURE

Although courses in popular culture are regularly framed using the theories and methodologies discussed here, they're often housed within more traditional departments and in interdisciplinary programs—communication studies, English and other national literature and culture departments, film, gender and/or women's studies, history, music, and sociology and anthropology—that may approach their analyses from within their own disciplinary framework. In short, analyses of popular culture—and the types of analytical work students are asked to do—come in many different "flavours."

So it's difficult for one textbook to cover the range of approaches and assignments that courses on popular culture can take, but we can sketch out a few general methodologies. Generally speaking, we can call these approaches the historical, the sociological, and the textual/thematic. Your instructor may wish you to take any one of these approaches in your assignments, or attempt a variety or combination of them. After all, the study of popular culture is an inherently interdisciplinary field, and very rarely would any one approach ignore issues of social context.

If one concept joins all these approaches, it is the concept of **discourse**, according to which all forms of meaning creation take place within concrete situations and contexts that are inherently part of all social communications. In other words, it's not possible to understand an object of culture in isolation; instead, we must analyze it within institutional, historical, and other social contexts. We can also discuss particular forms of social discourse (**gendered** and **racialized** discourses are two examples) as well as certain practices and forms of production that impact popular culture. Thus, a Tarzan film—as Frantz Fanon has argued—can take on different meanings according to the location and racial makeup of its audience: the context can effectively change the meanings of the film (see Chapter 12).

The following summaries of these approaches are offered to help students identify the goals and methods of their particular popular culture courses; in this way students can assess how their own work fits into the many fields of cultural studies. Instructors can use these descriptions, and the discussion of evidence and analysis that follows, to situate the approach or approaches taken within their own courses.

Historical

Traditional historical study maps out specific facts about a particular moment in history in the context of society's macro structures: the large social institutions and leaders as well as the significant and far-ranging actions they took. One would study the history of Canada, for example, by discussing its regional and national leaders and the important moments in the nation's formation and development (Confederation, for example, or the laying of the transcontinental railroad, or Canada's involvement in the two World Wars). With the advent of cultural studies, however, two things happened: historians began to study what's often referred to as "history from below"—the significance of people's everyday lives—and to recognize that their way of framing studies shaped knowledge rather than simply presenting facts (for example, traditional historical studies, often written by relatively privileged white men, excluded the roles of women, minority populations, and other socially marginalized groups).

More recent historical analyses, influenced by cultural studies, recognize what Louis Montrose refers to in "Professing the Renaissance" as the "textuality of history"

(Montrose, 1989, p. 20): the ways in which every moment in history is composed of heterogeneous discursive forces. Finding *the* historical Truth becomes an impossibility, but mapping out the interplay of discursive elements is at least partially possible. These historians will sometimes map a very particular moment in time (one year, or even one month or day) in great detail in order to show the complexity of forces at play. Or, they will map the role of a particular object through a vast span of time as a means of exploring the previously unsuspected complexities of social power that adhere to seemingly minor objects. This could include studies of how popular culture is invested in hegemonic power relations, and how popular and everyday culture respond to such distributions of power.

While studies of everyday or folk culture take a longer historical view, the historical study of popular culture often situates its rise within the industrial age and the capacity for mass reproduction. As an example, let's say one wanted to take a cultural-historical approach to science fiction. Such a study could look at the rise of the genre (and the term *science fiction* itself) in American pulp magazines of the 1920s and 1930s. At the same time it could analyze how scientific study and technological skills were becoming increasingly important to both the American workforce and the development of American global dominance. Such a study could, for example, analyze the convergence of these two trends in the pulp magazines' ads, which often tried to sell correspondence education in a scientific field. This analysis could be paired with a study of how the same period saw a transformation in American class identity.

The study's methodology would primarily involve the analysis of archival material—for example, the magazines themselves; local and personal records relating to the intersection of the magazines' readership and scientific study; and university and college calendars that track the rise in scientific and technological training. Such tools as statistical analyses (of, say, the workforce) would be used, but as with cultural sociology and anthropology, the focus would be more on particular groups' patterns of behaviour and knowledge in relation to cultural activities. In this case, then, a focus on one specific group or activity could lead to a detailed analysis of the intersections between the fictional representation of science, the rise of popular forms of scientific discourse, and scientific activity over time.

Sociological

While traditional sociology focuses on the role in societies of large institutional structures (religion, economic and class divisions, government, and so on), the **cultural turn** (the move toward analyzing cultural objects and practices, discussed in Chapter 7) meant examining everyday cultural behaviour and the multiplicitous force relations that exist in any given social moment. Society isn't necessarily seen as having an overarching structure (the economic or religious, for example) that determines everyone, but rather as being constituted of intricate and heterogeneous positions that are difficult to fully grasp but that may be invested in, or challenge, certain hegemonic social relations. Likewise, anthropology, and specifically cultural anthropology, analyzes how the cultural habits of specific groups are determined by and/or react against dominant institutional structures, and how anthropology itself functions within such discourses. While these two disciplines remain distinct, their approach to popular culture overlaps, with sociologists tending toward an analysis of popular culture as one social institution in relation to other institutions (economic, cultural, educational, and so on), and anthropologists turning to people's daily interactions with popular culture and other institutional structures. Finally, sociology tends toward numeric or statistical study while anthropology takes a more narrative approach (though, again, such distinctions are not rigid).

What we're calling the sociological approach to the study of popular culture is often treated as the accepted form within the cultural studies discipline, especially in the British tradition as developed by the Centre for Cultural Studies (see Chapter 7). In this approach, the structure, appearance, and general meaning of an object of popular culture may be considered significant, but much more important is how people interact with that object and how all such interactions are formed within a larger socio-cultural matrix. Thus, the actual materials of popular culture aren't the central focus of a sociological and/or anthropological approach. Instead, the focus is on *people* and their interactions as they take place through or in connection with popular culture.

The methodologies of a sociological and/or anthropological approach would thus focus on people's experiences with particular cultural objects or events in order to understand how those experiences are structured by institutional and other social structures and how people actually articulate these experiences, both in line with and resisting those structures. Cultural critics would analyze people's behaviours in order to make conclusions about how the surrounding social structures and their cultural apparatuses function (for example, Do they create social hierarchies or otherwise invest power differentials within the group?). These critics would gather data through archival research and reviews of other pertinent studies as well as analyze existing interviews, reports, and so on for patterns of behaviour and belief. Fieldwork assignments are also central, both to experience the cultural event first-hand but also to interview the people engaging in the cultural event or with the object. Individual interviews and larger, statistically significant surveys of people are often the ground of such analyses.

All of this data would be closely analyzed in order to discover certain underlying social structures (or the *breakdown* of those structures). Analysts would also study how a group (or groups) participate in certain cultural events or use certain cultural objects—and how those activities are viewed by **ingroups** (those participating) and **outgroups** (those on the outside looking in) as well as their perceptions of each other. Such an analysis wouldn't take these views as necessarily the "truth" about the event's social effects, but would see those beliefs as one set of evidence to be analyzed.

Just as, if not more, important is the role of the **cultural site**. After all, the experience of watching a film in the theatre differs greatly from watching with family on television in the living room, which differs again from watching it by yourself on a computer screen with headphones at a coffee shop. The setting can also influence how people talk about an event: people may discuss a film differently with an academic interviewer than they would with friends or anonymously in an online message board. In these studies, then, analysts need to be aware of their own positions in relation to the subject at hand, and develop an understanding of the complex relations that exist in any given social situation.

Returning to our earlier example, a sociological study would focus on how people interact with and through science fiction—for example, it could study the cultures of SF fandom. This approach could involve analyzing the behaviours and activities that take place at such popular SF conventions as the San Diego Comic Con. Approaching Comic Con from a Marxist perspective, and by using Dick Hebdige's theories about **subcultures** (see Chapter 7), one could hypothesize that, because the event appropriates the supposedly "outsider" status of science fiction fandom (in that it appeals to only a limited number, and therefore has what Walter Benjamin would call **aura**), it transforms this group identity into merely another form of consumerism. Or one could use a feminist approach, and hypothesize that while the cultural forms that bring the group together (popular science fiction films and comics, for instance) tend to represent women as passive objects, many of the women and men involved take on more active identities, playing with the gender expectations of those popular works in order to express resistant gender identities—either in the cosplay (costume play) at Comic Con or in the practice of writing fan fiction—and developing communities around such activities.

In order to prove these hypotheses right or wrong, one would have to examine the behaviours of people at the Con, identify patterns of group behaviour, look at how the event itself is written about by participants and outsiders (online, for instance), and interview people about their experiences through large data-gathering interviews and possibly one-on-one interviews with attendees. (Keeping in mind that, as noted in Chapter 15, most universities have ethics guidelines surrounding the use of human subjects for research purposes. Your instructor will familiarize you with any applicable guidelines.)

Textual/Thematic

The textual or thematic approach finds its home most often in disciplines that study the creative works of popular culture, whether they are literary, cinematic or televisual, or more generally artistic. Programs ranging from English to film studies and to music, and sometimes such interdisciplinary programs as gender and women's studies, can take a textual or thematic approach.

In this approach to popular culture, instead of focusing primarily on the use and social context of cultural objects, the objects themselves are seen as being important for study. Such an approach can generally lead in two overall directions. The first significantly overlaps with the cultural-historical approach discussed above, which examines how people discussed and used the cultural object over time or in a particular time and place. The difference is the emphasis placed on how the object itself does a certain amount of social "work" in terms of how these social activities are framed. This type of study can also look at the history of a particular work's reception in order to learn more about that work and about the societies and groups by which it was read, ignored, censored, and so on.

The second approach is sometimes referred to (often pejoratively) as what Rita Felski calls "symptomatic reading" (Felski, 2003, p. 512). Critics examine how a cultural object frames the larger social debates of a time. The critic can explore the work's representation of social structures, trends, and debates using the tool of close reading. Close reading involves the examination of a text or object for particular patterns of representation, which in turn present an opinion or argument about an aspect of the world: these patterns are often called "themes," and they can be found in linguistic, visual, or aural works. Critics can also look for disruptions of those patterns, which can indicate the presence of a larger social or cultural conflict regarding that particular theme. Important to recognize is that these themes are often not readily visible on the surface of the work: the patterns of metaphor in a story, or framing techniques in a film, need to be carefully observed and pieced together by the critic, and then placed into the larger context of the work's themes.

In traditional textual studies, the themes analyzed would often be represented as "universal" themes of literature and the human condition. But in textual analyses influenced by cultural studies, the themes are more specific to particular times and places, and there is an attempt to situate the work being studied within its larger social, political, and cultural contexts. This is often seen as the opposite of the sociological approach; practitioners of one will sometimes view the other as not performing "cultural studies" at all. However, the textual-thematic approach does apply the same theoretical lenses as the other approaches, and does situate the cultural work within its particular social and historical context. It's quite unlike the traditional "formalist" approach to literature, film or music, which examines works "in themselves"—or at most as part of a particular artistic history—devoid of the social questions of **class**, **sexuality**, or **race**, for example. Laura Mulvey's analysis of film (see Chapter 10) would fit in to this form of cultural studies.

Let's turn again to our example of science fiction. A traditional literary approach would focus on how the text creates meaning through its patterns of metaphor, symbolism, characterization, and other literary devices in order to assess what larger themes about the "human condition" (removed from specific social context) or (often) about literature itself are being addressed. Such traditional studies could also address the relations between texts in an attempt to develop a canon of literary works that best exemplifies the tradition. However, such popular genres as science fiction are often left out of traditional literary studies, following the split between high and low culture we examined earlier (see Chapter 1). Beyond the mere fact of wanting to study such popular genres, a textual-thematic cultural studies approach could examine how particular texts or a range of texts (including not only literary ones but also cinematic, televisual, and so on) work within specific social contexts to present science and technology in a particular light, such that science fiction may help to shape public assessments of scientists (one can think here of the TV series *Big Bang Theory*). Or it could analyze the portrayal of gender in such works, for example. As with the sociological approach, a textual-thematic study could also analyze fan responses to such works, but it would offer a close reading of fan fiction, for example, to analyze how such works engage and problematize some of the assumptions of the mainstream or mass-produced examples of the genre.

DISCIPLINES WITHOUT PUNISHMENT

There is no one set of practices or methodologies that define the study of popular culture; this wide range of critical approaches in fact demonstrates its inherently interdisciplinary nature. The theories we've studied often emphasize difference, heterogeneity, and the importance of not silencing particular groups, and the methodologies of the study of popular culture themselves reflect that emphasis on multiplicity.

That said, this textbook is designed to be taught in a wide range of popular culture classrooms, some of which may emphasize one of the methods over others. The "symptomatic approach" may be acceptable in certain humanities departments that have classes on popular culture (such as English or music), but would often be unacceptable in a social sciences classroom (such as sociology). Meanwhile, different courses or even different assignments in a dedicated cultural studies program may employ a combination of these approaches. Indeed, most popular culture classes, no matter their department or program, will inevitably employ some combination of these approaches. Make sure you know which approach or combination is closest to your particular class!

Equally important, you should make sure that the theoretical model you choose for a particular assignment is suited to the assignment's goals, its topic, and to the subject matter(s) it asks you to examine. In Chapter 15 we discuss some of the usual pitfalls and problems students face when incorporating theory into their assignments. We'll also look at what constitutes evidence and analysis as opposed to simple opinion on a topic.

Chapter 15
Opinion, Analysis, Evidence, Theory

INTRODUCTION

In Chapter 14 we discussed some of the primary disciplines that inform the study of popular culture, the different ways in which those disciplines approach it, and the different forms of evidence these approaches use. In this chapter we explore, in general terms, the difference between opinion and analysis, and how evidence and theoretical approach can interact in students' writing on popular culture.

OPINION, ANALYSIS, EVIDENCE

Every academic discipline focuses on different topics and uses certain kinds of evidence and forms of proof in its studies. To take two general approaches, physical sciences study physical evidence from the natural world (matter, its constituent atoms, their constituent subatomic particles, and so on), while cultural disciplines study the objects and creations of human society.

Human creations are especially complex objects to study. While many (though not all) scientific studies can be reduced to binary forms (a hypothesis is right or wrong, or can be proven or disproven), cultural objects, tools, and the ways humans interact with them are rarely binary in their meaning, but instead allow for any number of variations. While scientific studies will often attempt to limit the number of variables in an experiment in order to make that experiment more specific and therefore effective, any particular cultural study—involving, as it does, language and **discourse** at its core—contains innumerable, uncontrolled variables. Society often seems to function in black-and-white binaries, but cultural reality is made up of varieties of colours—and even multiple shades of multiple colours. (And even the preceding sentence can be read in several ways, using some of the theories we've discussed.)

One cultural object or moment can thus lead to many different interpretations. However, those interpretations *have to be* based on evidence. You can't say that the novel *Jane Eyre* ends when the electronic bunny rabbits eat Jane's digital carrots: there is no evidence for that. Likewise, you can't say that "Images of nature play no role in *Jane Eyre*," because there is too much evidence that they do. This brings us back to science: you can't say, in an academic paleontology paper, that Earth is six thousand years old; you may hold this as an article of faith, but there is no evidence for it (faith requires that there is no evidence), and an academic paper requires evidence. You *can* say that "Religious ideas concerning the origins and age of the planet, despite being contrary to scientific findings, are having an effect on climate policy debates": there is evidence for that (in online discussions, political speeches, and so on). But the second statement still doesn't make the first statement true.

Opinion

Unlike in physics, then, in the study of popular culture, we have no hope (or even desire) to find a "theory of everything." Instead, we're willing to believe that one piece of culture, one novel, one sentence, one piece of art, one song, one dress, one piercing, can mean different things to different people. But to write an academic paper, you still have to prove that your interpretation is viable.

We all have opinions on popular culture. Even if we don't watch a particular TV show (or watch TV at all) or listen to a certain kind of music, we will likely have an opinion on it, even if it's just to explain why we don't like something. As we learned in Chapter 1, such opinions can be informed by larger cultural standards of **taste**, which in turn reflect particular class or social structures. Still, we often either like or don't like some particular cultural object or form or trend, and don't spend much time analyzing why.

In an assignment for a course, such an opinion can inform your first thoughts about a particular cultural object, but if you were to simply write down that you did or didn't like something, or that you thought something was "good" or "bad," you wouldn't get a very good grade. Even if you were to write a more substantial opinion about a piece of popular culture—for example, that you thought a particular advertisement is or isn't sexist, or that a particular film presents a problematic vision of state violence—you still wouldn't be offering an analysis of that piece, but merely stating a personal opinion. Such opinions may be valid to you, but without evidence to support them, they don't necessarily constitute a scholarly analysis.

Analysis

There is often an assumption that humanities and, to a lesser extent, social sciences papers are "just opinion." Compared with papers in the physical sciences, this may seem true at first—but it's not. Our data simply leave more room for varied interpretations. But for those interpretations to be taken seriously, they still need evidence. The difference is one between a field with limited variables, which can often lead to a binary result of "right or wrong," and a field with nearly infinite variables (the intricacies of the use of language, for example). That can seem to be a very clear distinction, where one is "objective" and the other "subjective," but science and humanities are much more closely related than that. First, not all science leads to right or wrong responses—consider the "both/and" nature of quantum mechanics—and second, the development of arguments in humanities isn't really all that subjective. As noted above, one's "opinion" about a film or one's "taste" (whether one likes it or not) may seem subjective, but cultural studies deals not with opinion or taste, but with supported and proven arguments and specific analytical methodologies (just as in science). Evaluation, then, is based on the evidence provided, both in terms of formal written work and in class discussion. We may not have "right or wrong" arguments (as in some sciences), but we do have particular methodologies for providing weaker or stronger arguments, with the stronger argument providing more support in the form of evidence (verbal or written language, images, etc.) that is closely analyzed following those methodologies (i.e., those theories discussed throughout this text). The clarity of an argument—that is, the degree to which the writer demonstrates an understanding of and ability to implement and sometimes reshape those methodologies to produce accurate and convincing results—is the basis for evaluating the strength of that argument, just as in a lab in chemistry or biology.

Instead of simply offering an opinion about an element of popular culture, then, you must present an argument about it, and support that argument with fully analyzed and interpreted evidence. A clear argument proven through carefully interpreted evidence marks the difference between simple opinion and scholarly analysis. An example from a more scientific discipline may help: any person could form an opinion about the effectiveness of certain drugs or surgical procedures, but before you let someone prescribe medicine to or operate on you, you'd like to make sure that that opinion is backed up by careful research, studies of effectiveness, and so on. Likewise, we can all have opinions about popular culture, but in order to offer substantive analyses of it (which may be used in the development of new forms of popular culture, or in public policy on culture, and so on), a critic must provide evidence, and present that evidence in a coherent and convincing argument.

Evidence

Such evidence can take many forms, and what kind of evidence you use is often dictated by the approach you take, as discussed in Chapter 14. A sociological approach is likely to use more statistical data than would a thematic approach; a thematic approach is likely to use more close textual analysis than would a historical approach; and a historical approach is likely to use more archival research than would a sociological approach, but all of them can incorporate aspects of each other. The important thing is for the evidence to support your claims, and for your claims to be fully argued and fleshed out. Just as important, however, is the fact that what might count as evidence in one disciplinary approach to popular culture would not be evidence in another. The use of particular framing of scenes in a popular film, for instance, may constitute one kind of evidence in a thematic approach, but outside of readers' reception of or response to that framing, it would not be seen as evidence for a sociological approach.

One also has to consider the medium of one's data: Are you doing interviews and recording them? Are you relying on published material or archives? Each of these forms of data provides certain kinds of information while leaving out others, and each can include small, exemplary items of data, or large, statistically important sets of data. Each of these approaches has their strengths and weaknesses, and those strengths and weaknesses often depend on the disciplinary approach taken (as discussed in Chapter 14).

Digital Archives and "Big Data"   One particularly exciting development in recent years is the ability to use online archives and search tools to do so-called Big Data studies, in which massive amounts of data can be correlated, graphed, and analyzed. This form of analysis can be important for all the disciplinary approaches, whether you're interested in sociological studies (compiling the data from numerous surveys or polls, for example), historical studies (examining the interest in particular events at particular times by registering the number of hits on carefully chosen search terms to analyze records from various times in the past), or textual studies (examining the use of particular metaphors or other devices, again through careful textual searches). While such Big Data studies are often limited to textual or numerical study, visual (or image-to-image) search engines are being developed, and some archives of images are already encoded with specific search terms. Again, however, it can be tempting to see Big Data searches as exhaustive, and as offering final, firm fact (something that, as we've seen, many of our theories have questioned). But, as with all analyses, Big Data studies are limited by the contents of the electronic archive being used (these get especially weak the further back one goes in time, owing to what original material is available to be digitized, for example) and the search terms and mechanisms that the cultural analyst uses.

Scholarly Conversation

Last but not least, remember that all scholarly work should be approached as a conversation in which you can both teach something to and learn something from the reader on the other side. You want to make your points carefully so that the reader accepts and agrees with your argument, but you should also be willing to discover something new when your professor or peer reviewers respond to your argument so that you can improve your argument the next time. This is why drafting is so important: the more you work on your essay or assignment, set it aside, read it again, and revise to make it stronger, the better that argument will tend to be.

TYPES OF ASSIGNMENTS

In a cultural studies class, students may be assigned any number of possible types of work, from ethnographic surveys and interviews to literature reviews and to analytical essays, and so on. All of these assignments involve gathering data, analyzing that data, and incorporating it into a coherent argument or presentation of facts. In this section we discuss a few final products of such assignments, specifically in the form of written argumentation. Depending on the assignment, though, the gathering of data for such written work can take a wide variety of forms, some of which—specifically those involving interactive work with living people—may require involved processes of ethics reviews and monitoring, on which your instructor will give you guidance.

For our purposes, we will assume that the data being gathered come from popular culture itself and from previously published material on it, and that the assignments are constituted of close, written analyses of that material. Within this, we'll focus on three types of assignments: the theory response, the brief object analysis, and the longer analytical research paper. Chapter 16 offers an example of each of these forms, with a specific focus on feminist analysis in order to allow students to see how a topic might develop from a specific idea to a larger analysis. These different assignments are described below (along with variations on them) so that students can relate them to the types of assignments they're asked to work on in their own classes. In some ways, the first two assignments each teach one skill, which are then combined in the third assignment, which is why so many instructors use these three types of assignment or variations thereof.

Theory or Critical Response

Instructors often want to evaluate how well students understand the theoretical models being discussed, outside of or before particular applications of those models. These assignments can take the form of journal entries or reading diaries, of short mini-essays, or of Wikipedia-style entries on a particular theoretical text. Whatever the specific form, these types of assignments typically ask students to identify the central idea or goal of the theoretical text being discussed, to summarize that argument in their own words, and sometimes to gesture toward some aspects of popular culture that could be analyzed using that model. This type of assignment not only helps instructors and students identify potential difficulties in students' readings of the theoretical text; it can also help students to begin to consider the relationship between theories and popular culture, and to understand how to write about both. Further, it can help students try to boil down complex, difficult-to-read texts into more "digestible" bites, often giving them insight into a piece that they wouldn't otherwise gain.

Object Analysis

One of the more common assignments is the object analysis, or brief study of a specific item of popular culture. Such assignments form the backbone of many popular culture courses. Like the theory response, object analyses can take many forms, often as journal entries. The type of material can be pre-selected by the instructor, or it can be student generated, or a combination of these, with the instructor suggesting certain types of material (magazine advertisements, YouTube videos, and so on) while students find their own specific examples from within those categories. Unlike the theory response, these brief analytical pieces give students the ability to apply their knowledge of certain theoretical frames or models.

Longer Analytical and Research Essays

The research essay is often the capstone of courses on popular culture, requiring the student to engage in-depth with a particular object or topic in popular culture and analyze it using one or more of the theoretical models we have discussed, in addition to engaging with the wider academic dialogue on the object being analyzed and/or the theoretical debates being engaged. In other words, the longer analytical essay combines the two shorter assignments: it uses the ability to carefully articulate a theoretical model from the theory response assignment, and uses that in turn as a framework to do an extended version of the object analysis assignment. Research essays often include a literature review of materials relating to the topic (these are structured differently depending on the discipline), state how the current essay fits into larger debates on the topic, and provide an argument that attempts to push those debates in a new direction (the level of innovation expected varies according to the level of academic study, of course).

Choosing a Theoretical Framework

But how does one go about formulating an argument, and choosing the best evidence for that argument? Certainly, a hypothesis based on your initial reactions is one place to start, but you can't end there. Does an element of popular culture bother you? Why? Does another similar trend in popular culture seem exciting? Why the difference? Asking yourself why you react the way you do to a particular aspect of popular culture can be a way to begin your more scholarly thoughts on the subject. In answering that question, you may even find yourself changing your initial response: again in scientific terms, this is the equivalent of having a hypothesis, testing it, realizing that the original hypothesis was flawed, and then using that conclusion to form a new hypothesis to test.

But taste and personal reaction aren't necessarily useful indicators of why a particular piece of popular culture is interesting or useful for analysis. The theoretical approaches discussed in this text can help you to decide which approach to take to a cultural object and to narrow the argument concerning that object. Instructors may also ask you to use a particular theoretical lens. If they don't, it's important to choose the theoretical model wisely. While excellent insights can often come from using a theory relating to one form of popular culture on another (for example, using Laura Mulvey's theories relating to scopophilia and the gaze in film to analyze certain advertisements), there must be a clear connection between the theory being used, the argument being made, and the evidence used in support of that argument. If any of those three is weak or doesn't fit, the overall analysis will suffer.

Interest can also play a role in choosing one's interpretive framework or theory, but so can the material being studied: Are you focusing on gender dynamics in the role of advertising? Then a feminist approach may be appropriate. Is the particular ad or ad campaign you're studying aimed at men or spend a lot of time representing men? Then within feminist theory perhaps an approach from masculinity studies would be one way to study the text. But does race or sexuality also play a role in the ad? Then those approaches may also provide a solid framework, alone or in conjunction with a feminist approach. Additionally, advertising in contemporary Canada functions within a capitalist framework, and so a traditional or modified Marxist approach would also provide methods through which to view your object of study (Does the ad **interpellate** its viewers in particular ways? Is it aimed at particular economic demographics?).

In working toward an answer to why you feel or think a certain way about the object of study, it's important to understand that your theoretical perspective is an active part of your analysis and not necessarily part of an objective, unbiased analytical model: using Marxist analysis can help you understand the social inequities of class and wealth and how those transform different groups' interactions with culture; using a Foucauldian model of power will offer a different vision of the intricate power relations of given discursive moment; and approaching a situation from the position of particular identity theories will give yet other models.

It is thus important to know which model will give a clear picture of your subject, but it's also important to recognize that none will necessarily offer *the* whole truth about a situation. Each theory is a particular tool in a larger toolbox (to use a common metaphor), and each can help you examine more closely particular aspects of a given cultural moment.

Incorporating Theory into an Essay

Students often find it difficult to incorporate theory into their research essays, regarding the process as somewhat artificial, or feeling as if the theory has to be "jammed in" to their analysis. It's true that unnecessarily included passages from theoretical works can interrupt the flow of an argument, or be unnecessary for a particular point being made. So how does one incorporate theory smoothly into an argument, and in such a way as to make it clear that that theory is a necessary part of the overall work?

In addition to seeing theory as a tool that can help you decide on your approach, it's useful to consider it as a frame for your essay (just look at how often the *frame* or *framework* metaphor is used in this chapter!). In other words, just as the frame works for a painting or a window, the theoretical approach can provide a structure that holds the rest of the argument in place, even when it's the thing *in* the frame that people look at—in this case, the analysis of the popular culture moment, object, or event.

What does this theoretical structure look like in the final product of your essay? Many theoretically informed research essays begin with an introduction that, as in any essay, expresses the general topic and the specific object of analysis and includes a thesis statement that lays out a road map for the rest of the argument (most writing handbooks will give you this basic structure). But in an essay that is explicitly informed by a specific theoretical approach, that thesis statement will be informed or directed by the theory—a paper that uses feminist theory to study a film or advertisement, for example, will have a thesis statement that focuses on the role or representation of women, or the construction of gender, and so on.

In a research paper that explicitly makes use of theory, that *frames* its argument through that theory, the introduction will often be followed by a section that discusses the theoretical model being used, before it starts in on the analysis proper. This structure is used in order to lay out both the methodology and the related terminology being employed, so that the reader will be able to understand why the subsequent analysis takes the shape that it does. In effect, you're saying, "This model has been used to study similar situations or objects, and here are the specific principles of that model that I'll be using." This structure allows you and your reader to share a common ground in the essay. It also provides the reader with the ability to test how well the subsequent analysis applies that theory. Remember, all scholarly work is a dialogue, and you want your reader to have all the information necessary to engage in that conversation with you, and possibly to point out to you how your analysis or theoretical framing could be improved.

This opening theoretical discussion (depending on the length of the essay, it can be a paragraph or a section composed of several paragraphs and pages) is then used as a touchstone for the analysis of the element of popular culture being discussed. The terminology and structuring principles of the theory can be used to lend structure and flow to the argument. This is not the only structure that can be used (sometimes you need to introduce multiple theories throughout an essay, for example), but it is a common and effective one.

Chapter 16 consists of examples of the different assignments discussed above; these examples have been chosen so that students can see how the assignments can fit together. Taking Laura Mulvey's theories of the gaze, scopophilia, and the "pleasure" of "narrative cinema" (see Chapter 10) as its foundation, each assignment builds on the other: first, we have a summary of Mulvey's main points; then a brief application of those points to a commercial advertisement; and finally an extended analysis of the James Bond film *Casino Royale* (2006). While individual courses will vary in their assignments, depending on the instructor's preference, course level, and discipline, these models should give students an idea of how to begin writing about the rich field of popular culture.

Remember, though, that these are samples and are not intended to be "perfect." Quite to the contrary, there will be arguments or gestures in them that you find weak or that you disagree with, and that's good! Learning how to respond to arguments—deciding how you could add to, build on, or challenge those arguments—is a necessary step in the development of one's own analytical abilities.

Chapter 16
Sample Assignments

INTRODUCTION

This chapter provides examples of three commonly used, introductory-level assignments for popular culture courses: the theory summary; the object analysis; and the research essay (see Chapter 15 for more in-depth discussion of these assignments). Each example is prefaced by a sample assignment sheet, and is formatted using the MLA citation style. These sample assignments can also be used as springboards for discussion: What works well in each particular assignment? Are there aspects of a sample assignment that you think are weaker than others? Why? These samples are designed not to offer the "perfect" examples; instead, carefully analyzing these examples for their strengths *and* weaknesses, rather than simply using them as models, can help students improve their own writing.

THEORY RESPONSE

Theory responses are often used when instructors assign primary theoretical readings to supplement the textbook. Because theory response assignments are often very brief, they necessarily leave out a lot of detail regarding the theoretical model being discussed. In reading the sample assignment below, ask yourself what the author left out, and why. Are these the decisions you would have made?

Assignment Description

Course: Thinking Popular Culture

Assignment #1: Theory Response Mini-Essay

Assignment Description: In this assignment, you will offer a short response (of no more than 450 words, or one and a half pages, double-spaced) to one of the theoretical texts we will be reading. You can address one of the texts by either Sigmund Freud, Louis Althusser, or Laura Mulvey. The assignment will summarize what you see as the central argument of the text, and discuss briefly the ways in which this argument could be used in an analysis of an example of popular culture. You could approach this latter part of the assignment by discussing which types of works or material might be best analyzed by using that particular theory.

Structure: Your theory summary should be structured as a mini-essay, with a brief introduction, a main body that discusses what you see as the primary point(s) of the piece you are studying, and a brief conclusion that follows logically from the preceding material and that concerns the application of the theory.

Note: Because the assignment is so brief, you will not be able to cover every step or aspect of the theorist's argument; instead, you should focus on the one or two points that you see as the most central or the most generative for analysis.

L. Lane

Professor T. G. Arrow

Cultural Studies 101: Thinking Popular Culture

22 January 2013

Gazing at Yourself: Laura Mulvey, the Gaze, and the Ego

Laura Mulvey's "Visual Pleasure and Narrative Cinema" relies on Sigmund Freud's model of the psyche to analyze the structure and social functions of Hollywood film. She argues that the pleasure one feels while watching a film reinforces patriarchal gender roles: women are treated as sexual objects by men who are in turn represented as active and powerful figures.

Mulvey argues that "cinema satisfies a primordial wish for pleasurable looking, but it also goes further, developing scopophilia in its narcissistic aspect" (9). In other words, people reinforce their sense of self—this "narcissistic aspect"—through "scopophilia," which she defines as the "pleasure in looking at another person as an erotic object" (17). More specifically, men (both on screen and in the audience) are expected to view women not as self-motivated and self-controlled human beings, but as objects designed to give men pleasure. This objectification takes place through what Mulvey calls "the gaze." There are three central forms of the gaze in traditional Hollywood film: first, "that of the camera"; second, "that of the audience"; and third, "that of the characters at each other" (17). Because, in traditional narrative film, the first two gazes are ignored (the camera does not call attention to itself, and the audience is not referenced by the film), they are "subordinate[d] . . . to the third" (17). That is, the gaze "of the characters at each other" becomes central. Because traditional film tends to present the world from the perspective of the main male character, his gaze becomes the audience's gaze, and his pleasure in looking at, and subordinating, women becomes the audience's. In this way, the audience reproduces the patriarchal vision often present in the traditional films Mulvey discusses. Because the audience takes pleasure in that identification, Mulvey says, that pleasure must be destroyed if the patriarchal gaze of Hollywood is to be critiqued. Filmmakers should, she writes, make the audience aware of the camera in order to "destroy . . . the satisfaction, pleasure and, privilege" of feeling like "the 'invisible guest'" (18).

While Mulvey's argument is convincing, I would argue that one need not destroy pleasure in order to critique patriarchal filmmaking. *The Rocky Horror Picture Show* (1975) does what Mulvey asks regarding the camera's gaze (calling attention to itself on several occasions), and the audience participation at screenings calls attention to the audience's gaze as well. But people still identify with the characters and take pleasure in them. Unlike more traditional Hollywood fare, however, such identifications in *Rocky Horror* often call into question heteronormative and patriarchal assumptions, but make doing so *fun*.

Works Cited

Mulvey, Laura. "Visual Pleasure and Narrative Cinema." *Screen* 16 (1975): 6–18. Oxford Journals. Web.

Rocky Horror Picture Show. Writ. Richard O'Brien. Dir. Jim Sharman. Twentieth Century Fox, 1975. Blu-ray.

OBJECT ANALYSIS

Like the theory response assignments, object analysis assignments are usually quite brief, and so don't offer the sort of in-depth readings provided in research essays; they often leave the theoretical material covered in class more in the background. In reading the sample assignment below, ask yourself whether you think the author chose a good object to analyze, and whether the claims that are made about the object are strongly supported.

Assignment Description

Course: Thinking Popular Culture

Assignment #2: Object Analysis Mini-Essay

Assignment Description: In this assignment, you will offer a short response (no more than 450 words, or one and a half pages, double-spaced) to an advertisement (either print or television) for a particular product. You can discuss the product as well as its advertisement. Your analysis should employ one of the theories we have studied in this section of the course (i.e., from the Gender or Sexuality Studies chapters), but focus primarily on an analysis of the advertisement itself.

Structure: Your object analysis should be structured as a mini-essay, with a brief introduction containing a thesis statement that tells your reader what your argument is, a main body that proves that argument through analysis of the advertisement and discusses what you see as the primary point(s) of piece you are studying, and finally a brief conclusion.

Note: Because the assignment is so brief, you will not be able to analyze every aspect of the advertisement and/or product; instead, you should focus on the one or two points that you see as the most central or most generative for the type of analysis you are writing.

W. Rosenberg

Professor B. Summers

Cultural Studies 101: Thinking Popular Culture

05 May 2013

When a Pen Is Not Just a Pen: "Bic for Her"

In 2012, Ellen DeGeneres sarcastically endorsed a new line of pens produced by the Bic company and branded as "Bic for Her." Targeted at women and girls, the advertising campaign for these pens reproduces sexist stereotypes of women, particularly by representing women as passive, sexualized, and pleasureful objects for the "male gaze," to use Laura Mulvey's words (11).

On the company's website, Bic advertises the "Bic for Her" as a *"ball pen essentially for women!"* ("Bic for Her"; emphasis in original): the pen itself is clearly supposed to figure "essential" feminine qualities. But what are those qualities? The description of the pen's "Key Benefits" include "Fun comfort grip" and "Modern design." Femininity—or at least the ideal form of the feminine that Bic is seemingly marketing—is thus both "fun" and "comfortable": by extension, one can assume that women's writing is likewise "fun" and "comfortable," and never serious or challenging. If, as Sidonie Smith writes, women have traditionally been figured as "embodied" and men as "rational" (see Smith 5–11), then the "Bic for Her" description continues this figuration for the "modern" woman.

The television commercial for the pens—a copy of which is embedded in Emma Gray's article—reinforces this stereotyping. Set in a public school, the commercial represents femininity as inherently sexual and passive, while also being both superficial and objectified. The commercial begins with a young woman saying "Does anyone have a pen?," whereupon half a dozen young men rush up to her, offering her seemingly generic black and blue pens, which she rejects. Then a costumed arm with a cartoonish white glove holds out a pink pen, which she takes, saying "Thanks!" A voice-over interjects, saying "With its fabulous styling and smooth writing, 'Bic for Her' is the only choice." During this voice-over, a life-sized Bic icon (the figure who hands her the pen) stands proudly as the boys seem to congratulate him, followed by the young woman kissing him. The gender implications are clear: the young woman is a passive sexual object, which men can impress, and therefore win, through presenting the correct (notably phallic) consumer product. But to truly win her heart, they must understand feminine desire itself: she does not want a pen in order to write, but instead wants one that is superficially stylized and unthreateningly "smooth" or easy. The "male gaze" is always directed lustily upon a passive female, or admiringly upon the ideal masculine figure who wins her.

Presenting as ideals stereotypes of women as passive, superficial, sexual objects, the "Bic for Her" campaign is not so much "for" women as it is *against* them. As Ellen's own parodic commercial states, "Bic for Her: for best results, use while barefoot and pregnant."

Works Cited

"Product Detail for Bic for Her." *bicworld.com. Bic*. Web. 1 May 2013.

DeGeneres, Ellen. "Bic Pens for Women." *The Ellen Show. YouTube*. YouTube, 12 Oct. 2012. Web. 1 May 2013.

Gray, Emma. "Bic for Her Commercial Is Even Worse Than the Pink Pens Themselves." *Huffington Post*. 11 Sept. 2012. Web. 1 May 2013.

Mulvey, Laura. "Visual Pleasure and Narrative Cinema." *Screen* 16 (1975): 6–18. Oxford Journals. Web. 1 May 2013.

Smith, Sidonie. *Subjectivity, Identity, and the Body: Women's Autobiographical Practices in the Twentieth Century*. Bloomington: Indiana UP, 1993.

RESEARCH ESSAY

The analytical research essay combines certain elements of both the theory summary and the object analysis in order to provide a longer, in-depth study of a particular popular culture object, event, or site. The essay can also provide its own theoretical vision, often by combining and manipulating two or more of the theoretical models discussed in this textbook, and/or by gesturing toward ways in which the subject being studied necessitates a change in the model. Remember, too, that in research essays you must engage with the existing scholarly discussion on the topic: this is not just a "make work" task but a necessary step of the essay, one through which you situate your own argument and lay out the critical consensus on the topic, if any. (Note that the sample "Object Analysis" above incorporates multiple sources—two generally theoretical texts and two items of popular culture—but does not make use of any other scholarly discussion on the pens themselves or on product advertisement and the representation of women, and so on.)

Assignment Description

Course: Thinking Popular Culture

Assignment #3: Final Essay

Assignment Description: For this assignment, you will write a researched, theoretical essay of 2100 to 2700 words (approx. seven to nine pages, double-spaced) on the topic below. You must use at least one of the theoretical approaches we have discussed this term, and must support your argument by engaging (and properly citing) at least three critical works on the topic (following the research methods discussed in class).

Structure and Notes: In order to write a strong essay, you will have to narrow the topic below into a focused and well-supported argument about the primary work (with a specific and analytical thesis statement, a logical structure with points supported by carefully analyzed elements of the primary work, and other aspects of proper essay structure as discussed in class).

Topic: The depiction of gender in the film *Casino Royale* (2006).

D. Who

Professor D. Alek

Cultural Studies 101: Thinking Popular Culture

05 June 2013

James Bond's Mythical Masculinity

The James Bond film series, based on the character created in Ian Fleming's novels and short stories, has been a staple in theatres since the first film, *Dr. No*, was released in 1962. The first James Bond novel, *Casino Royale*, was published in 1953, at the height of the Cold War between the Western powers, primarily the United States, and the Union of Soviet Socialist Republics. Popular narratives, including Fleming's novels and the films based on them, have created the image of the suave and daring "secret agent" who risks life and limb to protect the democratic West from what is presented as an encroaching communist threat. Beyond international politics, however, such figures also helped to entrench what R. W. Connell would call the "hegemonic masculinity" of the age: a Western manhood at once rational and violent, cold and (hetero)sexual, and which could stave off an Eastern evil presented as overly emotional and effeminate, weak and queer. James Bond, however, continued after the Cold War came to an end, and was recently reincarnated in the 2006 interpretation of *Casino Royale*, starring Daniel Craig as James Bond. As in the novel, the film presents a Bond who is in the process of gaining his status as a super-spy. This James Bond presents a "proper" Cold War masculinity reformed for the post-9/11 age, and, more ambitiously, attempts to re-form the Barthesian myth of masculinity that earlier incarnations of Bond embodied.

In her foundational study of the patriarchal nature of popular narrative film, Laura Mulvey not only argues that Hollywood film objectifies women, treating them as mere objects of sexual pleasure, but also states that film subjectifies its audience, offering members of the audience specific models of identity that can help to shape an internal sense of self. She writes that "The image of woman" is treated "as (passive) raw material for the (active) gaze of man" (17). Because active women threaten the maintenance of masculine power—and thus the "representation" of such women "signifies castration"—this threat must be "circumvent[ed]" by presenting the woman as only and always a "voyeuristic or fetishistic" object of the "male gaze" (17). As fully formed, adult humans, women can threaten the patriarchal control of society; as mute objects designed to give pleasure to men, images of women can only reinforce that power.

But what of the images of men? If Mulvey is correct that the images of women on screen reinforce patriarchy, then images of men must do the same. Mulvey does address this, pointing to the ways in which the "gaze" of the camera, and hence of the audience, is "subordinate[d]" to the gaze "of the characters at each other within the screen illusion" (17). In other words, if the "gaze of man" in the film is active, and looks at the woman as a passive object, then the "male gaze" is necessarily that of the audience. Masculinity is thus presented as an active and forceful identity, one that audience members are necessarily invited to participate in. Men thus treat the image of the active male on screen as an ideal one to echo in their own lives, while women are left with a mere "desire to possess a penis" (7)—a desire to be as active as the man on screen, a desire that cannot, in a patriarchal world, be satisfied.

Sidonie Smith builds on this theory, arguing that in Western societies, masculinity has long been associated with both rationality and the ability to be completely "self-contained"—that is, to be in control of oneself, and invulnerable to the influence of outside forces. She writes that the ideal masculine self—of the kind Mulvey says is presented on screen—is "Independent of forces external to it" and that it is "neither constituted by, nor coextensive with, its class identifications, social roles, or private attachments" (6). The ideal man is, in other words, rational, independent, active, and able to act on his own without following the pressures placed on him either by his own body or his society.

This definition of ideal masculinity is also a definition of James Bond, especially as presented in film. Always rational and always in control, Bond may be threatened by others, but he always emerges victorious. As Christine Bold has written of the (pre-2006) film character, "Bond does not need to undergo physical and psychological trauma to achieve credible humanity: he is 'a fuller man' because he loves cars, vodka martinis, and women. Bond is, [Anthony] Burgess resoundingly concludes, 'a hero we need.' Shades of Kingsley Amis, who chortled nearly thirty years ago: 'We don't want to have Bond to dinner or go golfing with Bond or talk to Bond. We want to be Bond'" (169). As Bold goes on to argue, though, this "we" is one limited to those who wish to follow Bond's particular brand of Cold War masculinity. By the early 2000s, a period somewhat different in terms of women's rights in the West than Bond's original 1960s context, Bond's brand of masculinity would seem, at best, dated. But, as I argue below, Bond's "rebooting" in the 2006 adaptation of this first novel, *Casino Royale*, nostalgically rebuilds Bond's masculinity from the challenges it might face today.

In Fleming's novel, Bond is sent after a villain named Le Chiffre, who is a Soviet-funded union leader in France. Le Chiffre hosts a baccarat game in order to make up union monies that he lost in an investment in a group of brothels. Bond's job is to make Le Chiffre lose so that his Soviet backers will assassinate him. Bond is paired with a beautiful fellow agent named Vesper Lynd. After Bond, with the help of the CIA, bankrupts Le Chiffre, Le Chiffre captures Bond and threatens to castrate him, but is killed by the Soviets before he can do so. The Soviet agent then carves a Russian letter into Bond's hand, which identifies him as a spy. Bond goes to a hospital, and while there he and Vesper fall in love, and he plans to leave his job. But then she kills herself, and leaves a note saying that she's a Russian double agent ordered to make sure he doesn't escape from Le Chiffre. Bond calls up the office, says, "The bitch is dead now" (178), and goes back to work.

Clearly several themes are at play in this novel: the Cold War battle between the free market and socialism; the paired tension between government and unions; relations between women and men; and others. In his structuralist analysis of the Bond novels, Umberto Eco traces all of these themes. But he points out that, in the novel, Bond is briefly torn about his mission: "At this point Bond is ripe for the crisis, for the salutary recognition of universal ambiguity. . . . [H]e questions himself about the appearance of the devil and, sympathizing with the Enemy, is inclined to recognize him as a 'lost brother'" (145). However, M16 operative Mathis says to Bond, "Don't let me down and become human yourself. We would lose such a wonderful machine" (Fleming 136; also qtd. in Eco 145).

While Eco frames this as "Fleming exclud[ing] neurosis from the narrative possibilities" of the Bond novels (145), a more specifically gendered reading is possible. Falling in love with a woman and recognizing happiness in the world make Bond start to question whether he can so easily judge whether someone is good or bad, but when Vesper double-crosses him, he reverts to seeing everything in black and white. The novel's central theme is thus about the necessity of seeing the world in terms of good and evil, terms that are then framed as a gendered binary: if a man doesn't see the world this way, then he is liable to become weak and vulnerable.

The 2006 film alters significant points of the novel's plot. Set in the years following 9/11, the film transforms le Chiffre into a banker for terrorists: unlike his character in the novel, the film's Le Chiffre seems to have no political goals and is interested only in making money. In the film, Vesper is coerced into selling out Bond because her boyfriend is kidnapped, not because she's a double agent. But Bond is still tempted away by love, only to have it taken away from him, so that he realizes the dangers of falling in love. By changing plot details, the new film makes the character development less about the specifics of politics and more about character per se, and specifically about what makes a man a man. In order to protect the unambiguous forces of good, Bond must become a "blunt instrument," a perfect man who, in Smith's terms, is unencumbered by external commitments or forces.

By emphasizing character over politics, the film attempts to present a more "mythological" masculinity, to appropriate Roland Barthes's notion of myth: this is a masculinity seemingly not contingent on its specific surroundings, standing above them as a universal figure of manhood, what Barthes would call the "global sign" of masculinity (123). In order to reach this masculine myth, the film is constructed as a coming-of-age narrative, offering the development of a specific man into a mythological figure. In other words, throughout most of the film the viewer is presented with a troubled Bond, one who does not fulfill the role of the active, self-controlled figure of masculinity discussed by Mulvey and Smith. This is a Bond whose abilities and masculinity are constantly threatened, both by the forces around him, and—more importantly—by his own emotions.

Bond starts the film trying to be the all-powerful man, as evidenced in the opening scene. Presented in black-and-white, this scene offers the viewer the story of Bond's first two kills, those that allow him to become a "00" agent, one licensed to kill. The black-and-white picture functions to present the world of Bond through the morally stark, "Manichean ideology" Eco discusses (161): there are no shades of colour here, only black and white.

But this world may not be as clear-cut as its lack of colour makes it seem. Bond's fight in the bathroom with his first victim is vicious, bloody, and notably difficult. When asking him about it, Bond's second victim (a double agent) says, "Made you feel it, did he?" Bond may be *becoming* the ideal, emotionless man, but at this point he still has feelings. Connected to this fact is the opening scene's depiction of a constant struggle between the men over who gets to hold the gun. The struggle to gain mastery over one's feelings is thus symbolically tied to the struggle to master one's phallic power. Lisa Funnell makes a similar point about Bond's discussion with his second victim, which rests on Bond knowing where the other man's gun is hidden (Funnell 461–62). The rest of the film explores this connection, narrativizing Bond's struggle to become the ideal man, one who is devoid of feeling. Bond's superior, M, makes this clear when she says that Bond should be a "blunt instrument," telling him that in order to be the ideal agent, he must "take [his] ego out of it" and act "dispassionately," following Smith's definition of the properly masculine subject. But at this point in the film he is not quite there yet, as M points out.

Moments when Bond does display emotion are tied to a certain effeminacy or lack of masculinity. One of the more striking examples of this link, especially in relation to Mulvey's argument, takes the form of a visual allusion to the first Bond film, *Dr. No*, and to the iconic representation of a "Bond girl." In *Dr. No*, Ursula Andress famously walks out of the water, wearing a bikini, toward the beach. In *Casino Royale*, Daniel Craig, as Bond, mimics the scene nearly exactly. Indeed, Katherine Cox points out that "the male Bond . . . is offered up for the audience's voyeuristic gaze as he is born not once but three times out of water" (5). Bond/Craig becomes the passive, scopophilic object, in Mulvey's terms, fulfilling the stereotypically feminine role. This feminization and lack of control reach their climax when Bond is rendered weakest, when he is tied to a chair, naked, by Le Chiffre. Le Chiffre explicitly treats Bond as an erotic object, noting that Bond has "taken good care of [his] body." Le Chiffre then tortures Bond by hitting him in the testicles repeatedly, telling Bond that after too much of this torture, he will no longer be "a man." Funnell goes so far as to argue that Craig's Bond is a "Bond–Bond Girl hybrid" (467). Instead of the self-controlled masculine figure from Smith, or Mulvey's active subject of the gaze, Bond has become the effeminized, passive object, rendered into naught but emotions and his body.

And why is Bond in this position? According to the logic of the film, it is because he has become emotionally tied to Vesper, comforting her after she witnesses him kill two men, asking about her past, and generally indicating that he is falling in love with her. After he recovers from his torture, as in the novel, he decides to leave the spy game and instead travel the world with Vesper as a romantic couple. In the world of James Bond, as in the general world of Hollywood film described by Mulvey, women are a threat because they can "unman" even the strongest of men. Bond struggles to become Bond in this "reboot" of his introductory mission precisely because he wavers between the black-and-white, morally unambiguous, purely rational realm of ideal masculinity and the emotionally and morally compromised realm of femininity. Bond is, until the end of the film at least, better at being a Bond "girl" than he is at being 007. Cox reads the film as thus offering "welcome and unexpected additions to the character of Bond" that work against the "general depictions of the character as an embodiment of hegemonic masculinity" (11).

Working against such conclusions, however, is the fact that after Bond purges himself of feelings for Vesper, and of any feelings at all, he once again becomes the ideal agent, the ideal man, and the man with the biggest gun. Discovering that Vesper is a double agent (though an unwilling one, in the film), Bond follows her and finds out that she is betraying him, only to watch her drown. After this event, he calls M to say, as in the novel, "The bitch is dead," as he goes through Vesper's belongings and finds out who is responsible for the double cross. The final scene of the film has him shoot this man, and then stand over him, carrying the largest gun he has held thus far; at this point, he introduces himself to the wounded man below him, uttering his iconic, often introductory line, "Bond, James Bond," while dressed in his equally iconic black-and-white suit. Whereas in the opening scene he struggles to maintain what Barthes calls the Manichean view of the world, at the end he embodies it, and thus offers us the (new) beginning to this masculine myth: no longer an individual, this Bond is a hero, the quintessential active man whose gaze directs the audience: "Bond, James Bond" thus fights against any castrating evil that attacks hegemony, masculine hegemony.

Works Cited

Barthes, Roland. *Mythologies*. Sel. and trans. Annette Lavers. London: Paladin, 1973.

Bold, Christine. "'Under the very skirts of Britannia': Re-reading Women in the James Bond Novels." *The James Bond Phenomenon: A Critical Reader*. Ed. Christoph Linder. Manchester: Manchester UP, 2003. 169–83.

Casino Royale. Dir. Martin Campbell. 2006. Sony Pictures Home Entertainment, 2007. DVD.

Connell, R. W. *Masculinities*. 2nd ed. Berkeley: U of California P, 2005.

Cox, Katharine. "Becoming James Bond: Daniel Craig, Rebirth, and Refashioning Masculinity in *Casino Royale* (2006)." *Journal of Gender Studies* (2013): 1–13. *Taylor & Francis Online*. 28 March 2013. Web. 5 May 2013.

Eco, Umberto. *The Role of the Reader: Explorations in the Semiotics of Texts*. Bloomington: Indiana UP, 1979. First Midland Book ed., 1984.

Fleming, Ian. *Casino Royale*. 1953. Las Vegas: Thomas and Mercer, 2012.

Funnell, Lisa. "'I Know Where You Keep Your Gun': Daniel Craig as the Bond–Bond Girl Hybrid in *Casino Royale*." *Journal of Popular Culture* 44.3 (2011): 455–72.

Mulvey, Laura. "Visual Pleasure and Narrative Cinema." *Screen* 16 (1975): 6–18. Oxford Journals. Web. 1 May 2013.

Smith, Sidonie. *Subjectivity, Identity, and the Body: Women's Autobiographical Practices in the Twentieth Century*. Bloomington: Indiana UP, 1993.

Glossary

Afrocentrism: The political and historical school that argues for the centrality of African cultures and history (both in Africa and in the African *diaspora*) to the development of the modern world, that argues against *Eurocentric* bias in the representation of Africa, and that calls for a renewed centrality of Africa in academic, political, and social studies.

Agent: A term used to define identity as an active negotiation of different social forces, all of which function in (often conflicting) deterministic ways on the person. However, because these forces frame the person's interaction with the world, agential theories see them as generative and not simply repressive.

Anti-essentialism: In general terms, the theory that objects do not hold an inherent meaning, with the common correlative that any meanings attributed to specific objects are contingent and culturally constructed. Often used in discussions of human identity, where aspects of that identity are seen to be socially and culturally contingent rather than concrete and unchanging, especially in terms of specific identity categories (as in gender, race, sexuality, and so on). Anti-essentialism holds that such identities change over time and between social and cultural settings. See *essentialism*.

Archetype: In Jungian psychology, archetypes are the conscious manifestations of the collective unconscious. Mythology and dreams, for Jung, use archetypes to express universal human fears and desires.

Aura: In Walter Benjamin's writings, the effect generated by the experience of viewing a unique (and mostly unreproducible) beautiful object, whether it be a natural scene or a work of art. Aura is largely destroyed within modern mass culture, which is based on easily reproducible artifacts.

Base–superstructure model: Coming from the writings of Karl Marx and Friedrich Engels, this model sees societies as being structurally split into two mutually interacting levels or layers. The base is the basic economic and material forces of a society, while the superstructure is the social, political, and generally cultural aspects of a society.

Birmingham School: Name used for the Centre for Contemporary Cultural Studies at the University of Birmingham. Also used as the term for the form of cultural studies and theory that arose from the Centre in the 1960s, which took as its central tenet the role of *hegemony* in culture.

Blackness: The fact or experience of being constructed as being part of a black "*race*" in a racialized culture. In *white privileging* societies, this condition is often expressed within a hierarchical relation to *whiteness*, as discussed by, for example, Frantz Fanon.

Bricolage: The practice of reappropriating and redeploying objects in one's surroundings for alternative symbolic purposes; Dick Hebdige cites as an example the punks' use of safety pins as jewellery or clothing accessories.

Bricoleur: A person who practises *bricolage*.

British Cultural Studies: See *Birmingham School*.

Capitalism: An economic system combining the practices of private ownership of property and the means of production (such as resources, factories, education, and so on), and the open exchange of goods and services in the marketplace, often through the medium of currency (the open or free market).

Class; social class: In Marxist theory, societies characterized by a division of labour also group people in a hierarchical division of social worth, be it economic or cultural. The different groupings are known as "classes."

Class consciousness: In Marxist theory, a stage at which a (usually repressed) social *class* becomes aware of its relative position in the power structure of society and begins to work to improve that position; see *false consciousness*.

Class identity: A group of cultural practices specific to a certain social class, through which they identify as a group, but which does not necessarily entail a full recognition of or reaction against that group's relative position in the power structure of society, as with *class consciousness*; see *false consciousness*.

Cold media: For Marshall McLuhan, cold media are "low definition" media that require the active participation of the audience to understand its representations. See *hot media*.

Collective unconscious: In Jungian psychology, the term used to describe the unconscious structures of the psyche that are common to all human beings, which can manifest in similar ways across individuals, cultures, and time periods; the collective unconscious thus stands opposed to the Freudian, or "personal," unconscious.

Colonialism: A form of settlement, often associated with *imperialism*, in which the members of one state are sent abroad to form settlements (colonies) in another geographical region, which are controlled by the central state. Colonialism often involves the displacement and/or subordination of the colonial regions' indigenous populations.

Communism: A social system defined by a combination of the practices of public, rather than private, ownership of property and the means of production (such as resources, factories, education, and so on), a *class*-less society, and a centralized, state-operated market.

Complicit masculinities: For R. W. Connell, the masculine identities exhibited by those men who may not perfectly exemplify the hegemonic domination of women, but who still serve, in their masculine performance, to reinforce the dominance of those hegemonic behaviours and the patriarchy. See *hegemonic masculinity*.

Compulsory heterosexuality: Coined by Adrienne Rich in her 1980 article, "Compulsory Heterosexuality and Lesbian Existence," this term refers to the *ideologically* reinforced notion of the "naturalness" and "necessity" of heterosexuality, and specifically the unquestioned assumption that "heterosexuality is presumed as a 'sexual preference' of 'most women'" (p. 633). Rich argues that this ideology is used to reinforce patriarchal social structures and women's oppression, and that the erasure of lesbian existence from culture furthers those ends.

Connotative meaning: For Roland Barthes, connotation is a second-order meaning attached to a particular sign; when a whole sign (a signifier and a signified together) becomes a signifier in another series, it gains a connotative, or larger, symbolic meaning. More simply, connotative meanings are meanings that go beyond the literal, often within particular contexts, whether those are personal contexts (for example, an "inside joke" one shares with friends) or ideological contexts (adhering to particular historical moments, in relation to gender, class, and so on). See *denotative meaning* and *mythology*.

Critical theory: See *Frankfurt School*.

Cultural behaviour: Actions people undertake that go beyond what is required to satisfy basic physical needs, for intellectual, artistic, religious, or entertainment purposes, among others.

Cultural capital: A term (often associated with Pierre Bourdieu) that denotes the social value of particular cultural activities.

Cultural products: The objects that people make, use, or alter for cultural purposes (i.e., those purposes that go beyond our basic physical needs, for intellectual, artistic, religious, or entertainment purposes, among others); often refers specifically to those objects that are mass produced.

Cultural sites: The places that people make, use, or alter for cultural purposes (i.e., those purposes that go beyond our basic physical needs, for intellectual, artistic, religious, or entertainment purposes, among others).

Cultural turn: Generally used within the social sciences, this term refers to the disciplinary move toward the analysis of cultural objects and practices and away from material or empirical study. In the humanities, a similar movement occurred, but in reverse, moving toward more social scientific methodologies for the study of culture.

Culture industry: A term coined by Theodor W. Adorno and Max Horkheimer to describe contemporary mass culture, specifically as developed by large corporations for consumption by a mass audience.

Deconstruction: A form of critical analysis created by Jacques Derrida, and used by many poststructuralist thinkers following him. Methodologically, deconstruction involves the exposure and undermining of the binary logics lying behind any seemingly stable structure of meaning.

Denotative meaning: For Roland Barthes, the denotative meaning of any sign is its literal, or "dictionary," meaning. See *connotative meaning* and *mythology*.

Dialogism: A term used by Mikhail Bakhtin (especially in the form of "dialogic heteroglossia") to describe how various discourses in any given language connect and communicate with and through each other. For Bakhtin, the novel as a literary form is inherently "dialogic." *Dialogism* and *dialogic* should not be confused with a simple dialogue between characters or people, though the terms are related. See *monoglossia/monologic*.

Diaspora: Originally referring to the global Jewish population, *diaspora* has come to refer to any population that has become globally dispersed (either by emigration or forced relocation) from a specific geographical region; a diasporic people generally still share certain cultural and social traditions, and generally identify as being part of a larger racial, ethnic, or national group. Hence the African diaspora, the Irish diaspora, etc.

Discourse: Generally meaning "communication," *discourse* in cultural theory, following Michel Foucault as well as the advent of cultural studies, implies an approach to social communication that recognizes that such communication occurs within a large set of social structures, all of which impact or alter meaning. Thus, we can refer to certain "institutional discourses" (such as "medical discourse" or "legal discourse"), and we can also discuss the impact of different social structures on any given example of communication.

Écriture féminine: As defined by Hélène Cixous, a new form of language use, through which women could express a feminist-centric world view. This practice would undermine the binary and linear forms of *phallogocentrism*.

Ego: In psychoanalytic theory, the ego is our conscious self and our sense of who we are.

Empire: A political structure in which many previously separate states, across a significantly large area, are controlled by a central power that has extended its territories generally through military power.

Enlightenment: Also known as the Age of Reason, this term refers to both a time period and a set of concepts and world views. Historically, the Enlightenment is connected primarily to the eighteenth century, but is often seen to begin in the late seventeenth century. Philosophically, the Enlightenment describes a turn away from revealed or religious truth and authority as the centre of human life to the idea that humans can discover truth through empirical, rational observation. The Enlightenment is thus tied to the development of modern science.

Essence: See *essentialism*.

Essentialism: The theory that objects hold an inherent meaning, and that objects and their meaning are inseparable. Often used in discussions of human identity, where that is defined in concrete, unchanging terms, whether universally (as in "human nature") or in terms of specific identity categories (as in gender, race, sexuality, and so on). Essentialism can be framed within biological, spiritual, psychological, national, and other discourses. See *anti-essentialism*.

Ethnicity: A form of cultural identity defined by the generational passing down of cultural practices (including language, rituals, religion, etc.). Often, though not always, tied to specific geographical regions, *ethnicity* is often connected both to *nation* and *race*.

Eurocentrism: A term used to denote ideological positions that favour or are biased toward the cultures and people of Europe, often extending to the descendants of European colonial powers living outside of Europe (hence Euro-American-centrism). Often connected to *racist* practices and beliefs.

Everyday culture or folk culture: As the first word implies, this term denotes the cultural activities in which people engage as part of their ordinary lives; often used to refer to cultural activities engaged in by the majority of a population or group; often distinguished from *mass culture* as being something that arises out of the group's own activities rather than from mass production. Also see *popular culture*.

False consciousness: In Marxist theory, the ideological state in which the proletariat or working classes do not believe themselves to be oppressed or to be lacking in power within the social structure, sometimes due to the belief in class mobility.

Feminism: The term given to a wide range of political and cultural practices and theories that have the aim to improve women's position in society, to empower women politically and culturally.

Frankfurt School: Name given to the Institute for Social Research at the University of Frankfurt am Main, founded in 1923, and in exile in the United States during the Nazi regime and World War II. Through such thinkers as Theodor W. Adorno, Max Horkheimer, and Walter Benjamin, among others, the critical approach most commonly associated with the Frankfurt School is a *Marxist* approach that sought to combine Marxism with the practices of academic disciplines ranging from philosophy to psychoanalysis and literary study, and often critiqued the role that culture—especially commodity culture or mass culture—played in cementing dominant ideologies and social conditions.

Gender: The expressions of an identity associated with masculinity and/or femininity, or any of a vast range of other identities that challenge a masculine/feminine binary; in *essentialist* theories, gender is seen as the natural expression of one's *sex*. In non-essentialist theories, it is associated with certain cultural or *ideological* expectations, or resistance to them.

Hegemonic masculinity: For R. W. Connell, those forms of masculine identity that together most clearly express and help to maintain patriarchal social power. See *complicit masculinities, marginalized masculinities*, and *subordinate masculinities*.

Hegemony: In the Marxist theories of Antonio Gramsci, a development of *ideology* describing the underlying forces that maintain the status quo of society. Unlike traditional notions of ideology, which focus on ideas or *superstructural* practices, *hegemony* refers to forces throughout social practice that help maintain the ruling order.

Heteroglossia: A term used by Mikhail Bakhtin to describe the "multi-voiced" nature of living languages, indicating that languages are composed of several different, constantly changing discourses.

Heteronormativity: A term, like *compulsory heterosexuality*, used to indicate that heterosexuality is enforced, ideologically or through socialization, as a cultural norm or ideal, thus denying the validity of other sexual identities or orientations by representing them as "abnormal."

Heterosexism: The act (individual or systemic) of discriminating against a group on the basis of their sexual identity, when that identity is non-heterosexual or *queer* in some way.

High culture: Traditionally, forms of cultural production or objects that are seen as being unique, well-wrought, and meaningful in themselves, and as helping to distinguish, educate, or enlighten both individuals and the society of which it is a part. Often, this definition is restricted to certain forms of artistic production. Marxist-influenced and other later cultural critics often see the distinction between high culture and *low culture* or *popular culture* as serving certain class or other social interests. See also *cultural capital* and *taste*.

Historical materialism: Often used interchangeably with *Marxism*, historical materialism is an approach to the study of society that examines social developments by analyzing actual lived practices rather than philosophical, religious, or other cultural beliefs. This form of analysis focuses primarily on the economic forces of production in a society.

Hot media: For Marshall McLuhan, hot media are "high definition" media that fully engage one or more of our senses, and so require very little effort for us to understand what they're presenting. Hot media thus engage a passive audience. See *cold media*.

Hybridity: According to the postcolonial theory of Homi Bhabha, the indeterminate and adaptable forms of culture and identity, especially as created by those at the margins of society, especially within colonial states.

Hyperreal: According to Jean Baudrillard, to live in the postmodern world is to live in hyperreality: we have been completely removed from any connection with the "real" and experience only mediated visions of the world, which we mistake or replace for the real. See *simulacra*.

Id: In Freudian psychoanalytic theory, the name for our unconscious self, the repository for our libido and instinctual drives. The id is "interested" only in satisfying those drives.

Ideal ego: In Freudian psychoanalysis, our (largely unconscious) ideal image of who we feel we should be. The ideal ego is shaped by our surrounding culture and relationships with others.

Ideal-I: See *ideal ego*.

Ideological State Apparatuses (ISAs): For Louis Althusser, those state institutions that maintain the cohesion of society primarily through *ideology*.

Ideology: In Marxist theory, the ruling ideas of a society that function to maintain the status quo of class relations, specifically the position of the ruling class. Following Louis Althusser (and Antonio Gramsci's *hegemony*), often considered to be at least partly an *unconscious* mechanism.

Imaginary, the: The level of conscious identification in Jacques Lacan's view of the human psyche. See *real* and *symbolic*.

Imagined community: Benedict Anderson's term for the *nation*; contrary to the *essentialist* assumptions of *national characteristics*, the imagined community views the nation as a cultural construct rather than an essential aspect of a specific group of people.

Imperialism: A process in which a central sovereign governing body extends its control over numerous, often previously sovereign, geopolitical bodies, which are then subordinated to the central *empire*.

In group: A way of referring to the members of a socio-cultural group who all identify with that group to one degree or another. Examples range from such traditional socio-cultural institutions as religions and families to such recent popular phenomena as fandoms.

Individual: A term used to define identity as being specific to the particular person, who is seen as, following Paul Smith, a "self-contained" unit of conscious action.

Interdependence: An understanding of human social relations whereby people are, to one degree or another, mutually dependent on each other.

Interpellation: In Althusserian theory, the method by which society (through *ISAs*) "hails" or calls us into existence as *subjects* within *ideology*.

Libido: In psychoanalytic theory, especially that developed by Sigmund Freud, our instinctual, largely sexual drive.

Linguistic turn: The move in philosophy, social sciences, and other disciplines toward seeing language—and linguistic structures—as the primary structuring force in human existence.

Low culture: Traditionally, forms of cultural production or objects that are seen as being of lesser quality than those of *high culture*, as derivative and unoriginal, and as possibly having the ability to degrade those who interact with it and to further the larger degradation of society. Often this definition of low culture is associated with mass production and *popular culture*. Marxist-influenced and other later cultural critics often see the distinction between high culture and low culture or popular culture as serving certain class or other social interests. See also *cultural capital* and *taste*.

Marginalized masculinities: For R. W. Connell, those masculine identities that are defined in relation to other forms of social marginalization or oppression, such as *race* or *class*. See *hegemonic masculinity*.

Marxism: The general term for the political and economic positions taken by Karl Marx. See *historical materialism*.

Mass culture: Cultural objects that are mass produced, and the act of using or engaging with such objects. See *popular culture*.

Metahistory: A term coined by Hayden White to define the analysis of the functions of discourse as employed by historians themselves. Whereas traditional historians study a particular historical event, metahistorians study how those other historians analyzed that event.

Metanarrative: In the work of Jean-François Lyotard, the underlying logic that legitimates (or provides the ground for) any given discourse. Thus, scientific discourse is legitimated by a metanarrative that scientific research is always disinterested and based solely in fact, and hence beneficial to humanity. The term is also used to describe any large or "grand" narrative that asserts that a particular world view is a universal one; metanarrative is thus associated with the terms *ideology* and *mythology*.

Mimicry: From the *postcolonial* theory of Homi Bhabha, the ways in which a colonizing power forces an indigenous population to assume governmental, social, and cultural practices similar to that of the dominant group.

Mirror stage: In Lacanian psychoanalysis, the moment in a child's development when it recognizes itself in a mirror. The child at this point lacks motor control, but sees in the reflection an image of itself as self-controlled. This forms the beginning of the *Ideal-I* or *ideal ego* as well as other "secondary" identifications in the child's psyche.

Modernism: A loosely affiliated school of cultural production generally associated with the early decades of the twentieth century and incorporating forms ranging from literature to visual arts to architecture and others. Modernism is often seen as a response to massive social change brought on by the increasing role of advanced technology in society, growing urban spaces, and new philosophical concepts arising from psychoanalysis, Marxism, and others. It's often associated with a sense of fragmentation of meaning and a loss of grounded truth, both of which are often reflected stylistically in modernist works. See *postmodernism*.

Monoglossia/monologic: Terms used by Mikhail Bakhtin to describe theories that posit language as a unitary, fully ordered structure, and to describe the centripetal social and linguistic forces that pull living languages toward such an order. See *dialogism*.

Mythology: Following Roland Barthes, a common, socially shared *connotation* that is based on cultural codes and generally reinforces dominant world views.

Nation: A group of people united by language, culture, and/or ethnicity, and often associated with a particular geographical location.

Nation state: A sovereign political entity bound by specific borders, generally with one or more national languages and specific cultural practices. Best understood as a politically sovereign *state* that is also, to varying degrees, a *nation*, as those terms are defined here. See also *nation, state, nationalism, nationality,* and *ethnicity*.

National character(istics): Commonly associated with early forms of *nationalism* in the eighteenth and nineteenth centuries, the cultural, ethnic, and sometimes *racial* qualities shared by the inhabitants of a particular geographical region. Although an *essentialist* term not often used in contemporary works, the notion of a shared cultural and sometimes ethnic tradition of a nation's people is still commonly held.

Nationalism: A political position and *ideology* supportive of one's own nation or nation state and the sense that the members of that nation share an identity. See also *national characteristics*.

Nationality: A person's legal (sometimes hereditary) identification with a particular *nation* or *nation state*.

New Critics: A loosely knit group of American literary scholars from the early decades of the twentieth century who approached literature (and especially poetry) as generating fully self-contained meanings, such that the only thing a critic should do to analyze a poem is look at the work itself (especially its form) rather than place it in historical, cultural, or other contexts.

New Historicism: A form of literary and historical academic criticism popular in the 1980s and 1990s, which posited that literary or cultural texts had to be examined in relation to their particular context of production or reception and the discourses of those times. Likewise, other New Historicists argued that historical analyses needed to be aware of their own borrowings from literary discourse.

Nomadology: Coined by Gilles Deleuze and Félix Guattari, a set of political and critical practices that refuses to be limited by standard definitions or borders and so can threaten the dominant exercise of power (whether political, critical, philosophical, and so on). The term was further developed by Rinaldo Walcott to refer to the ways black identity in Canada and elsewhere is self-defined through multiplicitous relations between global diasporic black communities.

Normative: A normative discourse is one that both expects and demands a certain form of behaviour from people, behaviour that is seen as "normal."

Noumenon: In the philosophy of Immanuel Kant, the realm of concepts or the abstract laws that govern the universe. This realm is unobservable or unknowable by the human mind, and can only be understood through rational analysis of *phenomenon*.

Objectification: The treatment or representation of human beings as objects, as in the sexual objectification of women.

Orientalism: A philosophical, literary, artistic, and scientific school, generally associated with the nineteenth century, in which Western thinkers analyzed and represented the East. Following the work of Edward Said, Orientalism is generally associated with a *Eurocentric* approach to the East that justified Western *imperial* actions.

Othering: The process of representing a person or group of people as different from (and lesser than) the "norm" of the society in such a way as to reproduce the social status quo. Associated with racism, sexism, heterosexism, etc.

Out group: Those members of society who are deemed to be not a part of a particular *in group*.

Pan-Africanism: The political and social belief in the (need for) unity among all African nations and peoples, sometimes including the African *diaspora*.

Patriarchy: A social system in which men are given more social privilege and power than women, or that generally favours men over women; this can refer to those social systems that legally demarcate more power for men or that do so through social convention and tradition.

Performative: A particular type of utterance or speech act; as originally proposed by J. L. Austin, a "performative" speech act differs from a "constative," or a simple or descriptive statement, in that "the issuing of the utterance is the performing of an action" (p. 5). For example, as Austin states, "When I say … 'I do,' I am not reporting on a marriage; I am indulging in it" (p. 6). As proposed by Judith Butler, *gender* and *sexuality* are likewise performative; it is in the repeated social and cultural acts of performing gender (making gendered utterances) that gender comes into existence and continues to exist as a category.

Phallogocentrism: A *patriarchal ideology* that positions men on the positive side of a hierarchical binary, a binary that is encoded into language itself. See *écriture feminine*.

Phenomenon: In the philosophy of Immanuel Kant, the visible world of objects; the only world to which the human mind has direct access. See *noumenon*.

Popular culture: Generally speaking, those cultural objects or behaviours that are engaged in by a mass audience and often seen as standing apart from *high culture*; often related to mass production and *mass culture*. However, popular culture is

much more difficult and complex than this: see Chapters 1 and 2 for a more complete definition.

Postcolonial/postcolonialism: Literally, the condition experienced by a nation, state, or people after the removal of a *colonial* power, or the practices used to remove that power. More generally, the theoretical and critical school used to study such situations.

Postmodern; postmodernism: Both a period and a set of theoretical principles commonly associated with that period. The postmodern period is usually considered to begin after World War II and often following the 1968 political upheavals in France and elsewhere around the globe. Some theorists (notably Fredric Jameson) situate the postmodern as a period coinciding with "late-stage capitalism." Conceptually, postmodernism is an outlook on the world framed by a suspicion of *metanarratives* or truth claims more generally, with the argument that there can be no universal or original ground for meaning in any *semiotic* system, including language and culture.

Poststructuralism: A school of philosophy and criticism associated with such thinkers as Jean Baudrillard, Judith Butler, Jacques Derrida, Gayatri Chakravorty Spivak, and others. Poststructuralist thought is characterized by the belief that semiotic systems (such as language), while they may serve as structuring principles for meaning, are ultimately formed around inherent and unresolvable contradictions that result in the structure's never being able to ground meaning (poststructuralism is thus closely associated with *postmodernism*).

Power: In cultural theory, the unequal levels of control or influence people have over themselves or (especially) others in a given social situation. In Marxist theory, power is seen to lie with those who control the means of production. In Foucauldian theory, power is a more dispersed effect of social interaction that no one person or group can hold on to, and so is a constantly mobile aspect of society. For Foucault, power is generally seen as rising "from the bottom" of a social hierarchy rather than being in the hands of one particular group or individual "at the top."

Print culture: *Cultural objects* or *practices* that involve the act of printing; objects and practices that use the printed word (such as books, magazines, etc.).

Queer theory: A branch of poststructuralist theory proposing that sexuality is not an expression of an inner human essence but instead constructed as a set of unstable, malleable identity categories. Queer theory also works to actively undermine assertions of stability in human (sexual) identity and practices.

Race and "race": The subcategorization of the human species by certain biological traits, often phenotypical and often associated with populations from specific regions of the globe. The modern notion of racial identity began with the pseudo-scientific biological distinctions of skull shape and other traits by J. S. Blumenbach and others. Some theorists (notably Henry Louis Gates, Jr.) place ironic quotation marks around the term in order to signal it as a socio-cultural construction rather than a biological essence.

Racism: The act (individual or systemic) of discriminating against a group based on their race; in the West or Global North, generally used to support structures of *white privilege* or white supremacy.

Real, the: In Lacanian psychoanalysis, the order of the psyche that pre-exists the Oedipal and mirror stages; it is inaccessible to direct, conscious knowledge. See *imaginary, symbolic*.

Relations of production: In Marxist theory, the relative positions and interactions of different social groups *viz.* their connection to capital and labour. See *base–superstructure model*.

Repression: In psychoanalysis, one of two mechanisms (the other being *sublimation*) through which the *ego* mediates the competing demands of the id and the *ideal ego*. Repression involves a forceful rejection of certain desires from the conscious mind.

Repressive hypothesis: Coined by Michel Foucault, this term refers to the theory that the Victorian period can be characterized by its supposed repression of expressions of sexuality. Foucault critiques this position, instead pointing to the proliferation of sexual discourse during that period.

Repressive State Apparatus (RSA): For Althusser, those state institutions that maintain the cohesion of society primarily through the exercise of violence in one form or another.

Romanticism: Both a historical period that spanned the late eighteenth to mid nineteenth century and a set of concepts, literary forms, and world views based on a belief in the transcendent nature of the *individual* and of beauty. Romantics emphasized both reason and sentiment but argued that reason unfettered by emotion has deleterious effects on the individual and the world. Romanticism is thus often seen as a response to the *Enlightenment*.

Scopophilia: Defined by Laura Mulvey, through reference to Freud, as the "pleasure in looking at another person as an erotic object" (p. 25). See *objectification*.

Semiotics: The science used to study language and other sign-based systems, often associated with the work of Ferdinand de Saussure.

Sex: In some feminist theory, one's biological positioning as male or female (though these categories do not account for all human sexual biology, given intersex persons and other forms of genital or chromosomal sex that do not necessarily fit into this binary). See *gender*.

Sexism: The act (individual or systemic) of discriminating against a group based on *gender* or *sex*; due to the prevalence of *patriarchal* societies, generally used in reference to discrimination against women.

Sexuality: An identity category most often related to one's preferences in sexual partners and practices, and/or one's internal sense of sexual identity.

Signifier, signified, and sign: From Saussure's theory of *semiotics*, the basic structures of language. The signifier is the symbol we use when we want to transmit meaning to another person (e.g., a word). The signified is the concept that that word points to. Taken together, the signifier and signified (the word and the concept) create what Saussure calls the sign, the basic unit of meaning in language.

Simulacra: From the writings of Jean Baudrillard, simulations of simulations, which in turn are taken by their viewer as "the real." See *hyperreal*.

Socialism: A number of social and political systems that tend to share an emphasis on regulating the market, emphasizing group welfare, and reducing class divisions.

Sound culture: *Cultural objects* or *practices* that primarily engage people's sense of hearing (e.g., music).

Split subject: In Lacanian psychoanalysis, the theory that, while we consciously feel as if we have a "whole" and "contained" identity, in fact we gain that sense only through our identification with others. Lacan sees identity as functioning in a manner similar to the way in which Saussure defines language.

State: A sovereign political power that governs a populace within a set of clear geographical borders.

Stereotypes: A set of ideas ascribed to or representations of large groups of people, often according to race, gender, nationality, sexuality, and so on. Stereotypes can reduce particular people, with all their unique attributes, to crudely drawn caricatures of a larger group. It is often associated with *racism*, *sexism*, and other forms of group discrimination.

Strategic essentialism: Coined (and then critiqued) by Gayatri Chakravorty Spivak, a political act of representing a group through identities and behaviours often ascribed as *essential* to them; however, these identities are ascribed or assumed in only a limited fashion as a means of gaining political power or responding to oppressive structures.

Structuralism: A loosely affiliated school of critical theory, arising from Saussure's semiotic theory, which holds that various aspects of culture and human life are structured as language is structured, as a system of interrelated and interdependent signs, and that the best way to understand these systems is to examine their structures, or forms, rather than focus on content. Structuralism influenced thinkers in literary study, anthropology, psychology, and Marxism, among other fields and disciplines.

Subaltern: Technically a term for a lower-ranking military figure, Antonio Gramsci appropriated it to refer to the proletariat as a subordinated group. It was then reappropriated by Gayatri Chakravorty Spivak and other postcolonial theorists and activists to refer to the most subordinated lower classes of a colonized population.

Subculture: A small, identifiable social group within a larger society whose members self-identify, through clothing, musical or other cultural products, styles, or tastes, as being at a remove from the dominant culture. Subcultures often set themselves in opposition to the dominant culture, which is viewed as too generic or oppressive.

Subject: A term used to define identity as being constrained or determined by forces beyond a person's control, be they social, biological, or part of unconscious psychical structures.

Subject positions: In discourse analysis and other ideological analyses, the socially structured identities that people "inhabit" or "embody" in society. Closely aligned with Althusser's notion of *interpellation*, a view of social life in which our identities are largely determined by surrounding *discourses* or *ideologies*.

Sublimation: In psychoanalysis, one of two mechanisms (the other being *repression*) through which the ego mediates the competing demands of the *id* and the *ideal ego*. Sublimation involves redirecting libidinal desires onto socially accepted objects or acts, thus allowing both the id and the ideal ego to be satisfied.

Sublime: A concept that dates back to ancient Greece and has been defined variously by philosophers and artists from different periods, notably in the *Enlightenment* and *Romantic* periods. While there are significant differences between them, in general the *sublime* denotes a feeling of transcendence, whether emotional, intellectual, moral, aesthetic, or spiritual. An experience of the sublime implies a sense of the infinite, which leaves one feeling as if one has experienced something beyond the material or everyday sensations of the world.

Subordinate masculinities: For R. W. Connell, those forms of masculinity that are directly oppressed by, or denied access to, most forms of social power allotted to hegemonic masculine behaviour. See *hegemonic masculinity*.

Suffragettes: The term used to describe women involved in the fight to gain the vote in the early part of the twentieth century. Originally pejorative, the term was adopted by the more militant suffrage organizations to distinguish themselves from groups that took a more gradual approach (often simply termed "suffragists").

Superego: A term used by Freud to define the combination of the *ideal ego* and the conscience.

Superstructure: See *base–superstructure model*.

Symbolic order: The term Lacan gives to the larger social and linguistic ordering principles of human identity. The symbolic order is roughly equivalent to the overarching structure of language (i.e., the overall structure of the play of signifiers in relation to each other) in Saussure's semiotics. See *imaginary* and *real*.

Taste: In relation to culture, the relative ability of a person to distinguish between "good" or "bad"—often *high* or *low*—culture. In the work of Pierre Bourdieu, taste becomes a way of assessing and claiming *cultural capital*.

Three waves of feminism: A way of describing the history of Western feminist activism and theory as split into three overlapping periods, with concomitant theories or political goals: 1) the fight for suffrage; 2) the fight for equal rights and the struggle against the patriarchy; 3) a *postmodern* or decentred period of feminist activism that focuses on alliances with other marginalized groups.

Uncanny: In Freudian psychoanalysis, the feeling that arises when an object, situation, person, or so on is both familiar and strange, comforting and frightening, at the same time. For Freud, moments of the uncanny are related to the structure of our psyche, in which our ego watches over the desires of the id, and are thus simultaneously familiar (they are our desires) and strange (they are unconscious or repressed).

Unconscious: In Sigmund Freud's model of the human psyche, the unconscious is the repository for our libidinal and instinctual drives. Because we can never be fully consciously aware of these drives, we can only study or come to understand them indirectly. Later psychoanalytic theorists, including Carl Jung and Jacques Lacan, would build on Freud's notion of the unconscious.

Visual culture: *Cultural objects* or *practices* that primarily engage people's sense of sight (e.g., painting or graffiti).

White privilege: The explicit and/or implicit social benefits ascribed to people for being white, from legal segregation to traditional and ideological acceptance of certain racial inequities (such as when a legally democratic, racially diverse society still has public institutions—e.g., government or universities—in which white people are overrepresented in the higher echelons of power compared with the general population, or those institutions otherwise afford more social power to white people).

Whiteness: The fact or experience of being constructed as being part of a white *"race"* in a racialized culture. In *white privileging* societies, this condition is often expressed within a hierarchical relation to other racial categories (such as *blackness*).

Bibliography

Abrams, M. H. *A Glossary of Literary Terms*. 7th ed. Boston: Heinle and Heinle, 1999.

Adorno, Theodor W. *Prisms*. Trans. Samuel and Shierry Weber. Cambridge, MA: MIT Press, 1983.

———. *The Culture Industry: Selected Essays on Mass Culture*. Ed. J. M. Bernstein. London: Routledge Classics, 2001.

Adorno, Theodor W., and Max Horkheimer. *Dialectic of Enlightenment*. Trans. John Cumming. New York: Continuum, 1994.

Althusser, Louis. *Lenin and Philosophy and Other Essays*. Trans. Ben Brewster. London: New Left Books, 1971.

Anderson, Benedict. *Imagined Communities: Reflections on the Origin and Spread of Nationalism*. Rev. ed. London: Verso, 2006.

Arnold, Matthew. *Culture and Anarchy*. Cambridge: Cambridge UP, 1935.

Austin, J. L. *How to Do Things with Words*. 2nd ed. Ed. J. O. Urmson and Marina Sbisà. Cambridge: Harvard UP, 1975.

Bakhtin, M. M. *The Dialogic Imagination: Four Essays*. Ed. Michael Holquist. Trans. Caryl Emerson and Michael Holquist. Austin: U of Texas P, 1981.

Bannerji, Himani. *The Dark Side of the Nation: Essays on Multiculturalism, Nationalism and Gender*. Toronto: Canadian Scholars' Press, 2000.

Barthes, Roland. *Elements of Semiology*. Trans. Annette Lavers and Colin Smith. New York: Hill and Wang, 1967.

———. *Mythologies*. Sel. and trans. Annette Lavers. London: Jonathan Cape, 1972.

Baudrillard, Jean. *Simulacra and Simulation*. Trans. Sheila Faria Glaser. Ann Arbor: U of Michigan P, 1994.

de Beauvoir, Simone. *The Second Sex*. 1949. Trans. Constance Borde and Sheila Malovany-Chevallier. New York: Vintage 2011.

Benjamin, Walter. *Illuminations: Essays and Reflections*. Ed. and intro. Hannah Arendt. Trans. Harry Zohn. New York: Schocken, 1969.

Bhabha. Homi. *The Location of Culture*. London: Routledge, 1994.

Blumenbach, Johann Friedrich. *On the Natural Varieties of Mankind*. New York: Bergman, 1969.

Bordo, Susan. *Unbearable Weight: Feminism, Western Culture, and the Body*. 10th Anniversary ed. Berkeley: U of California P, 2003.

Bourdieu, Pierre. *Distinction: A Social Critique of the Judgement of Taste*. Trans. Richard Nice. Cambridge, MA: Harvard UP, 1984.

Burroughs, Edgar Rice. *Tarzan of the Apes*. Ed. Jason Haslam. 1914. Oxford: Oxford UP, 2010.

Butler, Judith. *The Judith Butler Reader*. Ed. Sarah Salih with Judith Butler. Oxford: Blackwell, 2004.

———. "I Must Distance Myself from This Complicity with Racism." 19 June 2010. *European Graduate School*. <www.egs.edu/faculty/judith-butler/articles/i-must-distance-myself>.

Cixous, Hélène. "The Laugh of the Medusa." Trans. Keith Cohen and Paula Cohen. *Signs* 1.4 (1976): 875–93.

Clark, Anna. *Desire: A History of European Sexuality*. London: Routledge, 2008.

Clark, Penney. "'A Nice Little Wife to Make Things Pleasant:' Portrayals of Women in Canadian History Textbooks Approved in British Columbia." *McGill Journal of Education* 40.2 (2005): 241–65.

Cleverdon, Catherine L. *The Woman Suffrage Movement in Canada*. 2nd ed. Toronto: U of Toronto P, 1974.

Cohen, Ed. *Talk on the Wilde Side: Toward a Genealogy of a Discourse on Male Sexualities*. New York: Routledge, 1993.

Connell, R. W. *Masculinities*. 2nd ed. Berkeley: U of California P, 2005.

Derrida, Jacques. *Margins of Philosophy*. Trans. Alan Bass. Chicago: U of Chicago P, 1982.

———. *Of Grammatology*. Trans. Gayatri Chakravorty Spivak. Baltimore: Johns Hopkins UP, 1974.

———. "Plato's Pharmacy." *Dissemination*. Trans. Barbara Johnson. London: Athlone, 1981. 61–172.

Devereux, Cecily. "Anatomy of a 'National Icon': *Anne of Green Gables* and the 'Bosom Friends' Affair. *Making Avonlea: L. M. Montgomery and Popular Culture*. Ed. Irene Gammel. Toronto: U of Toronto P, 2002. 32–42.

Drzewiecka, Jolanta A., and Kathleen Wong (Lau). "The Dynamic Construction of White Ethnicity in the Context of Transnational Cultural Formations." *Whiteness: The Communication of Social Identity*. Ed. Thomas K. Nakayama and Judith N. Martin. London: Sage, 1999. 198–216.

Dyer, Richard. *White*. New York: Routledge, 1997.

Eagleton, Terry. *The Idea of Culture*. Oxford: Blackwell, 2000.

Edelman, Lee. *No Future: Queer Theory and the Death Drive*. Durham: Duke UP, 2004.

Eliot, T. S. "The Love Song of J. Alfred Prufrock." *Collected Poems 1909–1962*. New York: HBJ, 1991. 3–7.

Faflak, Joel. *Romantic Psychoanalysis: The Burden of Mystery*. New York: SUNY P, 2008.

Fairclough, Norman. *Language and Power*. London: Longman, 1989.

Fanon, Frantz. *Black Skin/White Masks*. London: Pluto Press, 2008.

Felski, Rita. "Modernist Studies and Cultural Studies: Reflections on Method." *Modernism/Modernity* 10.3 (2003): 501–517.

Fleras, Augie. *The Media Gaze: Representations of Diversities in Canada*. Vancouver: UBC Press, 2011.

Fleras, Augie, and Jean Lock Kunz. *Media and Minorities: Representing Diversity in a Multicultural Canada*. Toronto: Thompson, 2001.

Foucault, Michel. *The Foucault Reader*. Ed. Paul Rabinow. New York: Pantheon, 1984.

———. *History of Sexuality*. Vol. 1. Trans. Robert Hurley. 1978. New York: Vintage, 1990.

Freud, Sigmund. *The Standard Edition of the Complete Psychological Works of Sigmund Freud*. Trans. and Ed. James Strachey in collaboration with Anna Freud, assisted by Alix Strachey and Alan Tyson. 24 volumes. London: Hogarth, 1953–1974.

Gates, Henry Louis, Jr. "Introduction: Writing 'Race' and the Difference It Makes." *"Race," Writing, and Difference*. Ed. Henry Louis Gates, Jr. Chicago: U of Chicago P, 1986. 1–20.

Gilroy, Paul. *Black Atlantic: Modernity and Double Consciousness*. London: Verso, 1993.

Gramsci, Antonio. *Prison Notebooks*. Vol. 2. Ed. and trans. Joseph A. Buttigieg. New York: Columbia UP, 1996.

Greenblatt, Stephen, ed. and intro. *The Power of Forms in the English Renaissance*. Norman, OK: Pilgrim Books, 1982.

Groden, Michael, Martin Kreiswirth, and Imre Szeman, eds. *Johns Hopkins Guide to Literary Theory and Criticism*. 2nd ed. Baltimore: Johns Hopkins UP, 2005.

Halberstam, J. Jack. *Female Masculinity*. Durham: Duke UP, 1998.

Hall, Stuart, et al., eds. *Culture, Media, Language: Working Papers in Cultural Studies, 1972–79*. London: Taylor and Francis, 1980. *MyiLibrary. com*. Web. 1 April 2012.

Haraway, Donna J. *Simians, Cyborgs, and Women: The Reinvention of Nature*. New York: Routledge, 1991.

Hebdige, Dick. *Subculture: The Meaning of Style*. London: Routledge, 1988.

Herder, John Godfrey [Johann Gottfried von Herder]. *Outlines of a Philosophy of the History of Man*. Trans. T. Churchill. London: Hansard, 1800. *Eighteenth-Century Collections Online*. 06 January 2003. Web. 07 July 2012.

"History of Women's Rights." ournellie.com. *Nellie McClung Foundation*. Web. 07 Feb. 2013.

hooks, bell. *Feminist Theory: From Margin to Center*. Boston: South End Press, 1984.

———. *Black Looks: Race and Representation*. Cambridge, MA: South End Press, 1992.

———. "Postmodern Blackness." *Postmodern Culture* 1.1 (1990): 15 para.

Hopkinson, Nalo. *Brown Girl in the Ring*. New York: Warner, 1998.

Hutcheon, Linda. *A Poetics of Postmodernism: History, Theory, Fiction*. London: Routledge, 1988. E-book.

Ignatiev, Noel. *How the Irish Became White*. London: Routledge, 1995.

Jameson, Fredric. *Postmodernism, or, The Cultural Logic of Late Capitalism*. Durham, NC: Duke UP, 1991.

Jung, Carl G[ustav]. *The Portable Jung*. Ed. Joseph Campbell. Trans. R. F. C. Hull. New York: Viking, 1971.

———. *Psychology of the Unconscious*. Trans. Beatrice M. Hinkle. 1947. Mineola, NY: Dover, 2002.

Jung, Carl G[ustav], M.-L. von Franz, Joseph L. Henderson, Jolande Jacobi, and Aniela Jaffé. *Man and His Symbols*. New York: Laurel, 1968.

Kant, Immanuel. *Observations on the Feeling of the Beautiful and Sublime and Other Writings*. Ed. Patrick Frierson and Paul Guyer. Cambridge: Cambridge UP, 2011.

Katz, Jonathan. "Queer Nation." *Gay Histories and Cultures: An Encyclopedia*. Ed. George E. Haggerty. New York: Garland, 2000. 725–26.

Keats, John. *The Complete Poems*. London: Penguin, 1988.

Klein, Naomi. *No Logo: Taking Aim at the Brand Bullies*. 1999. Toronto: Vintage Canada, 2000.

Kneale, J. Douglas. "Deconstruction." *Johns Hopkins Guide to Literary Theory and Criticism*. 2nd ed. Eds. Michael Groden, Martin Kreiswirth, and Imre Szeman. Baltimore: Johns Hopkins UP, 2005. 235–41.

KONY 2012. Dir. Jason Russell. Invisible Children, 2012. *YouTube*. Web. 17 May 2012.

von Krafft-Ebing, Richard. *Psychopathia Sexualis: A Medico-Forensic Study*. Trans. Harry E. Wedeck. New York: Putnam's, 1965.

Kunzru, Hari. "You Are a Cyborg." *Wired* 5.02 (1997). *wired.com*. 7 pages. Web. 12 June 2014.

Lacan, Jacques. *Écrits*. First complete ed. in English. Trans. Bruce Fink, in collaboration with Héloïse Fink and Russell Grigg. New York: Norton, 2006.

———. *The Seminar of Jacques Lacan, Book II: The Ego in Freud's Theory and in the Technique of Psychoanalysis, 1954–1955*. Ed. Jacques-Alain Miller. Trans. Sylvana Tomaselli. Cambridge: Cambridge UP, 1988.

Leavis, F. R., and Denys Thompson. *Culture and Environment: The Training of Critical Awareness*. 1933. London: Chatto, 1948.

Leeds-Hurwitz, Wendy. *Semiotics and Communication: Signs, Codes, Cultures*. Hillsdale, NJ: Laurence Erlbaum, 1993.

Lévi-Strauss, Claude. *Structural Anthropology*. Vol. 1. Trans. Claire Jacobson and Brooke Grundfest Schoepf. New York: Basic, 1963.

———. *Structural Anthropology*. Vol. 2. Trans. Monique Layton. New York: Basic, 1976.

Lorde, Audre. *Sister Outsider*. 1984. New York: Ten Speed Press, 2007.

Lyotard, Jean-François. *The Postmodern Condition: A Report on Knowledge*. Trans. Brian Massumi. Foreword by Fredric Jameson. Minneapolis: U of Minnesota P, 1984.

Macfarlane, Karen E. "The Monstrous House of Gaga." *The Gothic in Contemporary Literature and Popular Culture*. Ed. Justin D. Edwards and Agnieszka Soltysik Monnet. London: Routledge, 2012. 114–34.

Marx, Karl, and Friedrich Engels. *Capital*. Vol. 1. *Collected Works*. Vol. 35. London: Lawrence and Wishart, 1996.

———. *A Contribution to the Critique of Political Economy*. *Collected Works*. Vol. 29. London: Lawrence and Wishart, 1987.

———. *The German Ideology*. *Collected Works*. Vol. 5. London: Lawrence and Wishart, 1976.

McCullough, John. "Imperialism, Regionalism, Humanism: *Gullage's*, *Trailer Park Boys*, and Representations of Canadian Space in Global Hollywood." *Rain/Drizzle/Fog: Film and Television in Atlantic Canada*. Ed. Darrell Varga. Calgary: U of Calgary P, 2009. 151–70.

McLuhan, Marshall. *Understanding Media: The Extensions of Man*. 2nd ed. New York: Signet, 1964.

Montgomery, Ken. "Imagining the Antiracist State: Representations of Racism in Canadian History Textbooks." *Discourse: Studies in the Cultural Politics of Education* 26.4 (2005): 427–42.

Montgomery, L. M. *Anne of Green Gables*. Afterword by Margaret Atwood. 1908. Toronto: McClelland and Stewart, 2008.

Montrose, Louis A. "Professing the Renaissance: The Poetics and Politics of Culture." *The New Historicism*. Ed. H. Aram Veeser. New York: Routledge, 1989. 15–36.

Morson, Gary Saul, and Caryl Emerson. *Mikhail Bakhtin: Creation of a Prosaics*. Stanford, CA: Stanford UP, 1990.

Moss, Laura. "Preface: Is Canada Postcolonial? Introducing the Question." *Is Canada Postcolonial? Unsettling Canadian Literature*. Ed. Laura Moss. Waterloo: Wilfrid Laurier UP, 2003. 1–26.

Mulvey, Laura. *Visual and Other Pleasures*. 2nd ed. New York: Palgrave Macmillan, 2009.

Nye, Robert A., ed. *Sexuality*. Oxford: Oxford UP, 1999.

Osborne, Peter, and Matthew Charles. "Walter Benjamin." *Stanford Encyclopedia of Philosophy*. Winter 2013 ed. Ed. Edward N. Zalta. Web.

Plato. *The Republic*. Trans. Robin Waterfield. Oxford: Oxford UP, 1993.

———. *Symposium*. Trans. Robin Waterfield. Oxford: Oxford UP, 1994.

Rabaté, Jean-Michel. "Derrida." *Johns Hopkins Guide to Literary Theory and Criticism*. 2nd ed. Eds. Michael Groden, Martin Kreiswirth, and Imre Szeman. Baltimore: Johns Hopkins UP, 2005. 255–60.

Rich, Adrienne. "Compulsory Heterosexuality and Lesbian Existence." *Signs* 5.4 (1980): *Women: Sex and Sexuality*: 631–60.

Robinson, Laura. "Bosom Friends: Lesbian Desire in L. M. Montgomery's Anne Books." *Canadian Literature* 180 (2004): 12–28.

Said, Edward W. *Orientalism*. 1978. New York: Vintage, 1979.

de Saussure, Ferdinand. *Course in General Linguistics*. Ed. Charles Bally and Albert Sechehaye with the Collaboration of Albert Riedlinger. Trans. Roy Harris. Chicago: Open Court, 1986.

Sedgwick, Eve Kosofsky. *Epistemology of the Closet*. Updated with a New Preface. Berkeley: U of California P, 2008.

Smith, Paul. *Discerning the Subject*. Minneapolis: U of Minnesota P, 1988.

Smith, Sidonie. *Subjectivity, Identity, and the Body: Women's Autobiographical Practices in the Twentieth Century*. Bloomington: Indiana UP, 1993.

Spivak, Gayatri Chakravorty. *A Critique of Postcolonial Reason: Toward a History of the Vanishing Present*. Cambridge, MA: Harvard UP, 1999.

———. "Subaltern Studies: Deconstructing Historiography." *Selected Subaltern Studies*. Ed. Ranajit Guha and Gayatri Chakravorty Spivak. Foreword by Edward Said. Oxford: Oxford UP, 1988.

Stearns, Peter N. *Sexuality in World History*. London: Routledge, 2009.

Thompson, E. P. *The Making of the English Working Class*. London: Gollancz, 1963.

Walcott, Rinaldo. *Black Like Who? Writing Black Canada*. 2nd rev. ed. Toronto: Insomniac Press, 2003.

Wander, Philip C., Judith N. Martin, and Thomas K. Nakayama. "Whiteness and Beyond: Sociohistorical Foundations of Whiteness and Contemporary Challenges." *Whiteness: The Communication of Social Identity*. Ed. Thomas K. Nakayama and Judith N. Martin. London: Sage, 1999. 13–26.

Wertham, Frederic. *Seduction of the Innocent*. New York: Rinehart, 1954.

West, Emily. "Collective Memory on the Airwaves: The Negotiation of Unity and Diversity in a Troubled Canadian Nationalism." *Canadian Cultural Poesis: Essays on Canadian Culture*. Ed. Garry Sherbert, Annie Gérin, and Sheila Petty. Waterloo: Wilfrid Laurier UP, 2006. 67–83.

White, Hayden. *Tropics of Discourse: Essays in Cultural Criticism*. 1978. Baltimore: Johns Hopkins UP, 1985.

Wilde, Oscar. *The Importance of Being Earnest*. *Collins Complete Works of Oscar Wilde*. Centenary ed. Glasgow: HarperCollins, 1999. 357–419.

Williams, Raymond. *Marxism and Literature*. Oxford: Oxford UP, 1977.

———. *Problems in Materialism and Culture*. London: Verso, 1980.

Williams, William Carlos. "A Sort of a Song." *Collected Poems of William Carlos Williams*. Vol. 2: 1939–1962. Ed. Christopher MacGowan. New York: New Directions, 2001. 55.

Withnail and I. Writ. and Dir. Bruce Robinson. Handmade Films, 1987. DVD.

Index